Debi Marshall is a freelance j
Tasmania. She started her caree
now writes extensively for nat:
crime. She is also an experience
A qualified teacher (BA, Dip Ed), Debi also teaches Media and
English at college and university.

Also by Debi Marshall

Her Father's Daughter: The Bonnie Henderson Story
Lang Hancock
Justice in Jeopardy: The Unsolved Murder of Baby Deidre Kennedy

Killing for Pleasure

Pleasure

The Definitive Story of the Snowtown Serial Murders

DEBI MARSHALL

RANDOM HOUSE AUSTRALIA

*To my daughter, Louise, and my mother, Monica,
for their unconditional love and support.*

Note: Pseudonyms have been used to protect the identity of some people mentioned
     in this book.

Random House Australia Pty Ltd
Level 3, 100 Pacific Highway, North Sydney, NSW 2060
http://www.randomhouse.com.au

Sydney   New York   Toronto
London   Auckland   Johannesburg

First published by Random House Australia 2006

National Library of Australia
Cataloguing-in-Publication Entry

Marshall, Debi.
Killing for pleasure: the definitive story of the Snowtown serial murders.

ISBN 978 1 74051 248 0.

ISBN 1 74051 248 0.

1. Serial murders – South Australia – Snowtown. 2. Serial
murder investigation – South Australia – Snowtown. 3. Murder
victims – South Australia – Snowtown. 4. Serial murderers –
South Australia – Snowtown. I. Title.

Front cover photo (Haydon, Bunting, Wagner) and back cover photo
courtesy Newspix/News Limited
Front cover photo (barrels) courtesy Getty Images
Cover design by Darian Causby/www.highway51.com.au
Typeset by Midland Typesetters, Australia
Printed and bound by Griffin Press, South Australia

Foreword

Snowtown is one of the world's most bizarre and sadistic series of murders. If anything represents pure, unadulterated evil, then this case is it. Debi Marshall's book relives the nightmare that combined torture, cannibalism, dismembering and murder into a series of crimes that have shocked criminologists and law enforcement officials all over the world. It also opens the lid on the bleak, dysfunctional under class that spawned both victims and killers, in a confronting, no-holds-barred look at a group of people who preyed on each other.

Professor Paul Wilson
Chair of Criminology
Bond University, Queensland

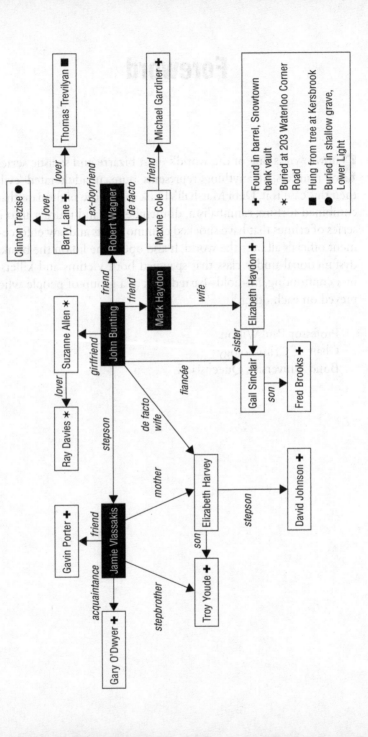

Preface

Mid-August, 1994. Farmers, going about their routine day's work, stumble on the skeletal remains of a young man in an isolated paddock at Lower Light, 50 kilometres north of Adelaide, South Australia. The identity of that man, Clinton Trezise, will remain a mystery for five long years, but he will come to symbolise a vital link in a murderous chain that is Australia's worst serial killing case. And it will be his death, too, that raises questions – serious questions – about the police and forensic investigation.

By the time the police investigation concluded in 1999, there were 12 bodies: eight found in barrels, two in shallow graves in a suburban backyard and a further two in the bush. Eleven murdered. One dismembered after death. Were there any more?

As the story unfolded and the body count rose, a horrified nation realised that the murders rivalled the savagery of the Ivan Milat backpacker killings, where seven young men and women were killed in the New South Wales Belanglo State Forest between 1989 and 1993, or the tragedy that was the Jaidyn Leskie case, set against the backdrop of Moe in central Victoria. Senseless. Evil. Internationally, the story was inviting comparison with that of the Rosemary and Fred West nightmare, the British House of Horrors. Details of what the so-called Snowtown killers – John Bunting, Robert Wagner, Jamie Vlassakis and their sidekick, Mark Haydon, who assisted his co-accused escape apprehension – did to their victims before and after their deaths were deemed so macabre, so depraved, that suppression orders were in place throughout the trial.

I first went to Snowtown – a sleepy, nondescript hamlet 150 kilometres north of Adelaide on the edge of a wheat belt – in

February 2001 to cover a feature story on the tensions in the town following the discovery of the bodies. Here, I found a community turning upon itself and resentful of the media intrusion on their lives. The residents did not welcome their town having been arbitrarily chosen as the dumping ground for Australia's worst serial killing. But there were deeper reasons for disquiet. As the *Adelaide Advertiser* noted: 'The state and the nation began to ask why. Why the killings? Why Snowtown? Why the bank vault?' And, they may well have asked: why South Australia – again? Its capital, Adelaide, was once known as the City of Churches; now it was disparagingly referred to as the City of Corpses. Driving back from Snowtown that first day, through the urban wasteland of the welfare-dependent northern suburbs, I wondered: have we grown an under class, born out of boredom and poverty and disaffection, that is becoming increasingly warped, increasingly violent and from whom we must turn away lest they catch our eye? Have we created a Gothic underworld of marginalised people?

I left Snowtown after two days, armed with enough information to write the feature and with a gnawing, uncomfortable feeling in the pit of my gut as I drove back down the same deserted road that the killers had taken with the barrels on the back of their vehicle. What, I wondered, had made them cross the line, the moral boundary? Were there indicators in their family backgrounds that drove them to such depravity? What fractured logic allowed them to continue to kill, despite the knowledge that their actions must arouse suspicion and, ultimately, apprehension?

Who were these killers? There had to be a mastermind behind the group, one individual with a Svengali hold over the others. Who was that man, I wondered, and why does this group come together – and stay together – to behave in such an abominable way?

Four men, marked by their outward normality, who seemingly tortured and killed for fun, for power. What was the motive? Many victims had been dismembered and de-fleshed, the ritual stuffing of the corpses into the barrels the killers' signature. Some victims were cannibalised, an act so repugnant and rare that criminologists could search for decades to find such cases. As Crown Prosecutor Wendy Abraham would say, 'It is one thing to murder a person. It is a completely different thing to go the next step.' Were the killers insane, or had they made deliberate choices to kill? The level of planning is extraordinary. They do anything they have to do – *anything* – to prevent the discovery of their crimes. It is a joint enterprise in murder.

A conspiracy of silence seemed to have protected the killers. If anyone suspected something was wrong, why was it that no one went to the police for years? Was it because where they live, police are regarded as the cultural enemy? Were people gaining opportunistically from use of credit cards? Was it because they were more frightened of the killers than the cops? Or perhaps they just didn't care?

And what of the police investigation? Why did the police fail to hand over a photograph that might have identified the first victim? Fail to take action after they received vital information via phone intercepts? Why were they so slow, despite mounting evidence, to piece together the human jigsaw puzzle? And who was responsible for failing to identify Clinton Trezise's skeletal remains?

There were too many questions, and too much to write in one magazine piece. I knew I had to write the book.

Nothing in my 20-year journalistic career, specialising in crime writing, prepared me for what I would encounter in this story. My portfolio is thick with stories of human depravity, of rape, abduction and murder. But nothing prepared me for this, the truly haunting story that the world would come to know as the 'Snowtown bank vault murders', the 'bodies-in-barrels case'. It was impossible to comprehend the magnitude of the crimes, their premeditation, planning and shaping; the blood lust and enjoyment of torture; the coldness of the psychopath;

the shocking reality of this country's under class and the apathy shown to those in it; the plight of the defenceless children.

This is a dark story of generational paedophilia and incest; physical, sexual and emotional abuse; neglect and despair. Of people with reduced intellect, mental and physical disabilities and a pitiful lack of education that dooms them permanently to the welfare poverty trap. There are no heroes: none in the welfare system that failed the children, and failed them badly; none in the suburbs where both killers and victims lived; and none in the middle classes that don't want to admit that these people exist.

As sole researcher and writer, I entered an environment where emotions are deadened and brutalised, an environment that challenged my parameters as a journalist, a woman and a mother from middle Australia. It will likely challenge the reader, too, as it did members of the jury. Of the original 15, three – unable to stomach the gruesome evidence – dropped out. This story offers no retreat into the safety of fiction. It is chillingly real.

Everything portrayed is factual, gleaned from numerous personal interviews, tens of thousands of pages of court transcripts, my own observations of people and events presented at the committal and trials, and from media reports. Most interviews were done face to face in Adelaide and Snowtown while others, for logistic reasons, were by phone. The colour in the story is based on my conversations with characters portrayed, their idiosyncrasies and what they told me about other people. This is how actions and thoughts are rendered with immediacy. For various reasons, many people I met frequently changed their names; for ease of understanding, once they use an alias that name is maintained throughout. For legal reasons, some names have been changed in line with on-going suppression orders. The names of children taken into the care of family and Community Services have been withheld.

There were times when I felt overwhelmed by the interviews and the unrelentingly black material. Out of my comfort zone, battling to retain a professional detachment and not get emotionally involved; to suspend my natural inclination to retreat back to my middle-class mind set; particularly on 11 September 2001 when terrorists slammed into the World Trade Center in New York after which, stunned and shaken, I returned to the court for another day of research, trawling through archives of lives and deaths. I suddenly felt bone-tired, wanted to go home to where I felt safe. Thirteen months later, I was again in Adelaide for the start of Bunting and Wagner's trial, when the Bali nightclubs were bombed. It all seemed surreal. The juxtaposition of evil.

There were logistic problems. No one involved in the case – police, lawyers or forensic experts – would speak during the marathon committal and trials, and details of the killers' backgrounds were sketchy. Did they follow the usual pattern for serial killers: environmental problems in their formative years; products of broken homes; a weak or absent father figure and dominant female; a consistent lack of discipline and care? It took years to piece the answers together.

Much of his co-conspirators' backgrounds and psychopathy was provided by the harrowing details offered at trial by the prosecution's key eyewitness, Jamie Vlassakis, and by people who knew them well. Lovers. Friends. Ex-wives. Neighbours. The exception to this was John Bunting: people were never sure if what he had told them was the truth; the juncture at which his fantasies collided with reality. Their recollections are included as they told them, but Bunting still remains an enigma, his 'not guilty' plea ensuring no sentence submissions or psychiatric reports were released. Psychiatrists speculate whether the cause of Bunting's abhorrent behaviour was rooted in shocking childhood abuse, and all agree he is a cunning psychopath driven by power and devoid of emotion, an egotistical sexual sadist whose bizarre fantasies reached their zenith in the act of cutting up his victims' bodies. The two people – his parents – who could possibly verify or deny significant events in his childhood or who could throw light on whether Bunting was insane or evil, never materialised, even as their son sat in the dock. I made every effort over the years to find them, but to no avail. For all intents and purposes, they have simply vaporised into thin air.

But if his parents remained silent, for the first time Bunting's last lover, Elizabeth Harvey, speaks out here about life with Australia's worst serial killer. For the first time, ranging far beyond the limitations of court transcripts, the definitive story of Australia's worst serial killings is told.

This book took more than five years to write. I came to see the story as a cautionary tale, a metaphor of our times. Another rural bank closes down, another town decays, the have-nots – the under class – degenerate into acts of sickening violence amongst their own and the bank vault becomes a secret place, hidden away under lock and key where we, a cut above them, shove our guilt. We only looked when they opened the vault. We had to. We could no longer avoid it.

I started out asking what had made Bunting and co. cross the moral boundary. At the end of the research, I came to realise they didn't have a boundary. Mark Twain said that 'all creatures kill – there seems to be no exception. But of the whole list man is the only one that kills for fun . . .' Justice Brian Martin echoed that sentiment when he sentenced Bunting and Wagner to life in jail. 'It's not an exaggeration to say . . . you were in the business of killing for pleasure', he noted grimly.

Many of the characters in this book – alive and dead – were frequently treated as nothing more than society's refuse: waste products. This is as much a story about those people, who never stood a chance, as it is an indictment of the society that ignored them. The real tragedy is that the cycle continues. And it is precisely because it continues that history is bound to repeat.

PART ONE
Crime

*Big fleas have little fleas upon their backs
to bite them, and little fleas have lesser fleas,
and so ad infinitum.*

Jonathan Swift, 1732

*What's done to children, they will do
to society.*

Karl Menninger, US psychiatrist, 1893–1990

Prologue

Not long now. Elizabeth Harvey wants to talk, but every word is a struggle. Drugged and drowsy, in and out of dreaming: of her kids and her life and John Bunting.

It is as though she has lived with two Johns. One – charming, gentle and kind – who held her tenderly, suffocated her with his attentions; the only man she ever loved. The other – domineering, sadistic, obsessed – who tortured and murdered her son and stepson, and who suborned another son into helping him kill four people. The man she lived with – lived for – for five years. The clever engineer of confusion and chaos who, too impatient to wait for her cancer to take its natural course, tried to murder her as well.

A life recalled in jagged pieces, bit by painful bit, as she slips in and out of the darkness.

Morphine eases the pain from the cancer that has insinuated itself through her lymphatic system, from her breasts into lungs and spine. But it can't stop her persistent cough of blood-stained sputum, her desperate inhalations for air and the wheezy rattle deep in her sallow chest.

All her life she has blocked out memories, but she can't block them now. Guilt and shame, shadows and voices fade in and out. A life as dismal and ragged in the retelling as it has been while she lived it. Dark, sad memories superimposed against the soft whirr of a tape recorder, a sputtering, hacking cough and the quiet gurgle of oxygen.

October 2000. She tells her story as she sits at a table in her Adelaide housing trust flat, the tiny unit reeking of the cloying, stale fumes of the cheap cigarettes she chain smokes. No food in the fridge and threadbare curtains failing to block out the heat. Come the start of summer, she will be too ill to sit up in a chair; her once obese frame is now reduced by cancer, crepey thin flesh covers her bones and she fights to breathe unassisted. Hospitalised by mid-January, she is desperate to finish telling her story but every word is a struggle. In and out of dreaming; of her kids and her life and John Bunting.

Elizabeth Harvey, John Bunting's last confidante and lover. Forty-seven years old, and dying. Not long now.

1

It starts as an idle thought, grows into an obsession.

He will fill the house with dead people; redecorate it as a charnel house. Sit the victim upright in a chair, cut his throat and place a live Chihuahua in his neck. Hide in the semi-darkness and wait quietly for the cops to arrive. He laughs as he imagines the carnage that will greet police: a barking corpse sitting in a chair, the room saturated with blood.

It pleases John Bunting to play God, to decide whether a person lives or dies. He spends hours fashioning fantasies in his head, and this is one of his favourites. He likes it so much that even when he is alone, he laughs out loud just thinking about it.

2

She is captivated with him from the start. Veronika Tripp is 18, a naive teenager with a noticeable intellectual disability who abandoned school at Year 8. Simply gave up: it was too hard. John Bunting is 21, educated to Year 11.

They meet at a metalwork course in the Adelaide suburb of Torrensville, a training course for people who need help finding work. John eats alone and watches Veronika from his corner of the lunchroom. Too shy to speak, he says nothing to her but he quietly, patiently absorbs the lessons: how to weld and use a guillotine cutter. Veronika and he catch the same bus to the course and John starts waiting for her, letting other buses go past until she arrives. She is flattered, if a little perplexed, at this bloke's attentions. She knows nothing about him, except he is learning how to weld and he seems nice. Pleasant, easygoing.

John sits next to her on the bus, looking at her through his mop of sandy hair with large hooded hazel eyes. They start talking over their sandwiches, just the two of them, well removed from the other people on the course. He follows her around, getting her lunch from the van that pulls up outside every day and his attentions make Veronika feel important, as though she suddenly has a spare set of legs to do her walking for her. She isn't used to the attention. Nobody has ever really noticed her before; not in a nice way.

Born with a severe hearing disability, undiagnosed until she was eight years old, Veronika has strained to hear conversations all her life. A regular school check-up proves she is half deaf and blind in one eye. She long ago worked out that when you can't hear, you are left behind and by the end of primary school she can barely read or write. But there is one saving grace: Veronika has finally made a friend, Caroline, who understands what it is like to be in a special class. Caroline is epileptic, and also the target of cruel barbs. They form a bond: the two girls against the world.

Leaving school didn't bother Veronika. All her life, it seems, she has been a prime target for bullies who pick on her incessantly, call her four-eyes because of her glasses. Tell her she is stupid, a rail-thin, buck-toothed girl with no brains. Judge her by the way she looks, and because she can't read or write.

But she can draw and paint intricately detailed birds and animals in beautiful colours; peacocks with violet and azure feathers, happy rabbits in tawny tones. She immerses herself in painting for hours, ignoring the bullies as best she can.

John circles around her on the bus and at the course, quietly zeroing in like radar. He seems to instinctively sense she is lonely. He is a loner as well. Veronika reckons he is as slow as a funeral. 'Thick as a brick', she would later shrug, as though bemused that they at least had that in common. 'He was thicker than me, that's for sure.'

Plaiting her words around each other, each falling with a flat thud. *Thicker than me, that's for sure.*

And it just sort of happens. Talking at first and then hanging out together as often as possible in their spare time. John lives at Pooraka, an industrial outer northern Adelaide suburb with his mate Kevin and Kevin's girlfriend, Michelle. It takes Veronika ages to get there by bus, out there in the place she christens the 'oobley whoop-whoop', but she makes the journey every chance she can.

She can't remember how long they hang around together – a month or two, if that – but it is long enough for her to fall in love with the bloke they called 'Big John'; a strange nickname, she thinks, since he is so short. Squat, pocketsized, with a broad chest. No taller than a jockey. It is also long enough for him to propose, in a fashion. Nothing fancy: more a statement than a question. 'What do you reckon we get married, Veronika?' She has to think about it, she tells him. Smacks her lips together over her protruding teeth, waits 10 seconds, then replies: 'Okay. Yep.'

She has already moved in with him at his Pooraka house, surrounded by factories and take-away shops. She is sick of the flippin' bus trip up and back from her parents' suburban home in Middle Park. They aren't impressed when she announces she is packing up and going to live with John; try to change her mind. Don't think it is right for her to shack up with a bloke before marriage. But Veronika doesn't listen. She has a mind of her own. She is 18 now.

John meets a bloke called Mark Haydon on the welding course, a taciturn dullard eight years his senior who never speaks out of turn. Mark owns a Toyota Land Cruiser, and they each bung in five bucks worth of fuel and run amok on the salt flats at Lower Light, isolated scrub and farmland an hour from Adelaide, off the highway heading toward Snowtown. Doing wheelies in this graveyard of vehicles and junk, on the excursions they call their 'five dollar lottery'. If a car has recently been dumped, they strip it, throw the parts into the Tojo and come home with spares to sell. They go out there all the time, get to know the area – and each other – well. It isn't long before Bunting and Haydon are inseparable. Thick as thieves.

They get a job together at a welding factory, an hour north of Adelaide, and John loves it. He would have stayed there if it hadn't closed down.

Veronika and John live a low-key, normal existence, watching videos, going to the beach. And after John proposes, they drive from Adelaide to Brisbane so Veronika can meet his parents. Like his young fiancée, he is an only child, born in early spring – 4 September 1966 – at Inala, an impoverished south-western suburb of Brisbane.

In 1950, the land in Inala – an Aboriginal name meaning 'good camping place' – was sold to the Queensland Housing Commission. It was developed to house returned servicemen and their families, and the plan was to locate residents – including high proportions of migrants from Europe and the United Kingdom – near industry. Instead, it became a government experiment that grew out of control: not the residential utopia it was planned to be but a monstrous creation, a cradle of high crime and high unemployment, economically isolated from Brisbane's services and facilities.

Today, efforts to repackage Inala in real estate parlance as leafy suburbia close to Brisbane CBD, a melting pot of different cultures, have had some success but cannot wallpaper over its grimy past. A large police presence was and is an accepted part of Inala's culture. 'In the past', a Queensland cop says, 'Inala was regarded as a fleapit. Now it's a slightly more fashionable fleapit.' Despite a strong community spirit, unemployment is still significantly higher here than in the rest of Brisbane. Gardens guarded by sombre Buddhas and front doors adorned with scarlet Oriental welcome signs testify to the higher-than-average number of residents from non-English speaking backgrounds, and it also boasts the highest number of Indigenous people in Brisbane.

In the early seventies, when Bunting was hoicking a school bag on his back, the streets teemed with kids from different nationalities who slogged past tentacles of dreary public housing and beehive units that seemingly mushroomed overnight. Inala, propped up by welfare, was an urban slum, a place dubbed by disgruntled out-of-work migrants as a culturally bereft backwater. Forget the tree-lined streets: three houses here would barely have afforded one in a better neighbourhood.

Bunting has no siblings to challenge or to compete with for his parents' attention. His mother, Jan, is upright and immaculate, both inside and outside the house. It is more a showroom than a home: a sterile, colour-coded showroom redecorated every three years. Everything in its place, never a cobweb, and visitors are asked to remove their shoes before entering. Jan, mud-brown hair, conservative in attitude and dress, frocks up in skirts, stockings and sensible shoes every time she ventures out. She sports a lopsided smile that can erupt into a grin, but aloofness in her manner doesn't easily invite people to smile back. She's a good head and shoulders taller than her husband,

Tom, with his pale skin, grey hair, glasses and neat-trimmed beard, and he is no match for his dominating wife. Tom has been in Australia for years but still, when he opens his mouth, the vowels of his native Manchester fall out. Both diligent, hard workers, they pay the bills and live a law-abiding life: Jan an office secretary, Tom a worker in a printing factory. His passion is strumming the guitar, soulful chords for hours at a time, until a freak accident with a guillotine at the factory severs his fingers. He grieves for them for years, for his fingers that had shaped the music he now can no longer play. But before and after the accident, Jan and Tom admit few outsiders into their insular world. They don't need to; they have each other. Fastidious peas in a pod.

Their lives run by rote and they go on holidays every year, trips other kids envy. Fishing down the coast, sight-seeing around country Queensland. His parents don't have a lot of money and don't spoil John; no sand is ever traipsed through the house after a day at the beach, nor mud pies thrown after a winter day's rain. Everything immaculate, perfectly in place. Even on holiday.

John drives them mad with his sloppy habits. He is a Virgo, fastidious himself in his own way, but with no apparent rhyme or reason to it. He throws everything into his drawers, his own private hiding place, and comes home to find his stuff strewn all over his room. 'Your drawers are a disgrace, John, clean them up', Jan admonishes him, and he feels violated and invaded, knowing his mother has rummaged through his private space, again. The secret places where he puts his junk. Inconsequential to someone else, but important to him. He can't keep anything sacred. His mother, he whines, has no respect for his privacy at all. He hates that.

3

John is happiest nutting out problems, working out solutions about electronics and chemistry. Particularly chemistry. He is disgruntled that he hasn't been afforded the chance to study physics and chemistry at Inala High School because his mathematics marks aren't up to scratch; is forced, instead, to pursue his interests in these subjects at home. He enjoys making his own rockets and stink bombs and once, before Tom has his accident, they build a boat together in the backyard.

When he isn't with his childhood friend, Kurt Bertrand, mixing chemicals that they use to develop photographs in the dark room at his house, John amuses himself. Experimenting with chemicals – nitric acid, brake fluid, chlorine – is his favourite pastime. He puts a glass over one of the redback or funnel-web spiders that nest under his house, watches as they float, convulse and then drown in the liquid.

Laughs, then repeats the experiment.

John spends a lot of time with his father, much more than with his mother. Still, he is different from them both, a gap that grows wider after he turns eight.

It seems to people who know him later that all John's memories are stuck in a time warp from that age. From the day a school friend's older brother locks them both in his room, a teenage retreat at the back of his house, straps them to the bed and sodomises them both. John's mate is terrified of his brother, who has been systematically raping him for years, but he is too frightened to do anything about it. John, tiny and under-developed for his age, lies next to his friend on the bed. He is punched in the mouth to stop him whimpering, and hog-tied face down, the pain savage and searing, his cries muffled by the mattress. His friend's brother entering that private place, that dark tunnel; penetrating, humiliating, hurting him and afterwards he is on the phone to his mates, boasting, 'I've got these two conditioned and we're all going to have a party'. Beaten and burnt with cigarettes, their flesh is singed and each bloke takes them in turns. John whimpers softly, too scared to move, and tears burn his cheeks until his friend's father suddenly materialises in the bedroom. 'Let them go', he yells, untying them and opening the door. Tells John to collect his things and dispatches him to a doctor.

Too traumatised to tell the truth about what has happened, John instead quietly goes home after the welts on his face are patched up. And when he does finally speak of it, years later, he refers to the rape as his 'accident'. Tells people his attacker fled the house to avoid his parents, tore down the street on his motorbike and ran straight under a bus. Tells the story over and over, his voice rising, high-pitched. The squeal of brakes, the bloke somersaulting through the air and landing dead on the bitumen. Raped by a dirty fag and robbed of any opportunity for revenge by the bloke's sudden, accidental death, John never gets any closure. But fantasy or truth; no one ever knows.

The way John tells it, his mother takes one look at him when he walks in the door and smacks him in the mouth. 'You're late, it's teatime and you had me worried sick.' That's all she says, he reckons, even after she notices the bruising on his face. He touches his swollen mouth, tells her he is late because he has fallen off his pushbike, goes to the bathroom and tries to stem the bleeding from his anus. He is too ashamed to tell her the truth, and never does. Bottles up his secret, keeps it close to his chest.

His schoolmates remember he was always close-mouthed. Even when the police start digging around in his past, that's the way they recall John Bunting. Reserved. Secretive. Arcane.

His parents don't know about his chemical experiments with spiders, or how he has been traumatised, but they find out about the underground tunnel he and his friend, Kurt, have dug under the house. A sophisticated, meticulously planned underground corridor that is 1.5 metres high and 5 metres long, reinforced with bricks and wood. John is furious when his father demands it be filled in. He can't, he fumes, keep anything secret.

And John's attackers tail him for months after the rapes, yelling obscenities, chasing him through parks and once running him off the road on his pushbike and dragging him into the back seat of a car. Threatening him: 'If we get hold of you again you're dead'. He lives in fear of his own shadow. Festering with anger and resentment, he keeps his shameful secret to himself.

At 13, John meets a bloke called Benny, who is in his 40s. Benny wears the scars of his own horrific boyhood with his father, a cruel bastard of a man who hacked off some of Benny's toes with bolt cutters, just for the fun of it. Persistently terrorised him, never knowing what his Dad would do next. Benny listens quietly when John summons the courage to ask for his help, and promises him protection, but with a catch. John will play bait for Benny, become his lure. Be his stool pigeon.

The name amuses him. *Stool* pigeon.

Loitering on street corners, tiny and under-developed for his age, John is the perfect decoy for the leering men who walk past and then double back for a closer look. 'Do you want to come with me, little boy?' John nods, 'Yes. But I have to tell my brother where I'm going first'. Leads the men around the corner, into the shadows of a side street where Benny lies in wait. Laughing as they smash the stranger to a pulp, leaving him begging for mercy and saturated in his own blood.

At 17, John gets a job putting up handball nets, travelling around mainland Australia and Tasmania, but based in Brisbane. The job saves him having to tell his mother he has left home; she figures he is just away working. And as soon as he lands back in Queensland, he hooks up with Benny again. He has a lot of acquaintances, people he calls great mates, but he is closest to Benny. Later, he boasts to Jamie Vlassakis that Benny taught him the ropes, how to deal with fags. 'He and Benny did a few murders', Vlassakis will later say. 'Benny taught him what to do.' Bunting's only other friend is a younger boy, Charles, whom he knew in his childhood. According to John, Charles committed suicide in his early teens.

And John also has another secret now: a daughter, Tammy, born when he was 17. He shares a casual custody arrangement with Tammy's mother, Lisa, even though they have separated before Tammy is born. Lisa is young, too, and wants a life, goes off on little jaunts with her latest boyfriend, comes back and picks Tammy up from him from the flat in which he is now living. 'Thanks, John', she says, and breezes out the door with the baby.

His parents don't know about Tammy. Another secret, stored away. He is like that: close-mouthed and tight-lipped. No one ever knows anything he doesn't want them to. The few people he does tell about his daughter recall he had his own reason for not telling his mother. 'He couldn't just walk up with this baby in his arms and say, "Here, Grandma"', Elizabeth Harvey explains. 'She didn't want grandchildren. She didn't want to be called Grandma.'

Lisa moves in with a boyfriend early in her pregnancy, tells the man it is his child. It is an on-again, off-again relationship that finishes altogether when Tammy is two, when the man finds out Tammy isn't his daughter. Terrible things he does to the little girl in his rage, physical and sexual things, so terrible Lisa asks John to pay for their tickets to England, to get them away. She has met another man whom she will marry in England, and she never returns to Australia.

And Tammy will not come back, either.

John and Benny are now inseparable, so close John calls Benny family. They become increasingly violent as time goes by: breaking into paedophiles' houses, up-ending furniture, defecating in the beds and killing their cats. Smearing 'faggot' on their walls with faeces and then going out in search of new victims. John hangs on Benny's every word. The younger man has not only found a father figure he can relate to. He has finally found a hero.

The police don't charge them with any crime, and Bunting becomes smug, self-assured. The cops are stupid. He is invincible.

And then Benny dies. John's friend, the man he regards as his 'family', is dead within months from the throat cancer that ravages him. A cruel death and nothing left for John in Queensland but dark secrets and Benny's ghost on every street corner.

1985. John is 18 years old, itching to hit the highway. He shares a house with a mate, Mark Day, after he is retrenched from his job. Day recalls Bunting talked incessantly about how he liked to bash up poofters. He doesn't believe John's rambling, thinks he is full of crap, but he travels with him anyway.

In February 1986, a junket of two cars and nine people – including John's friends Kevin and Michelle, Mark Day and Mark's 14-year-old girlfriend, Esmay – heads west, aiming for Perth. Bunting tells people he has been run out of Queensland by the cops, but they never know whether to believe him or not. So many stories, they never know if it is truth or lies. The car keeps breaking down and they pull stumps at Adelaide, book into a caravan park in the northern suburbs and stay there until the heat comes, when some of John's mates are done for break and enters. Still, Adelaide is a pretty place, seems like a good enough city to prop. John scores a job painting the concrete floor at a motor museum, a mind-numbing, menial task for a young man interested in chemistry and electronics. Painting the floor, smiling to himself. Fantasising about bashing up poofters, travelling back in time to his days with Benny. His work mates find him affable enough, though his high, sharp voice with the suggestion of a lisp can irritate. His reference, when he is retrenched, is glowing. Bunting is a diligent, enthusiastic and intelligent worker.

When Mark and Esmay break up, she and John start a year-long relationship; when that ends, John, Kevin and Michelle move out of the caravan park and into a house together.

The South Australian Meat Corporation offers John casual

shifts as a general labourer. This is much more to his liking: bagging meat and using his knife skills at the evisceration table on the beast's offal – spleen, liver and other organs. Much more to his liking.

He is busy in his spare time, too. Building his collection of guns that he secretes under his bed, and honing his reading skills: how to make home-made poisons, blow-torches and Molotov cocktails. The ceiling – that dark, enclosed space above the kitchen – is his favourite hiding place, where he stores his favourite things. Poisons, rope, knives, blow-torch. Guns are effective, too, as he has already discovered, after blowing a hole through a dog he didn't like. Instant death. Blood oozing from the wound. Hanging the animal in the shed for a few days before hauling it into a garbage bag and tossing it out in a deserted street on the edge of suburbia. Boasting to friends, who shake their heads at his stories about what he has done. But instant death bores him, leaves him feeling deflated, edgy. There is no challenge in the planning, or lasting thrill in the execution. Guns are too fast. Too impersonal. He wants to get up close. It is the things he hides in the ceiling, the slower instruments of pain, that he loves to collect.

It is his secret.

Life is good in Adelaide. Within months of moving in with Kevin and Michelle, John meets Veronika.

4

John revs the car all the way to Queensland so Veronika can meet his parents, and does most of the talking. When they are on their own, Veronika teases him that he could talk the leg off an iron pot, but she likes to listen to him.

Unlike Veronika, John can read, but he doesn't judge her. He isn't her first boyfriend, but he is the only fella who is of any use to her; not like some other witless boys she has known. They were practically glued to each other, she remembers. Always kissing and cuddling. John wasn't big on using the 'love' word but that was okay with her.

John cracks a lot of jokes, and Veronika laughs. But not everything he says is funny. He can be a big shot with his mouth. Hints at a sordid past, how he fled from Queensland, got out while he still could. Half the time Veronika doesn't believe his stories and she tells him to stop, particularly when he tells her things that really gross her out. She rolls her eyes, rests her tongue on her bottom lip and plonks her hands on her hips when she thinks about the things that he told her. How he loved to go into details about his time working in a Queensland crematorium and his fascination with dead bodies. Or when he detailed how he stuck skewers into a pig and bled it out before he cut off its head. She asks him why he would kill the dopey looking critter: surely not just for the fun of it? He just grins and she figures he has to be lying. Veronika can't understand why he would want to spin these sorts of yarns. She loves animals. The thought of hurting them upsets her.

Right from the start John tells stories, holding his audience in the palm of his hand, inviting them to enter his world. Leaves them shaking their heads, wondering if what they have just heard is true, but marvelling at his imagination if it is not. Stories so graphic they make people feel ill, but that doesn't stop him repeating them. Skiting that one of his former girl-friends had been sexually abused as a young child, and how he and his mate had grabbed the bastard who molested her, strangled him and cut him up as they drove along the highway between Adelaide and Melbourne. Hacked him up and threw him, piece by piece, out the window. One driving and the other cutting, both laughing and singing, soaked in blood and the car interior sticky and scarlet. It is one of his favourite stories. He tells it often.

John's mother, Jan, doesn't say anything but Veronika gets the impression that she doesn't approve of her. Something in Jan's tight mouth and sideways glances suggests Veronika isn't quite good enough for her son. The house is spotless, and it makes Veronika uneasy. John's father, Tom, is a lot less intimidating but still, Veronika is glad to get back to Adelaide, where she and John step into the registry office on a warm day in mid-September 1989. A 19-year-old bride in a dress suitable for a woman twice her age: a calf-length sky-blue frock with ruffles on the shoulders, accessorised with flat white shoes. Her husband in a white shirt and black tie and coat, too-long trousers falling in folds around his ankles. Veronika can't remember her vows, simple utterances of loyalty and love, but John prompts her and she follows his cue, words rising and falling in her strident, singsong voice underpinned with the monotone of the half-deaf. I, Veronika Leanne Tripp, 'I, VeROniKA LeANNE TrIPP', take you, John Justin Bunting, 'take YOU, John JUSTin BUNting . . .'

A moment frozen on Polaroid: parents and relatives standing beside the bride and groom, in the street outside the registry office, twenty-six guests in all. John holding his new wife's hand, squinting and grinning at the same time; a wide grin encircled by thin lips; hair tied in a ponytail at the back and flopping over his forehead like a Muppet. Veronika loves John's light-brown hair, especially the way it curls slightly when it hangs loose past his shoulders. John loves his hair, too.

Veronika's parents stand next to their daughter, her mother joyless, her face already starting to crease into dry craggy lines that will, through stress and fear, later run deep as crevices. Her father leans slightly backwards, one hand thrust into his pocket, laughing at the camera. John's mother's hand is chained into the crook of her husband's elbow, her lips set in a studied grin almost wide enough to reach her red earrings. His father, Tom, in pale blue suit and brown shoes, stands awkwardly, hands clasped together at the front and staring away from the camera. Aloof and distant as a Buckingham Palace guard, his body language screaming that he doesn't want to be there.

They spend their wedding night – their honeymoon – at a hotel. Veronika isn't much into sex, has not developed an appetite for it. She is never quite sure what she is meant to do so she does nothing, suffering John's attentions with resignation. If he is a good lover, or an indifferent one, she neither knows nor cares. She was a virgin when they met, and has no means of comparison. But he isn't kinky or weird, she knows that much. He just does what she knows men do, while she lies still on her back hoping he won't take long. 'Sex is just flippin' over-rated', she will later say, shaking her head vigorously as she speaks. 'I dunno what the big deal is. Can't work that one out.' Worse, John wants to do it every day. She thinks that's a bit much.

Two weeks before Christmas 1991, they move into their first real home together, at 203 Waterloo Corner Road, Salisbury North. An unremarkable, double-fronted weatherboard identical to its neighbours, on a street clogged with traffic in a housing trust area an hour north of Adelaide. For a wedding present, John's parents buy them a washing machine; soon after, they also move from Brisbane to Adelaide to live. Jan hates the sweltering Queensland weather and John constantly harps at them to move to South Australia.

But they rarely visit. It is John's biggest complaint, that his parents live quite close but hardly ever stop to see him. He recalls how they would drive past his house up to five times a week, but he usually had to visit them. It makes him really mad. Elizabeth Harvey ruminates on his relationship with his parents. 'He didn't have a close relationship. On the surface it was, "I'll play being the good son, I'll visit", but underneath they couldn't understand why John was always angry and what they'd done. It was because of their attitude towards him . . . they were very, very conservative.'

Veronika's parents visit more often, though Jim hates his new son-in-law. 'He's got a cruel mouth', he complains to his wife, Patsy. 'I think he's trouble.' But Patsy likes John well enough. He is harmless, she thinks, and Veronika is happy. 'Give them a go', she tells Jim. 'They're only just starting out.'

5

Sometimes mischievous, sometimes surly, Robert Wagner was born in late November 1971 – the same year astronauts first drove on the surface of the moon. His father abandoned the family when Robert was nine months old and at three, he moved with his mother and sister to Adelaide from New South Wales. Within months they settled in the housing trust area of Elizabeth West and by five, Robert had started school. Hulking and slow right from the start, he gawped at his teachers with dull eyes and slyly shifted sideways in his seat to see what the other students were doing. Dyslexic, he never grasped how to read or write. School was to be endured.

Robert fights constantly with his mother's new lover, Les, who once beats him when he refuses to pick up things from the floor. Another time, he cops a hiding when he baulks at mowing the lawn, because he knows the grass cuttings will bring on a severe asthma attack. It is a childhood strained by blues with his stepfather, being barely able to read or write and isolated from his peers.

Shortly before his eighth birthday, Robert is sexually abused by the teenage son of his mother's friend who is staying at their house for a short time and occasionally looks after him. Michael has a go at him when no one else is around, but Robert doesn't tell. Only a child, he is so traumatised he tries to commit suicide afterwards. He wants out of this world, wakes instead from an overdose of drugs found in the bathroom cupboard, whimpering and talking to himself, lost in his own private pain: 'Michael, don't hurt us. Leave me alone'. He develops even more severe learning difficulties from this time on, growing into a tall, churlish heavy-set boy who jostles uneasily amongst people.

By the time he reaches his teens, Robert stops going to school altogether, but his mother doesn't know. He walks out the door at the same time as other students do, his school bag slung over his shoulder, and comes home after the last bell. Regular as clockwork until the truancy officer knocks on the door and gives up his little game.

Barry Lane knows Salisbury North well. It has been his stomping ground for years, this run-down suburb next to Elizabeth where he stands out from the crowd with his dyed, dirty-blond shoulder-length hair and luminous pink shorts. He is different, but those who know him suffer his eccentricities with a shrug.

Born in Snowtown in August 1955, his birth name is Barry Venables, the fourth of 11 children in a family whose bloodline is an eclectic mix of Irish, Scottish, German and Aboriginal descent. Taken from his family at eight months, he is returned into the arms of his grandmother from foster care when she gains custody of the small boy. His father, a violent alcoholic, terrorises the family, regularly bashing his mother, Sylvia, even as she is swollen with child. Barry's oldest brother, Cyril, remembers their upbringing as harsh and joyless: Sylvia begging for food, their father menacing in his drunkenness. He picked Cyril up by his armpits once, banged his head on the ceiling so hard that the boy sustained concussion. No one cried when, before they reach adolescence, their father died of a stroke.

Barry spends his formative years in the mining town of Port Pirie, where baking heat and isolation have earned it the name, 'the Iron Triangle'. Men brawl in the streets and sissies are condemned. His mother, Sylvia, lives nearby and the Salvation Army plays a large role in the family's life. But he is always something of an oddity. His two younger sisters, Suzanne and Gillian, cope with the unrelenting, grinding poverty of their childhood by trying to fit in, blending into the school playground despite their clothes being held together by a thread, sitting slightly apart from other students when they eat the lean offerings in their lunch boxes.

But Barry doesn't ever fit in, never tries to. The family's penury seems to ingrain itself on his personality. He quickly works out that the best way to escape reality is by pretending he is someone else. Inwardly, he is Barry Lane, from a destitute family. Outwardly, from the age of nine, he metamorphoses into a glamour puss, a female incarnation who calls herself 'Vanessa'. At first, alone in his room, Barry dolls up in gaudy glass bauble earrings, fish-net stockings and a hot pink skirt; two years later, peeking out the door, looking up and down the street, wonders: dare she make her debut yet? And by 15, he is sashaying in stilettos and satin, lips painted and false lashes fluttering, waving to the men in cars who slow down to honk and ogle.

But Vanessa can be a real bitch. Sometimes she doesn't want to go out to play, and so Barry has to go in her place. And Barry's favourite playmates are young boys.

In 1980, aged 25, Lane receives a four-month prison sentence for the sexual assaults of two 12-year-old boys. He has become something of a regular in the court for similar offences, and the judge is harsh in his caution. Lane, he says, clearly has problems establishing his identity, but that does not give him the right to behave in this manner for his own gratification. Lane's response is to blame his family who, he grizzles, prevent him from living his life as he chooses. 'If I done such a foolish thing again . . . I'd rather be chucked away for life and the keys chucked away.' Even in prison, Lane stands out from the rest of the inmates. Tagged as a 'rock spider', he is regarded as the lowest link in the prison food chain. Other prisoners vent their contempt for him by spitting on his food and regularly threaten him with violence.

He is glad to get out of there and has some counselling sessions when he is released, sitting in a room with a well-meaning person who wears a benign expression as he unravels Barry's life, stitch by stitch. The counsellor nodding sagely, 'Mmm, mmm . . .' as he gently leads Barry down a path of understanding about why he fancies young boys: 'Now tell me, Barry, what drives you to this behaviour; do you still feel the desire to touch a boy?' And Barry sits there, thinking: 'This is like being in confession, this is a waste of time'. As soon as he can, he stops attending. He becomes a regular sight around Salisbury North, trying to engage in conversation with pre-pubescent males, fluttering his eyelashes and fluttering his hands, pouting, 'I'm only *talking* to them', if people look sideways at him as they walk past.

Lane's house is frequently pelted with rocks and he is constantly derided when he walks the streets dressed as Vanessa. In an effort to stop his three-day growth showing through, he tries pills to make himself more feminine. It doesn't work. Trying to find his soul, he joins the Salvation Army but that doesn't work either. He turns up outside the gates where his sisters go to school, frocked up in his Salvos' Army Band uniform, embarrassing the girls as he blasts away – badly – on a trumpet. When he grows tired of the Salvos, he moves on. Church shopping becomes a hobby. Church shopping and young boys.

Robert Wagner doesn't tell his mother but she finds out anyway, that he is spending his days with a transsexual instead of going to school. 'Her name is Vanessa', he says, 'and she lives just a fingertip away, around the corner from our home.' Robert wants his mother to meet her. Wagner has met the much older man at a party, and Lane will later boast to people that he asked the young man to perform fellatio on him.

She is horrified that her 13-year-old son is with this 'thing': a man trying desperately to pretend he is a woman. But there is no mistaking he is a bloke. It is as though someone has stamped the memory in her mind. Yellow, unkempt hair that he continually flicks back from his shoulders, a blue strapless dress and feminine, white high-heeled sandals ridiculously out of place at the end of hairy, mannish legs. Boasting to her about the presents he has given her son: expensive remote control cars, other gifts she can't afford on a sole parent pension. Touching Robert in front of her, and her son uncomfortable. Still, when Carol tries to cajole Robert into coming home, he refuses. He wants to stay with Vanessa, he says.

Carol rings the police, gets them to go and bring him back, and the pattern has started. Robert disappearing, the coppers bringing him home, him staying for a few days and then gone again. Even the school has given up, tells Carol he may as well leave permanently; he is never there anyway. Welfare doesn't want to know about it, either, and Carol is contemptuous of their inaction, how they rubber stamp her son's safety and file it away in a drawer. They just put it in the 'too hard' basket, she reckons. They say Robert will soon be of the age of consent and can then do what he likes. Unless he makes a complaint himself, they cannot act.

Two months after his fourteenth birthday, Robert vanishes into thin air. It will be years before Carol sees him again.

Not one word from her teenage son for four years, until he suddenly turns up again in Adelaide with Vanessa in tow. Now 18 years old and at the age of consent, Robert Wagner is more than 183 centimetres tall and broad-shouldered. He hasn't kept in touch, he tells his mother, because his lover won't allow him to. He can only see Carol now if Barry is also there. Vanessa, Barry. It's hard for her to keep up.

Carol is determined to maintain contact with her son this time. She detests Lane, but visits the couple at the home they rent through the housing trust at 1 Bingham Road, Salisbury North. Right opposite a school, where Lane has a bird's-eye view of the young boys who play in the grounds at lunch-time. He can't believe his luck; surely the housing trust knows of his criminal history?

Carol doesn't have five minutes peace alone with Robert. It seems Lane is always hovering, mincing about in the back-ground. The creep just won't go away.

Tall and angular, Lane has a high, protruding forehead and receding hairline, his broad nose set against gaunt cheekbones. Glasses frame cold, staring eyes but his mouth is feminine, a cupid's bow on his top lip ripe for lipstick. He cuts an odd match next to his truculent lover.

Neither man holds down a job, both surviving on disability

pensions; medical certificates ensure a reduced reporting time to Centrelink than other pensions, for permanent illness or incapacity to work. Lane often complains of debilitating back pain, and Wagner's illiteracy ensures that no employer will give him a look in the door.

Robert Wagner worships Hitler. In deference to the dictator, he names one of his Alsatians 'Adolf' and has a computer screen saver that trumpets 'Adolf Hitler is still alive'.

Wagner's neighbours often comment on how 'weird' he is; as snarly as the Alsatians he keeps. They recall him as a tough sort of bloke, with rough manners. Nicknamed 'Lurch' because of his height; covered in tattoos, he is a walking art gallery. But the tattoos aren't enough. He wants a swastika emblazoned on his forehead, a brazen symbol of defiance against the world. Tattooists shudder when he approaches them to do it: Adelaide, with its large European population, including Germans and Jews, is too small a city. Wagner contents himself with his growing involvement in National Action, bully boys with extreme reactionary neo-Nazi views who preach racial purity and employ terror tactics similar to the Ku Klux Klan. To prove his allegiance to National Action, Wagner's upper arm proudly displays the group's emblem, the Eureka flag. He is only a member for a year until, with Bunting (whom he has yet to meet), he is thrown out for being too radical. Still, it is long enough to make Wagner boastful and rambunctious about his allegiance to its cause.

Wagner's slender, long fingers seem out of place on the end of an arm inked with an emblem symbolising violence and hatred. Fingers that could belong to a professional pianist but instead curl into fists when he is angry or annoyed. He is angry and annoyed often, as surly and savage as his Alsatians.

The Alsatians, and Doberman they also keep, prowl the perimeters of Lane and Wagner's property, kept in by a 2-metre iron fence that they erect. The dogs growl and bark incessantly at neighbours who walk past, scaring them half out of their wits. But if the noise is bad enough, the smell that wafts over the fence from the animals' excrement is nauseating. Sometimes the neighbours complain to the couple about it, but nothing is done. They don't notice the stench, tell the neighbours to mind their own business.

And if the yard is filthy, the house is unfit for human habitation. Piles of dog and cat excreta on the floor. Bird droppings. Mountains of dirty dishes covered in mildew. Fleas in the carpet. Neighbours give up trying to talk to them, get the Health Commission down instead.

Wagner likes to play church music, lengthy funereal pieces that blare from their house. The music matches his personality: brooding, melancholy. He smirks, never smiles. They are only renting the house, but they still rig up an expensive alarm system and security doors. The neighbours think it is odd, but then, Wagner and Lane are odd, though they seem devoted. Call each other 'love', hold hands in the street and look coyly into each other's eyes. Wagner often introduces Lane as his fiancé, and they boast to anyone who will listen of their plans to marry.

Bestiality is one of their favourite party tricks. Cornering a Doberman out in the backyard, while kids walk past on the street. The other dogs in a chorus, growling, barking while Wagner, frigid and impassive, holds the Doberman. Lane mincing, fluttering and fretting at the animal: 'Oh, keep *still*'. A neighbour hears them skite about it once, how they tried to 'do' a dog in their backyard, but he doesn't find out if they are successful. Doesn't like to ask. He often hears them bragging about their exploits. They would invite themselves into his house, he says, and talk incessantly about sex.

But there is a downside to their relationship. It is fractured by constant violence: punching, screaming, kicking each other, doors slamming in temper. The violence adds to the din; their home is a madhouse.

6

Robert Skewes is looking for a quiet life when he moves into 205 Waterloo Corner Road. Orphaned from childhood, he sustained mild brain damage from his traumatic birth and has suffered migraine headaches all his life. He left school early – 'I didn't do very good at school' – and has lived on a disability pension since the age of 20. Lived a lean, gritty existence in Sydney, where he bunked down for a time at the Matthew Talbot hostel for homeless men. Corpulent with greasy, grey hair, he has an untrimmed moustache and beard that collide with each other on a face as lined as railway tracks. His tongue constantly flirts with his lips as he speaks, poking out like a lizard's.

In his late fifties, but looking at least a decade older, Skewes is grateful to have a patch of dirt to call his own when he wanders back to Adelaide. His sunless housing trust house is no palace, but it beats the hell out of the streets. He fills it with vinyl furniture and decorates it with empty Coke cartons, old tobacco tins, plastic bags and anything else that falls to the floor after he has used it. For company he keeps large, black dogs, and cats that sleep throughout the house and have litters season after season. The house reeks with the overwhelming smell of dog and cat urine, unwashed dishes and pizza boxes gathering mould. There is not a spare centimetre of the place that isn't cluttered from floor to ceiling. Pure squalor.

Robert Wagner and Barry Lane live a short distance away from their new friend, Skewes. The three men are introduced to John and Veronika Bunting the day the young couple move into 203, and soon all of them are hauling boxes and lifting furniture. Helping the newlyweds settle in. Soon, Wagner and Lane are hanging around the Buntings' house all the time.

★ ★ ★

Mark Haydon is another neighbour who hangs around, too. Barely educated, he is often described by people who know him as backward, slow. Monosyllabic when he speaks at all; but most of the time he is silent. He looks old; even as a boy, his face creased into scowl lines. An only child following the death of his 26-year-old brother in a car accident years before, when he isn't hanging around Bunting's house he spends his time tinkering with cars in the backyard of the home he shares with his father in Catalina Avenue, Elizabeth East. A backyard littered with broken-down FJ Holdens that he reckons he will fix up one day. He loves cars, scoring his first job at General Motors Holden where his old man has worked for a decade. Haydon doesn't last that long: sacked after two years, he never works again.

Resigned to never marrying, he doesn't participate in life at all, instead just lets it drift past him. But he can sometimes show reasonable intelligence, answering quiz show questions and getting them right. It surprises people, who know him to be an introverted, meek follower, to hear him speak with authority. His schizophrenic mother was in and out of mental homes all her life until her death in 1996, and Mark is on the carer's pension, looking after his Dad.

Wagner, Lane, Haydon, Bunting and Skewes wander in and out of each other's homes, whenever the fancy takes them. Skewes doesn't have a car, and Bunting sometimes drives him places, particularly on pension day when the older man collects his cheque. But Skewes notices something about his neighbour that he keeps to himself: John likes to get his own way, expects people to jump to his tune. Skewes's eyes gleam when he psychoanalyses Bunting. 'There was a real mean streak lurking under his placid persona', he smirks with a hint of self-congratulatory revelation. He wags his head up and down as he speaks. Yep, no question about it. Bunting could be a cruel son-of-a-bitch.

★ ★ ★

From the outset, Bunting enjoys an easy relationship with Wagner, who hangs on his every word. But he despises Lane, sniggering behind his hands when he introduces him to other people. 'Come and meet this freak', he sneers.

7

Without work, both Lane and Wagner have plenty of time on their hands and they spend much of it at another neighbour's house watching TV and drinking coffee. In his early fifties, unemployed and bored, Geoffrey Williams is glad of the company and John Bunting is also a frequent visitor. Williams has Lane and Wagner in his home, but he won't go to visit them. They are filthy dirty, and so is their house. Still, they hang out together.

Although he is a regular visitor, Bunting hates Williams. He once grabs a can of paint and scrawls 'fag' on his fence, before going home and boasting to Veronika in an exaggerated lisp about what he has done. 'I just painted pretty words on Williams's fence', he crows. He starts to fantasise about how he can fix Williams up. He will fill his house with dead people, sit Williams's corpse upright in a chair, plant a live Chihuahua into his neck and wait for the cops to arrive. Laughs as he imagines the scene that would greet them: ventriloquist corpse barking like a dog, cops backing out the door and going mad for years after, needing psychiatric help.

John Bunting spends hours fashioning fantasies in his head. This is one of his favourites. Even when alone, he laughs out loud just thinking about it.

For a short time in 1991, Barry Lane and Robert Wagner are friendly with 17-year-old Clinton Trezise. Born in the first quarter of December 1973, at the tail end of the hippie flower-power movement, Trezise spent his early years in care facilities and with foster families. Divorced when Clinton was three, his mother placed the little boy and his brother, Scott, into care, but the fractured family maintained frequent weekly visits. Throughout his young life, Trezise's moral, physical and emotional wellbeing was controlled and administered by a welfare officer.

Craving security and attention, Trezise, with his freckled face, gap-toothed ready smile and small eyes that insinuate deep inner sadness, spends his early adolescence meandering through the maze of evangelical churches that hold out their loving arms and collection bowls to all who enter their portals. Trezise crosses many, as if going through a car wash: entering with dirty soul, washed clean, rinsed and left to drip-dry. He finds another church each time he tires of the old one. Attempting to better himself, he returns to school as a mature age student and teams up with a classmate, spending time hanging around the city with him until the friendship sours when Clinton sexually hits on him. Now an adult, 16 years Lane's junior, he is a gay, happy-go-lucky drifter who sports dyed copper-blonde hair and orange nail polish, his bum wiggling in the full technicolour of his flame-red and purple trousers.

John Bunting hates him, too. Christens him 'Happy Pants'.

By mid-1991, Trezise finally has a place to call his own, a small flat amongst hundreds of others in the grim northern suburbs, compliments of his landlord – South Australia's Housing Trust.

John and Veronika are going to Bingham Road for an early tea with Wagner and Lane. It isn't an invitation Veronika relishes: the fetid smell of dogs and cats turns her stomach. The men sit in the lounge room after tea, watching TV while Veronika plays on the floor with a cat, idly tickling its tummy. She recalls the occasion: 'John, Robert and Barry disappeared. They told me to stay there and mind the cats'. She remembers the cats, she will later say, because one was 'somewhere between the lounge room and the kitchen at the time. It had two legs in different places.'

She is used to John, with Robert, going out and giving her little notice of their movements. Day or night, they come back with things; the ceiling at 203 full of things. Video recorders, electrical items, computer equipment. All in good condition, and much more than she and John need for their house. The gear is never stored in the junk room, but she doesn't query why.

'Did you think maybe they'd been naughty and they'd been stealing them?' she is later asked in court.

'It's possible', Veronika replies petulantly. 'I didn't know what to think about it.'

And now they have gone out again. Just locked the door behind them and disappeared. Veronika thinks nothing of it.

It is light when the men leave the house, dark when they return. Night and day, dark and light; simple measures of time for a woman with poor eyesight and a very poor memory, a grown woman who will give evidence in court clutching a teddy bear.

Tired of sitting on the floor and playing with the cat, Veronika curls up on the couch in front of the television and falls asleep.

Happy Pants is gone. Simply disappeared, but no one notifies the police. Occasionally someone inquires, 'Where's Clinton?' and it will usually be Wagner who shrugs, 'He's a drifter, could be anywhere'. Barry flutters his eyelashes and flutters his hands in a vague, helpless way and says nothing. He once dares speak to his sister, Sherie, about Clinton, standing outside the front door of his house, his voice low and eyes nervously darting to see if anyone is listening. And then Wagner appears at the door and furiously interrupts the conversation. 'What have you been saying, get back inside!' he screams, his face purple with rage. The door slams in Sherie's face.

By August 1992, Sherie is wondering where her brother, Clinton, has got to. She rings his flat constantly, but there is no answer; finally, by September, she and her father go around to see him. The Housing Trust has notified her that Clinton's tenancy has been terminated and, armed with a key, they drive to his flat. Sherie isn't in the habit of visiting him regularly; she also regards him as reasonably tidy. But when she stands outside with her father and they peer through the gap in the drawn lounge room curtains, she instinctively senses something is wrong. There is no sign of life inside the messy lounge room, and when they eventually go inside, they are floored by what they see. The flat looks disgusting. The smell is the first thing that hits them; Sherie, a nurse, likens it to a wound or ulcer dressing. It is putrid, makes them want to throw up. There are half-empty cans of food around the place, with flies crawling through them, and dog faeces on Clinton's bedroom floor.

They close the door behind them. God only knows where he has gone to.

When he isn't physically reinventing himself, Barry Lane is making up yarns. He is a daydreamer, a bullshitter; couldn't lie straight in bed. He has a fantastic imagination, often telling people that he menstruates every month, just as women do, or that he is pregnant. And so Veronika doesn't believe him at first as Lane, starkly agitated, stands in her lounge room, looking around to make sure no one else is there. Nervously rubbing moist hands over his tight satin shorts, trembling as he begs her not to tell anyone about this conversation. Particularly John, he says. He is petrified of John. She asks him, why are you telling me? And he replies, I've got to tell *someone*. And after Lane leaves, Veronika takes a cursory look around her lounge room. Shrugs her shoulders impatiently, huffs as she gets down on her hands and knees and checks under the couch. Nothing here, flippin' nothing to back up Barry's story. No blood on the floorboards or walls. Furniture intact. No evidence of cleaning or mopping up.

Veronika tells John about the conversation as soon as he comes home. Not a muscle moves in his face while he listens impassively as Veronika recounts what Barry has told her: that John killed a man, a friend of theirs. Barry didn't say who it was, and she didn't ask. 'Well, what reason would I have to ask?' she will later counter. 'And you didn't flippin' muck around with John, I can tell you that much.' She tells John that Barry reckoned he had helped him dispose of the body. Describes how he shuddered and shook when he told her, his skin pale and clammy, terrified the walls had ears.

John denies it, reminds Veronika that Barry is a bullshitter with a big mouth. Remember the time, John says, that he had a gift for Veronika, a microwave oven, but Barry ruined the surprise, blabbed about it? Barry just can't shut up. John tells her to ignore the story, so Veronika does as he suggests. Forgets about it, puts it out of her mind. Besides, she argues, she only ever put up with Barry. She didn't never *took* to him much.

A month later Lane is back again, more distressed, gabbling the same story but adding awful details. How John had crept up behind the man in the lounge room of John and Veronika's home at 203 Waterloo Corner Road, hit the man on the head with a shovel, felled him like a tree. Shovelled him up and with Haydon and Lane's help, threw his body in Lane's station wagon and drove to Lower Light, 20 minutes from Salisbury North, and dug a shallow grave. Tossed him into this makeshift tomb in a lonely, windswept paddock and covered the body with soil. After, Lane whispers, John wiped his hands on his jeans and drove off, not so much as a backward glance at the grave. Acted normally on the way to Lane's house to pick up Veronika, who was still fast asleep on the couch with the TV flickering snow in the darkened room.

Lane, pale and sweaty, takes off his glasses and rubs his eyes which are smudged with dark shadows. A waterfall of words gushes out, terror punctuating his sentences. He pleads with Veronika: 'Please don't tell John. He'll come after me if he knows I've told someone'.

This time, when Veronika mentions the conversation, John admits it. Says Lane isn't making it up after all. He is implacable, indifferent about the killing but savage about Lane and his big mouth. His eyes blaze as he tells her that Lane has been told to say nothing, but the filthy faggot just can't keep his trap closed.

Veronika can, though. She has been warned to shut up, and

she does. It helps that she has a lousy memory, and that John threatens her, too: 'Say anything to anyone, and you'll end up like the person at Lower Light. So shut the fuck up'.

She is silenced by the same sort of fear that protects her husband from his friends. She doesn't tell her parents, doesn't tell the police. Veronika is a good wife, does as she is told. She shuts the fuck up. Doesn't tell a soul.

They are bleached by the elements, years of exposure to the sun and wind and rain in sheep grazing country at Lower Light, 50 kilometres north of Adelaide. There is no doubt in the two farmers' minds what they have stumbled on. Brothers Ronald and Jack Finch, who have been spraying weeds on their 1600-hectare property, crouch closer to the earth to take a look. It is the close of winter, 1994, an imminent spring heralded by a warming sun. Bones, the colour of chalk, scattered by wildlife. Human remains: skeletal parts and skull strewn around the isolated paddock and legs disconnected from the torso. But who it is, and how long the corpse has been here, is a mystery. Ron nurses the skull in his large, weathered hand, before returning it to the earth. The farmers stand up, push their Akubras to the backs of their heads and leave the rest of the bones as they found them. They drive the tractor back to their homestead, carefully avoiding what they had at first thought was a fox hole. It unsettles them to now accept they have tramped over someone's burial ground.

Within an hour, police, including detectives from the Major Crime branch, converge on the paddock. Their numbers will swell within 24 hours, as they fan out on hands and knees to find any physical clues to aid identification.

In Adelaide, forensic pathologist Ross James painstakingly pieces the dry, odourless bones together to form a human whole. He notes the skeleton is that of an adult, white Caucasian male, around 17 years old, 172 centimetres tall and of slender build. An elongated jaw, tapered nose and large teeth with a prominent gap crowding a small mouth. Left-handed, judging by the development of his left shoulder joint compared with his right. Hair dyed copper-blonde and a hole in the left side at the back of his skull that marks death as consistent with traumatic brain damage. A facial reconstruction approximating similarity to the victim's is forwarded to the media and $100,000 reward for anyone with information is posted. Fruitless. The skeleton does not match any police records of Missing Persons, and a public appeal for help yields no results. 'Somebody, or a group of people, has lost a mate', a police officer tells the press. 'He's got friends, his friends must have missed him. Someone knows something.' But it appears they don't. So this white, Caucasian male joins the ranks of the unidentified: another mystery death, another unclaimed individual who has been perhaps a vagrant, an illegal immigrant, a drunk, a junkie. Without identification, there is no way of knowing. He remains a tag, a number, a question mark, seemingly belonging to no one and from nowhere. Just skeletal remains, stored at the State Forensic Science Centre in Adelaide.

In 1995, a woman contacts police and reports her son missing. His name is Clinton, she says, Clinton Trezise, and he was last seen in 1992. No, she tells the police operator, the family has had no contact with him since. He is a bit of a drifter, a young, impressionable bloke who just floats about from one place to the next. His ties with the family aren't that close but they are curious now about where he might be. After all, it has been over two years since she has had any contact at all. That's a long time. Even for a drifter.

The police check what they know of Trezise. He has not come to their attention since May 1992 and last attended a Community Services office for financial assistance two months after that. But it is his bank account details that most interest them. He has not accessed funds paid in from his disability pension since that same month. For a man who needs financial assistance, that is certainly unusual.

Clinton's mother provides a photograph of her son to police, one of the rare pictures of him in existence. The photograph is forwarded to the Forensic Science Centre, and the task of comparing it with the mystery skeleton falls to forensic odontologist, Jane Taylor. Taylor has a trace of crispness in her tone; her father-in-law is Dr Kenneth Aysley Brown, known in forensic circles as 'The Father of Forensic Odontology'. He is better known to the wider public as the dentist whose theory – that damage to baby Azaria Chamberlain's clothing was not caused by dingo teeth marks – re-ignited the highly controversial Chamberlain debate and brought about a second inquest.

Taylor brushes an occasional wisp of hair away from her face when it escapes the confines of its rubber band. She writes her report.

The skeleton will remain unidentified for another five years.

8

They have been in the house at 203 Waterloo Corner Road almost a year, and John starts digging a hole under the tank stand. Blind in her left eye with extremely limited vision in the other, Veronika asks him once, out of idle curiosity, what the hole is for. He tells her it's an underground bunker, or maybe a TV room. She doesn't ask any more questions after that. That was a good enough explanation.

The hole gets bigger. To Veronika it is a way for John to amuse himself when he isn't working at the local abattoir. Just a silly pastime.

John and his mate, Kevin, are now working on the slaughter-house floor of an abattoir at Gepps Cross in Adelaide's northern suburbs. Bunting, with his thin lips, bulbous nose and shock of brown hair that falls over his forehead doesn't stand out physically from the other blokes at the abattoir, but he is a legend with the knife. He can do Kevin on a break, wielding the blade with flair, slicing through the carcasses in record time. He skites he is possibly one of the fastest blokes that ever worked there. A legend.

John is more than good at his job; he loves it. He starts to bring his work home, obsessing about what he has done that day at the abattoir. He has an aversion to blood but is transfixed with it, talks incessantly about how he slices through the carcasses suspended from meat hooks, cuts the beasts clean at the joints and chucks their entrails into buckets. Describing the colour of the entrails, purple and cream and scarlet, writhing in the bucket like jelly. Boasting all the time how he is so fast with the knife. Continually talking over the dinner table about cutting up animals until Veronika feels ill, but he won't shut up about it. It is an obsession.

He has a sick sense of humour, too, occasionally hiding

something in his jacket and goading people to guess what it is: 'Go on, bet you can't fuckin' work it out', and smirking when he says it. They never can, so he has to tell them: 'It's a lamb's foetus', or 'It's a sheep's foot'. Then he opens his jacket. There is never anything there.

John hates sheep, complains constantly to Veronika that they are stupid. Hates pigs, too; reckons they stink. Loathes beasts because they have no brains. Brags about how they die at the abattoir, how he likes to watch. Always blustering.

He comes off a shift tired, his hands stained with the blood of slaughtered animals. He reeks of it, even though he has showered at work before coming home. But John can't smell it. He has no sense of smell at all. Was born without it. Women will later complain there was no point wearing perfume around him. It was a waste of money.

He loves food, the spicier the better, but he can't smell it. One of his favourite spots is an Italian warehouse, where he wanders around and asks people to describe to him the aromas of herbs and soaps and spices. Standing next to a stranger and closing his eyes: 'Tell me what it smells like'.

His mother, on the contrary, has a fine sense of smell. Veronika whines that Jan started meddling from the beginning, a combative mother-in-law pursing her mouth, telling Veronika the house isn't clean, complaining it is a pig-heap and asking how often she uses the washing machine they were given as a wedding present. Always telling Veronika off for not being clean enough. Not like her; her house is spotless. Visitors have to remove their shoes before going inside.

John tells Veronika to ignore his mother, but his own untidiness doesn't help. He is a slob, and Veronika tells him so when he throws wet towels on the floor and leaves them there, or when he refuses to pick up his dirty socks. But John doesn't change. His mother has picked up after him all his life. Now Veronika can do it.

After a few months, Bunting enlists Mark Haydon's help to dig the hole. Haydon shares Bunting's interest in tunnels, has once dug one under his bedroom floor. They love cars, too, pulling vehicles apart in the yard, spanners and wrenches littering the cement. Now they work hard putting their backs into shovelling dirt; John in the hole, Mark ferrying buckets back and forth. Sometimes Veronika watches from the back door, staring blankly with her one good eye. She figures John is just going about his business, doing things that men do, but she is growing tired of it, his obsession with this hole that gets bigger every week. It seems to consume him, particularly when he is aggravated. He is fascinated with it, starts bringing home books on the subject with pictures of tunnels and holes. She complains to him: 'You seem to spend half your life out in that flippin' yard', but it doesn't make any difference. Out in all weather digging, digging. Rock-hard ground under the tank, yielding under the force of a pickaxe and shovel.

And still the hole gets bigger.

Someone has painted graffiti on the wall out the back, but Veronika can barely read and doesn't know what it says. John won't tell her, just says it is nasty stuff, before he grabs a tin of paint and whites it out. Veronika never finds out what was written, or why, but she loves John for protecting her. Admires the way he just takes charge.

John loves motorbikes as much as cars. Motorbike bits all over the cement, engines pulled apart waiting to be rebuilt. He once uses one of his cars for collateral to buy a bike, but he doesn't make the repayments. The debt collector comes visiting, walks up the drive while John orders Veronika and the other visitors there to form a human chain to stop the man reaching him and serving the papers. Tells the man to fuck off, turns the hose on him and sends him drenched back down the driveway, Veronika recalls. A bath and bad language is all that that bloke got for doing his job. It doesn't bother John that the bloke might come back with a cavalcade. Laughs, says the fucking mongrel got what he fucking deserves. It appeals to his dark sense of humour. The bastard wouldn't show his face in his driveway again in a hurry.

John never shows any respect for people in authority. Cops, process servers, government officials: they are all the same to him. He and Veronika are living in public housing, but he brings home a sheep to keep the grass down. Breaks every council by-law in the book and could have been thrown out, but he just shrugs when Veronika says the sheep has to go. It doesn't bother him. Rules are for other people.

Robert Wagner joins the dig, putting his back into it with the others. He starts spending so much time at 203 with Bunting that Barry Lane gets in a huff, throws a jealous little tantrum, pouts and ponces about. Veronika thinks Wagner is a creepy piece of work, but she knows he is gay and no threat to her. He is a huge, boorish man with thick, Neanderthal features and a permanently sour look, as though he has been pickled in vinegar. But he isn't surly around Bunting. Though he physically towers over him, Wagner grovels to the shorter man's demands, happy to do the dogsbody jobs of emptying buckets and moving bricks. He is as strong as an ox. Wagner could hoist Bunting under his armpits, hold him up vertically and his feet wouldn't touch the ground. But Wagner doesn't mess with John, in any way. Bunting has an air about him. He is in charge.

Bunting offers to teach Wagner how to read and write, but he can't absorb the lessons and gives up almost before they start. Veronika suffers Lane but she avoids Wagner, with his glacial stare and huge hands. She is scared of his dog too, that nasty-looking Alsatian critter he calls Adolf.

Shadowy, grubby figures, Wagner and Lane barely acknowledge Veronika in her own home, eating her food and drinking her coffee. Unlike most of the people he mixes with, John doesn't smoke, very rarely drinks and is openly disapproving of drug use. Veronika can't understand why he hangs around with these blokes. She wishes he didn't, but John is starting to become a bit testy, so she doesn't say much. Most days, she doesn't say anything and isn't expected to. Everyone who comes to the house knows she is a bit backward and that her vision is so impaired that she is, in effect, legally blind.

And still they are out in all weather. Digging. Digging.

Veronika is not interested in having kids, but John is. That is one of the problems that surfaces between them after their first year of marriage, though by no means the only one. He nags at her continually to have a baby, despite the same response he always gets: 'You've got a fascination with flippin' kids, sunshine. But I'm not havin' any'. Veronika can be like that – determined when she makes up her mind – and it reflects in her voice, singsong, deep with emphasis on certain words. 'I TOLD him I'm not HAV'in any.'

John starts to bring strangers into the house, young people he has met around Salisbury North. Teenagers with drug problems, strays off the street. They slouch in the corner of the lounge room and John counsels them, playing the father figure. He hates drugs, reckons he wants to start his own rehab place but doesn't have the money to do that. So all he can do is ply them with coffee and talk at them, bleary-eyed smack addicts and edgy speed freaks, listening to him rave about how he wants to save their lives. He puffs up a little when he sermonises, and Veronika stands in the kitchen and thinks, he's playing the bigwig again, they'll get bored in a minute and take a hike. But there are always plenty more where they came from in this welfare ghetto where they live. When John isn't at work, or out in the yard digging, he is entertaining strays. Saving the world.

Stray people and stray animals. Sometimes the house resembles a menagerie. Cats prowling the benches, birds in cages. John finds a German shepherd bitch on the salt pans, half-dead from dehydration. Brings her home, flushes the salt from her guts, doesn't leave her side until he is sure she will pull through. He can't bear to let her go after that so they keep her, call her Kelly.

A broken arm from a motorbike accident spells the end of Bunting's casual employment at the abattoir. He grouches around the house for months after, bemoaning his fate. He misses his job. When his arm heals, he starts with Mark Haydon at the local foundry. He loves this job, too: not just pouring molten metal into moulds to produce castings, but working out all the calibrations. It is like chemistry: how much metal to put in to make steel. It pumps him up to work out measurements. What fits where.

It is a potentially dangerous workplace, and John has to cut his long hair off before he gets a start. He isn't even permitted to tie it back in a ponytail. He comes home spewing about that, but he doesn't go to the barber. Too tight to spend money on a haircut, he instead asks his mother to lop it off and she obliges, using kitchen scissors. His brown hair flutters onto the lino, waves of hair at his feet. Chop, chop. Veronika stands by, watching as Jan cuts. And when it is over, John flips out into the filthiest temper Veronika has ever seen. Snarls at her, kicks the furniture and bolts out the back door. Grabs the pickaxe and spade. Digging, digging.

It seems to Veronika that John's moods get worse from that time on. Appear to seize him from out of nowhere; suddenly, when least expected, a plate will be hurtling towards her. It doesn't take much to provoke an outburst: a shirt not washed, lid left off the toothpaste. 'If he got into a real 'uff', she recalls, 'he would push his motorbike over.' But, ever faithful and loyal, Veronika tells people her husband just has a bad temper. Big John isn't violent. He only throws plates.

She is becoming increasingly fed up, though. First his obsession with animal carcasses, now the hole in the backyard. Seems like he brings half the flippin' foundry home with him, bits and pieces he has scavenged: bricks, metal, wire, rocks. A bower bird building his nest in the backyard. Stuff everywhere. Veronika is almost relieved when, after eight months, John resigns from the foundry after hurting his back at work. He tries for compensation, though he doesn't succeed. And after he stops working, the house seems to be always full of people: Wagner, Haydon, Lane and the strays that John pulls off the street. Again, he is in his element, playing the bigwig, saving the world.

When he isn't talking at people, he is watching them. Wandering into their bedrooms uninvited, his eyes travelling over their possessions. Looking through their things, mentally taking notes. What they own, what they do. Obsessively, mentally recording small details. Obsessively, clandestinely watching.

And still he is out in all weather. Dirt from the diggings is shovelled under the pine trees next to Skewes's fence. The hole is so awkward that even years later, Veronika remembers that John couldn't fit in it, that if he had tried to stand up under the tank stand he would have knocked his block off. He is forced to crawl in on his hands and knees. Veronika is always afraid their dog, Kelly, will fall in the hole, but she only ventures to look in it once, when there is no one else home. Wandering around the backyard with a torch, calling out the dog's name and shining the light into the pit. No dog in there, only a dark, deep hole taller than the ceilings inside her house, empty apart from a makeshift ladder, a fan to circulate air and Christmas lights. John has used the welding skills he learned to make the ladder from scraps he picks up at the foundry, and when that doesn't work, he and Wagner have roughly tied it together. The ladder is a necessity: after weeks of shovelling dirt, the hole is now so big, once John is in there, he can't get out.

Digging, digging. A tunnel that becomes a giant hole.

9

The father of Elizabeth Harvey's first child is a married man she has been seeing for six years. 'Well, look for a star in the East – it must be a virgin birth', he says when she tells him she is expecting. No way he wants anything to do with it. Elizabeth is 23 years old.

The arrival of her son, Troy Youde, in 1976, follows a painful and protracted birth that nearly kills mother and baby. Desperate to escape her mother's drunken, controlling behaviour, when Troy is two, Elizabeth answers an ad for a housekeeper at Broken Hill. She is 26, and Spyros Vlassakis, a flamboyant restaurateur 17 years her senior, is waiting for her at the airport. A big man with swarthy features and a dominating, charismatic personality, he has been married before but has no children. He takes her straight to the restaurant, wines and dines her like a date instead of a prospective employee. Born in Port Said, Egypt, to aristocratic parents, he attended a French college and worked his way up on Greek liners, learning cooking and PR skills. A hard man with a high intelligence who speaks a number of languages, he married a wealthy Dutchwoman and gave up the sea. Bought a restaurant in Holland, but his wife wanted to come to Australia, to save their failing marriage and start again. It lasted six months: Spyros stayed in Australia, his wife returned to Europe.

Elizabeth never starts as his housekeeper and never falls in love with him, but she is attracted to his confidence, his dynamism. The way he just takes charge. Elizabeth likes that in a man. Needs that in a man. Premier Don Dunstan, who is openly gay, is Spyros's mate, and Elizabeth struggles to understand why Spyros surrounds himself with homosexuals. It just doesn't make sense.

Spyros dotes on Troy, never lets him out of his sight. It isn't the best reason to marry him, but it is good enough. The brutality starts on their wedding night, three months after they met.

Troy is a difficult child, in constant pain with gastric reflux and extremely demanding. He refuses to sleep in his bed and throws temper tantrums frequently. At three, lying on his back outside the bathroom, legs thrashing like beaters, demanding Elizabeth let him in. 'Open the fucking door, Mum, open the fucking door', he screams and she leans on the other side, exhausted and crying. By four, Troy bites her if she refuses him a treat, and by the age of six, if she locks him in his room to settle him down, he lights a fire under the bed. Elizabeth takes him to Child Health and Medical Services, but they only seem to want to dig around in her past, so she gives up.

But if Troy is uncontrollable, he is also very bright. He can count to 100 by the age of two, and recite all the colours of the rainbow, including its variants. By 10, he can speak five languages. But he is always in trouble. He frequently sets fires in the back paddock, and Elizabeth takes him to see a psychiatrist. She is scared he is a pyromaniac, but the shrink doesn't seem alarmed. 'I used to set fires at your age, and I turned out okay', he says, eyes glinting behind his glasses. Elizabeth thinks the shrink is a nutcase, and she never takes Troy back there. Teachers constantly describe Troy as disruptive and troublesome, failing to understand that the curriculum just cannot cater to his high IQ. He is bored witless.

A professor at Adelaide University once reads his poetry, says he has a huge talent and a big future. An articulate story-teller, Troy writes an entire, complicated episode of Dungeons and Dragons, which works and is played. He teaches himself to play the guitar and the drums. It seems that anything he touches, he picks up immediately.

Elizabeth lives in fear of Troy's outbursts, but he can also be the most loving child. Always the first to throw his arms around her with a cuddle, and a smile that can light up a room. But if he is loving and affectionate one minute, he is a walking black cloud the next. Unruly, difficult, particularly when he has to stay with Spyros on his own. Elizabeth can't go anywhere without him clinging to the car door, begging her not to leave him. Just a speck in the rear vision mirror as he runs after the car, screaming hysterically: 'Don't leave me, Mum, don't leave me. Dad's not nice to me when you go'.

Jamie's conception is a nightmare, so bad that Elizabeth will always remember it with fear and distaste. On their honeymoon, Spyros brutally rapes her, and the next morning he comes into the bedroom and offers to take her back to her mother's house. It is the worst thing he could have said. She would have been grateful if he had offered to leave, but returning home is not an option.

She starts shaking when she realises she is pregnant, petrified Jamie's birth will be as traumatic as Troy's, relieved when it is as quick and simple as popping a pea. Jamie is a good baby, chubby and cheerful, but the marriage quickly degenerates into farce, each of them fighting the other in court for custody of the children.

They have been sleeping in separate bedrooms for 12 months when Spyros, the veins standing out on his neck and his eyes frenzied, bursts in and rapes her again. Pregnant with another son, she moves out into her own home in 1981. Troy stays with Elizabeth, while Jamie, not yet two, spends time with her during the day, and sleeps at Spyros's house at night. It is an arrangement that continues for 18 months.

At three, Jamie develops a condition that doctors initially think is leukaemia. His hair turns white and falls out in patches; skinny as a Biafran waif, he is constantly tired. He takes months to recover. And it is tearing Elizabeth apart, being separated from her son. 'You might as well move back in with us', she tells Spyros in a voice that cannot disguise her dread. Within days, the merry-go-round starts again.

By five, and now recovered from his illness, Jamie smiles innocently at the world from a cherubic face framed by blond hair. Elizabeth calls him the Professor, after his habit of picking up junk in the backyard and hammering it together. He makes a car out of a broom handle and a pushbike steering wheel, improvising a small piece of wood as a gear stick.

But something is wrong with her youngest son. Although he babbles in his cot, he is never coherent. The doctors scratch their heads, tell Elizabeth all the tests are clear and that he is just a late bloomer. She is still waiting for him to bloom by the age of six. He has a strange habit of grinding himself against his teddy bears, but Elizabeth doesn't understand why. 'He's humping his teddies again', she tells people who drop in. Must be a boy thing, she reckons.

He isn't diagnosed with epilepsy until he is 15, when doctors tell Elizabeth his circuitry is switching on and off up to 300 times a day. It is now too late for him to absorb even a special education, and the family accepts he is borderline intellectually impaired.

On one occasion, seeking adventure, Jamie and the youngest son decide to run away from home. Elizabeth, sitting in the lounge room, hears an almighty racket in the street. She runs out to find him on the car floor operating the pedals and Jamie steering the wheel. The car has been revved up to top gear, blowing smoke but is now stalled in the middle of the road, traffic weaving around it.

Bright, loving and constantly seeking attention, Jamie is the teacher's pet every year. He is a little monster – but a loving one. Always the leader of the pack, he is nonetheless introverted and not interested in sport. He likes to do his own thing, his own way; once fills up paint tins with mud and paints the house eaves, just for the fun of it.

Troy is three years older than Jamie and there is tension between them from the beginning. Troy frequently backs his half-brother up against a wall with a knife and they constantly jockey for parental attention, a tug of love. There is no contest with Joyce, Elizabeth's mother, who loves Troy but never accepts Jamie. He has foreign blood. Joyce treats the baby as persona non grata.

It is a household of boys, all monstrously behaved: breaking things, throwing tantrums, demanding their own way. Of them all, Jamie is the most subdued.

Tired of the unexpected pregnancies, and planning to go back to college, Elizabeth has her tubes tied, a botched operation that necessitates repairing her bladder and uterus. Eight hours under anaesthetic. The doctors assure her she has only a 2 per cent chance of falling pregnant, but four months later, the all-too familiar morning sickness starts again. Five years on and she gives birth to another son. Elizabeth is forced to leave teachers college, where she has been accepted with extremely high marks.

She tries to be a good mother. Strict, but caring in her own way; the kids call her 'Dragon Lady' with some affection. Jamie pinches a chocolate bar when he is six and she punishes him for it, explains that stealing is wrong.

Ever since he can remember, Jamie's world has seemed warped. An emotional void exists in his household like a never-ending winter; no stability, no warmth, no encouragement. But what Jamie hates, the thing he dreads most, is his father touching him up, poking his fingers around his private parts, making him touch him in the same places. It is a memory that will surface later in one of his frequent psychiatric sessions, though it pains him to remember his father that way. The other boys, too, are abused. All of them. Darkness in the house and in Jamie's head. Tormented by a black shadow he can't escape.

Jamie Vlassakis is only seven years old, watching as his father staggers and falls to the floor, crying out with the pain in his chest. Three o'clock in the morning when the ambulance arrives and carries his father out on a stretcher. That is the last he sees of him. Dead by 6am, Friday 13 June 1986. Jamie doesn't go to the funeral: his mother, Elizabeth, says it is no place for children.

Spyridon is only 49 years old when he dies.

Much of the time Elizabeth appears deeply unhappy, dragging herself around and rarely smiling. The marriage has been marred by physical and sexual violence, but after Spyros's death she puts his memory on a pedestal, mourns the man she had wanted him to be.

She is still a young woman, but lacks exuberance for life. Usually depressed, and looks it. Jamie gets used to that, her despondency interspersed with manic outbursts of energy. The house always reeks of cigarettes and of something less tangible, a feeling that something bad is about to happen. They all live on edge, out in Adelaide's northern suburbs. A household of gloomy people.

But there is another side to Elizabeth. Articulate and intelligent, after Spyros's death she works as an accounts clerk and for a year studies psychology at university as a mature age student, having another go at getting an education. When she was younger, photographs show smiling blue eyes and a freckled face soft as snowflakes. But she ages quickly, and badly, her cornflower eyes dulled to a lifeless blue, her skin lacklustre.

There is so much tension in her life, particularly from her mother. The nasty old bitch can't help herself, even at Spyros's funeral. Troy believed Spyros was his natural father, and is distraught the day they bury him. Grandma Joyce, paralytic, sneers at him, 'What are you snivelling for? He isn't your real father anyway'. From that moment on, Troy uses Elizabeth's maiden name: Youde.

10

Elizabeth Harvey has always known torment.

Elizabeth's father, Peter, was intelligent and theatrical but also distant, unapproachable; a legacy of his own strange family upbringing. Her mother, Joyce, was a vicious, abusive alcoholic. Elizabeth reckons hard isn't the word to describe her mother. She says she was like granite.

Elizabeth's maternal grandmother married a returned soldier whose body was a scarred patchwork of shrapnel. They endlessly moved from farm to farm to earn a quid and their first-born, a boy, died in her arms at a godforsaken country railway station, while she waited for the train to take him to hospital. And when, three months later, their daughter was born hideously deformed with a cleft palate, she blamed the disability on her grief.

Their second daughter, Joyce, was born a couple of years later and three years after her, Marjorie. They still moved from town to town, three young kids and a husband, increasingly delusional with shell shock, who dies when Joyce is nine. Joyce will never recover from her father's death.

Joyce, 18, and Peter, 24, met at a dance hall in the exuberance of post-war 1945 and married within months. A son, Peter, quickly followed and later a daughter, Diane. Their third and last child, Elizabeth, was born in September 1953. By the time Elizabeth is six, the marriage has ended.

Joyce starts to leave the children home alone, frocking up and sallying out the door to a cabaret, lurching home well after midnight. The girls figure she was probably smashed when she met George, leaning against the cabaret wall inviting attention with her crimson lips slightly parted; legs too, probably, and the music loud enough to drown her slurred words. George, a mountainous brick of a man, moves in with the family shortly after, signalling the start of a relationship splintered by such extreme violence that Elizabeth and Diane huddle in bed and pray the night will swallow them. Joyce taunts them mercilessly, forces them to dance and dangle on her thread like a spider controlling the web. All her life, she sneers at Elizabeth: 'You should have ended up in an abortion bucket'. She is furious that her daughter survived despite the fact she had hurled herself off a wardrobe when she found out she was pregnant.

Elizabeth Harvey's first memory: waking up, screaming that snakes are writhing in her bed pot. A woman picks her up and soothes her, 'Shhh, shhh', and years later she finds it was her Aunty Marj. Joyce had asked her sister Marj to adopt Elizabeth, said she didn't want the child; but her sister knew it was hopeless. Joyce was tough, hard as nails. Adoption papers or no adoption papers, she just would never have let go. It would have been a nightmare.

So Elizabeth stays. Four years old, helping her grandmother dig in the garden. A dot of a girl with sandy curls and enormous blue eyes, she is so small a toad jumps straight over her head. She likes being at Grandma's house much more than at her own, and visits her whenever she can. It is the only semblance of a normal childhood she can remember. Dressing up in high heels, putting her dollies in a pusher, and perambulating down the garden path to the front door. Grandma opens the door when she knocks, expresses surprise at this unexpected visit and invites her in for a cup of tea. Elizabeth opens an old cigarette packet with twigs in it, tuts, 'Oh dear, oh dear, I've run out again', and Grandma passes her a Craven A cigarette to put into the packet. She finishes her tea, slides off the chair and announces she is taking her baby home now. Teeters back up the garden path, pushing the pram.

Elizabeth is safe at Grandma's, but she barely survives her childhood at home. Learns to shy away, stay invisible, peeking helplessly through a small crack in the bedroom door as her mother and George drink together and the inevitable, brutal bashings that follow. Chairs smashed over Joyce's head, cigarette burns on her body and heavy, hard blows to a face already scarred by frequent beatings. Black eyes, broken bones, and the house stinking of sherry.

Their older brother, Peter, has long since escaped to the army and the girls are constantly on edge, waiting for the blue to start. It is always a free-for-all: the girls jumping in the middle – 'Hit me you bastard, instead of Mum' – and never a Saturday night or a Christmas Day without a fracas. They come to dread weekends and public holidays.

Elizabeth has to call George 'Dad'. She hates him, calls him 'Slops' behind his back, and hates him even more when her lovely dog, Prince, runs away. George tells her: 'Come out to the car and have a look in the boot', and inside is her precious animal, dead and mangled, run over and left to die.

Elizabeth is seven when George molests her the first time. Holds her sore 'front bottom' as she tells Joyce what happened, and her mother backhands her so hard, she topples over. Smacks her in the face, screams that she is a slut. And that is the pattern from then on: sexual abuse increasing with both sisters, escalating to rape by their teen years. Joyce steps in occasionally, but mostly she is too drunk to care. The girls are hot little tramps, she hisses. Just hot little tramps running after her man. Sunday afternoon was George's speciality, when Elizabeth's mother had an afternoon nap. Even the day after her favourite Auntie Olive, Joyce's sister, committed suicide; even then he had a go at her.

Living in the shadow of secrets and lies, Elizabeth's childhood is so traumatic she will spend her adulthood trying to escape the pain. 'It's not that we weren't allowed to have friends', she later recalls, 'but who would want to in an environment like that? And you had big secrets you couldn't tell anyone. Mum tried to commit suicide that many times, we'd go to school and she'd be spewing her guts up because the night before she'd swallowed all these tablets and you couldn't talk to her about any of this, it is a big taboo . . .'

Fifteen-year-old Royce is Elizabeth's first boyfriend. He knocks on her door to take her out, and George punches him for his troubles. 'No boyfriends,' he screams, and slams the door. But Joyce reneges, says she'll throw Royce a sixteenth birthday party. She does more than that: gets paralytic and seduces him into bed. Elizabeth stays with Royce until she is 18, but her mother's seduction of her boyfriends is a repetitive pattern.

She tries to run away at 15. 'But I had nowhere to go; there was no support system, no welfare, no crisis care, no nothing. Nothing. Now there's a number that kids can ring.' She grew so tired of it all. 'When I was in high school, I remember being so depressed, I couldn't stop crying. I was cranky about the whole situation, sick to death of everything.'

At 17, she takes every tablet in the house she can find. She is so close to death, resents her drunken mother for taking her to the doctor and saving her life.

11

Elizabeth is scared of being alone, without a man. Within months of Spyros's death, she starts a relationship with Marcus Johnson. Pint-size with bat-wing ears and waxy skin the colour and texture of peanut butter, he runs on nervous energy, watery-grey eyes endlessly darting and hand caressing his bald pate. He wants to impress Elizabeth, peppers his conversation with grandiose words he often uses out of context. But it is doomed from the beginning. Living in an on-again, off-again de facto relationship for years, by the time they eventually marry in 1992, Elizabeth has her eyes on divorce. She resents having had two terminations with his children, but a deeper problem is emerging. Elizabeth is skidding headlong into a major depressive episode.

Marcus had hoped to become the family's knight in shining armour, their saviour, but despite his best efforts, he instead becomes a parody, an obsequious, suburban Mr Malaprop. Elizabeth, drifting in and out of her private world, is immune to his idiosyncrasies. Her increasing reliance on prescription drugs – Valium, Benzodiazepams – helps.

David, Marcus's son from a previous marriage, moves in with them. At 15, David, a twin, is only four years Jamie's senior. Much of the time, they all live under the same roof: Elizabeth, Marcus, Jamie, his half-brother Troy, her two youngest sons and stepbrother, David.

David is a good kid, eight years old in 1983 when his mother, Carlyne, remarries and takes her husband's surname, Cheeseman. He studies hard at school, and with the rest of his family is a committed member of the Christian Fellowship. Tired of the city, the Cheeseman family moves in 1990 to a 10-acre, self-supporting hobby farm at Hamilton, Victoria, when David is 14. But he is bored in the country, misses the bowling alleys and game parlours, and starts asking questions about his father, whom he hasn't seen since he was a young boy. Carlyne cries when he packs to go and live with Marcus.

It isn't a happy arrangement. Carlyne bitterly recalls David hated his stepmother, Elizabeth, and that he was treated as an asset who would bring money into the household. Still, he periodically returns to Hamilton and every time he does, Carlyne is alarmed at the change in her son, how the standards he has grown up with are being eroded away. The way he has started talking about easy money, what he calls 'filthy lucre'. She frets over the changes in him, but takes comfort that at heart, David is a good boy. He will be okay.

Elizabeth's version of why David comes to live with them is at odds with Carlyne's. He has, she claims, been dumped off at their place because Carlyne has found *Playboy* magazines under his bed. But Carlyne is right when she says David takes one look at Elizabeth and hates her. She tries to like him, but finds him impossible to get on with, breaking the other kids' toys out of sheer jealousy and once lunging at one with a Stanley knife. She has a theory that David hates all women, and that he looks down on people, even though he is only on the dole. He has never paid board, she says, and never contributes a penny toward household expenses. Nothing.

Marcus tries hard, but fails spectacularly in his bid to become close to his four stepsons. Elizabeth's inner darkness, later diagnosed as bipolar disorder, is worsening and she shows extreme signs of obsessive-compulsive behaviour: constantly shopping, or spending all day playing the pokies.

She starts a craft class, and does nothing but that for months. She makes a friend there, and talks a lot about her. The woman's name is Elizabeth Sinclair.

Sometimes the depression is so severe, Elizabeth's mind seems to fragment. Her family find her crying or watching TV without registering one word of what she sees. Sometimes the doctor diagnoses nervous exhaustion and admits her to hospital for a few days and when she is home, she uses anti-depressants and prescription drugs, which she arbitrarily doles out to her sons like lollies.

Elizabeth doesn't notice how disordered her household has become. She misses a lot in her foggy, stoned world; has no idea that Troy is regularly raping his half-brother, Jamie. Younger, frightened and compliant, the younger boy is forced to do things he finds disgusting. But nobody knows. He doesn't tell.

Obsessive-compulsive and bipolar, Elizabeth is either flitting in and out of the house unable to keep still, or brooding in her own world. And Marcus has problems, too. He likes a drink, but likes the pokies more. Shovels most of his pay down the machines, oozing sweat as he feeds in a stream of coins, oblivious to the punters around him. Scared to move in case someone takes his seat, he sits there until closing time every night, his eyes darting around the machine for a jackpot. On the rare occasions he wins, the only sound is his laboured breathing and coins hitting the tray before he shovels them back into the machine again.

The family moves constantly, taking their problems and addictions with them. They rent a shop outside Adelaide that goes bust. Return closer to the city and move again and again. Salisbury North. Campbelltown. Kudla. Burton.

Elizabeth has tried to commit suicide at 18, and she tries again at Kudla when she is in her early 30s. Sits in the car with the exhaust hose spewing carbon monoxide, willing Marcus to get home before the kids arrive, so that they don't find her first. Watching the clock in the car, almost unconscious but starting to panic – where the hell is Marcus? – and staggering out of the car, gasping fresh air into her lungs, sick as a dog but alive at least. She starts seeing psychiatrists after that attempt, but they are of little benefit.

She hates her life, spends her time screaming at the kids, screaming at Marcus and popping pills.

In 1991 the family moves again, to Kilsby Street, Elizabeth

Park; another soulless housing trust home virtually identical to the others they have lived in. Jamie, now 12, has attended five different primary schools. Never had time to make friends he could keep, or to settle into a school routine. It seems that from the time his father died, his family does little else but jump around like jack rabbits, endlessly shifting house, a rootless existence devoid of security. By the time Jamie turns 18, they will have moved 23 times.

In 1992, Joyce, whom Elizabeth calls 'the spider at the top of the web', is diagnosed with cancer of the oesophagus and complications from alcoholism. Elizabeth, drifting in and out of dark depression, nurses her mother through that final illness, turning her back on her own children, leaving them alone for long periods of time. Largely unsupervised, they roam the neighbourhood at their leisure.

Their neighbour, Jeffrey Payne, sits out the front of his house at Kilsby Street and watches the boys, who live across the road. Sometimes he even dares to take photos of them when he knows no one is looking. He particularly likes to watch Jamie: tall, broad-shouldered with Cimmerian colouring compliments of his Greek heritage, he is easy on the eye. His hair is now darker than it had been as a child, but his demeanour is, too. Just 13, Jamie is pre-pubescent with a vulnerability Payne finds alluring. Emotionally deprived, obviously lonely, and physically a boy–man. A perfect combination.

In 1993, Elizabeth finds a mass in her breast. She waits two months before seeing a doctor and is referred to one specialist after the next. She instinctively knows something is very wrong, but no-one will do a biopsy, no one will agree to check it further. The mammogram shows a node, half in her rib cage, half in her breast, and a mass on the right side. She frets every time she looks at her breast but keeps being assured the mass is benign and that there is no justification for her fear. She gives up.

Nothing ever seems to go right. Paranoid from the dope he

is smoking, Troy tries to hang himself from a curtain rod when he is 14. Crisis Care is called in; not the first or the last time they will engage with this family. Troy is so angry with the world, but Elizabeth doesn't know why. He can be such a gentle soul. It breaks Elizabeth's heart when he comes home one morning with a rough tattoo of an iron maiden on his arm. He has carved it on his skin using a pin, when he was stoned. It looks like a jail tat.

Even when Troy starts work – a stint as a labourer, then packing orders for a poultry place – he sabotages himself. He can't accept the boss's praise, acts up and ends up back on the dole. He has some fine qualities: he pays his debts and is kind-hearted – but he just can't seem to help himself. He always self-destructs.

Elizabeth hates him smoking dope, but he doesn't listen. They fight all the time: *you're not using that shit in my house*, but he does, anyway. He starts dabbling in heroin, bingeing on it, but never becomes addicted. He likes a drink, too, but he doesn't know when to leave it alone. He never drinks to enjoy alcohol, but to completely wipe himself out.

Jamie wants to be a motor mechanic or an electronics engineer. Always mucks around with cars or electronics gear, deftly building radios and putting motors together. He just has the knack. He is as bored at school as Troy, thinks he can take the short cut without the education.

Elizabeth is struggling with her mental stability, at times feeling as though she is melting into her own darkness. And in that darkness she doesn't notice their neighbour, Jeffrey Payne, smiling at Jamie and the boys, inviting them to join him on push-bike rides or beckoning them to visit him in his home. Payne watches the family and creeps closer, closer; circling, then finally moving in. Sidles up to Marcus, tells him the boys are welcome to sleep over the night. Marcus hesitates, unsure, then agrees.

First, pornography. Soft, and then harder, porn images. Jamie looks away, but Payne's threats are real. Co-operate with me or your brothers are next. Touching Jamie, making Jamie touch him. First with his hands, then his mouth. It makes Jamie feel sick. Later, hard porn video playing in the background, Payne's trousers down to his ankles exposing the white flabby flesh of his thighs, Jamie bent over while Payne penetrates him, panting, 'Shut up about this or I'll kill your mother'. Every day. No one knows. Jamie doesn't tell.

In November 1993, at the age of 66, Joyce dies. Elizabeth now has to face her greatest fear. Her mother has always controlled her; who now is going to hold the thread to make her dance? She shuts down, noticing nothing.

Jamie constantly misses school. He can't deal with his trauma, his dirty secrets. Can't deal with his dysfunctional family, but has to shield them. His mother's safety, his brothers' protection, depend on his silence. Every day – his skin crawling, obsessing about cleanliness, showering for hours, scrubbing himself until he bleeds. Sitting around the house brooding, scared he is now a homosexual. Sketching endless doodles, images of hell.

Walking in a dark tunnel, with no way out. Sickened with himself, self-medicating to stop the pain. Mixing grog and dope with the drugs his mother gives him – Valium, benzos. The world is a nicer place with its sharp corners knocked off. Jamie has learned how to light the darkness. Get stoned, mellow out. Forget about the world.

Barry Lane wants some of the action and is pissed off that his mate, Payne, won't share the boys with him. Payne wants to keep them all to himself. All the boys. All abused, all sworn to their own code of silence. Lane decides he will get even. He will tell their mother.

Elizabeth doesn't know who this man is, standing on her doorstop babbling obscenities about her sons. 'Your neighbour is a paedophile and he's been molesting your boys. All your sons, except Troy.' He introduces the hulking man standing next to him as his fiancé: 'This is Robert Wagner'. Stumbling back inside, Elizabeth slumps at the kitchen table, Wagner saying nothing as the filth continues to pour from Lane's mouth. He seems to be an expert on everything, even about where there is a house just outside Adelaide that auctions kids to paedophiles. Gives her a running commentary on what the auctioneer says. 'What do we give for this little beauty, no reserve – five dollars, eight dollars, twelve dollars, do I hear more than twelve? Going once, going twice . . .' Barry Lane, she comes to realise, is the middle man. 'He was tangled up with the Family', Elizabeth recalls. 'He used to procure little boys for these little boy auctions. He would talk about it all the time.'

They are sick people who attend these auctions, and the boys aren't always alive. Dead boys, offered up for necrophiliac activities. Part of a secret network that allegedly operates clandestinely. Adelaide's infamous, shadowy 'Family'.

But these are Elizabeth's kids he's talking about now. Telling how he's seen her sons showing their arses and having five dollar notes stuck up there. Elizabeth hates Lane, figures he's lying about some things, but she keeps both the men hanging around for a few weeks until the police take action against Payne. Wagner plays games with the boys – Nintendo or football – and is just like a big kid himself, barely brighter than a child. But Lane is impatient. He knows someone who can fix up Jeffrey Payne. Scare him off. The man's name is John Bunting.

12

1993 is a terrible year for Elizabeth Harvey, capped off by Joyce's death. And now the flashbacks start. Previously tucked away in Elizabeth's subconscious, they spring to the surface: hideous memories of her stepfather, George; what he did to her, how he ruined her childhood with constant sexual and physical abuse. Just a girl, holding her breath while he touched her bottom, cringing from the outstretched hand that cuffed her around the ear to keep her silent. Watching her as she grew older, staring at her developing breasts, brushing himself against her as he walked past, whispering in her ear what he was going to do to her when Joyce wasn't around. Touching her at first and then raping her. Right through her teens.

And suddenly it all adds up. Why Troy hated staying alone with Spyros. The subtle undercurrents in the house. Spyros's homosexual friends. Sustained sexual abuse: not just of Troy, but of Jamie and the youngest as well. Her sons, who were conceived in rape.

And when she talks to Troy about her suspicions, he finally breaks down and tells her. It started when he was a small boy. Spyros holding his head so he can't break away, saying, 'This is good for you, you're really enjoying this, aren't you?' The same things he has done to Elizabeth and later to his own sons. Now it all adds up. He hated women. They are the wrong sex. He preferred to penetrate his sons.

Troy: a strapping tall young man, with jet black hair, huge blue eyes, cleft chin, slim build and broad shoulders. Eighteen years old, unburdening his secrets, sobbing helplessly in his mother's arms.

★ ★ ★

Elizabeth crashes into a complete psychiatric collapse. She is again suicidal, endlessly scrubbing her body, disgusted she did not recognise that Spyros was a paedophile, did not notice the abuse of her sons. Little wonder they have not wanted to go to school; it would be impossible to concentrate, with so many depraved secrets.

Sitting in the bath, pounding the water, the floor a quagmire and not answering when people speak her name. Whispering in a baby voice, 'My name is Laura', moving to the lounge room in a vacant trance, rocking and asking for her doll. Splintering into her alter ego, the little girl from her imagination. Poor Elizabeth has had to endure her mother's alcoholic demons and her stepfather's sexual abuse, but Laura has been much smarter than that. She has always saved Elizabeth when she needs her most. She always arrives on time. Laura helps Elizabeth escape.

Jamie finds it difficult to talk about his abuse, even to the police who act on the family's information eight weeks after they file a report concerning it in early 1994. Eight weeks, as Payne sits on his front doorstep all night, staring at her house while Elizabeth waits for the cops to do something. Not a wink of sleep for two months as Payne walks around her house, his tread heavy outside the windows as he stalks the family.

And when he finally talks about what happened, Jamie gags on his words. Even then, at the Sexual Assault Unit, he can't bring himself to admit the penetration. On three occasions, Marcus takes Jamie to see a social worker at the children's hospital, who writes a report. 'It is critical that Jamie have some peers who will confirm that he is a good person worthy of friendship and trust . . . Jamie presents as a pleasant, well-spoken, caring teenage boy . . . Apportions blame to Jeffrey [Payne] for the abuse that he and his brothers suffered.' The social worker makes recommendations about how Jamie can address his complex psychological problems, but with the household shattering, none of the recommendations are acted on.

'Her records reveal that Elizabeth is a profoundly disturbed woman with a serious psychiatric illness, certainly a serious depressive and anxiety disorder, but perhaps more important a very disturbed personality', child sex abuse expert, Professor Mullen, later notes. 'It's clear from her records that she is a woman who would have found it very difficult to provide any form of consistent or effective care to children. The disorganised and disrupted life which Mr [Jamie] Vlassakis experienced throughout his childhood and early adolescence is clearly a result in large part of his mother's disturbances . . . [he was] exposed to an inconsistent, constantly changing and ineffectively caring environment . . . leaving him vulnerable, dependent and really with very little strength of character . . .'

Professor Mullen goes further. 'Sexual abuse in and of itself is a distressing, disturbing and potentially damaging experience for any child', he writes. 'But sexual abuse which occurs to someone from a disrupted and disorganised background, who is already developmentally vulnerable, is far more damaging. They fail to develop the capacity for effective and close intimate relationships, have considerable problems with instability of mood, particularly high levels of anxiety and a tendency to depression. There is a very strong association between severe child sexual abuse and suicidal and self-damaging behaviour.'

Mullen would write that given Jamie's depressed state of mind, he had become vulnerable, dependent on others and desperately sought comfort and support. Added to that, his drug abuse prevented mature development as a normal adolescent, creating a pathetic dependence not just on the drugs but on any person around him who would sustain either the drug abuse or other aspects of his life.

Arrested in early March, 1994, Payne is promptly bailed and returns to live at Kilsby Street. He again sits out the front of his house, taunting 'his' boys and taking photographs, bearing out a psychiatric report of him that he has little willpower over offending against young children. Jamie seethes with indignation. Where the bloody hell are the cops?

Then John Bunting arrives. Rides into Elizabeth's life on a BMW motorbike which he parks outside the Kilsby Street house, a .38 pistol hidden under the seat. Simply materialises on the doorstep, flanked by his silent sentinel, Robert Wagner. He does all the talking, while Wagner nods his head up and down, a ventriloquist's dummy.

Elizabeth's world has collapsed, and so has her marriage to Marcus. And on her doorstep, this short stranger is warning her that Barry Lane is a sicko, that her boys could become a target for him as they have been with Jeffrey Payne. Looks her straight in the eye, as if daring her to disagree. Just takes control. 'That's why we're here', he says. 'We are people who take care of these types of people.'

Elizabeth is mesmerised by Bunting from the start. Drawn to him like a magnet; something about him she can't quite explain. Perhaps it is his voice, or how he enters a room and fills it up with his presence. She takes one look and melts into his hazel eyes. It is a memory that will never leave her, even as she lies dying. 'He isn't very tall, only slightly taller than me. He wasn't chubby when I met him, but he has a round face and was clean-shaven. I thought he was quite good looking. Decent.'

He isn't tall, but he has attitude, the way he talks about people he doesn't like. Poofs and paedophiles. Transvestites. Fat people. The intellectually disabled. He doesn't like a lot of people, and he just takes charge. She likes that in a man. Needs that in a man.

He becomes her white knight, roaring up Payne's driveway in the middle of the night, shining the light from his motorbike onto the veranda and sending Payne scuttling inside like a crab, hiding. The boys love him for it and so does Elizabeth. She will never forget how she felt about him then. Head over heels for the first time in her life, even though he is 13 years younger than herself. She let him into that special place – her heart – that she has never let anybody into before. That part of her that has never opened up, because of the sexual assaults when she was a child. But Bunting opens her, like a flower. She thinks he can walk on water.

Marcus deeply resents the intrusion of this stranger into their lives but raises no fight, slinking out of the marriage with far less fanfare than when he entered it. But he keeps in touch with Elizabeth and the boys, who are by now living in a continuous crisis of poverty and despair. She has renamed herself Christine, though most people still call her Elizabeth. She and Marcus loosely share the boys, a fluid arrangement noticed by outsiders as a complete absence of a normal family life.

Elizabeth's kitchen becomes the meeting place for paedophile vigilante meetings. All of them sit around discussing the fact that the children have been interfered with, Bunting the ringleader. Marcus often joins the group, and recalls that the conversation frequently turned to violence. Later, he clumsily pieces together the conversations in his convoluted, verbose way. 'There was a consistent feeling that some action should be taken against Payne. It appeared, for quite a while, that the police were not going to do anything about it, and as my visits got more often over a period, the expressions and the speech patterns became more and more violent . . . I said we should push him off a bike, off a cliff. Some of the discussions were about the types of methods in which they would kill him . . . The funny thing was – Barry Lane was present in a lot of these conversations and I couldn't work out where he fitted in at any time, as being on both sides of the fence, as it may be.'

13

Bunting moulds and shapes Elizabeth Harvey like a piece of pottery. Warns her that single women are prey for paedophiles who only really want to get to the children. She finds John's presence cathartic, melts every time he enters the room. Giggles like a schoolgirl and feels the anger, bottled up so long, harnessed into energy. 'What was I to do with all this anger and hate? The stories John told me about paedophiles and what they do to kids, it was horrific: like, they would stick batteries up little girls, things like that. We used to sit around the kitchen table and just feed each other hate, hate, hate about what I was going to do if I got hold of Jeffrey Payne. It went on for months.'

Veronika sits back and watches as Elizabeth storms into her marriage. There is nothing she can do about it.

It is months, too, before Jeffrey Payne is jailed: sentenced to four years in prison, paroled in two. The delay in justice has a profoundly disturbing effect on Jamie's psyche. All his life, he has been abandoned by adults. Now he feels abandoned by the police. It is a betrayal that will tell.

But if he blames the system for failing him, for the pitiful lack of police protection, he also blames himself. It must be his fault. If he had admitted he had been sodomised, Payne's sentence would have been longer.

Every day his skin crawls, and he scrubs himself until he bleeds. Walking in a dark tunnel, with no way out. Sickened with himself, he self-medicates to stop the pain. The world is a nicer place with its sharp corners knocked off. Jamie has learned how to light the darkness. Get stoned, mellow out. Forget about the world.

John makes Elizabeth feel young. At 41, she no longer has the soft face promised in her youth; her pale skin has lined, she has ballooned to size 18 with the medication and lack of exercise. But now she is getting tattoos carved on her skin and riding pillion on the back of his motorbike, her leather jacket billowing in the wind and sweet freedom from the kids. Medicated to the eyeballs on Lithium and Zoloft and Valium, heavy-duty prescription drugs, she thumbs her nose at authority for the first time in her life. She is madly in love with John, but at first there is no sexual relationship between them. Madly in love, mad as a meat axe and mad with the world.

The family moves house again, away from the memories. Elizabeth has broken down mentally and emotionally, and the kids spend some time at Marcus's house, making friends with the teenagers across the road. The youngest of Elizabeth's children is raped by the young men, but nothing is done. 'A cop told me he couldn't give chronological evidence, because he is intellectually handicapped. But I found out one of the lads [who raped him] had worked for Payne and he'd been writing to him from prison', Elizabeth says. 'Payne told him to make friends with him and keep him bent until he got out of jail and could have him back.'

It doesn't seem to matter where they go. They just can't escape the ugliness.

Marcus Johnson reckons Bunting is one of the biggest bums in Adelaide. Always cadging petrol money or angling for a cup of coffee. Never a quid in his back kick. But people are drawn to him, and he to them. One way or another, everyone Bunting knows will wind up on his hit list. Male or female, gay or straight, married or single, disabled or healthy. Constantly manipulating people to his own ends, gathering his followers around him like Australia's answer to Charles Manson. Deciding who will live and who will die. Clever, controlling, the king of his domain; creating mayhem, sermonising to the damaged and the traumatised. Totally paranoid, warning people that paedophiles are everywhere, there are rock spiders on every corner. And they listen to him. He has the answers, he has the power. The cops are stupid, he rants, and the legal system doesn't work. His way is right. He is the Managing Director, running a business outside office hours. An industry.

Robert Wagner, shifty and cold-blooded, is only his hatchet man and Mark Haydon, a dullard and moral coward, does their bidding. Elizabeth is entranced with Bunting and now Jamie is hooked in. Utterly magnetised by his mother's lover. An emotionally fragile child–man handed to Bunting on a silver platter. *Here, take me.*

Bunting collects spiders, a gallery of venom he hangs in the spare room. The junk room, his wife Veronika calls it – and Bunting fills it with his junk. Pictures, photographs, details of paedophiles – rock spiders – written on a Post-it pad and stuck to the wall connected by a web of wool. Names, addresses, phone numbers, all stemming from a central name: Barry Lane. Bunting tells Veronika what the names mean. 'He said they were people who knew Barry and that some of them had done horrible things to children. I don't really know more than that, that's all he said.' She doesn't ask any more questions.

He tells other people he has been sexually abused when he was young, and that's why he hates paedophiles, why he has a pathological obsession with them. But he doesn't ever divulge his past to Veronika, even when they are married. Years later, she looks blank, quizzical, when the subject is raised. 'First I've heard of it, sunshine. And he would have told me. I would have known about that one, for sure.' She only went into the spare room to store things away, but she knows where he got the wool from. 'I would have gave it to John because I was into finger stitching and knitting.'

Veronika wraps everything that she stores in boxes. Plastic toys, telephone books. John can never find a thing once she's stored it. He nicknames it the room of no return.

He tells visitors, anyone who will listen, about how he has been abused as a child, ranting and raving about what was done to him, talking about it obsessively in the same way he has talked about the animals at the abattoir. How he has sliced through the carcasses suspended from meat hooks and watched the blood flow, cut them clean at the joints, chucked their entrails into buckets, skinned them and all, how he is fast with the knife. Bunting is proud of his wall of spiders. He adds to it every chance he gets.

Lane and Wagner discuss who are 'dirties', casually sitting around a table with Bunting, Haydon and Vlassakis. And it becomes Bunting's Friday night ritual to close his eyes and walk up to the wall, take down the card he touches and telephone the person whose name is on it. Let fly with a stream of abuse: 'You're a dirty, you're breathing valuable oxygen' – and end the call with a threat. 'Disgusting piece of waste. Watch out.' He always hangs up looking self-satisfied, regaling his audience with details of how the recipient of his phone call whimpered and begged to be left alone. How most homosexuals are just filthy paedophiles.

And he explains that paedophiles aren't always men. If females know abuse is happening and do nothing to stop it, they are paedophiles, too. Female paedophiles have their own special name: tooth fairies. Tooth fairies. John smiles enigmatically when Elizabeth asks him why he calls them that, but he doesn't answer her question. She tries to work it out herself. What do tooth fairies do? Quietly enter a room at night, remove the child's tooth from under the pillow, and leave cash in its place. It seems harmless. They take something. They put something back. It seems harmless.

She can't understand why tracking down dirties and tooth fairies is such an obsession for John. He acts like he is saving the world.

Now Elizabeth has virtually moved in, dragging her sons with her. Moving in and out, spending half her time there and half at her own house. Friends of Jamie's, Mark and Douglas Townsend, move in as well. Complete strangers to Veronika, they constantly smoke dope, which offends her. She suspects other guests use harder drugs as well and nags John to throw them out. But he won't. John is king of his domain: this small, suburban house crowded with people sleeping in the junk room and on the lounge room floor. A doss house.

John throws Veronika out in mid-1995, tells her to take a hike, he doesn't want her living with him at Waterloo Corner Road any longer. In a way, she is relieved: she is jack of him; tired of his obsessions, his digging in the backyard, the comings and goings of strangers, the way he plays the big-wig all the time, his flippin' wall of spiders. And she isn't stupid, can see that he and Elizabeth are fascinated with each other. She can't quite remember how she came to know her: 'She come – I met her – well, John met her and I met her after John knew her. John knew her first'. But she remembers John playing Daddy to Elizabeth's kids and her hanging off his every word.

Veronika goes as she is told. Says, 'You want Elizabeth, sunshine, you have her', and moves back to her parents' house. Intellectually disabled, blind in one eye with extremely limited vision in the other; where else is she to go? Takes clothes and toiletries with her, but leaves behind the furniture. She has no call for that.

Veronika is upset that her marriage has ended. She has been a good wife but she has had enough.

Jamie is besotted with Bunting, shadows him everywhere. He finds him polite, well spoken. And as soon as he could, he had asked John if he could move in with him at Waterloo Corner Road, to escape from Kilsby Street and the memories that make him cringe with guilt. Jamie is seeing social workers, trying to disentangle his fractured past, deal with his sexual abuse. But Bunting makes more sense than all of the psychologists put together, encourages Jamie to not let up on Payne, to pursue criminal injuries compensation, to keep at the bastard. Bunting knows a lot about these sorts of people. Jamie can tell him everything.

Jamie has to sleep in the lounge room, but he doesn't mind; anywhere is better than being at home. And Bunting is happy for Jamie to move in. He genuinely likes him, and they share an easy rapport. He also notices other qualities about the young bloke. He is vulnerable. Impressionable. Disturbed. Damaged.

Jamie trails Bunting everywhere. 'So', a social worker will later write, 'at a time . . . that Jamie Vlassakis needed appropriate peer support and he needed trusted adults that would never betray him, he came into the most dangerous relationship of his life . . .'

Bunting is 28, Jamie 14. The young man has not only found a father figure; he has finally found a hero.

14

She dies in England, clutching John's picture in her hand. Fifteen years old, another teenage suicide statistic, diagnosed with AIDS after being sexually assaulted by a teacher at a private school. At least, this is what Bunting tells Elizabeth Harvey. Truth or lies? How will she ever know? 'John told me the school teacher had sexually molested Tammy and her girlfriend, locked them in a classroom and raped them, and they got arrested and everything for all that. So then Tammy was having tests because her kidneys started to pack up and that's when they found out she had HIV and she committed suicide. And she died with her father's photo in her hand.'

The day John Bunting finds out his daughter is dead, Elizabeth sits up with him for a marathon 48 hours, holding his hand, lending support, a shoulder to lean on. By the time dawn breaks on the second day, she knows she can never leave him. 'When Tammy died, John was so cut up that he said to me, "Come to my place. Please". I knew that he was very devastated but I didn't know why. He was just lying on the lounge in the dark, crying his heart out. Veronika was at her Mum's house and I walked in and said, "What's the matter?" He told me then that Tammy had committed suicide and I just held him and we went to bed that night, both naked, and held each other. We slept like that for a fortnight, just holding one another, no sexual overtures. I comforted him for a fortnight. Two people reaching out. I was grieving because of my kids being sexually molested and he was helping me, and I was helping him with Tammy. I didn't go home, and helped him through the grief, and then after a fortnight I said, "This is silly, I've got to go back home". That's when he begged me to move in.'

The bond has been sealed: shared secrets, nursing him

through his grief. A dark bond: tied to his past, and to his future. And he tells her another story, about a girl he knew from Brisbane who stayed with him for a short holiday in Adelaide before she returned to Melbourne to live. Pregnant with John's baby, she miscarried at four-and-a-half months; devastated, she took her own life. It seems to Elizabeth that he is surrounded by death. Suicides, accidents, friends dying from illness. Truth or lies. She doesn't ever ask. She doesn't ever know.

She is drawn to John like a magnet. He needs her. She loves him.

But he drives her crazy, suffocating her with love. Holds her hand 20 times a day. She can't even do the dishes without him putting his face close to hers, telling her he loves her, smothering her with affection.

Sex isn't the basis of their relationship, but it grows to form a very active part of it. John, Elizabeth recalls, could be very tender.

15

Like her mother before her, Elizabeth Haydon has seven children and lives in a revolving cycle of poverty, unemployment and violence that lasts until the end of her tragically short life. Like her mother before her, she is ground down and world-weary, with none of the advantages that middle-class women enjoy. But unlike her mother, Pat Sinclair, who had only one disastrous marriage, Elizabeth tramps from one relationship to the next, most of them abusive, most of them casual and all of them unfulfilling. She never learns from her mistakes; never finds the love she desperately wants, never dreams to set her sights higher. Dreams die young where she is from, and hearts break early.

Elizabeth Haydon is one of the under class, a woman the world neither cares about nor nurtures, whose own dysfunctional upbringing has left its mark, left her tainted and tired. She doesn't fit in anywhere outside the norms that she understands, and she surrounds herself with losers. Like water, she finds her own level. Sex is part of the bartering process: give some affection, get some back. Rough love, if any love at all, and the sure knowledge that Elizabeth is up for it. In the back of cars, usually: an unromantic grope in the dark and a desultory grunt when the bloke is finished. So many men, people whisper, that surely she isn't just giving it away?

The only constant in Elizabeth Haydon's life is pregnancy. Year after year, she walks around with a bulging belly. And year after year, her children are either voluntarily surrendered to welfare, dumped with family or with a father they barely know, or taken from her. A growing army of kids, directionless as broken weather cocks, swinging between institutions and their fractured home. A litter of children.

* * *

Elizabeth's parents, Pat and Reg Sinclair, started going steady in the buoyant post-war years, going steadily toward the altar of St Patrick's Cathedral, Parramatta, where they married two years into their courtship in 1950. Pat, a slip of a girl at 18, had only two dreams – to marry and to have children – and she adored her husband, Reginald Sinclair.

A spray painter by trade, he was a few years older than her, a larrikin and a rebel. Pat called him Reg, lovingly at the beginning but later she called him a lot of other things besides. There were few occasions – pathetically few after her wedding day – when she wore a dress, or a splash of lipstick on her mouth. But on her wedding day Pat was deliriously happy, slender and feminine in a white gown, a young girl from, she would boast, a decent home, who had just fulfilled one of her two dreams.

Their first daughter, Christine, was born in 1951, the year after they married and other children – Garion, Diane, Gail, Tony, Wayne – followed in quick succession. Life was unrelentingly tough, and the family was often forced to take refuge in emergency accommodation.

Once, an Irish woman wrapped a two-shilling piece in a baby's shawl the day they left their temporary digs. 'With the blessin's of the saints', she said, 'to bring good luck to you and your girl.' But the family will need more then an Irish blessing. Pat is reaching the end of her tether. 'My husband decided I wasn't a good mother and he called welfare. I was having blackouts and was comin' to in Sydney. Didn't know where I was. He just reckoned I was havin' a good time and neglecting the kids.' So does welfare. Entering the house when Pat is bathing Diane, they don't stop to ask questions or listen to explanations. They take Diane – only nine months old – Christine, almost six, and Garion, three. Her hands still wet from the bath water, Pat ran after them, screaming *don't take me kids, give me back me kids*, but they keep walking toward the car, lock the doors and drive off. She slumps to the floor and weeps. 'I tried me hardest to get 'em back, but I only got Garion after a few months. Not the girls.'

Within months, Pat returns to her old habits, wandering off for days, weeks at a time. It will be years before she sees both her daughters again, who are sent to foster parents.

Reg picks up a few hectares of land for a song at Warner-vale, a sprawling estate near Wyong, where he jerry-built a two-and-a-half room shed into which he shepherds his burgeoning family. Primitive in the extreme, a kerosene lamp casts a ghostly shadow over the sparse interior, which has little furniture. The children play on the dirt floor. There is no electricity and no running water.

There is also little love left in the marriage and virtually nothing to keep out the elements during the long days of winter. Wind tears through the galvanised iron sheeting that clads the house, and when holes develop, the rain comes visiting, dripping onto the kids' heads and turning soggy the bread and dripping they regularly eat for dinner. There is often nothing else to eat: take it or leave it. The Sinclair kids are poor, dirt poor, the butt of many neighbourhood gibes from other children. 'Bush coons, bush coons!' they taunt as they pass them on the street. In their bare feet and rags, they are cold, chilled to the bone. And usually hungry.

Elizabeth, christened Verna Audrey Sinclair at her birth on 29 August 1961, was their last child. She is known in the family as the 'flying baby' because she came out after only the third push; the doctor literally caught her, mid-air. Seven children, and five miscarriages. Pat was exhausted; there would be no more babies. An enforced hysterectomy following Elizabeth's birth – a 'butcher's job' as she calls it – infuriated Reg. 'You're only half a woman, Pat, only half a woman', he sneered, and she stormed out, the youngest kids clutching the back of her cardigan. Pat and Reg's marriage had degenerated into mutual loathing. 'We had some terrible rows over him saying those things to me. Some terrible rows.'

A former neighbour at Warnervale recalls that the Sinclair mob were the queerest lot of buggers he'd ever met. Half gipsy, half hillbilly. Jumping around like jack rabbits. Here today, gone tomorrow.

A heart attack in 1962 spells the end of Reg's working career. He just turns grey and clutches his chest, that's how Pat remembers it: that, and the fact that from that day on, she has to work when she can to make ends meet. Mostly they lived from day to day.

Christmas for the Sinclairs was always a lean affair. Once, they ate beetroot sandwiches for lunch; another year, they tied pinecones to a broom handle and pretended it was a tree. When Elizabeth was still very young, a local man who played Santa Claus gave all the children a small gift. It was the only Christmas present any of the children could remember receiving.

Elizabeth is only five when Pat starts going walkabout. Slatternly around the house and sick and tired of the noise, the fights and the struggles, Pat waits until Reg has left home, as he frequently does, and she takes off, too. The kids are never warned when she is leaving, nor told where she is going, but they learn to scrounge and beg and steal, if they have to, until she comes home again. They are never sure how long she'll be away – sometimes one week, sometimes two – but the one thing they do know is that she rarely takes any of them with her.

Welfare sometimes come sniffing around, sticking their beaks into the family's business and turning up their noses at the squalid state of the house. Dirty washing piled on the floor, high as a mountain, and dishes caked with food stacked in the sink. Reg once comments, in front of Pat's mother, that the house looks like a brothel. Pat comes up fighting after that insult, gives him the first black eye he has ever had from her, but not the last.

Welfare knows the Sinclairs only too well, from their experiences with Christine and Diane who are both living in foster care.

For all the kids, it is more an existence than a childhood, a war zone of parental blues, fighting amongst themselves and little else but unremitting misery. Garion, the oldest boy, often has the dubious responsibility of being the stand-in parent, doing the best he can with what there is. But even so, conflict resolution is always dealt with in the same way: a smack around the head. The authorities don't do much, apart from raising their eyebrows and issuing ineffectual warnings, gingerly picking up their feet as they wind their way through the mess in the house and write notes in their books.

And so, in the minds of the children, 'the welfare' becomes just another set of useless authority figures, as useless as the teachers who know they are hungry or the neighbours who don't want to get involved. If they know nothing else, Elizabeth and the other Sinclair kids know that people turn their heads away a lot and pretend they don't see. The only authority figures that do take notice, it seems, are the cops. One way and another, they come to be on a first-name basis with most of the brood as the years wear on.

The trick for the cops, though, is to catch them. They move, endlessly. Baulkham Hills. Castle Hill. Currabubula. Werris Creek. Parramatta. Into the city, then back to the scrub. Endlessly.

They are a tormented band of gipsies, a rag-tag clan whom most people avoid. But Pat is growing sick and tired of tramping around. Fed up. The moving around, the to-ing and fro-ing, is a pattern that will reflect in Elizabeth Haydon's adult life time and again, but as a child she accepts it. She has a vulnerable and trusting disposition. She mostly manages to avoid the maelstrom that surrounds her by refusing to be drawn into it.

Elizabeth later tells her brother Garion that Pat sometimes made her feel guilty she had been born at all, reminding her that she had been crook all the way through the pregnancy with her. But Elizabeth doesn't fight back. It isn't in her nature. Instead, she builds a brick wall around herself and her emotions, although it is really more like a galvanised iron roof with holes in it. The rain still comes in, drip drip dripping over the years. She just can't seem to escape it. And like her brothers and sisters, she makes do with what she has. Elizabeth has never had a doll to call her own, and so she does what her siblings do. She pinches them.

★ ★ ★

Christine, the prodigal eldest daughter, comes back to the family when she is 15 and Elizabeth is five. Nothing has changed. Pat is still disappearing, Reg is still hostile, abusive and violent and the kids are still as wild as hawks, barefoot, hungry and running around the neighbourhood. They rarely go to school. Christine now takes on the burden of the family when Pat is absent, but her 10-year separation from her mother has taken its toll. It will be many years before they forge anything resembling a decent relationship, and even then it will not last long.

Garion, too, is becoming increasingly bitter. A talented artist, at 15 he has won a worldwide competition to become a copy-artist with the Walt Disney Corporation in America. But Reg won't sign the guardian permission form to let him go. The Sinclair kids don't rack off to the other side of the world, filling their heads with big ideas. Reg will not sign that form, no way, no matter how much Garion begs him to.

There is rarely a peaceful evening. 'The table was tipped over at every flamin' meal', Tony says. 'It was always a free-for-all.' He finds it vaguely amusing now, with the passage of time to blur the harsh edges, but some situations are worse than others. Cops turn up one day looking for Pat, who has taken off again. They suspect that Reg has finally achieved what he often threatened to do – to kill her – and so, in front of the kids, they search the house and the backyard, even shining their torches into a well that Garion has helped his father dig. Elizabeth, just a toddler, follows behind and no one tells her to go indoors. But Pat isn't in the well; a few days later she saunters in, unaware of what has happened.

Another time, she takes a handful of pills at the dinner table, the children an audience to the bizarre spectacle of their mother trying to commit suicide. Reg watches, taunting her with his silence. And when he finally does speak, it is only to gibe, 'Make a good fuckin' job of it, will ya'. Someone gets her to hospital in the end, and a doctor makes her vow she won't do it again. Many's the time after that she wants to end her own life, but she's made a promise, and sticks to it. She is still proud of that.

The worst blue of all is indelibly etched in Tony's memory. 'One night Garion threatens to blow Mum's goddamned brains out and she's yelling at him, "You'd better make sure it counts, otherwise you'll wear it!" There weren't no bullets in the gun, but he doesn't know that. He pulls the trigger, Mum grabs the gun and breaks the rifle butt over his shoulders. Then they is all into it. Dad slaps Gail, Mum and Gail take off to welfare, and Dad's telling welfare to get her out of the house, otherwise she'll go out in a box. I went with Dad in the car and Mum, who has loaded the gun by now, blew the windscreen out as we was driving off. Flamin' near got me with the bullet.' Pat shakes her head from side to side, interjects as Tony tells the story. 'Noo, son, nooo. If I'd wanted to get you I would've. I'm too good a shot to miss.' The neighbours can hear the ruckus, but there is nothing unusual in that. They reckon the Sinclair family is easily the queerest lot of buggers they've ever met.

Elizabeth, not yet nine, runs around the backyard screaming until the car disappears from sight. 'Mum shot through for good, that time', Tony recalls. 'Elizabeth went to stay with Mum's mother for a time while Mum went fruit picking with Gail and Wayne, but Dad and her never got back together.'

By 1969, despite the family background, Pat has gained legal custody of her children.

For a while, the kids follow one or the other of their parents like pied pipers. And then, two years shy of his fiftieth birthday, Reg dies from a combination of lung cancer and a bad heart, turning grey and dying where he falls. Reg's passing is so unremarkable that no one claims his ashes, which are tossed out after a respectable length of time.

Elizabeth and her mother, Pat, stay together, forming a close bond. The roller coaster of welfare department housing and government handouts continues. That is what they know, and that is what they do. Now in her mid-seventies, Pat admits that she wasn't the best mother. 'I loved my kids – my word I did. Every one of them. But it was self-preservation, see? Self-preservation. That's why I used to take off.'

★ ★ ★

At 14, and living with some of the family at Mt Druitt, Elizabeth Haydon falls pregnant for the first time. Pat doesn't know and if her brother, Wayne, does, it doesn't stop him from deliberately toppling his sister off her pushbike. At the hospital where she is taken after the bike accident, Elizabeth's 13-week pregnancy is terminated. Pat still blames welfare for that, bitter that they conned Elizabeth into believing that she – Pat – has signed the papers agreeing to her daughter's abortion. After the termination, Elizabeth finds out that she had been carrying twin boys.

At 17, she is pregnant again but the relationship with the father doesn't last. Placid most of the time, Elizabeth can be a fiery piece if a man ever raises a hand to her, which he does. He wants her to terminate and when she refuses he pushes her down the stairs, hopeful it will bring on a miscarriage.

It doesn't, and though she can barely change a nappy – she has never been taught and has little interest in learning – she keeps having her babies. Contraception is available, but she chooses not to use it. She only ever 'falls', she says, when she is on the pill. Children bring with them the promise of love. They are a bargaining tool: if she has a man's baby, he won't leave her; and a child's love is unconditional. But it doesn't work out like that. The bloke inevitably shoots through, sooner rather than later, and she is left with the kids on her own again, unable to cope with the daily grind of cleaning dirty bums or wiping dirty noses.

And so, like her mother before her, Elizabeth Haydon discovers that she is not a great mother, that it is an art that has eluded her; and she abandons some of her kids to relatives and others to welfare. That is how she has been raised, that is what she knows. And that is what she does.

At 21, and now with three children – Leslie, John and Elizabeth – to two different fathers, Elizabeth moves in with Gary Grey, who has previously been married to her sister, Gail Sinclair. Elizabeth's union with him produces a son, but not long after, that relationship also fizzles.

Gary has known the family since they lived at Warnervale

in 1953, remembers the blues and the taunts – 'Bush coons, bush coons' – and he is still Tony's best mate. He has two kids with Gail, but there is a long pause before he remembers their names. Daniel, in 1972. Nanette, 1973. Gary was in love with Gail, he says, but he admits he was only ever fond of Elizabeth. 'All up, Gail had seven kids', he says. 'My two, and another five, all different fathers, all in and out of welfare. She give me merry hell in our marriage, and she goes by so many different names now, I don't know how she keeps up with herself.' The relationship turns him right off marrying again. 'Oh, God no', he grimaces, tweaking the gold earring in his ear. 'You marry someone like Gail, you never want to do it again. Never.'

Gary Grey has known the family so long he wanders into the house without knocking, sitting down and staring at the carpet when he speaks, fixating on a spot and absently flicking his hair, thick as a lion's mane, off his forehead. He is part of the furniture, part of the changing kaleidoscope of the Sinclair family.

Pat no longer speaks to her daughter Gail, and neither does Gary; the lines are clearly drawn and he has chosen his side. He now lives with Sharon Ball, who plays her own walk-on, walk-off role during the court cases. Gary has known the Sinclair family so long that he can say what he likes about them, and no offence taken. They are dysfunctional, he says. Very, very dysfunctional. Pat opens her mouth to speak, showing a pronounced line of stained, obtruding teeth, but Tony gets in first. 'He's right, Mum, he's right. We are dysfunctional.'

Elizabeth's next relationships follows the same pattern as the others. At 22 she gives birth to a son whose father she met at a ten-pin bowls club and whom she marries. Pat lives with them, but not for long. The marriage only lasts five months. Elizabeth can't cope with all the kids and so her sister, Christine, takes the oldest two boys, raising them from early childhood. The following year, Elizabeth gives birth to another son.

With welfare help, and pooling their meagre resources, Elizabeth, Pat and some of the children decamp to New Zealand in search of a better life. This is a good lurk. Pat gets money from both the Australian and New Zealand governments and Elizabeth, with her children, pulls in a fair amount each fortnight in welfare. Her last son is born in New Zealand when Elizabeth Haydon is in her mid-twenties.

But the run of good luck doesn't last. Thieves invade their home and take off with their booty, and Pat's beloved dog is baited and dies. Their final refuge before they combine their money and high-tail it back to Australia is a halfway house, where they share stories with the other residents about how unlucky their lives are.

They seem to attract disaster everywhere they go. Like shit-magnets, a journalist would later comment. They move again, this time to the northern suburbs of Adelaide.

It has to be a whole lot better than New Zealand.

16

This is suburbia without a soul. Adelaide's grey northern fringe, on the outer edges of the city's metropolis, is hard-bitten, hard-edged and hard done by. Distinguished by declining economic opportunity and residents with 'severe multiple disadvantage', Salisbury North is described in a 1997 report commissioned by the Housing Trust and Salisbury City Council as an urban crime ghetto.

In the down-at-heel suburbs of Salisbury North and Elizabeth, sun-starved little boxes, masquerading as houses, are clumped together and rented out by the government for less than a hundred dollars a fortnight. There is a standing joke in the welfare office: if people don't pay their rent on the housing trust homes they live in here, they are sent to Whyalla, another housing trust area, further from sight.

Salisbury North, like its sister housing trust areas, is overwhelmingly multicultural and blue-collar, with pockets of middle-income earners. Behind the doors in Salisbury North, many families eke out an existence on their pension money. Fathers who long ago have given up hope of finding a job and who have lost the heart to try; mothers who week after week never have enough to buy anything beyond the bare necessities; children who can't see the point in going to school and who opt out of the system early, half illiterate and with no aspirations beyond packing boxes at the local supermarket or working at the check-out counter at Coles or Woollies. They can't choose their neighbours here, take what they are given, so if there are brawls or screaming kids or drunks throwing up in the backyard, that's too bad.

This is a suburb where dreams turn early to dust, where kids with baseball caps on back to front loiter on street corners, looking for trouble and often finding it, a fag in one hand and a joint or beer can in the other. Video games, television and more sleep than they need fill their days in this enclave of the idle poor where life on the dole is a given. Here, youth unemployment is as high as 36 per cent – amongst the highest in the nation – and there is little chance of that changing. Grog and smokes and dope are a way of life, a means of breaking the boredom of waking up to endless days of nothing. Faces become ravaged while they are still young. By the time they are 40, these faces are the colour of concrete, just as grey and set just as hard. Violence is commonplace, knives tucked into socks and jocks. Young girls, barely more than children themselves, slouch as they hold their babies on their hips. There is no one to go home to: their boyfriends usually take off as soon as they hear the word 'pregnant', and often they have no extended family. So they hang around on the street until the babies get hungry.

There are drifters, who have moved away from their families and not bothered to keep in contact, and street kids who have washed up like debris. Takeaway food outlets are abundant, and the new growth industry is 'SmokeMarts' – snazzy drive-through cigarette outlets as big as McDonald's.

The commissioned Housing Trust report recognises the problems: that the high level of public housing has resulted in a melting pot of residents with particular socio-economic profiles.

It wasn't meant to be like this; an Orwellian nightmare. This is a social experiment that has gone hideously wrong, resulting in generational unemployment, lack of education and poverty; whole suburbs of people isolated by geographic disadvantage and removed from the opportunities afforded the middle class. Whole suburbs of early school leavers, single parents, social security recipients, and below-average household incomes. Generations with no resources to scrabble back up the welfare ladder.

It wasn't meant to be like this.

Named after Queen Elizabeth II, the town of Elizabeth was

the brainchild of the South Australian Housing Trust, intended to accommodate the predominantly British post-war migrant population whose passage to the land of opportunity was boosted by the Migrant House Purchase Scheme. Built on the sheep grazing plains between Salisbury and Smithfield and designed into twelve sub-divided districts, it was initially envisaged as a satellite town, touted as the 'City of Tomorrow'. The development of major industrial sites, including General Motors Holden, ensured it became self-sufficient, though it is generally regarded that 'polite society' ends at Gepps Cross, in Adelaide.

But for all the hoopla of Elizabeth's opening, and the boast that it was the 'greatest venture of Australia's most active housing agency . . . perhaps unparalleled in Australian planning', history records that 'consistent rain in the first winter turned the dirt roads into quagmires where cars and people would sink deep in mud'. Critics of the City of Tomorrow argue that with the slump in its industrial base, Elizabeth has been sinking ever since.

The Housing Trust has looked for areas that can accommodate people in desperate need of public housing, and they choose Elizabeth and its surrounding suburbs. It is here that Bunting, Haydon, Wagner and Vlassakis live, and from here that their victims are drawn. A former community worker at Salisbury North vents her disgust that people with multiple social problems have been channelled into the area. 'They have been dumped in there', she seethes. 'People who are desperate. The Trust will say, "You want priority, you say you're desperate, here's a house". Barry Lane has a conviction for paedophilia, which the Trust is aware of, but they gave him a house opposite the local primary school. It isn't as if they didn't know his past.'

Following the Housing Trust report, the green light is given to a 10-year renewal project for the suburbs, with a focus on dismantling the existing communities and introducing wage-earning home owners into the estates to balance out the social mix. Many, particularly the elderly who have lived in the neighbourhood for decades, do not want to leave and opponents of the dispersal policy argue that the disadvantaged, though less visible, will still exist and relocation will simply move crime, unemployment and other social problems from one area to another. But for those in favour, change – if it works – can't come soon enough.

Elizabeth Haydon isn't looking for somewhere better when she returns from New Zealand. With her kids and Pat in tow, she is looking for somewhere cheap to live. And cheap housing in Adelaide isn't in the beachside suburb of Glenelg, the conservative elegance of North Adelaide or the leafy peace of the hills. Cheap rentals are in housing trust areas. This is where she goes looking.

Bunting, Haydon and Wagner aren't looking for somewhere better, either. This urban crime ghetto, with its high rate of unemployment and social disintegration, is just right for them. A perfect place to live, work and do business.

17

Mark Haydon is a bit backward, mentally slow. But to Elizabeth Sinclair, he is good enough. She is a bit backward, a bit slow herself.

At first, Elizabeth fancies John Bunting, giggles like a school girl when she is in his presence, gazing at him with the blank stare of the slightly bewildered. 'Don't let me get pissed around you, I'll put on the hard word', she tells him, moving closer towards him. But she turns his stomach, particularly after he finds she is plagued with thrush and herpes. 'That really put John into a spin', Elizabeth Harvey recalls. 'From that time on, he'd call her a dirty, a slut. He has nightmares about herpes crawling all over the bed and he doesn't really like her to start with. She brought up her kids atrociously, the house is always filthy and she never does housework. She is just a slut, as far as he is concerned.'

The stories Elizabeth Sinclair tells her friend: being dumped by her mother with a farmer who chased her around with a cattle prod; living in the Cross and being sold into a brothel; the children and the men and the violence. Elizabeth Harvey doesn't know what to make of the stories, especially the ones when she says she had been an escort to politicians. Hardly likely, she shrugs. Like, she says, if you saw Elizabeth Sinclair, she was no oil painting. Hardly bloody likely.

Elizabeth can't have John, so she settles for Mark Haydon instead. He has no social skills, is a complete misfit, but he will do. She dumps her kids off at his place while she goes out and has a good time.

Mark Haydon's friends are a scruffy lot, but Elizabeth doesn't notice. She has long ago learnt to accept the good with the bad. With her two youngest boys, she moves in with Haydon and his father and two years later, when he finally suggests marriage, she doesn't hesitate. Haydon isn't all that keen to marry her, has to be talked into it by Elizabeth Harvey, but he wants Elizabeth to have his babies and harps continually on the subject.

Although given to sudden mood swings, Elizabeth is still easy-going and the constant presence of drop-ins and drop-kicks who frequent their home doesn't bother her. Her wedding to Mark, at the Church of Latter-day Saints in Elizabeth Downs, is low-key, but happy. The Mormons accept the couple, even if they don't entirely abide by the church's edict that caffeine, alcohol and cigarettes are a sin against their prophet, Joseph Smith, and the teachings of the Bible.

Mark is on a carer's pension to look after his father. Once they are married, Elizabeth nags Mark to leave Adelaide, to pack up and move to Queensland to live and they do, carting whatever they can with them in the car. There is no room for Mark's father, so they leave him behind. Give him no warning they are leaving, organise no domiciliary care, leave no food in the house. An elderly man, frail from a stroke, he is reliant on a walking frame and incapable of feeding or showering himself. It will be almost a week before Mark's aunt discovers her brother lying on the floor with a broken hip, when he is admitted to a nursing home for care.

Queensland is a disaster. Mark and Elizabeth run up credit and then run out of the state, Mark changing his surname from Lawrence to Haydon along the way. They high-tail it back to Adelaide with the boys and move straight back into the house with no explanation and no apologies to Mark's father.

On some days there can be up to half a dozen people at a time in the driveway of their Elizabeth East home, all milling around a vehicle with the bonnet up. A Holden ute or beat-up Torana with mag wheels, a souped-up engine and something dangling from the rear-vision mirror: plastic skull, black spider or knitted footy mascot. Huddling there for hours on end, oil spilling onto the pathway and mixing with their discarded cigarette butts, the ground charcoaled and sodden underfoot. And Elizabeth might join them sometimes, lumbering down the path with her massive thighs and ugh boots slopping up and down, dragging herself along, sometimes holding one of the children on her hip, looking bored and baffled, slumping against the car and doing the same as the blokes, just staring into the engine. It is something to do to fill up the day, in between the endless moments of squealing kids, dirty nappies and snotty noses.

Elizabeth turns to fat when the kids start coming, now a substantial woman, vast around the beam, with a face resembling a Russian peasant.

Mostly she is okay with the kids, placid if a little vacant, a little bored; unsure what she is meant to do with them or for them. But sometimes she loses her temper and shouts at them to shut the fuck up. She has a foul mouth and a hot temper when she is put out, particularly if a bloke ever tries to raise a hand to her. She can put up with a lot of things, but she won't put up with that. The kids cop it sometimes from her, a mouthful when they are noisy, but mostly she keeps her hands off them. And they do what she has done as a child: run barefoot and unsupervised around the house, the driveway, the streets. Like a litter of wild puppies.

With her other kids in welfare or living with her sister, Christine, Elizabeth tries to make a better fist of motherhood with her last two children, but it is near impossible. Lacking the necessary motherhood skills, she also has another problem. The boys aren't Mark Haydon's kids, and he treats them as if they are bloody nuisances, devising ways to keep them in their place.

At night he locks them in their room, not allowing them to come out even to go to the toilet. They can't escape, even through the window, which is nailed up. So if they wet their pants or soil them, that is too bad. They are sent to school unwashed and if the teachers notice the smell, little is done. This time welfare doesn't come, the police don't come, the neighbours don't report it and Elizabeth watches it happen and does nothing. Silence is the better option.

Gary Grey reckons Haydon is a 'moody bastard' whose black temper worsens when he suffers a migraine headache. 'He is mean to those boys, real mean. He'd pick them up by the ears and belt the crappers out of them.' The youngest is working out that the smartest way to escape the abuse is to lie low, to duck and weave and tiptoe when Haydon is in another of his foul moods. The boys spend a lot of time hiding under the kitchen table, but it doesn't take much for them to get into trouble. When they are hungry, they steal food from the cupboards, which earns them a hiding. But there isn't much in the cupboards to pinch: their mother doesn't cook, and they virtually live on takeaways: Hungry Jack's, McDonald's, Kentucky Fried; anything that comes in a cardboard box. And when they have finished with the food, they leave the takeaway containers on the floor where they fall. The house is filthy, littered with rubbish and half-eaten, fly-blown food. A mess that a lawyer will describe as 'almost indescribable squalor. If they lived in the States, they'd be known as "po' white trash"'.

Haydon's frail father signs his dilapidated house over to Mark, who sells it to a developer for $22,000. They don't clean up their mess behind them when they leave; oil soiling the driveway, sodden cigarette butts, the filth inside the house. Within a short time, renovated by the new owner, the house is again on the market and fetches almost three times that amount.

The family moves to the house Mark has bought in September 1998 at Blackham Crescent, a less than salubrious address at nearby Smithfield Plains. The chaos that surrounded them in Elizabeth East – the comings and goings of strange characters, souped-up cars and nailed-up windows to stop the children leaving their room at night – all follow them to Blackham Crescent. But Elizabeth is chuffed to finally have a place she can call her own. She hangs a kitsch, pink sign over their new front door: 'Home Sweet Home'.

18

Jamie Vlassakis is inculcated into John Bunting's world in the most subtle of ways. Groomed and shaped, week after week. Initially, it appears a benign relationship: Jamie riding pillion on Bunting's motorbike, or the two of them going to the movies together. They get on well. For the first time in his life, Jamie feels secure, wanted.

Drugs help. Blocking out the world with his cocktails of dope and grog, Valium and benzos. By 14, he is also doing speed – at first sniffed and swallowed, later injected. Pumping the vein, gripping the tourniquet between his teeth and fastening it tight on his forearm, before he slips the needle in. Bingeing on speed, off his face for days and topping up with LSD or cocaine. Crushing benzos and shooting them up, using Valium to help bring him down.

He lands a job at Hungry Jack's when he is 15, but that only lasts a few days. He is off his face most of the time, figures he doesn't need the job. His youth allowance, combined with his natural ability to scam and scheme, keeps him financially afloat. He buys a car engine for a packet of smokes, puts it in a vehicle he's bought from some desperate junkies for next to nothing, then flogs it to someone else for three times that amount. He is a survivor. And he has John Bunting: 'Will you be my father?' he asks him. 'Will you, John?' Jamie is bloody tickled pink when Bunting says yes. Elizabeth Harvey recalls with distress how Jamie came to live with Bunting, 'One of his friends, Anne Cordwell, went and got Jamie exempted from school so he could sell chemicals for her door to door, and she made herself legal guardian over Jamie. This was all going on without me signing a piece of paper. Very cluey woman, and I wanted Jamie out of her clutches, and I said to John, "Can he live with you?" "Oh yeah, no worries", John said, so Jamie came.'

She sighs, lights another cigarette, coughs until she dry-retches.

But Anne Cordwell's version is utterly different. '[My partner and I] were hoping that we could provide him with the most normal – show him what a normal family home was like . . .' she tells John Bunting's Counsel, Elizabeth Shepperd, in court.

'And over a period of time before you became [his] guardian, did you come to see the way his mother dealt with him?'

'Yes, I did.'

'Did that upset you.'

'Yes, it did.'

'Did she appear to reject him?'

'She rejected all of her children.'

'Jamie,' she adds, 'was a fantastic kid, who would do anything for anybody. But with her, I felt like there was just no maternal instinct there at all.' Once he moved back in with Elizabeth, she says, he became ratty and rebellious.

His mother is now permanently living with Bunting at 203 Waterloo Corner Road, and it's a tight squeeze with all the kids. Human traffic, in and out of the house, day and night. Human flotsam and jetsam, sleeping wherever they can find a place to put their heads. Usually it is the floor.

And all the while, Jamie is listening to incessant talk of paedophiles and homosexuals. Bunting never differentiates between the two, never shuts up about them. They are filthy waste. Dirt. Rock spiders. Tooth fairies. He is totally preoccupied. Paedophiles are everywhere. There is no escaping them.

John's role is to hunt them down and expose them; it's his job to save and protect children. He is obsessed with the idea of exposing paedophiles and what he will do to the dirty bastards when he gets his hands on them. People who knew him in Queensland and when he first arrived in South Australia remember he has always talked like that. Obsessed with hatred and talk of violent retribution.

Jamie listens and absorbs the lessons. Hangs on his hero's every word, a stoned human sponge. He is gradually brain-washed, drawn in deeper and deeper, drowning under the weight of Bunting's beliefs. Bunting's obsessions. Bunting's missions.

Barry Lane, frightened of Bunting yet desperate for attention, still spoon-feeds him information. Who is a rock spider and who is a fag. It makes Lane feel important and, based on his information, Bunting constantly adds to the wall of spiders. A web of wool snaking between names on his wall that grows bigger by the week. And Bunting shares all he knows with Jamie, feeding him a steady stream of information. On and on. Inculcated, desensitised. Then, finally, initiated.

First, victimising paedophiles. Abusing them and vandalising their property, pouring brake fluid onto their cars, spraying graffiti on their houses. Exposing them, abusing them, hunting them down. They are no-good waste. Dirties. Human pollutants, breathing good air.

Bunting is also fixated with guns. A .38 with a fitted silencer is hidden under the seat of his motorbike. He grins when he talks about what guns can do. The mess they can make. Blasting a hole in skin, exposing blood and guts and gore.

Then, animals.

Killing and skinning cats, reeking carcasses rotting in the backyard, stench drifting into the house. Visitors turn up their noses at the fetor, but it doesn't bother Bunting. He has no sense of smell and no sense of their pain. Cats can cry and bleed but they can't fight back and can't talk. Dogs next. Swerving deliberately to run one over in the street, laughing and leaving the animal yelping in pain, dying helpless and wounded in the gutter. Telling Jamie to lock another dog in the laundry after it tries to bite him, giving him a .22 zip gun, ordering him to blow the animal's brains out. Jamie tries not to shake, to hide his aversion, aims at the dog cowering in the corner, pulls the trigger and misses. Bunting laughs and takes charge. Music blares through the CD player. One shot and blood, brains and fur splatter all over the laundry. Jamie wants to retch but can't show his revulsion. He has to impress his hero.

And all the time, Bunting's incessant talk of paedophiles. Hurting them, punching them, kicking them. Sticking the boots in, listening to their bones break. Over and over. Shaping and forming and crystallising his ideas. Sharing them with his protégé.

His mission is to do the world a favour, to kill the dirties. Rid the world of waste. Send them to the clinic.

Make them good.

Elizabeth Harvey is law abiding until she meets Bunting. She listens to his talk of retribution against paedophiles, nods her head, sometimes her thinking lucid and clear but mostly foggy from the Valium. Goes with him to spray-paint graffiti on the house of a woman who, Bunting says, has abused her own children. He has no proof, but an air of authority and power about him. He just takes charge.

She likes to spoil him. Buys him biscuits that he dunks in milk, up-down, up-down in a yo-yo action until they are saturated and soft. The sweeter the biscuit, the more he likes them and no one else is allowed to share. Elizabeth lovingly shapes a pottery container at ceramics class in which John can store his special treats. His very own biscuit barrel.

He hates coffee, drinks only cordial and milk that he guzzles like a child before wiping his mouth with the sleeve of his jumper. Loves expensive cheese; the house reeks of blue vein, but he can't smell it. He can't smell a thing.

Elizabeth can't control Jamie anymore. He has his first whack of heroin at 16, around the same time he is raped again. All the old feelings of self-disgust rise to the surface, his skin crawling, scrubbing himself in the shower until he bleeds. This time it's an acquaintance of Marcus Johnson who is staying at his house, a man named Richard, who takes a fancy to him. It happens after a party at Marcus's house; the man, drunk, invites Jamie to the nearby park for drugs. Jamie, pissed and stoned, is scared stiff as he is forcefully held down and sodomised. Richard staggers off into the night and Jamie blames himself again, increasingly self-medicating to stop the pain. He doesn't tell anyone, doesn't report it to the police. Who would believe a 179-centimetre-tall young man could be raped? Better to say nothing.

He loves the way heroin makes him feel. The way he can hear voices around him but doesn't need to connect with the world. No pain, no drama and no time at all before he has a raging habit. Alternating between speed and smack. Anything he can get his hands on.

Wagner and Lane's relationship started well, but now it is fractured by increasing violence. Barry minces around demanding Robert spends more time with him, and less time with John Bunting. Throwing jealous little tantrums. 'You just can't seem to keep away from that man', he pouts.

There are terrible rows, even in public. Once, Robert's mother, Carol, is in the car with him when Lane drives up behind them, rams the boot and pushes their vehicle out into traffic. 'Robert flew out of my car and started kicking and bashing Barry's car and told him he'd see him back at my place. Barry came up behind us, and when he got out of the car, Robert started belting into him', Carol remembers. And that was one of their least violent blues.

All hell breaks loose when John tells Elizabeth that Barry Lane has touched up her son. She smacks Lane in the mouth, screams the house down and then Robert gets involved. Punches Barry, who is running up the street in his effeminate way, yelling, 'Please don't hit me, don't hit me again, Robert'. The bunches of keys he carries jangle from out his back pocket and he is fleeing, calves flying out sideways in what they have called 'Barry's chicken faggot dance'. Robert bashes him for weeks after, every day another hiding and the verbal taunts that go with it: 'You bastard, you took me when I was 14'.

The police, increasingly involved in their domestic dramas,

advise Barry to move out, to put distance between them. They warn him that if he doesn't go, God knows where that sort of violence could end. As his gear is being loaded on the truck, Barry timidly knocks on Robert's door.

'Robert. Robert?' he wheedles.

'What do you want, faggot?'

'Can I have the telephone directory, please?'

Robert rips out a page and hands it to him. 'Here, that's the only page you need. "P" for paedophile. Now fuck off.'

Robert Wagner is alone in the house and lonely now that Barry has gone. But his anger at his former lover is fermenting. John visits him frequently, and they make a decision: Robert will move in with John and Elizabeth for a while. First, Wagner moves to his mother's house for a short stint, and then to John Bunting's house at 203 Waterloo Corner Road.

Elizabeth Harvey remembers her first meeting with Robert Wagner. 'He was like this 12-year-old child and very angry when he and Barry broke up. He thought John was God. He and John joined National Action shortly after that, but they got kicked out because they were too radical. Robert started going out with girls straight away. He was determined to show he isn't gay.'

Robert Wagner proves to be the perfect incubator for John's ideas. Soon, he is walking up and down Hindley Street, a seedy nightclub area in the middle of Adelaide, bashing faggots. In training for working with John.

Later, when Bunting, Elizabeth and her family head to Bakara, Robert follows John like the Messiah before finally settling at 36 Mofflin Road, Elizabeth.

A volunteer with the Country Fire Service, Wagner struggles with the theory but manages to pass. He walks around in his uniform with his pager and mobile phone, pumped up and important, but the crew find him intimidating and strange. His cold eyes stare right through them and a constant vitriolic stream pours from his mouth.

The Country Fire Service and John Bunting: the two

things in Robert Wagner's life that make him feel important. Everything else comes second.

Now that Barry is out of the picture, Carol enjoys a much better relationship with her son. When he asks her to store a four-wheel-drive, and later a Nissan Pulsar for John Bunting, she doesn't hesitate. Robert wants it to sit in her backyard until he gets the parts for it. It needs fixing.

So many things need fixing. It is their code, their way of blocking outsiders with their own secret language. 'This is falling out of the car, we need to fix it.' 'That job we got for the landscaping, we need to meet to do a quote.'

There is a car in Robert's driveway, with a barrel in the boot. Carol remembers the barrel is black and big, with a screw-top lid on it. Later, she stumbles when she explains to police about the barrel. 'The lid is – it is – the lid isn't screwed on properly, so it is empty; otherwise, if there had been anything in it, I'm sure I would have smelt it', she says. The barrel doesn't fit properly in the boot, and the boot lid is held down by an octopus strap. She asks Bunting what he needs the barrel for.

'To store compost', he says.

At the end of 1995 Bunting rings Veronika out of the blue, says he is moving out of 203 Waterloo Corner Road and relocating to an old farmhouse at Bakara, in the Riverland district two hours from Adelaide. A decrepit, isolated settlement boasting a handful of shabby houses and one garage, Bakara is perfect for their needs: far from the prying eyes of city neighbours, a bigger place where he, Elizabeth and the kids can live. He orders Veronika to move back into Waterloo Corner Road, says he doesn't want just anyone living in the house. It doesn't occur to her to refuse. 'I had to go back there', she recalls. 'I didn't have a leg to stand on. He just said I had to and that was that.' Recited in a matter of fact voice, her words plaited around each other and each falling with a flat thud. *That was that.*

The lease on 203 is transferred solely into Veronika's name; by January she has resettled at the house, with the little bits of furniture John has left behind. He has promised that it is a house she can call her own, but it doesn't turn out like that. 'There were all sorts of people waddling through the kitchen', she says. 'Robert Skewes used to come in all the time and drink coffee, he never had any money to buy his own. Elizabeth and her kids seemed to always be there when they were in town. Jamie, and his mates Mark and Douglas Townsend lived there at various times, and then later on Marcus Johnson and Troy moved in.'

Elizabeth has told Marcus there is a room available at 203 and, as is frequently the case, he has nowhere else to go. It is a workable, platonic arrangement: Marcus and Veronika have come to know each other during their respective marriages and Veronika knows the boys. Veronika particularly likes Troy, feels an affinity with him.

John Bunting drops in frequently after he has moved to the country. Sometimes he is on his own, sometimes with other people: Robert Wagner, Jamie Vlassakis or occasionally Mark Haydon. Veronika doesn't question why they are there.

Bunting is not aware that he is under surveillance from Work-Cover for reporting he has a crook back. He climbs 6 metres up onto the roof at Bakara to put some fly wire over the chimney, free falls, shatters his ankle. Needs pins and rods to hasten its healing and grumbles around the place that no one will give him a job now. He vents his anger on WorkCover staff, abusing them at the counter and sneering threatening remarks. Elizabeth watches him out of hooded eyes, listening as he obsessively continues the tirade against WorkCover when they get home. He never shuts up.

They don't last long at Bakara, rattling back to Waterloo Corner Road with their goods and chattels – mostly stolen – early in 1996. But they won't stay there long, either. Bunting has his sights set on moving to the country again, this time to the housing trust community of Murray Bridge, a river town 70 kilometres to the south-east.

It seems to Veronika she never had any peace at 203 Waterloo Corner Road. Indignantly, she comments that John reckoned it was her place, but he'd left people behind.

19

Suzanne Allen adores Bunting. Writes him love letters signed, 'I love you Johnny Angel', and plasters them with lipstick kisses. If she knows of his on-again, off-again relationship with Elizabeth Harvey, she never comments. But Harvey does. 'This Suzanne just wouldn't leave John alone', she says. 'I said nothing, just sat back and watched, wondering how long this little caper would last. There was no way John was serious about her, him and me were so close.'

Suzanne leaves him little notes. Until he moves to the country, she drives past his house at 203 Waterloo Corner Road every day. Drops in unexpectedly, always at his door with her wide grin and obsessive questions. 'What have you been doing, Johnny?' 'Do you want to go for a drive, Johnny?'

A post-war baby, born in June 1949, Suzanne is one of seven children born and raised in Mildura, Victoria. She left home at 14, a backward girl trying to make her own way in the world in rural New South Wales. Desperate for affection, she attracts the wrong type of men. By the age of 24, buxom and beaming, she has left behind two marriages and four children with whom she will only periodically stay in touch. She will head to South Australia, try her luck there.

With little money, she settles in the enclave of the welfare dependent at Ghent Street, Salisbury North, 200 metres from 203 Waterloo Corner Road. She waves to neighbours during the day and at night drags back to her house men that she has picked up at the local karaoke club. The neighbours get used to her peculiar choice of men. Without exception, one sneers, they are all half-wits.

Chubby-faced, Suzanne doesn't have a quarrel with the world, going about her business with a friendly smile and an open, cheerful manner. Her hobby is painting: birds and flowers in full bloom and in full colour, work that shows a modicum of talent. The flowers – daffodils, irises – reflect her sunny nature and she is proud of them, offers them as gifts.

But there is another side to Suzanne Allen, a side that Bunting recognises when he courts her attentions in 1996. Underneath her happy-go-lucky surface, Allen's simplicity fosters an inferiority complex that allows her to excuse men who abuse her, mentally or physically.

Plagued with ill health through her thirties, she repeats, parrot-fashion, what her doctor has told her. Rattling off her problems and counting them on her fingers. Asthma. A bowel disease. Obesity. Carpel tunnel syndrome. High blood pressure. Occasional chest pain. She doesn't add her intellectual disability.

In 1996, Bunting, Wagner and Lane are frequent visitors to her small house. At 47, and pre-menopausal, she is 16 years older than Bunting, but he dominates her. He is good at that, has an air about him even though he is short. A man of ordinary appearance; incredibly ordinary. Pass him on the street, think: tradesman, council worker. But there is something about him.

It is his attitude that sets him apart. Like a desert dingo sensing prey, stock still, ears pricked and sniffing the wind. Hardly a flicker of his eyes, but alert. As though something is ticking over in his brain.

Ray Davies lives in a caravan at Port Pirie. His parents, both intellectually handicapped, are incapable of looking after their son, born in June 1969, and the role falls to his aunt. She loves the boy who has been christened James but who later changes his name to Ray. She passes off as a childhood phase his penchant for dressing in girls' clothes and showing an interest in dolls. But his perverse sexual predilections become deeply disturbing to her. When Ray is 13, she finds him having sex with the family dog in the backyard, and berates him for being a dirty boy. It doesn't change his habits. As he grows older, he will come to the attention of police for various offences on different occasions, including indecent behaviour with a dog, assault and stealing.

In 1989, Ray Davies moves into the city's northern suburbs. Between the welfare offices and gay nightclubs, it is inevitable he will collide with people who share his sexual appetites.

Lane and Wagner offer to help move Davies's caravan to Adelaide and Suzanne Allen, with her cheerful and sunny nature, agrees he can park it in her backyard. She has met him a few times and he seems okay. They become engaged for a time, but it is an odd relationship. Davies lives out in the van, she lives in the house.

He proves to be a strange boarder. Bisexual, Ray also continues his fetish for bestiality, having sex with dogs in the caravan. When he tires of that, he tries to seduce children into his caravan, or ambushes neighbours, standing on the street and masturbating as they hurry past. They tell him to stop it, to go inside, but as they will later recall, he isn't quite right. Not quite all there. Intellectually compromised and with a speech impediment, he often walks around with a ghetto blaster plastered to his ear, the thing he calls his 'boom box'. Elizabeth Harvey once meets him when he visits John, and can't understand a word he says. 'He could hardly string four words together', she says. She reckons it is on account of his bad genes.

Suzanne Allen suffers more than her neighbours from Ray's bizarre behaviour, and is frequently on the receiving end of his physical abuse. He beats her until she cowers against the wall until finally it gets too much, even for her, who is used to abuse from men. She puts a restraining order on Davies, and then he vanishes. Suzanne thinks little of it; she has already fallen for Bunting.

December 1995. They take Ray Davies for a drive in the car, Bunting driving and Wagner sitting with him in the back seat, pounding him down, keeping him down. He doesn't want other people to see what is happening, keeps punching and punching, Davies's bones shattering under his mammoth fists. Beats him and tells him to be a good little faggot when they stop the car for lunch. Psychopathically detached, Bunting and Wagner share a take-away meal in front of Davies before driving on to the farmhouse at Bakara. Elizabeth Harvey and the kids are in Adelaide for Christmas, staying at 203 Waterloo Corner Road. The coast is clear.

Davies is whimpering with terror as they guide him through the empty house and into the bathroom. Water is streaming from his eyes and nose and he is forced into the bathtub and repeatedly smashed in the groin with a metal pole. He is overpowered by Wagner's physical strength and Bunting's maniacal energy; his testicles are swollen to twice their size from the beating. They laugh as they whack him again, screeching at him as the pole impacts with savage force on his groin and thighs. No one can hear them, the sustained beating accompanied by a verbal tirade. 'Nappy raper. Waste. Filthy faggot.'

They don't want him to die in this bathtub, so they force him to stand and subject his wrists to handcuffs before frog-marching him back to the car. 'Be a good little faggot', they order him, before they start to drive away. Davies, bloodied, bruised and terrified, lies scrunched in the foetal position in the dark, airless tomb of the car boot as they make the two-hour journey back to Adelaide. He can't hear Bunting and Wagner's hysteria over the noise of the car engine. 'His balls have swollen to the size of golf balls', Bunting gloats. Wagner sniggers and keeps driving.

Suzanne Allen's daughter, Annette Cannon, who lives near her mother, asks where Davies has gone. They dropped him off in the middle of the scrub somewhere, they giggle, and made him walk back towards town. It's a long walk.

But Davies doesn't come back, simply ups and disappears sometime over the festive season of 1995, just after Cannon has told Bunting that Davies had sexually interfered with her children. Left behind a filthy caravan and a filthy reputation. No one ever sees him again.

But Elizabeth Harvey knows where he is.

Sitting at the kitchen table at 203 Waterloo Corner Road,

souped up on anti-depressants and downers; up to 25 Valium a day. So medicated, she can barely keep her eyes open. John had disappeared without explanation but now he is walking in the door, elated, jumping up and down, telling Elizabeth that he has someone outside. She's doped up to the eyeballs, what she calls 'la-la land' and furious at him for going away without telling her.

'Where the hell have you been? I've been worried sick you were in an accident', she slurs, but Bunting can't get the grin off his face. He is joyful, energised. He has a surprise for her in the boot of the car, he says.

'Well, bring it in.' Elizabeth's head is lolling to the side and she can barely hold her cigarette. She watches as Bunting and Wagner march Davies into the bathroom, listens to them scream abuse at him before they steer him into the bedroom. Sitting half comatose at the kitchen table, she looks vacantly into the bedroom as they strip him naked and continue their verbal tirade. 'Faggot. Dirty faggot waste. Nappy raper.' Davies, exhausted and beyond pain, speaks only when he is told to. 'Yes, Lord. Yes, Sir.'

There is a knock at the door. Jamie Vlassakis is standing outside, impatiently tapping his feet as he waits for someone to answer. He looks back at Marcus Johnson sitting in the car, gestures with a shrug of his shoulders that perhaps no one is home. But he can hear noises from the back of the house, the sound of running feet and now the door is opening. His mother, wild-eyed, is standing in front of him, flanked by Bunting and Wagner. 'Go away', Bunting hisses. Wagner, holding a metal pole in his hand, stares emotionlessly after him as Vlassakis walks back down the driveway.

The door closes behind him.

They lie Davies on a mattress on the floor of the spare bedroom, the room with all the junk in it. The room with the wall of spiders. They have beckoned Elizabeth to join them and she is stabbing the naked, petrified man and helping strangle him with jumper leads to make him good.

'Do you like your present?' Bunting nudges Elizabeth, as he

beams down at the lifeless man. And what to do with him now but drag him through the house, throw him in the hole out the back, the underground bunker, the tunnel, toss him in and giggle that he lands holding his balls.

John's coup de grace is telling Jamie of his mother's involvement. 'After I found out he killed Ray Davies, he also said my Mum was involved . . . He said my Mum stabbed Ray Davies with a garden tool and that she and Robert Wagner strangled him.' At first, Jamie struggles to believe it is true. Elizabeth is in and out of psychiatric hospitals, mentally unsound. But the gnawing has started, the doubts and the fear. He has to protect his mother the best way he knows. Her safety depends on his saying nothing, just as he has done with Jeffrey Payne.

All silent partners in the business of killing.

Elizabeth later says that it is six months before she can bring herself to mention Ray Davies to John. All that time, she is stoned on medication and mute with shock; six months before she accepts that she actually helped John and Robert murder a man. She knows she has to stay quiet, say nothing. She is terrified of John now, and what he is capable of. She remembers the time, very early in her relationship with John, that she went out with another man, Mervyn Hameister. John stormed in with a gun in his hand and she stood in front of Mervyn and said, 'If you shoot him, you shoot me'. John made Mervyn beg for his life, sobbing, before he fired the empty gun. In late 1994, Mervyn takes out a restraining order against Bunting. Elizabeth knows John is capable of anything. Her safety depends on her silence.

Suzanne Allen and Bunting spend a lot of time together for the first few months in early 1996, but by May, the relationship has soured. Bunting encourages her at first, but he quickly tires of her obsessive attentions and incessant visits. When he sees her arriving, he gets in his car and drives off. She never gets the message, keeps visiting him and he gripes to his neighbour, Robert Skewes, that she is getting on his nerves. It gets so bad he tells her to her face that he is busy and she will have to piss off.

In the end, Suzanne Allen makes him mad. Really mad. He tells her daughter, Annette Cannon, that he can't take any more of her mother's behaviour. Tells her to warn her mother to back off. After the message is relayed, Suzanne hides in her house, heartbroken, not emerging for weeks. She has adored her Johnny Angel, even helped him clean out Ray Davies's caravan after Ray's sudden disappearance. And all the thanks she gets is to be dumped again.

It seems she can never get it right in love. She falls for men quickly, and like a teenager in the first flush of infatuation, announces that they plan to marry. It happens so often, her relatives grow tired of it, know it is another of her fantasies. The men leave her and she chases them, obsessively writing love letters, throwing herself at their mercy. But they never come back. Ever. Suzanne Allen is a loser in love.

She chases her Johnny Angel, too. Writes him love letters, with the help of her daughter, Annette, which he reads out loud to other people. Gathering his audience around him: 'Listen to this'. Adding facial expressions, hooting.

'Dear John. I am finding it hard to be away from you all the time. I wish that you would stay with me for good because I love you so much . . . I hope you are feeling the same way about me.

'So my darling John, please don't take too long to come back to me, I will always wait for you.

'All my love, Suzanne.'

He thinks it is hilarious. She can't even spell the word 'angel' right when she uses it. Spells it 'angle'. She's a fruit bat. A ding-a-ling. She's a kangaroo short in the top paddock. A filthy, fat fucking whore who won't fuck off.

The tooth fairy will pay.

He won't answer the door to her so she drives past his house, slowing down to see if she can get a glimpse of him. All hours of the day and night. 'You there, John? Woo-hoo. Anyone home?'

Then her daughter, Annette, falls pregnant to one of Suzanne's ex-boyfriends. It is too much, adds to John's rejection. Suzanne starts telling people she is going to take a drug overdose. She sports a hang-dog look on her plump face as she talks about her own suicide.

And then she is gone. Simply disappears, between mid-spring and the beginning of summer. She has left no suicide note but her distressed, unfed animals are proof to her family that she has gone quickly. She loved her animals. Her artwork is still there on the kitchen table, brightly coloured birds and flowers that reflected the happy side of her personality. Annette is bewildered. Surely she would have said goodbye to her?

Strange things start happening. Suzanne's car is there one day and gone the next. Nobody sees it driven away. Then weirder things; noises in the night, men moving around her house with torches, flashes of light into dark corners but no electric lights turned on. A truck pulling up, muffled voices, three or four men going into the house and coming out with furniture, bits and pieces, loading it onto a truck marked Steptoe and Son at 3 o'clock in the morning. Two men standing at the end of the driveway on lookout, watching, silent, and a neighbour peeking through the curtain, too scared to move, petrified she will be observed, too scared to walk outside and past Suzanne's house to call police from the phone box on the corner.

Suzanne's brother, John, is the first to notice she is missing in November 1996, frowning as he surveys her usually tidy home. It's an unholy mess, furniture gone and her animals hungry. He reports her missing. It is out of character for his sister to go to ground. It's all too weird.

Annette is also perplexed at her mother's sudden disappearance. She contacts Centrelink, appealing for help to locate her, but is barred by bureaucratic rules. Privacy regulations prohibit them telling her anything, they reply. Joan Potts, Suzanne's sister, also tries to make contact, forwarding a letter to Centrelink asking a message be passed to her. She never receives a response.

The police fare better. Accessing Centrelink records, Missing Persons staff discover that Suzanne's bank account is still active. Her pension goes in every fortnight, and is promptly withdrawn. They trace her change of address to a house at Murray Bridge. And to the lessee: John Bunting.

He is ineffably polite when the police ring. Yes, his name is John Bunting. Yep, he knows Suzanne Allen. She stayed with him for a while but is no longer there. Suzanne has moved interstate with a bloke called Andy and doesn't want her family making contact.

'Thanks for your help.'

'Yeah, no worries. See ya.'

Bunting hangs up, looks around the room at Suzanne's furniture that now adorns their lounge room. Part of his swag of trophies. He laughs out loud. Dumb fucking coppers wouldn't have a fucking clue.

The police contact Suzanne's family. People who disappear in mysterious circumstances don't access their bank accounts. Everything, they reassure them, appears fine. She obviously just doesn't want to be found.

According to Bunting, Allen is a tooth fairy, a woman who tolerated Ray Davies sexually interfering with her grand-children. She knew what he did, and though she had already kicked him out, Bunting figured she was responsible. 'John reckoned she tolerated Davies exposing himself to all the little boys and little girls in the street', Elizabeth Harvey recalls. 'Ray had that many warrants for indecent exposure and Suzanne was getting police knocking on the door at Salisbury because Ray was standing in the front yard with no pants on . . . so accord-ing to John, she was a paedophile because she tolerated it.'

After she is dead, they mutilate her in her own bathtub. Slice off both her legs. Sever her left arm from the shoulder joint, her right arm and shoulder-blade. De-flesh her, meticulously. Skin and tissue. Slit out her heart and right lung. Cut off her ample breasts. Slice her genitals. Saw both feet through the ankle joints, sweating with the labour. Take to her hair, although it is never clear how. Either hold it up by the roots and hack it off, or tear it from her scalp. Kidneys, adrenal glands, pancreas and spleen rot away. Remaining organs wither and decay. Teeth gone, possibly yanked out.

Cut off her head with a knife, sawing through skin and muscle to reach the windpipe, thick and sinewy and tough. The awesome satisfaction of dismemberment, thrusting the knife, in-out, in-out. Sawing, grinding. Taking her apart, piece by piece. Through the blood vessels and carotid artery and jugular vein to the oesophagus, sweating as they work and finally carving through cartilage to the bone of her spine. Excited, exultant, slathered in gore, hand-passing her bald head between them, back and forth, back and forth like a bloodied football, playing with her, humiliating her, holding her face the colour of chalk up to their own, puckering to kiss her lips as blanched as cherries too long in the sun, her gummy mouth agape, laughing to each other, 'Kiss the puppet'.

Gut her, humiliate her and then bag her up, separating her torso and legs and breasts and genitals. Throw the garbage bags in the back of their car and cart her around the corner to 203 Waterloo Corner Road. Throw her in her grave on top of Ray Davies, her left hand shaped through the mechanics of rigor mortis in an impotent fist. Shovel dirt and bricks to cover her and leave her to rot, for the maggots to do their work.

Bunting returns to Murray Bridge and throws Suzanne Allen's ID on the table. He admits to Elizabeth that they have broken into Allen's home with the intention of robbing her. They found her slumped over the bath, he says, dead from either an overdose or a heart attack. Elizabeth believes him. Suzanne had a history of illness and a bad heart. It makes sense.

But she can't understand why he has to dispose of the body. Why he just doesn't go to the police and report she has died of natural causes, instead of interring her body in the hole out the back of 203, on top of Ray Davies. Why does it all have to be so secretive? But John is like that. Close-mouthed, when he wants to be.

A lot of Allen's property is moved to their house at Murray Bridge. They sell her television to Cash Converters and give her stereo to Vlassakis. Some is hocked to a second-hand shop, 'Steptoe and Son'. Allen's possessions are dispersed as casually as her body.

Elizabeth buys his story that he will get into trouble for moving the body and does as he asks, going to the bank posing as Suzanne Allen to activate a new card. She collects Suzanne's pension for 12 months, and pays off Allen's debt to Radio Rentals. 'I'm a moral person', she explains as the reason she has paid a dead woman's debt. It appeases her guilt. 'I thought that it's not fair for Radio Rentals.' But she can't live with the deception. She tells John they have to cancel the pension and he agrees.

He gives the card to Elizabeth Haydon's sister, Gail Sinclair. Overnight, she metamorphoses into Suzanne Allen.

By October 1996, Veronika is finally alone at 203. John still drops in without notice but Marcus has moved out, throwing the junk he doesn't want to take with him over Skewes's side of the fence. Bits and pieces, even a ladder. And by Christmas of 1996, Veronika decides to move, too. John and Robert help her, John taking some of the bigger pieces of furniture to his house at Bakara and telling Veronika not to worry about the rest. He has rented a U-Store-It at Gepps Cross, in the northern suburbs. Everything else can be stored there. All the junk.

After the move, Bunting occasionally knocks on Skewes's door to say g'day. Accustomed to a lonely existence, Skewes thinks it is nice that his mate – friendly, chatty, the sort of bloke you'd have a beer or a coffee with – stays in touch. Unexpectedly, John drops in on Skewes one day and wants to check the hole under the tank at 203 because he thinks it has sunk again. 'He called a friend and they went to the hardware shop, bought some concrete and filled it up. They mixed it up in my front yard, using an old plastic bucket of mine.' Skewes, leaning by the side of Bunting's house, scratching his belly and whiskers, doesn't want to just stand and watch them work. The least he can do for the bloke who has kindly driven him to the pension office is to offer help. 'Do youse wanna hand?' he asks and Bunting says yes. There are spider webs and crawly creatures underneath, so Skewes doesn't bother to get right down and look inside the hole. They spend the afternoon filling it in with old bricks and soil.

More than 50 bricks were passed in a human chain, Skewes will tell the court. 'Veronika was handing them to me, I was handing them to Barry, Barry was handing them to Robert and Robert was handing them to John.' An organised line. Bunting tells Skewes it has to be fixed, otherwise the Housing Trust will class it as a repair.

20

Nicole Zuritta is born in January, the same month and year that her first cousin, Maxine Cole, is conceived. 1968, the year Martin Luther King's voice for civil rights is silenced with a bullet and Robert Kennedy is gunned down. The year *Hair* opens on Broadway and Simon and Garfunkel sing *Mrs Robinson*. But international affairs and social change are of no interest to the girls' mothers, sisters Beverley and Nerrill, who live next door to each other in the unpolluted air of the Blue Mountains, and who share a bad gene passed on from their father. A mental impairment so pronounced that each is, effectively, only 10 years old.

Beverley and Nerrill share children's minds, women's bodies. And Eric.

He has slept first with their mother. More than 183 centimetres tall, handsome and athletically built, Eric is intellectually normal, with the pick of the women in the district. He soon tires of Mum and next woos her daughter, Beverley, with little more than a suggestive wink and a careless arm slung around her shoulder. Twenty-three years old, Beverley blushes and giggles like a 10-year-old from his attentions and cries like a baby when nine months later she goes through the hells of labour. Their daughter, Zoe, is still only tiny when Eric turns his attention to Beverley's sister, Nerrill. Nerrill's son Robert is born and four years later a daughter, Nicole. Eric is 55 years old when Nicole enters the world, a lecherous, middle-aged man with a plethora of party tricks for children. Throw money in the middle of the lounge room and look up little girls' dresses when they dive to collect it. The first to grab the money can claim it. Every child wins a prize.

Nicole is seven days old when her Nanna takes her in to raise her. Even the hospital agrees that Nerrill doesn't have a clue about looking after children. Nerrill and Eric have separated, and he sometimes stays at his caravan parked on a block out of town. Nicole still can't look at a caravan without seeing Eric's leering face, beckoning her inside. Six years old, not much taller than the card table that stands in the middle of the musty, claustrophobic interior. He locks the door, slides down his zip and Nicole knows what will come next. It happens right into her eleventh year, and she never gets used to it, forced still with her head clamped in her father's hands, gagging on that hard thing he shoves in her mouth and being sick in the sink after. Sometimes she sleeps in the back of his ute in the bush, but after she almost strangles in her sleep on the canopy rope, Eric makes her camp in the front. Stretched out on the seat with her father on top, that thing rubbing up and down in between her thighs and she wishes he had let her strangle, instead of putting her through this. She senses some people know what is happening, but that they just keep their silence. She does, too. Mute and alone, Nicole doesn't trust people enough to make friends.

Nicole is known in the area as the girl who runs everywhere. Running to school, running home. She figures if she keeps moving fast enough, no one can catch her.

She is 12 when Nerrill remarries a bloke called Don and they move to Cootamundra. Pretty country; wattle blossoms in the springtime and the birthplace of Donald Bradman, but that's not what Nicole remembers. What stays with her is being stuck in the middle of nowhere and her stepfather refusing to drive the half hour to town unless she sits crammed next to him on the bench seat, his elbow jammed into her crutch all the way. He frequently storms out of the room in a violent temper if she doesn't sit practically on his lap while they are watching television. Don never misses an opportunity, and nor does his father, who wrenches her head around to give him a proper kiss after he has visited the house. She is 12 years old, and fair game.

She is relieved when, after a couple of years, Don leaves Nerrill for her sister, Beverley.

Nicole loses her virginity at 12, a memory she blocks until she is well into her twenties, well into the counselling she will continue for the rest of her life. Staying at her girlfriend's house, half an hour from her home, and her friend's brother creeps in and jumps on top of her as soon as she turns out the light. Screaming the house down – why can't anyone hear? – and he is belting her to shut her up; raping her, belting her, over and over. She crawls under the bedclothes when he is finished, praying he doesn't come back again and knowing she won't tell a soul what happened.

Back home the next day she swallows every pill she can find, resentful that when she wakes up she is taken to hospital to have her stomach pumped. Both Nicole's and Maxine's self-esteem is shot to bits, what little they had to begin with. The only decent man they know is Maxine's natural father, the only male in their lives who doesn't have a go at them. Nicole later muses, wryly, that God deliberately gave her sons to stop her hating men.

At 12, Nicole runs away to Sydney on her own; returned by police, she is deemed uncontrollable and put in a home for recalcitrant girls. Within a month, she has escaped over the wall, spending the next five years wandering between Sydney and Melbourne. Nicole regularly hitches the Sydney–Melbourne highway where Ivan Milat trawled for victims. Dangerous, for sure, she says, but better than what she'd left behind. Fifteen years old, barrelling through the darkness, sitting in the front of a truck with a stranger. And he suddenly pulls off the side of the road and gives her an ultimatum. 'Hey, this is where you fork it, or walk it.' Climbing out of the truck, two o'clock in the morning, a forlorn, hungry figure on the side of the road and not a vehicle in sight. 'Dangerous, sure,' she says, 'but better than what I'd left behind.'

Maxine wheels her own daughter up and down Sydney's Kings Cross in a pram as she visits her street friends. Nicole steps in, as she will frequently do over the years with her cousin, berating her. 'Your daughter is only six months old, Max. It's dangerous in the Cross.' But she understands why

Maxine behaves the way she does. She is so scarred from her past, Nicole reasons, who can really judge the way she lives? Nicole confides in Maxine about Eric and Don. 'You too, eh?' is all she says.

Now comfortably numb, at 23 Nicole gives birth to a son, in 1991 and another a year later. Separated from their father, she heads to Adelaide in 1992 to start again. Settles in Salisbury North, the only area where she can afford to buy a house. Maxine follows, living with Nicole for a while before getting her own digs. Both of them are on the move, but they live close to each other. Maxine starts going out with a man called Peter Gardiner. He has a brother, Michael.

Michael Gardiner prefers to be called Michelle. Desperate for a sex change that he cannot afford, he instead dresses up in women's clothing when he is at home. Maxine sees him in drag, and other people do too. Running around the house in women's stockings and dresses, with a female wig covering his brown hair and a five o'clock shadow evident.

Nicole thinks the world of Michael. Introduced to her through Peter Gardiner and Maxine, 19-year-old Michael moves in to board at Nicole's house in July 1997. She doesn't care about his high-camp mannerisms or his cross-dressing fetish; he is a beautiful person, one of the few decent men she has ever met. He isn't angry or violent, and certainly not sexually drawn to her. Cheerful to be around, he doesn't drink, smoke or do drugs. He is a delightful house mate.

But Michael is damaged, too. Following the death of his father during his early childhood, his mother remarried, and he did not enjoy a happy relationship with his stepfather. Ugly scenes were constant and by 14, after being sexually abused by a man close to the family, Michael was shoved into foster care. He resented being there as much as he resented his stepfather, and started meandering between family members or mates. By 19, when he moves in with Nicole, he is openly gay and proud. And Nicole understands his past. She recognises immediately he is yet another victim.

Maxine Cole is now single again, living on the same street as Jamie Vlassakis. She has met Jamie through her sister Iris – five years younger than herself – whose boyfriend has given her a hiding. He hauled off and punched the daylights out of her, and Iris wants vengeance. She tells Jamie's girlfriend, who sometimes looks after her children, what has happened; inevitably, Jamie's girlfriend tells him. So, it is a simple equation, Nicole says. Maxine got to know Jamie because he was going to bash her sister's boyfriend.

In time, Jamie meets Maxine's cousin Nicole, and Nicole's house mate, Michael. Jamie ridicules Michael as he prances to the music of Kylie and Madonna. Bunting has schooled Jamie well. He just hates poofs.

It takes Robert Wagner months to ask Maxine out, but when he finally does, early in 1997, they start to share each other's houses. A few days at his place, a few days at hers. Fluid living arrangements, jumping around like jack rabbits. Robert's visitors camp on the couch or floor and Maxine meets them all as they file through the door. Jamie and a much shorter man, John Bunting. Mark Haydon, who gives Maxine the creeps; he is a scruffy, dirty looking bloke with too much facial hair. She shudders when he turns up. And she finds Jamie Vlassakis unpredictable and highly strung. Once, he jumps on Maxine's guitars, smashing them to smithereens; another time, he bounces on a car roof, as though it is a trampoline. He has fearful mood swings, changing in an instant, particularly when he can't get his hands on the drugs he needs. On another occasion, Maxine recalls, he tries to burn down her house when her kids are in it. 'He couldn't get any drugs and he was really in an agitated state. He started throwing things down the hallway, then he went outside, grabbed a paper, lit it up and tried to burn the outside of my house. Then he grabbed an aerosol can and struck a match to the fuel. I had a shadecloth and he burnt that down.' Edgy. Unpredictable. A typical junkie.

Maxine's kids are sick of moving around, and it is way too hard now she is pregnant with Robert's baby. They pool their resources and Bunting helps them move into another housing trust rental, a soulless fibro like all the others on the street: 36 Mofflin Road, Elizabeth. Bunting is now living at Lohmann Street, Murray Bridge, but he will soon be on the move again, too. By May 1997 he, Elizabeth Harvey and the kids will move into new housing trust accommodation in the river town: 3 Burdekin Avenue, Murray Bridge.

A trust home, just like all the others. Fibro with tiled roof, bland concrete driveway and a shed out the back. Just what Bunting needs.

Robert Wagner and Maxine's house is filthy, so putrid that police will later express dismay and disgust that children have had to live in it. Dirty dishes in the sink, unwashed plates on the floor, clothing strewn throughout every room. Maxine moves amongst the mess, shapeless in size 22 track pants.

Bunting, Haydon and Vlassakis always seem to be at her house, clamming up whenever Maxine gets close enough to hear their conversation. First, when she asks Robert what they are talking about, she is told it is 'men's business'. After a while, she stops asking. There is no point. 'I asked Robert once and he told me the less I know, the better I am', she will tell the court. Maxine doesn't ask questions about Robert's former relationship with Barry Lane, either. He goes ballistic when she raises it the first time, smashing his hand into a brick wall and hurting himself so badly he has to drive himself to hospital. She queries him about it a few times after that, but it always makes him furious. So she stops asking.

She doesn't ask him, either, where he is going on the frequent occasions he goes out with Bunting, or why he sometimes takes clothing with him. Robert tells her he is driving trucks, making a quid on the side to supplement his disability pension. That makes sense, explains where the extra money is coming from.

Nicole and Michael live just around the corner from them. A fingertip away from Mofflin Road.

★ ★ ★

In September 1997, Nicole Zuritta leaves Michael to mind her house and goes away for a couple of weeks. Ten days later, a friend calls her, advising her to come home as she has been burgled. And Michael is gone, too. Just ups and disappears, no warning or phone call. Gone, along with his clothes and Nicole's furniture: TV, videos, even her vacuum cleaner.

It appears the bastard has betrayed her, just like all the other scummy men she has known. She is disappointed in him. Michael is one man she believed would not have let her down. But something doesn't add up. There is no sign of forced entry into her house and the only other person who has a key to her home is her cousin, Maxine Cole. And there is no way Maxine would steal from Nicole.

Nicole looks for Michael over half of Adelaide, draws blanks at every turn. She is pissed off and wants her stuff back. She asks Wagner and Bunting if they know where he is and they do, they say. Robert says he saw him at a service station, talking to other gay men; says he yelled out to him that he is a 'poofter thief' and that Michael accelerated furiously away from the group.

Jamie Vlassakis will later admit to Nicole that it is he who broke in and stole her property. A TV and stereo, pawned for money to buy the drugs he shot straight up his arm.

Bunting and Wagner often repeat the story that they saw Gardiner at a service station. Nobody twigs that the pair are the only ones to purport to have sighted people who, for all intents and purposes, have vanished into thin air. If anyone has suspicions, they don't share them with the police.

Bunting likes it that way.

He stands at the window and watches as Nicole drives away from his house. 'She's a meddling whore', Bunting fumes. He is not the only one who is fuming. Nicole can't get anyone to tell her anything that sounds remotely credible about Michael's disappearance and her belongings. Every time she mentions his name, she is stared at, blankly. The only people who appear to know anything are Bunting and Wagner. But Adelaide isn't that big a city to hide in, surely *someone* would have seen Michael?

Michael has been gone a week when Nicole finds his wallet under his bed, with all his identification in it. There is also a letter addressed to her, a thank you note for allowing him to stay at her house.

Nicole is suspicious. 'This made me think that definitely, something was wrong, that perhaps he had got into the wrong company and they were misguiding him.' She is not concerned that something bad has happened to him, never suspects foul play.

Then a message from Michael is left on Maxine Cole's answering machine, a message that Nicole listens to over the phone. A hollow, echoed message that doesn't sound quite right. He wants his wallet back, he says, and he sounds desperate. 'I'm sorry about your stuff, but I need the money. If you go to the cops, I'll go to the Tax Department.' By the time Nicole gets to Maxine's house to retrieve the tape from the answer machine, the message has been wiped. She is furious with Maxine for mucking it up, but her cousin is six months pregnant. Not a good time to upset her.

The phone calls keep coming to Nicole's house, via a male friend of Michael. 'He really needs his wallet for ID, he's got no money . . . would you meet him in the park?' And then Michael himself is on the phone, but it isn't his voice. 'This is Michael . . .' and she knows it isn't. Yeah, right, she thinks. 'I just want to tell you your kids taste nice.' She hangs up, shaking, but still the calls come, increasingly darker and more threatening. 'I don't appreciate you mucking me around, and I'm probably going to have to come and gut you myself.'

Nicole works out a plan with her good friend, Jamie Vlassakis. Jamie will take Michael's wallet, stage a break-in at a business premises and deliberately leave the wallet behind. Instead of other people looking for Gardiner, the cops can do it. Save them all a heap of time.

★ ★ ★

They lure or force Michael into the car from Nicole Zuritta's home, driving from Adelaide through straggly traffic up to Bunting's house at Murray Bridge. March him into the back shed and subject him to the same kind of torture the other victims have had to endure, laughing and screeching at him as they watch him beg for his life. Burning his skin and testicles with a cigarette, chortling as he winces with the pain and cries out from the electric shocks.

Wagner grabs Michael from behind, starts to strangle him. He is falling to his knees and Bunting is taking off his feminine voice, demanding he stand up. 'Oh, Michael', he wheedles, as he staggers again. 'Thstand up. Thstay on your feet. Naughty boy.'

His knees are giving way but he has to try and stay standing. There is a slipknot at the back of the rope, tied to an overhead beam. If his legs falter, he will strangle.

Wagner pulls the rope tighter and Bunting watches the life expire from Gardiner's eyes. He will endlessly repeat the sordid, sad details of the teenager's death to Jamie Vlassakis, who will, in turn, repeat them to the police. 'He was laughing his head off about how he had murdered Michael. When John Bunting said to Michael to stand up, Michael stood up until, basically, he couldn't. That was the big joke to John, the fact that he, Michael, tried to stand up . . . and fell down and he died.'

21

Sylvia Lane remembers the last conversation she had with her son Barry; how she woke in the night to the phone ringing, jostled out of sleep in the early hours of the morning on 17 October 1997. How Barry spoke calmly to her for a few minutes then suddenly started abusing her, a tirade of abuse. And it was terrible, she recalls, the dreadful, hurtful things that spewed from his mouth. He screamed at her that she wasn't his mother, that he didn't want to know her. Announced with no to-do that he was moving to Queensland; a simple statement of fact, that he was leaving Adelaide. And then the phone just went dead.

But Barry isn't alone when he makes that call. There is somebody else in the background and Sylvia recognises the voice, recognises that it is Thomas Trevilyan, the chap that he is living with at that time, in the same house he shared with Robert Wagner. She knows Robert very well. He has been close to her family, has called Sylvia 'Mum' and so, she will say, it is as if she has two sons. He calls her mother 'Nan' and sits by her bedside when she is dying.

But this is a new boyfriend. Thomas Trevilyan.

Barry is hysterical on the telephone, calls her a lot of bad names that she finds hard to repeat. Her lip quivers when she says the words. He calls her a 'moll' and 'arsehole'.

Barry is not a heavy drinker, but he always marks the anniversary of his grandmother's death by getting drunk. He's a two-pot screamer. His inner demons surface in alcohol and he often becomes abusive and belligerent before sinking into a melancholic, self-piteous stupor. Tonight he is tripping over his words, sneering and screaming down the phone, swearing at her, but the thing that haunts Sylvia most, the image that wakes her up at night, is what terrors Barry must have gone through when they were trying to strangle him. 'Poor Barry. The horror of it all. He would have been terrified. He didn't deserve that.'

His final gift to her was a picture of Jesus dying on the cross, and it has become symbolic of the way she will remember him. He has told her about Clinton Trezise, how scared he is that he helped dispose of the body. Knowing his predilection for telling stories, she has given him the best advice she can. 'Go to the police if it's true, Barry. I can't do nothing about it.'

Michelle Bihet met Barry Lane at a Salvation Army meeting in December 1996. A slow, plain woman, she has known him a month before they start talking about marriage. Welfare doesn't need to know about his filthy temper, how he slaps her around the mouth and splits her lip, but Michelle has three sons, not yet in their teens. Given Lane's history of paedophilia, that is a concern to the Welfare Department. Family and Community Services step in as soon as they hear talk of the marriage between Bihet and Lane, and insist on a compromise, with Lane having only welfare-supervised access to Michelle's children. That soon becomes a farce. 'He was supposed to have non-access visits to those kids but she would ring him up when they were in bed asleep and he found a way to get to them', Elizabeth Harvey recalls.

Lane, who is now sharing a house with Thomas Trevilyan, doesn't turn up for a scheduled access visit. Trevilyan calls Michelle, says the two men have gone to Clare for a few days' break and will be there longer than expected. Michelle isn't that surprised: her relationship with Barry has soured since Thomas came on the scene and she feels that Barry is slipping back into his old ways. Going back to men. He is over 40 and Thomas is only 18. They are sharing a housing trust rental at Hectorville, deep in Adelaide's suburbia. Sharing a bed, too. She is not impressed.

They have gone to Clare, and their car has broken down. Next thing Michelle knows, Barry is on the phone saying, 'I love you and I love the kids', and asking her if she can collect his mail and feed his dogs. She does that until she realises that his car is missing, and he must be home from his trip. But he's not home; instead, the back door has been jemmied open and the air conditioner has gone, hoicked out of the wall. Michelle thinks back to how he sounded on the telephone. He hadn't been his normal self. His voice had a nervous, strung-out quality; just not right.

A rolled up bandage has been shoved into his mouth to absorb his screams, and tape wound around his head and under his mouth. They torture him through the night of 17 October, squishing his toes with pliers, laughing as he squeals in pain. He screams loudest when they apply pressure to his toenails, an orgy of torture that lasts for hours. Handcuffing him, shoving their faces up to his as he lies on the floor; goading him. He is a filthy paedophile who has defiled Wagner. A dirty, stinking fag. A big-mouth who can't keep quiet. He is fainting and Bunting is slapping him awake, demanding his bank cards and PIN numbers. 'Wake up, you slimy waste. Ring your mother. Call her a Christ moll and tell her you're moving to Queensland.' Slapping him again as he slides into another faint.

Thomas Trevilyan is ordered to join in, to help put the fag down. Wagner, with brutal force, applies the final pressure to his former lover's neck, Bunting gleeful as they wrap Lane's body in tape, pour him into a garbage bag and roll him in carpet.

Michelle goes over to the flat to feed Barry's dogs as he has asked, walks over a protruding mound of carpet on the floor as she is leaving.

They have left his corpse in the house. It will be four days before they return for their trophy.

Satisfied that no one can see them, they drag Barry Lane's body out of the house, giggling as they stuff him into a barrel. The paedophile poof knew too much. It is good he is now out of the way.

Michelle Bihet reports Lane missing on 27 October 1997, after she finds the door wide open and his house a shambles. There

is nothing unusual in that, but she has a sixth sense that something is wrong. Months later, she gives a formal statement to
the Missing Persons Unit, and it is typed up by Detective Craig
Patterson.

She remembers, too, to tell the police something else Lane
has told her: that sometime in April 1997 he had to get rid of
some bags, but he didn't know what was in them. But he had
guessed what they contained, had a hunch that they held the
remains of his friend, Clinton Trezise. Michelle had increasingly come to distrust everything that Lane said, until she saw
a program featuring Missing Persons on *Australia's Most
Wanted*. Then she started to take it seriously.

A mate of Bunting's, Greg Cannon, inquires a few weeks after
Lane disappears where he has gone to. Bunting grins, one side
of his mouth turned up. 'Barry's gone on a holiday', he says.
There is no further explanation, no colouring of details about
where he has gone to or when he will be back, and no further
questions from Cannon. That is it: Barry is on holiday. Wagner
and Haydon hear the conversation, and snigger.

They are gleeful when they discuss his murder. 'Like,'
Vlassakis will later tell the court, 'when you go to a shop with
a young kid and you buy them a toy and the kid gets really
excited. It was like that.'

They call Wagner 'Papa Smurf', after the small, blue dolls with
the same name. He boasts how he enjoys making smurfs:
killing people and watching as they go blue in the face. 'First
they go blue, then they go poo . . .' he crows. He enjoys
making a smurf of Barry Lane.

22

Thomas Trevilyan is fixated with the army. He has not been accepted as a recruit, but that doesn't stop him from pretending that he is, decked out in the khaki military gear he picks up at army disposal stores, parading around the streets of Elizabeth like a soldier on a spy mission. Telling people he is going on a bivouac. The 18-year-old bolts outside the house with a carving knife in his hand every time he hears a noise, and puts aluminium foil in his hat to stop the satellites targeting him. The enemy is everywhere.

He hopes the same enemy can't hear the voices in his head. They are quiet sometimes, when he takes his medication, but lately they have been very loud. He is sick and tired of taking the tablets the doctor has prescribed him for paranoid schizophrenia, decides to give them a miss for a while. He hasn't used them for three months now and the hallucinations are severe. The Grim Reaper is out to get him and he cowers from the menace. Everyone who meets him can see that Thomas Trevilyan is a deeply disturbed young man.

Born in 1979, he has always been 'different'. His relationship with his parents is fraught with strain. He is closer to his grandfather, Thomas, and to his cousin, Lenore Penner. At 11, he makes his first failed suicide attempt, trying to hang himself at a scout meeting. Within a year he leaves home, drifting from place to place. His voices are getting louder: at 14, the year he is diagnosed with schizophrenia, he again twice tries to commit suicide. Once with a loaded gun, and then by hanging. Close to Christmas 1996 the young man is psychiatrically assessed at an Adelaide hospital. The diagnosis is grim: Thomas Trevilyan, the doctor writes, is suicidal and worn out, hurtling toward a nervous breakdown.

Then he meets Barry Lane.

★ ★ ★

Now that Lane has gone, Thomas Trevilyan is dossing down at Maxine Cole's house with her kids and her fiancé, Robert Wagner. He has been here six weeks and it is now Melbourne Cup day, the first Tuesday in November 1997.

Maxine has got that look about her, like she's scared of him. She likes him okay at first, when Robert unceremoniously turns up with him and says he is staying. 'We've got him away from Barry', he says matter-of-factly, and now this lunatic is outside her house, running around with a carving knife, threatening to kill the puppy that Maxine's nine-year-old daughter is holding in her arms.

'Leave the dog alone', Maxine screams.

'No, it's just a mutt. It doesn't deserve to live.'

She knows he will kill it. A lady walking with a child down the road hears the screaming and commotion, asks Maxine if she wants her to take the dog.

'Yes, for Christ's sake, grab it', Maxine stutters.

The kid and Maxine are scared to hell and scared the puppy will be run through with the knife. Later, when the household calms down, Thomas gets in the car with Bunting and Wagner to go for a nice drive in the country.

'Where's Thomas?' Maxine asks when they return without him.

'He's gone to Gawler', Bunting says, looking at Robert and laughing. She doesn't ask any more questions after that. There is no point.

It is dusk. The nation is celebrating the end of Melbourne Cup day as Thomas is walked to his scaffold, scared as a blind man in unfamiliar territory. They are prodding him with a sharp stick: 'Go on, keep walking. Keep going, keep going, stop now. Step up on this crate.'

An elderly couple have stopped their car behind Bunting's Ford Marquis, peering down over the embankment. They can't see the rope or the terrified young man but they can see Bunting and Wagner. If their car has stopped on this quiet stretch of road, perhaps they need some help? Bunting looks up at them through his large-rimmed glasses. 'We're fine', he says, smiling. 'Thank you anyway.' They watch as the couple shuffle back to their car, before kicking the crate out from underneath Trevilyan.

'Fuck, that was close', Bunting grunts, as he rifles Trevilyan's pockets for identification. He leaves a few dollars in the pockets, to fool police into thinking it is a suicide. But he can't resist taking one trophy, that he hides in the ceiling with the rest of the junk. Thomas's precious Scottish hat.

His feet swollen in the army boots he is wearing, Thomas's toes touch the ground and his body sways slightly on the spring breeze. That is what the truck driver notices as he drives past the area known as Humbug Scrub at Kersbrook. Police cut him down so that other motorists can't see him from the road; cut the blue nylon cord from around his neck and lay him on the ground underneath the tree at the bottom of a steep embankment near a dirt track.

The red crate he stood on is stark against the camouflage of his army fatigues, head to toe in green t-shirt, shirt and pants. His face is blue, his neck swollen and he has injuries to his left upper arm, where he has been poked at.

The police have taken him away and a middle-aged man is standing in the morgue as they pull back the sheet. He looks quickly at the corpse before turning away. 'Yes, that's my grandson', he weeps. 'That's Thomas Trevilyan.'

Maxine had told Robert about the incident with Thomas and her daughter, how he threatened to kill the puppy, but Robert hadn't changed expression. 'He looked as placid as what he usually does, but with Robert, you never knew', she will later say. He is shocked and stunned when the police call the next day to say Thomas has committed suicide, has hanged himself from a tree at Kersbrook and that his girlfriend Maxine's phone number has been found in his pocket. He hangs up the phone. Suicide. Shocking.

Bunting and Vlassakis often travel past the area where Trevilyan was hanged, and the older man likes to point out the spot to Jamie. 'There, over there', he chortles. Vlassakis later shows police the area.

Thomas Trevilyan's cousin, Lenore Penner – one of the few relatives he is close to – did not take it seriously when, a week before his death, he told her that he had been involved with two other people in killing Barry Lane, that they disposed of his body in a drum and were using his Social Security PIN to access his account. The money was being shared amongst them, he told her, and they were taking great pains to make it look as though Lane was still alive. He was gibbering, dressed in his army fatigues complete with camouflage paint. The killers, he said, clutching at his army helmet, were now out to get him. Lenore kept him talking until he calmed down. Poor Thomas, she thought. He must be having another psychotic episode.

But she doesn't believe that anymore.

Shortly after Thomas spoke to her, in October 1997, Lenore contacts the police who listen to her story and take down her statement. A detective reads what she has said and comforts her with the information that she has no need to be concerned. It is their belief that Barry Lane is in Queensland.

Pathologist Dr Ross James surveys the lonely area where Thomas Trevilyan died. Police have found $6.90 in his pockets, and the sum of the evidence seems to prove that there are no suspicious circumstances. The body has only minor injuries; bruises on his forehead, grazes on his left arm. The tell-tale injury appears to be from the rope around his neck, tied in a slipknot with three loops below the jaw. The young man was not taking his medication. He has tried in the past to take his own life. The rope, the position of the slipknots, the crate, are consistent with self-harm.

Ross James notes his findings. In his opinion, Thomas Trevilyan has taken his own life.

23

Maxine Cole never hides her relationship with Robert Wagner, even though she knows about his sexual past. She doesn't try to hide it even after he is charged with multiple murders. Her cousin, Nicole Zuritta, figures she protects Robert for the sake of their son, born on New Year's Eve, 1997: three months after Michael Gardiner's murder and two months after the murder of Wagner's former partner, Barry Lane. Births and deaths.

New Year's Eve, 1998. Party time for the nation, fireworks and sparklers as the clock counts down into what will become Robert's busiest year yet: five murders, one a month from August through to November. His son's birth sparks a celebration and there will be some party touches in the deaths, too: lit sparklers stabbed into the heads of penises and the gurgling sound of air expelling when Robert stands on a victim's chest, like a child's whistle run out of air.

Robert will have a busy year, but he is determined to be a good father. There is no way his son is going to go through what he endured as a child. Tied up when he did something wrong, systematically abused, physically and emotionally. Robert enrols to serve on the school's kindergarten committee with Nicole Zuritta. Their kids go to the same school. He will be a good father.

Now Gavin is dead.

He is lying on the shed floor of their home at Murray Bridge, sprawled out cold and blue under blankets and cushions, his knees raised in a defensive pose and his neck with tell-tale strangulation marks.

The stench in the shed is so overpowering, Vlassakis's stomach somersaults. This is his best mate, Gavin Porter. Now

Bunting is lifting the lid on the barrel and pointing. Laughing. And it will come out in a rush, with no commas or full stops, like taking the cork out of a bottle, when Jamie later tells police what he saw. 'John pointed to me and said "That's Barry's arse" and it is ugly all shrivelled and the stench is disgusting the shed reeked of the smell it is horrible I went outside and spewed my guts up.'

The gooey, stinking mess makes Vlassakis heave, but Bunting is impressed. They are rotting very nicely.

Two days later Bunting arrives with another barrel, and now they are picking Gavin's lifeless body off the floor, and shoving him in. The barrel is placed next to the one that holds the corpses of Michael Gardiner and Barry Lane, and Bunting has a great idea.

He demands that Jamie baby-sit Gavin's barrel. It makes logical sense. Gavin is Jamie's friend. His responsibility. Jamie is scared to death. He can't stop throwing up but he must not show his fear.

John hangs over him all the time, with a terrible, dark power. So powerful that even when Bunting is in custody, Vlassakis will not feel safe. He overdoses on heroin during a break in an interview with police, as scared as a little boy. 'The power over me and stuff, he was very manipulative, he would play mind games . . . There was real occasions I was going to ring police and lag him in and I couldn't because I'd end up in a drum next to them. If I turned to my mum he could have killed my mum, instead I turned to my mate, Gavin.'

Jamie wants to overdose, can't live with the fear. The ambulance officers inject him with Narcan to revive him after he overdoses during the interview, and every day after that, a squad car sits in front of his house and follows Jamie to make sure he doesn't OD again. They have not taken him into custody, allow him to remain at home, but the coppers can't afford to lose their star witness.

Now Gavin is dead and Bunting is laughing. 'He needed to go to the clinic, just like the others. They are the disease', he tells Jamie. 'We are the cure.'

Gavin Porter was born in Victoria in 1967, and his parents divorced when he was young. Black depression stalks his mother following his birth, and his grandmother raises the young boy. Later, working as a telephone technician, Gavin spends some time in the Philippines before he returns to Australia in 1992. But he has a monkey on his back: seduced by heroin, from the age of 23 he starts a hopeless, futile battle to overcome his addiction. When he is 24, his mother dies of cancer; a year later, he has found his way to South Australia, working for a time at the harsh and hot mining town of Mintabie before throwing his swag in at a hostel in Port Adelaide. He spends a lot of time wandering the streets, looking for people who share his own interests, getting the feel of Adelaide CBD before venturing north to Elizabeth and Salisbury North. His eyes, set in a pinched face, have the dazed expression of a junkie, bewildered and spaced out.

By Christmas 1994, Gavin is admitted to the methadone program, where he meets Jamie Vlassakis. But neither man lasts long. It is the second time Jamie has developed a habit; he is renting a Housing Trust house at Salisbury Downs and needs a house mate. He and Gavin share the rent and share their fit. Needle. Spoon. Tourniquet. They are good mates.

Jamie really likes Gavin, trusts him. They doctor-shop for prescription drugs between them, and once grow a dope crop together. When smack is on the street they help shoot each other up, even though they are so scarred it is almost impossible to find a vein. They use a cap a day for six months, losing time and memory. The two of them, getting stoned, mellowing out, forgetting about the world. Blocking it out.

Jamie now spends up to $300 a day on drugs. 'I had to do a lot of burgs, shit like that, to keep the drugs goin'', he admits. 'At one stage I ended up dealing drugs, doing interstate deliveries for other people, driving hookers around. I enjoyed doing that. I'd get about $250 cash, $250 worth of heroin, plus fuel. It was worth it.'

They do methadone together, too, in a desperate bid to kick their habits, but they end up abusing that as well, saving up their take-aways and using it all at once.

Gavin moves in with Elizabeth, John and Jamie at Murray Bridge in the first part of 1998. Bunting hates him because he is a drug user, particularly after he steps on a syringe Gavin has used in the bathroom.

He shoots up in the shed, lying on the old couch. 'That bloke is a fuckin' waste', John snarls to Elizabeth, but she is fond of Gavin. She finds him to be pleasant and mild-mannered. But he drives her mad, falling asleep so often, mixing a cocktail of methadone, Temazepam and heroin together, on the nod regardless of where he is. She once comes home from shopping and finds Gavin face-down in the car motor. He staggers in hours later, marks from the battery terminals imprinted on his face. Elizabeth has to keep an eye on him inside the house, asking him to sit down to stop him bouncing from wall to wall or toppling into her television set. He falls asleep anywhere, even sitting up against the wall in the hallway, where people trip over him in the dark. Always on the nod.

Gavin lives with them for three months, but something has to give. Elizabeth tries to warn him. 'If you want to live here, you'll have to cut down on your drug use. Cut down and stop leaving syringes everywhere. It's bad for the younger boys and it's making John really mad.'

John gets even madder when he sits on the couch in the shed and gets a needle in his elbow. Two days later, early April 1998, Gavin disappears.

No one but John and Jamie and Robert are allowed in the shed. They are not even permitted to put pushbikes or storage items in there. 'No one needs to go in there', John intones as he pockets the key. Nobody questions why, not even Elizabeth. Especially Elizabeth. 'Why would I question him if he wants to keep the shed locked, it's his business?' she will say. Defensive, guilt-ridden. 'I was on medication and everything was too big and if I started asking questions, well then – John made sure chaos was always around. People crashing into my social security file, letters in the mail, Jamie getting broken into, things missing out of the house, wheels coming off my car. Looking back, it was all John. He stage-managed all of it.'

The shed. John's private space. His secret area. The place no one can enter without an invitation. Where no one can snoop through his personal things. Not like his mother did.

They ambush Porter in his car when he is on the nod. Creep up and loop a rope around his neck before he fights back with a screwdriver, stabbing Bunting in the hand. Elizabeth is sitting only metres away in the kitchen, doesn't hear or see a thing. Bunting is on top of him, watching him die as he exerts pressure on his chest to squeeze out his last breath.

Wagner is enjoying a Chinese meal with Bunting when Jamie returns home from the drive-in later that night. Fear claws at him when he sees Wagner is there from Adelaide. A portent of something bad.

They wipe the food from their mouths and beckon Jamie out to the shed. Rigid with terror, his eyes move from his friend's lifeless body to Bunting's mouth, that seems to be moving wordlessly. He will try to explain his emotions to police. 'I remember I was pretty scared at the time of seeing this, and I remember . . . the way [Bunting] was looking at me. But I can't remember any words now. I know he was talking to me.'

They pilfer his possessions: clothes, papers, and Vlassakis and Wagner drive his car to Adelaide, running out of petrol and sleeping the night in the dead man's car. After they re-fuel and drive to Wagner's house, Maxine eyes off the vehicle.

'That's Gavin's car', she says.

Wagner shakes his head. 'No it isn't.'

She shrugs, goes back inside.

Two days later, back in Murray Bridge, Bunting instructs Jamie to go out to the car and bring the new barrel he has bought into the shed. They lay it down and shove Gavin's body in, head first. The barrel is moved to Wagner's house, a transitory stopping point before its final destination at Snowtown.

Bunting plays Father Christmas, gives Jamie his friend's keycard to access his social security benefits. Jamie shoots most of the money up his arm.

It helps him forget.

Vlassakis is stoned, sick with fear, desensitised. Bunting has prepared his protégé well.

24

Bunting hates football, but it impresses Elizabeth no end that he drives miles every week to watch her kids play. He goes to the footy club when Troy gets his first trophy, beaming smiles, so proud of his stepson. But he rarely tolerates TV, complains when people in the household watch soapies and drama. It's all rubbish, he says, flicking it off. But in July 1998, a story appealing for information about the skeleton found at Lower Light appears on *Australia's Most Wanted*. Detective Trevor Couch, then heading the investigation, is blunt. 'I think it's really sad that nobody knows who he may be, and it is important that it is found out. We've been throughout Australia with Missing Persons records, Interpol and the Department of Immigration where people have overstayed their visas.' Bunting, watching the television with Elizabeth and Jamie, knows exactly who that person is. 'That', he grins, 'is my handiwork.'

John keeps nothing on the outside of his dressing table, no photos or knick-knacks. Everything is crammed inside. Little scraps of paper with phone numbers, old phone cards, letters from WorkCover. His little secret place where he can put his junk. He never clears it out, keeps accumulating it over the years. Elizabeth regards it as one of his eccentricities. 'He might have seen a stamp that he likes. "Oh, I'll put that in the drawer", he'd say.' It is John's drawer, with John's personal stuff. Even though there is nothing important in there, it is where he can keep his private things, undisturbed.

His favourite novels are written by Stephen King, and he particularly likes macabre horror. He flies through them voraciously and swaps books with Elizabeth. Reads the book, then rents the video and whinges it isn't the same. *Bag o' Bones* is his favourite King book, and the movie *Silence of the Lambs*. He likes to study the mannerisms of the murderous psychopath Hannibal Lecter, especially his slight shiver as he runs his tongue over his teeth and teases personal details from potential victims. A definitive book on serial murderers – *The Serial Killers* by Colin Wilson – is underlined throughout. One of his heroes is Ted Bundy. He shares Bundy's enthusiasm for the power of murder. As much as Bunting pretends to like women, he loathes them. They are nothing more than playthings, to be manipulated, controlled, turned to his advantage. Used for sex, for impersonating victims, never love or friendship. Bunting prefers the cold, impersonal companionship of his blow-up doll. The plastic woman demands nothing of him, and he does not need to give anything back. The doll is frigid. Silent.

Perfect.

Elizabeth takes up ceramic classes and John decides to have a go. He has never made a mould before, but shapes intricate, eight-piece designs that require precision and concentration. Elizabeth reckons it is an act of love, to learn how to make moulds for her. She would tell people, 'My bloke is a borderline genius'.

He doesn't drink, apart from the occasional Cointreau, but he likes to eat. He treats Elizabeth to pub lunches, which she thinks is special.

But he isn't always like that, sweet and cuddly. They have some huge blues, mainly over the kids, when Elizabeth invariably comes off second best. She always seems to be in the middle. Troy and John niggle at each other all the time, particularly when Troy argues that homosexuals have a right to life. 'They're harmless', he would say. 'If they keep to themselves, I don't give a shit.' Troy's calm reasoning infuriates John. He huffs around after a debate, slams doors and stomps out.

Her youngest boy can't sleep with the light off but John complains that he is only lying there looking at the light to keep him awake. Elizabeth counters that he is scared of the dark. 'Bullshit', John says and flicks the light off. John likes to get his own way and she learns not to argue, learns to keep the peace. There are lots of fights, especially after she develops cancer and he nicks off all the time with Robert. 'Don't go out tonight', she beseeches him, and immediately wishes she has said nothing. That familiar dark cloud scuds across his face and he punches his fists at the door and heads out for a long walk. Elizabeth senses he wants to hit her, but he never does. Sulky silences follow their rows and last for days. The smallest things upset him. Once, when he is making an egg and bacon sandwich, the bread falls apart. He hurls the frying pan in the sink and the sandwich against the wall, and Elizabeth cleans up the mess. 'I'll make you another one, John', she offers, but he doesn't want another one. He glowers, punches the door, storms out.

John Bunting can be delightful, but he is never easy to live with. He is, Elizabeth recalls, stubborn, moody and as volatile as all get out.

It is as though she lives with two Johns.

He likes to look into their eyes. Stares at them as they are being tortured and strangled, his face so close to theirs they can feel his breath. Intently watching their pain and fear, he laughs and jokes, prodding them like cattle, boasting he can pinpoint the precise moment when they die.

This is one of the best parts, just watching them.

Troy Youde is great fun. It is almost a pity he has lost consciousness. Bunting could have played with him all day.

It is August or September 1998; no one will ever be sure of the exact date. Wagner is visiting Bunting at 3 Burdekin Avenue, Murray Bridge; Haydon, too. Elizabeth and the younger boys are elsewhere. Vlassakis is woken by Bunting, shaken from sleep like a rat out of a slumber; hauled from his bed in the soulless housing trust home he shares with his half-brother Troy, who is asleep in the next room. Wagner and Haydon are armed with jack handles, the two men silhouetted in the bedroom's shadows. They are handing Vlassakis the leg of a lounge suite and handcuffs and he thinks Troy is going to be given a beating; he deserves a beating for what he did to him as a child, the sexual assaults he has been forced to endure. All four men advance quietly toward Troy's bedroom. 'Now!' Bunting screams and Troy, asleep on the floor, is woken by a slam to the head from the jack handle. He is on his feet, backing up against the wall, shielding his face from the blows, yelling to Jamie: 'What are you doing? What are you doing?' Jamie hits him on the leg with the lounge piece, handcuffing one wrist while Bunting handcuffs the other. And Jamie walks away as Troy is frogmarched into the bathroom, staggering, afraid in this early morning. Begging them to answer him – 'What are you doing, what is happening?' – and his head shoved down so he can't speak.

Jamie returns to the room as Troy is put into the bathtub, where his t-shirt and track pants are cut from him with a Stanley knife. He is beaten again, blubbering now, and savage welts are appearing on his body. Bunting produces a tape recorder and Troy, handcuffed in the bath, stares at it, wild-eyed and fearful. Jamie is angry at Troy, disgusted that his half-brother has systematically raped him as a child, but another part of his brain is starting to rebel: *I don't want him to die.* Years later he staggers sobbing from the witness box as he recalls kneeling down next to his half-brother and forcing him to say sorry, listening to Troy's tortured cries resounding from the tape that is played to the court: 'Leave me the fuck alone, I've had enough, I've had enough'.

But Bunting and Wagner have only just started. Blood is pouring from Troy's nose and ears and Bunting is trying to punch him in the testicles. Bunting leans in closer, whispers for him to shush and gently wipes away the blood with a tissue. Relieved the beatings have stopped, Troy relaxes for a moment. Thwack. Bunting lands a punch and sniggers.

'Call me "Lord Sir"', Bunting orders, and Troy does so. 'Lord Sir', he whimpers. 'Call Robert "God"', he demands. 'God.' Mark Haydon is loitering in the bathroom doorway, pale as a medieval hangman, and Bunting leans in close to

Troy's ear. 'Choose a name for Mark', he whispers. 'Be a good boy and choose a name for Mark and we will take you for a drive and drop you off somewhere. Name?'

'Chief Inspector.' Bunting smiles, malevolently. 'Good. And Jamie? Choose a name for Jamie.' Troy's hair is matted with blood, his lips parched and swollen. 'Moses.'

'That's a Jewish name!' Bunting shoots a thunderous look to Wagner and they start raining blows again to Troy's groin, legs and chest. 'That's a Jew's name! A Jew's name! Pick a proper name!'

'Master.' Spittle is dribbling out the side of his mouth and tears stain his cheeks. Bunting looks satisfied. 'That's better.' Crushing his toes with pliers, cuffing him around the head to shut him up when he screams. He screams loudest when the pliers crush his toenail. He is begging them to let him go, leave him alone, but he is told to speak when he is spoken to. 'Shut the fuck up. Speak when I say.' Forcing him to speak into the tape recorder now, to recite phrases after Bunting. 'Mum, I can't handle it in this house no more. It's all around me. I'm going to see the earth before there's none left. Wish me luck.'

More phrases. Forced to say them. To sound like he is angry. 'You're going to stay the fuck out of my life.'

Twenty phrases, blood and perspiration and spittle dripping into the bath.

And suddenly Jamie understands, as Bunting demands that Troy tell them his PIN, that he is about to witness his first murder. He staggers out into the hallway, wanting to vomit, and would keep walking if he could. But Bunting is calling him back, in that high-pitched, feminine voice that signals he is excited. It is time for Troy to atone, to say he is sorry for raping Jamie. He will do anything now to appease Bunting. He has said sorry already, he cries. And he is sorry. Really sorry.

A rope is around Troy's neck and Wagner is grimacing on the end of a lever to try and tighten it, to strangle him, while Bunting squeezes his toe with pliers. Bunting slides down at Troy's side, peers into his face and slowly recites the names of the people he has murdered. Happy Pants. Ray Davies. Barry.

Michael. Gavin. He pauses briefly, turning to Wagner and Haydon. 'Have I left anyone out?' Wagner grins, repeats the names in his slow, thick voice.

But Wagner does not come out of this murder unscathed. 'Robert Wagner's hand was broken, is that right?' lawyer Wendy Abraham later grills Vlassakis. 'How did he break his hand?'

'I smacked him with a club.'

'You did?'

'Mm. Broke his hand. Not bad, eh?'

Troy is now starting to lose consciousness, but Wagner has released the pressure on the lever and he is coming around, groaning. Bunting has that look Jamie has seen before, dark and sadistic. He wants it to go longer but Jamie does not. Troy has suffered enough. He grabs the lever to tighten the rope and hasten his death but the rope snaps. Wagner grunts, re-ties it. In the seconds before Troy passes out, music plays loudly. Bunting's favourite song, 'Selling the Drama' from the band Live's CD *Throwing Copper*. A song about Judas and justice, death and power, pain and retribution. The chorus swells and Bunting's eyes grow black, his anger peaking at the mention of rape and scarring. 'Selling the Drama' is the murderer's theme song.

There is a knock at the front door. Bunting stiffens, distracted from his purpose. 'Who the fuck is that?' Elizabeth has driven to Adelaide for the day and will use her key to come inside. Whoever is at the door, they are unwelcome guests.

Friends of Troy's are standing on the doorstep, smiling benignly at Bunting. He keeps the door half closed and glowers at them that Troy is not home, before slamming the door in their faces.

A gag is shoved into Troy's mouth and Jamie can't stand to watch any more. Bunting is chortling, 'This is fun', kneeling down and watching intently as life fades from Troy's eyes. Satisfied he is dead, Bunting turns to Jamie. 'Kick him in the head', he orders.

They have to get him out of the bath before Elizabeth comes home, but there is nothing to put him in. Bunting commands his minions, Haydon and Vlassakis, to drive to the local supermarket to pick up some gloves and rubbish bags. Strong ones.

Troy is stretched out on the bathroom floor when they return, his flesh bruised and already starting to mottle with the bluish hue of death. Wagner stands on his chest to make sure he is dead, and gurgling air comes from his nose and mouth.

The four men heave Troy's body into garbage bags they have draped over it and carry him out to the shed, balancing him on a weights bar that they lift, two on either end. The shed reeks with the cloying stench from the two barrels with the three bodies inside that have sat there for months. Bunting and Haydon can't smell it, but Wagner can. It doesn't bother him but Jamie wants to throw up, is doubled over, dry retching.

Troy's murder is hungry work. Bunting and Wagner want to eat and Haydon and Jamie follow obsequiously along in their wake, forcing down a McDonald's before heading back to the house. They leave Troy's corpse on the floor and two days later Wagner and Haydon drive to Adelaide to purchase another barrel.

Troy has been made good, Bunting boasts. He won't hurt anyone no more. He is at the peak of his elation, overwhelmed with a sense of power and domination. Troy has been made good. But Bunting's joy is tempered with irritation. Troy died too fast. He will make him pay for that when they can't fit him into the barrel. He grins when he works out the solution. This will be a slice and dice.

He cuts off his foot, first.

Vlassakis's description of the further mutilation of Troy Youde at the bank vault is so ghastly, reporters visibly pale.

'Bunting and Wagner started cutting up Troy . . . They chopped off his legs and that. Robert cut off all the . . . muscles and that, so it was down to the bone, and threw that into the other barrel.

'During the process . . . I walked out of the actual vault . . . Mark was outside . . . [he] said something like he couldn't handle it . . . it was too gruesome.

'I . . . entered the vault again, just to see how long John was going to be. He said . . . Troy's balls . . . were filthy. I can't remember the exact words. He cut them off, or started cutting down there and then just started stabbing with a knife.'

There are also safety lessons to be learned. Always be careful when handling corpses, Bunting tells his protégé, Jamie. You could catch a disease.

Inculcated in the most subtle of ways. First talk. Then animals. Then a passive onlooker. Finally, a participant.

Bunting wants to know what Jamie thinks of participating in his first murder. He tells him he enjoyed it, but in truth he is terrified. Bunting hangs over him, dark and menacing. Jamie's safety depends on his compliance. 'I kept the lie going for him because, you know, I thought, well, if he could do that to my brother, he could do it to me.'

Bunting lifts the lid on the barrel that contains the corpse of Gavin Porter and asks Jamie to tell him what it smells like. He closes his eyes as he hears the description, shivering slightly as he rolls his tongue along his lips. His eyes are dark in their sockets and his mouth flirts with a smile. 'They're rotting very nicely', he says.

Vlassakis didn't know Troy was on the hit list, but the money is handy. He uses Troy's keycard to withdraw his social security benefits, and scores a double dose of methadone. The world is a nicer place with its sharp corners knocked off. Get stoned, mellow out. Forget about the world.

Elizabeth is greeted when she arrives home by John babbling that Troy has gone, that there has been a fight and some people have picked him up. The boys are crying because Troy hasn't said goodbye, and Elizabeth is crying, too. Exhausted from the chaos and the long drive back from Adelaide, she does what she has always done – heads straight in to take a bath. It will be a long time before Jamie tells her what happened in that bathroom, how Troy wet himself, trembling and weeping as he asked, 'Why are you doing this to me?' and John going berserk because he died too quickly. Taking a bath where her son has been murdered the night before, where her lover has tortured and terrified him. It is a thought she will never be able to erase. How John killed and dismembered her son.

She doesn't understand why Troy doesn't contact her, but John and Jamie keep up the illusion. 'We've run into him, he's okay, he's got a job, got a girl.' Elizabeth writes a letter to the people who were supposed to have picked Troy up after the fight, but she never gets a reply. She frets that she doesn't hear from them. She never knows that John didn't post the letter.

Bunting and Elizabeth are on the move again, this time to number 26 Burdekin Avenue, a few houses from where they now live. It is too risky to leave the barrels in the shed, and he can't take them with him. He'll have to organise another hiding place.

He likes to know they are close, the trophies he can salivate over to re-live the murders. He plays the tapes when he gets a chance, closing his eyes and listening, smiling as he again hears his victims plead and scream. Bunting has the power to choose whether a person lives or dies. He is all-powerful. Lord, Sir.

It irks him to have to move the barrels but there is no choice. And it is better that if something goes wrong, someone else cops the heat.

Quiet, dull Mark Haydon. He will become the happy recipient of barrels containing the stinking corpses of Barry Lane, Michael Gardiner, Gavin Porter and Troy Youde.

They wait until nightfall, Wagner and Bunting lugging the three barrels onto the back of a vehicle and driving down to Haydon's address at Blackham Crescent. Haydon nods silently as they manoeuvre the load into his garage.

It is only a month after Troy Youde's murder, but the old feelings of self-loathing and despair are already surfacing in

Bunting. He is itching to play, has cast his net and is zeroing in close to home. Elizabeth's son is perfect.

This time, though, Elizabeth whisks John's target out of town. Perhaps it was sixth sense, she ruminates. She drives to 3 Burdekin Avenue and tells her second youngest to pack his bags. 'I drove him down to Marcus's to live', she remembers. 'So that saved him because John couldn't get to him once he was down there.' Elizabeth had wanted to remove him from the mayhem, but she has no idea he is on the hit list.

And no idea that she is, either.

Weeks after her son moves to Adelaide, Elizabeth is home by herself, feeling stifled and bored. She fancies a drive, heads out of town with the car windows down and the sun beating through the window. Hits 100 kilometres per hour once she passes the last town sign, leans back into the seat and pushes pedal to the metal, winding the car up to 140 kilometres per hour. She feels a thump, a sickening thud as the back wheel suddenly spins off. The car is lying on its side in a ditch, Elizabeth is in deep shock and an old couple are helping her out of the vehicle. Someone has loosened all the wheel nuts. She rings John in Adelaide and asks him to come straight home. He is ranting that either Jamie's friends have sabotaged the car or the local Aborigines are playing a sick joke. But it doesn't make any sense to Elizabeth. Why would they have done that? It takes her years to figure out the truth. 'Me dying with cancer wasn't quick enough probably, because he was very heavily involved with another woman, Gail, by that stage.'

But John can always convince her to ignore her doubts. He has that way about him: strident, determined, controlling. She always gives in, says, 'Oh, whatever'. Like she does when he announces he wants to buy a boat. They have been living at Murray Bridge, with its lovely wide river, but never once in all that time has he shown a skerrick of interest in anything nautical. He gets back to Adelaide and suddenly he wants to buy a bloody boat. Wants to go fishing, he reckons, and Elizabeth fires up, tells him not to be so stupid. But once he gets that look about him, she knows better than to keep arguing.

'Oh, whatever', she shrugs and Robert, Jamie and John huddle over the *Trading Post*, working out how big the boat needs to be. They figure that if they pool their finances next pension day, they can afford to buy it then. Elizabeth just can't work John out. All his chaotic schemes that just don't seem to have any rhyme or reason.

And now this. A bloody boat.

25

By May 1998, the number of people living in Mark Haydon's home has swelled by two. His wife's sister – Gail Sinclair – has fled from Queensland with her 17-year-old son, Fred Brooks, in tow, leaving behind another failed relationship and a swag of unhappy memories. Like her mother and sister, Gail Sinclair just can't seem to get anything right.

Mark and Elizabeth Haydon have shifted to another house at 4 Blackham Crescent, Smithfield Plains, a clone of other bland housing trust areas that suffocate suburbs like creeping vines. With three adults and three teenagers living under the same roof, space is limited. Gail moves out the back to the rumpus room, and Fred dosses on the couch. He is not used to anything better.

Within days of moving in to Blackham Crescent, Gail meets John Bunting. She is immediately smitten with the dominating, squat man. He is polite, well-spoken, unlike most of the ruffians she mixes with. Gail affects a coquettish manner around Bunting, and he notices her flirtations. He notices other things, too.

Gail Sinclair is emotionally vulnerable, easily manipulated and entirely lacking in self-esteem. She is also overweight, unemployed and on a pension.

She disgusts him.

Perfect.

Fred Brooks was born in early March 1981, and his parents separated when he was a toddler. Fred spends his early childhood running the gamut of foster homes. Naive and not too bright, he has a trusting, cheerful disposition that lands him the role of becoming his mother's primary caregiver. Gail Sinclair is deeply disturbed; her fragile mental health and highly dependent personality are burdens the young man does not need. He doesn't get on, either, with John Bunting, who seems to spend a lot of time at Mark Haydon's house where Fred is living.

Fred feels he has to get away, returns to school to try and fulfil his dream to join the Airforce Cadets. He meets a girl there, who will later describe her friend to the police. 'Fred was always friendly, he would never hurt anyone. I do know he had a lot of problems. I know he had problems with his mum and the guy that was living there with his mum, Bunting. He told me that his mother treated him like shit; they didn't cook for him or anything like that . . .'

No one in the house has a job. Their days are filled with trips to Centrelink, filling out endless paperwork and drinking endless cups of coffee. The sisters talk – mindless chatter – while Mark Haydon listens, catatonic. His rangy eyebrows hang like a veranda over his close-set brown eyes that seem to register nothing.

The last time Gail Sinclair sees her son, Fred Brooks, is on Thursday, 17 September 1998. He tells her he is going to a party at Victor Harbour, boasts that he is going to get lucky, get pissed and get laid. Gail thinks this is more information than she needs from an 18-year-old.

Bunting hates Brooks, partly because he is the nephew of Elizabeth Haydon, who is so fat she makes him feel ill. Obesity disgusts him. She is nothing more than a backward dirt-bag, with a heap of kids to different fathers. Fred Brooks has learning difficulties at school, where he is classified as intellec-tually slow. He has also recently touched Jamie's leg, to steady himself when he lost his balance and threatened to fall over. That accidental touch seals his fate. He is a paedophile. A dirty. A waste. He needs to go to the clinic. Needs to be made good.

Bunting reforms people by killing them. In his own mind, he is a cause célèbre.

Brooks is out the front of the house talking to Bunting, Wagner and Haydon before he leaves to go to his party, pumped up, excited. Fifteen minutes later the trio leave, telling Gail they are going away to do a job, and will be gone for a few days.

Next day, Gail is fretting. Fred hasn't come home and she needs him. He is her primary caregiver. By eight o'clock that night, she reports her son missing to the police but a few days later Bunting and Haydon tell her that they have seen Fred. He is 'off his face and aggro' they say, and they have given him five bucks to call home. Gail thinks that is odd. Why would he need five bucks when his Centrelink benefits – paid into an account he shares jointly with her – are untouched? She will later deny giving police a number of different explanations as to why Fred left Blackham Crescent and disagrees that her son did not get on with John Bunting. 'That's not true', she tells a lawyer petulantly, as she nervously clutches a teddy bear. 'He admired the man.'

Big John. A legend.

He admired the man.

Brooks's murder is meticulously planned to the last detail. It has been weeks since Troy Youde was killed, and they are desperate to play again. They will increase the level of torture this time. Fred Brooks will die a horrible death.

Bunting justifies it all, endlessly. The victims deserve it. Society is a mess. He is not breaking the law, he is fixing society by getting rid of the waste. Doing what other people won't. The police. The judges. The welfare agencies. The psychiatrists.

Dumb fuckers, all of them.

Brooks did not make his party; instead was tricked into joining Wagner and Bunting at 3 Burdekin Avenue. They are going to do a break and enter on a computer warehouse, Bunting says. If he joins in, he will score a hot computer. Vlassakis, meanwhile, has been asked to give Bunting a hand to move some 'goodies'. He assumes they are stolen goods, feels a cold dread when, outside the house, Bunting tells him there is a surprise waiting for him inside.

They welcome Brooks into the house with a smile and he

beams with excitement when Vlassakis puts a set of hand and thumb cuffs on his own wrists and then encourages him to do the same. Put your wrists out, Fred. Snap. Trick him, make it appear to be a fun game. Brooks has never had handcuffs on before, and his dull brain slowly ingests the information. This is a great adventure, perhaps leading to an erotic game before they do the break-in. Then Wagner and Bunting grab him and drag him into the bathtub, the same bath in which Troy Youde was murdered. They cut off his clothing and press 'Play' on the tape recorder. Troy Youde's whimpering voice, begging to be let go, fills the room. 'It's not that one, that's someone else', Bunting whines. His voice has taken on the high-pitched, effeminate edge, his eyes black.

Punching Brooks in the groin, forcing him now to repeat phrases into a tape recorder that they will play back to his friends to convince people he is alive long after they have murdered him. He must call Bunting 'Lord Sir', and Wagner, 'God'. Jamie. What will he call Jamie? Brooks's eyes are glazed and bewildered, and he stutters out a name. 'Master?' Bunting nods.

Evening becomes night, that inches towards dawn. Fred's flesh is singed with a cigarette lighter and a machine, used for inducing electric shocks, is attached to his testicles with an alligator clip when he refuses to admit he has touched up a young girl. Bunting explains what the machine does in slow, calculated language. 'It is called a Variac machine. It goes from zero to 260 volts.' It is turned up to 20. Brooks convulses in agony from the electric current and Bunting repeats the question. Tell them he touched up a young girl. Admit it.

He admits it.

Brooks's testicles are as shrivelled as a walnut and a lit sparkler is rammed into the tip of his penis. When it burns out, they drive another wire sparkler in.

Vlassakis needs an ashtray for the cigarette he is smoking and Bunting finds the solution. 'Use the dirty', he says. Butting it out on his arm, lighting another and shoving it up his nose. Wagner smirks, stubs his cigarette out on Brooks's forehead to give him a smiley mark and lowers his lighter to the young man's nipple, the stench of singed flesh colliding with his screams. Bunting holds a lit cigarette tip inside Fred's ear, crouches down beside him, gently, gently blowing on the smoke to keep it alight.

Bunting tells Jamie to punch, punch and he hauls off with his fists into Brooks's stomach and chest. Brooks is gibbering, repeating what Bunting tells him to. Phrases, sentences. 'Yeah Mum, you're just a user, you just want my money. I don't want to see you again. I'm going to Perth. Bye. I'm fine. I don't know why you're fucking ringing me. Fuck off and leave me the fuck alone.'

Bunting picks up a pair of pliers, targets Brooks's right toe, gleeful as the soundtrack to death swells. Bones crushing under his pressure.

A gag now stuffed into his mouth and the Variac machine turned on again. 'Indicate the level of pain', Bunting orders. A number between one and 10. 'Ten', Brooks motions with his hands. The machine is turned up to 100. What is it now? 'A hundred out of 10.'

Water injected into his legs and groin. Sobbing as he admits to everything Bunting accuses him of. And the sound of Wagner punching, punching, all recorded on tape, the sound-track to death which Bunting will play and replay, over and over again.

Repeatedly, savagely beating him on the shoulder with a jack handle, raining blows on his bloodied, bruised shoulder as Brooks drifts in and out of consciousness.

Death, when it finally comes, is a merciful release. Bunting leans over him, leering, watching intently as the 18-year-old dies. His face is so close to Brooks he can feel his final breath and smell its acrid tang. This is Bunting's favourite moment. Playing God. The orgasmic power of life over death.

And after he murders her son, showers and eats, Bunting goes to Mark and Elizabeth Haydon's house at Blackham Crescent, where Gail and Fred live, and sleeps with Gail. He calls her the 'village idiot' behind her back, but she has her uses. She is emotionally damaged and fragile, a prime target for manipulation. John isn't the best lover, but sex is a powerful weapon. A great distraction. Gail often fugues off into her own world, and lately she has taken to incessantly babbling to people that John is going to make her a special Valentine's Day tea. They make a cuckoo noise, tell her, 'Yeah, sure'. She whines to John that they spend virtually no time together, but it doesn't change anything. He is just always so busy.

They haul Brooks's broken body out to the boot of a car, where it stews and sweats in garbage bags until the vehicle is towed away by Mark Haydon. The body is tossed onto Mark's garage floor with the accessories used for Brooks's torture. Even in rigor mortis Fred's face holds an agonised grimace.

Gail Sinclair calls her son's mobile phone. He answers, but his voice sounds strange. 'I don't know why you're fucking ringing me. Fuck off and leave me the fuck alone.' Within days, Elizabeth Haydon answers a call from her nephew, and is stunned at the abuse he hurls at her. But at least he is alive.

She calls the local police who retrieve the Missing Persons file that had been activated nine days before. Frederick Robert Brooks. DOB 7 March 1981. Last seen 17 September 1998, 4 Blackham Crescent, Smithfield Plains.

The officer hangs up and stamps the file. 'No Longer Active.'

Brooks has been receiving a Youth Training Allowance, 'at home' rate, but the benefit isn't high enough. Bunting knows if they can successfully impersonate him and receive the allowance at the independent 'homeless' rate, the benefit will rise.

Vlassakis will metamorphose into Fred Brooks.

Bunting accompanies him to the doctor's surgery, announcing himself to the receptionist as Gavin Allen. The name tickles his fancy. 'Allen' is Gavin Porter's middle name.

These doctors are so easy to fool. For all their university degrees, Bunting can still outsmart them. He plays his roles to perfection. Loves the power.

Vlassakis sits unsteadily in his chair, running off symptoms of schizophrenia and paranoia as Bunting has taught him to do. It is so easy to do: the trick is to stay calm, remember your lines. The doctor is satisfied 'Brooks' needs a medical certificate and they try not to grin as he hands it across the desk.

A week later Vlassakis, again posing as Fred Brooks, personally lodges the medical certificate and other forms at the Centrelink office. He now needs to change Brooks's address to Haydon's home, 4 Blackham Crescent, but he strikes a hitch. For the benefit to be changed, 'Brooks' needs to be assessed by a social worker.

This person isn't quite as malleable. She checks the paperwork, gives him a cold glance, tells Brooks she wants to see him again in a fortnight. For the moment, she recommends the Training Allowance be suspended.

Vlassakis baulks at returning for the next appointment, but Bunting is determined, accompanying 'Brooks' in mid-October 1998, again representing himself as Gavin Allen. Robert Wagner, surly and blunt, also attends for a short time, grunting that Brooks will be living with him at his 36 Mofflin Road address. This time, the social worker agrees to the lifting of the suspension, and now there is only one final hurdle: to arrange for Brooks's benefits to be redirected from the joint account he shared with his mother, Gail Sinclair, into Gavin Porter's Commonwealth Bank account.

26

Maureen Fox falls in love with Gary O'Dwyer as soon as she sees him. He is 19 months old, and no one wants the tiny infant. Pitifully underweight, with severe epilepsy, he has been abandoned to welfare from the time of his birth in 1969. But, unable to have children, Maureen and her husband are thrilled to be asked by welfare to take the little boy home and love him. A warm and loving couple, they have already fostered six children when Gary joins the family at their farm in the Adelaide Hills.

Almost two years old, Gary weighs only 9 kilograms and wears size 0 clothes. And as he grows, Gary O'Dwyer knows that he is loved in the most unique way. He is special.

Maureen's bond with her foster son grows even stronger after her husband's death. Gary has dreams of marrying and starting a family, but there is little chance of that. He sustained brain damage after being left to die by a hit-and-run driver on Christmas Day 1994 and has few friends and no lovers, either male or female. And he has gone off the rails. From the age of 15, he lives an increasingly isolated existence, wandering around Adelaide's streets, drinking heavily and using drugs. The brain damage triggers black, angry moods and he commits petty crimes for which he is usually caught. Slow and trusting, Gary O'Dwyer is a perfect target.

Gary keeps in close contact with his mother, Maureen, but compliments of a substantial payout following his accident, he lives independently and alone in a housing trust home at Frances Street, Murray Bridge. Just a fingertip away from John Bunting's death house: 3 Burdekin Avenue.

By the end of October 1997, Bunting is itching to murder Gary. The pathetic, epileptic piece of waste needs to go to the clinic, to be made better. Vlassakis recalls Bunting was just hanging out for it, couldn't wait to get his hands on him and fantasised endlessly about what he was going to do to him.

This time, the murder will take place in the client's own home. But first, the groundwork needs to be laid.

Bunting stops Vlassakis in the street at Murray Bridge, flashing his lights at him to stop, turn around. Dispatches Jamie to find out if Gary is on a pension, and whether he has any court cases pending. Whether it is worth the trouble of killing him, and who, if anyone, is likely to go to the cops if he suddenly vanishes. Jamie recalls the moment: 'What about Gary?' Bunting says. 'Can we do Gary? Tell him you've got a couple of friends that want to come for a drink.'

Vlassakis tries to hide the tremble in his hands as he nods agreement. He suddenly feels violently ill.

Gary is grateful for the unexpected attention, excitedly answers all Jamie's questions like a puppy wagging his tail. He is on a disability pension, he says, and doesn't need to lodge regular forms. He lives on his own, no wife or kids. Jamie listens, moves in to offer the bait. 'I've got some mates who want to come over and meet you, have a drink', he tells him. Gary is thrilled, nods his head emphatically, grinning fit to burst. He hardly ever gets any visitors.

Bunting has the instincts of a dingo sensing prey. Knowing who is unlikely to be missed if they disappear. The ability to just radar in on a ragged life. That is his speciality. Always on the prowl for new recruits. Watching, waiting, pouncing.

It has been five weeks since Fred Brooks's murder. He has waited long enough. He needs to play.

Bunting, Wagner and Vlassakis arrive en masse at Gary's house. Bunting doesn't drink, but he has organised alcohol for this session. 'Skol, skol', Bunting demands. He will stay perfectly sober, perfectly in control. The others down their grog before Bunting slyly nods and Wagner hooks the crook of his elbow around Gary's neck and hurls him onto a mattress on the kitchen floor. Gary is so stunned he can't speak; stares, confused, at Bunting who is looking down at him with cold disdain. Wagner's arm is still around Gary's neck and he is gagging on his own words, falling, struggling to get back up, gasping. 'What's going on? What is this for? What have I done?' The strength of Wagner's lock has sent him into convulsions, and Bunting is displeased. 'Ease off a bit', he growls. 'Let him go, or you'll kill him. It must not be premature. There is gratification in watching their suffering, in bringing them in and out of consciousness. He decides when his victims die.'

Wagner is flexing his fingers in and out of a fist, itching to get to work, while Vlassakis goes to the car and brings back the equipment to induce electric shocks, the same equipment they road-tested on Fred Brooks.

Gary whimpers in panic as they attach the alligator clips to his testicles and abdomen, and turn on the electric shock machine. 'Selling the Drama' blares to drown out his screams. He has burns from the alligator clips and angry welts on his chest and arm, underneath his blue windcheater with the brand name IOU.

They ignore his tormented cries as they assault and torture him. Handcuffed and held down on a mattress on his kitchen floor, Gary – only 163 centimetres and extremely underweight – would have found it difficult to fight back, even without the restraints. Vlassakis plays along, punching him. He will justify why, later. 'All these murders and stuff, I just could not handle it any more . . . [I did it] to reassure him that I was still playing . . . still doing what he was doing, I was still with him that way, that I wasn't a threat to him, to reassure me not being murdered.' Jamie leaves to go to a party, downing so many beers on the way he almost totals the car, but Bunting and Wagner stay behind, enjoying the moment. They force Gary to speak into the tape recorder, to repeat the phrases they place in front of him.

The crackle of a tape recording and Bunting's girly, lispy voice demanding that Gary repeat what he says. A hideous silence, a nanosecond follows as he struggles to keep the terror from his voice, tries not to cry and the desperation, the hope that shows in his speech that if he does what he is told, they will let him go. 'I'm Gary O'Dwyer. I'm a paedophile. Now I'm feeling really happy I've had treatment.'

Bunting's voice resonates, cold and detached. 'Do you like the treatment, Gary? Do you like the clinic?'

'No.'

'Does it hurt?'

'Yes, it does hurt, lots.'

'Are you ever going to fuck another little girl or boy, Gary?'

'No, I'm not.'

'Good little faggot.' Bunting chuckles.

Mark Haydon – the Chief Inspector – has entered the room and Gary has to speak to him. He has to address him properly, with reverence and respect in his tone. Has to talk as though he is bowing to the man. Bunting has no doubt he will oblige.

'Say, "Hello, Chief Inspector".'

'Hu-llo, Chief In-spec-tor.' Gary falters, crying, and he can't go on.

And now he is dead. They throw him into a barrel, use his keycard to access his disability benefit and return to his house to steal his furniture. Gary's neighbours, Kim and Stephen, could prove troublesome so Bunting knocks on their door, invites them in to take whatever furniture is left over. Gary has been bashed up and has fled Murray Bridge, he tells them.

There is a smell in the laundry area that repels Kim. She crinkles her nose but is reassured by Bunting. The stench is from meat that Gary has taken out of the freezer, he smiles.

They disperse the goods among themselves and return the key to the Housing Trust. Gary O'Dwyer, Bunting says, has gone away.

Maureen doesn't understand why Gary has suddenly become so quiet. It will be months before she knows why, before the police call and inform her he has been identified as one of the bodies in the Snowtown vault. Then she goes numb, a blessed numbness of shock and disbelief that buffets her but which quickly wears off and becomes something else, an excruciating pain in her heart that will not leave her. At night, when the shadows close in, she imagines Gary crying out to her but she can't reach him, can't help. She endures unrelenting terror, night after night, thinking of his pain and fear. And after Gary's funeral, there is little left but memories of the intellectually disabled boy who knows he is loved in the most special way, and who is murdered at 29. That and a victim impact statement, the only way Maureen can share her sorrow with the world. 'Does he think of me and the rest of the family? I will never know. So the tears go on. The fear is constant. The pain and heartache has not eased. Will it ever? A million tears have been shed since I learned of my son's death. There will, more than likely, be millions more, but will the ache inside of me ever stop? I doubt it.'

Gary's sister, Denise, had tried to find him after he mysteriously vanished, but she never came close. She has no doubts at all, even after Vlassakis is imprisoned and Bunting and Wagner sent down for life sentences. 'I don't think it will be concluded for us', she laments, 'until they pass away.'

27

In November 1997, the Missing Persons Unit is given a brief to investigate the disappearance of Barry Lane, known to the local police as a curious character with some very unsavoury habits. It is four months since police instigated a routine review of Missing Persons cases, including that of Clinton Trezise. Robert Wagner grabs their attention. He has already come under suspicion when it was discovered that Clinton Trezise lived with Wagner's former lover, Barry Lane. Monitoring the running sheets of Major Crime detectives at Elizabeth CIB, the Missing Persons Unit submits a report to Social Security to access Barry Lane's banking records. Money is still being taken out of his account, judging by the regular withdrawal pattern at an ATM machine at the BP Express, Main North Road, Elizabeth Vale. It is a full nine months since Lane disappeared.

Liaising with different branches, the police set up video surveillance at the ATM machine in July 1998. Bingo. It isn't Barry Lane who is making the withdrawals. It is Robert Wagner. His pattern is to saunter into the service station and hit Lane's account shortly after dawn.

Frustrated by the lack of resources, Detective Craig Patterson – tall and solidly built with an impenetrable demeanour – repeatedly asks for increased surveillance, using specially trained police officers, on Robert Wagner. None is available. An application to use the resources of the Federal Police surveillance team is also rejected.

Over a six-month period, Wagner is shadowed by a surveillance team on only six occasions. Patterson's application, in October 1998, to have telephone intercepts placed on Wagner's calls, is also rejected. There are only six lines available in South Australia, and none to spare. Whatever Robert Wagner is doing, it is not considered a high priority. The investigation would need to be declared a Major Crime in order to be given the necessary resources and manpower. Once a Major Crime declaration is made, accountability and management of the case can be tightly controlled; without it, investigators cannot invest their sole energies into Missing Persons. There are other inquires to make.

Four months after police finally start surveillance, another Missing Persons report appears on a police desk. Elizabeth Haydon. The report is forwarded to Detective Greg Stone, based in the northern suburbs.

Mark Haydon has told his brother-in-law, Garion, that Elizabeth has up and left following a domestic argument. He says it casually, throws it into the conversation – 'We had a fight, she took off' – but Garion doesn't believe him. It just doesn't ring true. Where would she go? The couple has had arguments before, but Elizabeth hasn't taken off. Something is wrong.

Mark Haydon has been indiscreet, an indiscretion that will have deadly ramifications. He has taken Elizabeth into his confidence, he tells Bunting, about Happy Pants's body being dumped in a paddock at Lower Light.

Bunting listens with a slight nod of his head and turns away. No worries, he says. But he is more forthcoming when he speaks to Jamie Vlassakis. Elizabeth Haydon knows too much, he grumbles. And Mark Haydon has a big fucking mouth.

Neighbours remember the Haydon family – Mark, Elizabeth and the kids – only too well. They remember, too, that Elizabeth's sister, Gail Sinclair, lived in the granny flat out the back. Up to 10 people at a time in the house, and always a riot. They are really active at night, a real pain, one winces. They never speak to them and have told their children not to play with the kids from the Haydon house. One neighbour offers an opinion as to why Elizabeth has suddenly disappeared. There was a terrible row, she says, between Haydon and Elizabeth in

November 1998, when Elizabeth rebelled against the attention her husband was showing Gail.

Within days, Elizabeth has simply disappeared. Just upped and shot through, never seen or heard from again.

The last time Garion sees his sister is when she drops off the two boys to be baby-sat. Elizabeth and Mark, he will tell police, were going to a restaurant, but after she hasn't rung their mother for a few days, instinct tells him something is amiss. And she would not go that long without contacting her boys. 'She didn't have the best upbringing and she flitted from one relationship to the next, but she is trying to change, to be a better mother. She's already lost most of her kids to welfare and doesn't want it to happen again.'

But if Garion thinks Elizabeth's disappearance is out of character, other people don't. It is a weird household, with weird people. They jump around like jack rabbits. Half gipsy, half hillbilly. Now she has vanished into thin air.

At sunset on Saturday, 21 November 1998, Mark Haydon leaves Blackham Crescent to go for a drive with his sister-in-law, Gail Sinclair, to Reynella, an hour and a half's drive from his home. Bunting has asked him to take her to look at a Chihuahua that she can mate with her own dog.

It is a futile journey. The dog owner does not show up.

Haydon is unaccountably jumpy, stops the car at a phone box on the return journey, and slides back into the driver's seat after he hangs up. 'We've gotta get home', he tells Sinclair. 'All hell's broken loose.'

Elizabeth Haydon is pleading for her life, wailing and crying, imploring the two men trying to restrain her to go away, leave her alone. It requires brute force to keep her down: at 115 kilograms, she is no lightweight. Her eyes, usually as dull as her mind, are bright with fear and her voice sounds strangled, far away, as if it belongs to someone else. She is sobbing for them to stop but they are staring impassively at her, unresponsive as strangers. Can't they hear her? She knows these men, John Bunting and Robert Wagner: they have been to her house plenty of times. Wagner is Bunting's puppet, an over-sized oaf with a frigid expression and a taste for violence. Bunting isn't much better, has often abused her to her face, called her a fat pig, made it clear he despises her because she is overweight and has far too many children to far too many men.

She was sweet on him for a while but he never wanted her, made that abundantly clear. But she is desperate, gulps back tears and grabs Bunting's shirt, tugging at him with the frightened expression of a deer caught in headlights. 'If youse just want sex', she whimpers, 'youse only have to ask.' He shrugs her off and laughs, a bitter, malevolent sound that comes out hostile and threatening. 'Get off me, you pussy slag', he sniggers. Now she turns to the only other man in the room: Wagner. 'Help me, Robert, please.' But he is ignoring her and now she is trying to fight back, screaming, 'Don't you lay a hand on me, you bastards, fuckin' leave me alone'. They're not listening, frogmarch her into the bathroom and force her into her bath. She is covering her face to stop the blows, blood dripping from the punch to her nose and there is loud music playing, the sound of music mixing with her screams. Wagner has his hand around the back of her massive neck and is forcing her to kneel in the position of a soldier under the Samurai sword.

Bunting wants her to speak into a tape recorder and shoves a hand-written message in her face. 'Read this', he orders. 'And don't make any fuckin' mistakes.' There is a slightly feminine tone in his voice, the whisper of a lisp. The music has been turned off and the script – 'Leave me alone, I'm all right' and 'You're a dirty slut, you're nothing but a dirty fucking slut' – is swimming in front of her eyes. Elizabeth is opening and closing her mouth, but no sound is coming out. She is trying, she is trying but she can't think straight, her head is hurting and she wants to be sick, has an overwhelming urge to go to the toilet, any minute she will wet herself. 'Please, please leave me alone', she begs, but Bunting cracks her hard around the head and she is gabbling now, repeating parrot-fashion the words on the page. Tears are mixing with dribble on her chin and she is shaking violently, perspiration dripping from folds of skin. She has recited it, over and over and is wailing, 'Please don't hurt me, please let me go', crying and dribbling and shaking. But there is a knee in her chest, her ankles are held still and her arms are flailing wildly. She is screaming, 'No, no!' and a gag is being rammed in her mouth to shut her up and tape wound around her head. 'Shut up, you fat slag', Bunting sneers, and Elizabeth is choking on her tongue, her head craned backwards, eyes dilated and terrified. And then she sees it as it is looped over her face and feels it as it teases her neck. Lightly at first, and then harder, harder.

Rope.

She is a massive weight and they struggle to lift her out of the bath, heaving her up between them as she stares at them with dead eyes rolled back, bruises on her neck and blood coagulated on her chin. The garbage bag is ready and they are heaving, straining again to lift her, pushing her in head first and there is so much of her, so much body weight it threatens their balance. They are in a sweat, ticking down the minutes. Her head is in face down, her shoulders and now her torso and finally her feet. They are tying off the bag and dragging it, throwing the bag into the pit underneath the garage of her home with the sign over the front door, 'Home Sweet Home'. They will have to move her again, later, unscrew the lid on a barrel that is designed to preserve pickling vegetables, take her out of the bag and shove her inside the barrel. But right now they are walking back inside for a rest.

Bunting is triumphant. It's been a hard night's work. He hadn't figured this disease-riddled whore would be so heavy. But they got there.

This is a memory to salivate over, and he doesn't want to miss any details. He writes it down, so he doesn't forget. 'The routine of confession that has to be got through. The grovelling on the floor and the screaming for mercy, the crack of broken bones, the smashed teeth and bloody clots of hair.'

The herpes-ridden scab deserved to be wasted. She knew too much. She needed a cure, just like the others. Needed to go to the clinic.

Bunting does not mince words with Gail Sinclair. Elizabeth tried to make a pass at him, he glowers, and when he rejected her unwelcome advances, she stomped off to her room. Mark goes in to see his wife, while Gail and Bunting drive to the local Hungry Jack's for dinner.

A curtain flutters in Elizabeth's bedroom as they walk down the drive. Gail and Bunting turn back to the window. 'Disease-riddled moll!' he yells. 'You don't need to tell all the fucking neighbours', Gail objects. She will go and talk to her sister when they get home, she tells Bunting. His response is calm. Better, he says, to leave her to cool down overnight.

Sharon Ball is upset, and more than a little perplexed. She has been told that Elizabeth Haydon, her girlfriend, is missing and that no one has heard from her. Sharon waits four days to see if Elizabeth will call and when she doesn't, she rings her phone. 'Elizabeth?' she says when the phone answers. There is a split-second silence before Elizabeth answers. 'Leave me alone, I'm all right.' The phone line goes dead and Sharon waits a moment before trying again. This time, there is a long pause before Elizabeth's voice comes on the line. 'You're a slut, you're nothing but a dirty fucking slut', she yells. Now Sharon is visibly shaken. She knows that Elizabeth is capable of speaking like that, particularly when she is angry with someone, but in all the years she has known her she has never been on the receiving end of any abuse. What the hell is going on? Why has Elizabeth suddenly disappeared without telling anyone where she is going, and what's wrong with her voice? It sounds miles away, as if it doesn't belong to her. Like a voice from the dead.

She tries the number for the third time, but all she gets is a male's voice saying 'Um'. 'And then', Sharon will later recount, 'it, like, hung up.'

Sharon rings Gail Sinclair, who has previously been

married to her present de facto, Gary Grey, and who has borne two of his children. She wants to know where Elizabeth is, what is going on. Sinclair is her usual blunt self, with a shrug in her voice. She repeats what she has been told. Elizabeth had been drinking and had got dressed up to go out, she says. There was some sort of argument or something. How the shit would she know where her sister is?

And John Bunting keeps the rumours circulating, telling an acquaintance, Anne Cordwell, that Elizabeth Haydon has 'done her vanishing act again'. 'It was not out of the ordinary for her . . . to just up and leave her children and take off with another man', Anne later comments. 'It was mentioned that the police were trying to blame Mark for her disappearance which we had all laughed about, saying, "This is just ludicrous". It was a normal thing for her. She had children scattered all over the country. She had just left them with the partner she was with at the time. They weren't even their children; they were the partner *before's* children . . .' Anne recalls a conversation she had with Bunting. 'At one stage, John Bunting had actually said to me that she had been spotted at the Cross in Sydney, which is nothing out of the ordinary. She had apparently been a prostitute, so we were just led to believe she had gone back to prostitution.'

It is all worked out. Mark Haydon will collect Elizabeth's welfare benefits and not tell the police she is missing. Just keep going on as if nothing has happened. But now Elizabeth's kids have thrown a spanner in the works, run off to their uncle Garion's place and told him their mum is not around. Haydon had picked them up from Garion's place the night before, after they stayed the weekend, and told Garion: 'Elizabeth is home, asleep'. But now the kids are back on his doorstep, babbling that Elizabeth is missing. Within hours, Haydon's story changes. Elizabeth, he says, came home drunk in the early hours of the morning, packed her bags after she woke up, and left with her new bloke. She also wiped out his bank account.

Garion frowns. Report her missing, he advises. Haydon shakes his head. No.

Within 36 hours, Garion fronts to the local police station and fills in a Missing Persons report. The next night – 25 November 1998 – Detective Greg Stone, a bright copper with a reputation for professional brashness, is working a late shift. He runs his fingers through his hair and looks at the name on the report that has just landed in front of him. Elizabeth Haydon, 36. Reported missing by her brother.

He looks again. That's odd. The woman is married, and her husband's name is Mark Haydon. Why hasn't he reported her missing? Very bloody odd.

Stone checks his watch. It is just after 11pm. He picks up the telephone and calls Mark Haydon, impatiently tapping his foot as he waits for him to answer. Could he and Gail Sinclair come down to the station please?

28

Mark Haydon glowers at Detective Stone and peers at his ID. Gail Sinclair, as amply proportioned as her sister, hovers next to Mark.

Only half literate, Haydon fills out a rambling page-and-a-half document reiterating Elizabeth's last movements. She had made a pass at his friend, John Bunting, he wrote, which was witnessed by another mate, Robert Wagner. Haydon struggles to keep his pen steady as he clumsily signs his name. Stone studies his demeanour. A copper's instinct tells him something is just not right.

In a nearby interview room, Gail Sinclair fares little better. Her statement, recorded on tape and heavily laced with Australian ockerisms, is as clumsy as Haydon's. But her story is the same.

Stone looks at the statements. With Elizabeth Haydon's disappearance, Robert Wagner's name is now connected to three missing people. It is starting to push the boundaries of credibility to believe that this is a coincidence.

Mark Haydon and Gail Sinclair leave the police station as the clock ticks towards 1am. Gail is pissed off that they have been there so long, grumbles that she's tired and hungry. But Haydon is worried sick. He has to get a message to John Bunting before the cops get to him.

It's too late. Stone has dispatched a patrol car to go around to Bunting's address to ask him to call the detectives at the Elizabeth police station. Over the telephone, Bunting agrees to see Stone that night at 6pm. He materialises three days later.

And Bunting repeats the story he has rehearsed: that he had spurned Elizabeth Haydon's advances and she had stalked off into her bedroom.

★ ★ ★

They have to move the barrels out of the city. Fast. With the cops sniffing around and Mark Haydon under scrutiny, it is far too risky to leave them where they are. Bunting sits in his car at Murray Bridge and tells Jamie what has happened. Stoned, Jamie barely reacts. 'Fucking wake up!' Bunting screams at him. 'Don't you know how serious this is? The shit has really hit the fan!' Jamie looks through bloodshot eyes at Bunting. His hero seems to be unravelling.

With five barrels containing the dismembered remains of seven victims, the move needs to be quick and low-key. They will use the Toyota Land Cruiser now parked at Mark Haydon's house. To avoid arousing police attention since the vehicle is unregistered, it will be towed on a trailer on the back of Robert Wagner's car.

They start moving the barrels at midnight, asking Gail Sinclair to keep a lookout for the cops. Everyone was edgy, she recalls. 'I thought . . . they might have some stolen property or something . . . They had stuff they had to move, right . . . and they took some stuff out of the manhole in the house and they . . . wrapped stuff in a whole heap of old blankets and put that into the Land Cruiser . . .'

They can only fit four barrels in the four-wheel-drive. The fifth will have to be stored in a car at Vlassakis's house at Murray Bridge until they can move it.

Bunting asks his mate, Denis Cordwell, to store the Land Cruiser at his Hoyleton property two hours north of Adelaide, where he lives in an isolated cottage concealed behind a thicket of trees.

The house is set on a low knoll. Wind whistles through the trees, roaring in across the barren, open plain. The cottage grounds are strewn with detritus that has become a playground for Cordwell's three children, junk like car engines, tyres, old radiators. Junk outside the house, and junk inside. Dirty windows, cobwebs, stains in the kitchen sink and in the bath. Not just the yellow discolouration of age or dirt but a spooky place, made all the spookier by the untrue rumours that circulate later, that some bodies had been cut up in there.

Shortly after the discovery of the bodies at Snowtown in May 1999, a journalist went alone to the Hoyleton property and the hairs stood up on his neck. Years later, they still do when he remembers what he saw. 'It was so eerie', he shudders. 'There was a sense that evil had visited there, one way or another. A lonely, scary place. I couldn't wait to leave.'

Cordwell's partner, Anne, starts complaining immediately about the terrible stench that wafts from the vehicle. The barrels stand there from November 1998 through to January 1999, when the oppressive summer heat accelerates the rancid smell. On windy days, the odour drifts through the house, impossible to avoid. 'For Christ's sake, Denis,' Anne whinges, 'that car reeks. Move the stuffing thing.'

She frequently demands to know what is in the barrels and is repeatedly told that they contain kangaroos. The explanation is enough for her: the stench is so overwhelming she can't get close enough to prove it one way or the other. Bunting and Wagner, during regular inspections, often tease her. She owns a kangaroo named Rina. They will, they tell her, put Rina in with the happy roos.

Anne wants the barrels moved, but John has told her partner it is too risky. The kangaroos were shot with an illegal weapon that belongs to Mark Haydon, he says, and if the cops find out, he will get into strife.

In the weeks leading up to Christmas 1998 and into January 1999, police investigations into Elizabeth Haydon's disappearance intensify. Suspicions that Elizabeth has met with foul play are heightened when, on separate occasions, police find personal documents belonging to the missing woman. Purse. Bankcard. Diamond engagement and gold wedding rings. Dirty clothing in a garbage bag. Why, they ask Haydon, would his wife have left these things behind? He shrugs. He doesn't know.

Elizabeth Haydon's disappearance is now officially a Major Crime.

Elizabeth Harvey has always hated Christmas, but she hates it even more this year, 1998, with her breast distorted and painful. She sees her doctor on Boxing Day and he tells her she's got a tumour the size of a golf ball and that the cancer has spread to her lymph nodes. She is whisked straight into surgery in Adelaide, where doctors remove her breast; and John paces the hospital corridor, calling on Robert Wagner to come in as well. She is in hospital for a week but John only lasts two days, can't handle hanging around any longer. 'He just left me in the hospital and took my youngest with him', she recalls, bitterly. 'He pissed off to continue his affair with Gail Sinclair. And I didn't know where he was, I didn't know how to contact him, I didn't know how I was even going to get home from the hospital. So that was that. Yet he was so sensitive and caring afterwards about the fact that I'd lost my breast and wouldn't get undressed in front of him and couldn't sexually feel like a woman. He was so understanding about that, yet he just up and left me in the hospital.' He was so preoccupied.

Elizabeth Harvey comes to understand it is part of Bunting's game: to keep her souped up on medication, so she won't notice the chaos. Just part of his game. Even as she looks down at the place where her breast has been and cries with fear and self-loathing, even as she shies away from her lover in the bedroom, he is gentle. It is this contradiction in his nature that confuses her most. 'I was the one who backed off, I was the one who felt inadequate; but John nurtured me through that to make me feel a woman again and this is the John that I can't come to terms with. I mean, if it was an act, it was a damn good one.'

By early January 1999, Detectives Stone (who has been on leave) and McCoy are again back at Blackham Crescent. McCoy stays inside with Gail Sinclair while Stone, with Haydon, decides to have a look in the back shed. Police have been tipped off about the existence of a 'secret passage' that will prove to be non-existent. Stone picks his way past the mess in the backyard and enters the shed, littered with the shell of an old car, tools and cigarette butts. He descends into the pit, which allows access for working under cars.

It is like entering hell. The smell hits him immediately.

Stone is no rookie. He joined the force in 1985 and he has attended many deaths and autopsies since. He knows this distinctive odour. Gesturing to McCoy to come out the back, he subtly indicates towards the shed. Something, he says, has died down there.

The detectives had presented at Haydon's home looking for unregistered firearms and ammunition, which they found. He is charged with those offences, but now the situation is accelerating rapidly. They find it increasingly difficult to separate the two inquiries.

By 13 January 1999, police are doorknocking Haydon's area. Neighbour Suzanne Dickenson repeats to them what her daughter has told her: that she has recently seen a male person loading up a Toyota Land Cruiser with garbage bags. And, like Elizabeth Haydon, the four-wheel-drive has disappeared.

Investigations continue. A mark on the laundry wall illuminates under Luminol, which is used by forensic investigators to detect blood stains. Haydon and Sinclair explain that the mark is the result of a dog whelping in that room. Maggot casings are also found in the pit area. They would have been feeding on something.

What started as a Missing Persons investigation is now becoming a probable murder inquiry. But it will take until the second week in February for police to finally declare the entire case a Major Crime.

Vlassakis is panicking. The forms to claim the Independent rate from Centrelink have to be lodged fortnightly, but he has failed to lodge anything in the past six weeks. He is starting to fall apart, sick from the drugs and the pressure of the murders. But he can't let Bunting notice. His safety depends on his silence.

Bunting is determined that they will keep going until they get Brooks's benefits. They haven't been able to get any for Trezise, because their operation wasn't sophisticated enough then. Trevilyan's murder, staged to appear as a suicide, has back-fired: his benefits were automatically cut off when Centrelink heard of his death. He has missed out with Michael Gardiner, too: his social security payments have been cancelled after Nicole Zuritta kept sniffing around and asking questions, telling Centrelink he had taken off without a forwarding address. They have dipped out, also, with Elizabeth Haydon. It is far too hazardous to try and claim her supporting parent benefits, as the cops started a Missing Persons inquiry soon after her brother reported her disappearance.

Bunting is determined not to miss out on Brooks's benefits. It isn't why they murdered him, but it is the icing on the cake. A bonus.

Elizabeth Harvey loves living at Murray Bridge, with all the amenities so close. She only needs to go to Adelaide to shop for clothes: if she had been thinner, she says, she wouldn't even have had to do that. She likes the sense of community at the Bridge, too, but then the Aboriginals start drifting down from Alice Springs and congregating in the park, binge drinking and making a racket. John reckons they are bad news, says it is time he and Elizabeth moved back to the big smoke. They have chosen a house at Bunderra Court, Craigmore, another housing trust home that fits in perfectly with identical houses in the street.

They pack up for the umpteenth time. Nothing is placed in boxes; it is all tossed willy-nilly in the back of their vehicles and Elizabeth, sick with cancer, is told to go on ahead and unload at the other end. John stays behind to continue loading up: clothes, pots and utensils thrown in and later tossed out on a country road when no one is looking. He doubles back to the empty house with Wagner and loads on the barrel left behind at Vlassakis's house. Elizabeth, waiting in the city, can never understand why packing up takes so bloody long and why so much gear is always lost in transit.

'Can't you be a bit more careful, John?' she whines to him, but the rebuke brings on a dark look, and she shuts up.

In early January 1999, Anne and Denis Cordwell move to Snowtown, 45 kilometres from Hoyleton. They take their detritus with them and leave behind things they can't use again: old tins of paint, a woman's shoe abandoned in the backyard and a dead sheep that has become a feast for the flies and vultures. But to Anne's chagrin, instead of the Land Cruiser staying behind with the rest of the rubbish, it is towed to their Railway Terrace property by Bunting and his mates.

He seems reasonable enough to Rosemary Michael, this unremarkable looking man she meets in January 1999, inquiring about renting the State Bank building she and her husband own at Snowtown. He says he wants to store equipment in there for rebuilding cars and motorbikes and needs to ensure there is enough room. His friend, Mark, says nothing but John Bunting is loquacious, wanting to know if there is a key to the unlocked vault. He is short, polite, unobtrusive; asks if it is okay that they store drums with acid in there and could they start moving in right away? He says he is satisfied with the size of the property, declares it should be big enough and everything should fit, hands over $240 on the spot for bond and a fortnight's rent. They have a neighbour, Mrs Michael explains, an old lady who lives next door in the house adjoining the bank. Fine, Bunting says.

Mrs Michael leaves the rental book and tenancy agreement at the bank, and the men sign it in their own handwriting. John Bunting and Mark Lawrence, Haydon's real name.

Vlassakis – again impersonating Brooks – twice calls Centrelink to ask about the social security payments. Four days later, he materialises in the Centrelink office, explaining that schizophrenia has prevented him lodging the forms on time. Proof of his medical condition is again required, and Dr Khoo ushers Jamie, posing as Brooks, and Bunting, impersonating Allen, into his office where he fills out the necessary paperwork.

It requires all Jamie's concentration to remember to sign the forms in the name of Brooks, his alter ego. He has practised signatures in sketchbooks, which are later shoved into the ceiling at Bunting's Bunderra Court house. The signatures of dead men: Brooks, Porter, Youde and later, O'Dwyer. Once, Jamie was relieved when, instead of signing 'Brooks', he mistakenly signed a document in his real name and no one noticed. He hurriedly crossed it out and shoved the paper in the ceiling.

Now, for the second time on the same day, Vlassakis, armed with the medical certificate, returns to Centrelink and lodges the necessary forms. His perseverance pays dividends: the benefit is reinstated. In light of 'Brooks's' schizophrenia, Centrelink also makes it easier for him to operate within the system, changing his lodgement time to every three months, instead of fortnightly.

It is the icing on the cake. A bonus.

Vlassakis has to return to see Dr Khoo on several occasions, and he sometimes takes Mark Haydon with him. They shove appointment cards and other documentation in Haydon's car and leave them there, unless they are hiding them in the ceiling at Bunderra Court.

A week after the benefit is reinstated, 'Brooks' is back in Dr Khoo's surgery, providing a blood sample. Bunting has telephoned earlier to ask about the appointment time. Cocky, confident. This is all so easy. The dumb bastards don't have a clue.

It has been a busy Easter, and now there is only one thing left to do: change Brooks's payments from his mother's joint account into his own. Haydon drives Vlassakis and Bunting to the credit union, and waits with Bunting while Vlassakis goes inside.

His voice is steady as he speaks to the teller. 'I want to open an account', Vlassakis says, handing over identification. 'My name is Frederick Brooks.'

Vlassakis leaves Murray Bridge in late December 1998 to live independent of Bunting. In March 1999, arrested for riding an unregistered bike, police look him up for non-payment of previous fines. It is the first time he is incarcerated, and he is petrified. If he goes to Yatala prison, the paedophiles will get him. He calls his mother, who sells some of her possessions to pay his bail on the condition he returns to live with her and Bunting. Vlassakis is now back under Bunting's control.

By April 1999, John Bunting is making his feelings plain to police about their heightened interest in his activities. Declared a Major Crime the month before, when they had secreted listening devices at Blackham Crescent, they also have information gathered by surveillance that Robert Wagner is accessing his former lover Barry Lane's money. There is no doubt that Lane is a missing person: there has been no proven sighting of him since 1998. Police do not act on the third-hand claims that Lane has been sighted around Adelaide nor attempt to call Wagner in for questioning. John Bunting, they also know, is collecting pensions from other people's bank accounts. Bunting has already warned them to stay away from Mark Haydon's home at Blackham Crescent, but they don't seem to be listening. Now, sitting in the office of Barry England, Detective Superintendent for the Elizabeth area, his feet barely touching the floor, Bunting is whining that he and Wagner are being harassed. Wagner sits next to him, silent. Bunting's specific target is the tall, granite-jawed copper, Greg Stone, who he says has been rude and aggressive towards people he knows. England's face betrays nothing as he invites them to make a formal complaint.

They decline.

29

Former FBI investigator Robert Ressler, who pioneered criminal psychological profiling, coined the term 'serial killer' in the mid-1970s. Wherever people become alienated from society, neighbours hardly know one another, families do not keep in very close touch, runaway teenagers roam dangerous streets and violence is made to seem a viable response to troubles, he wrote, an upsurge in serial murder will be one troubling response.

Serial killing is almost exclusively an urban phenomenon. The killers live among us, but their activities are well beyond our definitions of 'normal'. They can be our next-door neighbour, our friend, our father, our colleague. Blending into their environment and gaining the trust of their victims, they are often mild-mannered, cheerful and beguiling: it is an art that they practise. 'Dress him in a suit and he looks like 10 other men', said a prosecutor for the notorious all-American boy, Jeffrey Dahmer, a gay 31-year-old who confessed to dismembering and cannibalising 17 men. But Dahmer didn't stand out from the crowd. On the contrary, he blended into his environment.

Serial killers are the Hannibal Lecters of our society, who frighten yet fascinate. We are drawn to them as we are to reptiles, yet repelled by their behaviour. Psychopathic individuals, their lust for blood and power over their victims deafens them to the screams of the children, men and women who beg for their lives. These killers are immune to the emotional pleas of the victims' families when they beg to know where their loved ones are. Emotionless, calculating thrill-seekers unburdened by conscience, they kill for fun, for pleasure. And they prey on the weak and the vulnerable, the young and the old. They give way to the evil within, succumb to their insatiable appetite for inflicting pain and suffering. Serial killers are cunning, cagey and often intelligent, avoiding arrest, planning and executing their crimes in cold blood, and producing myriad excuses for their anti-social behaviour when they are caught.

What is it that unscrambles these individuals, sets them apart from the average human being whose conscience is their moral barometer? Jeffrey Dahmer's excuse was that he was 'born with a part missing'. Ted Bundy, who killed 23 women across the United States, blamed pornographic material for triggering his murderous urges. John Wayne Gacy, who liked to dress as a clown and entertain children in hospital, admitted to killing 32 boys and later boasted to police that his victims 'deserved to die'.

The reasons serial killers offer psychologists and police for their macabre behaviour are as diverse as their modus operandi. Adoption. Childhood abuse. Rejection by their natural parents. Exposure to violent events during childhood or adolescence. Genetics. School-yard bullying. Brain injuries. Sexual abuse. Ridicule. Rejection by their peers or by women. Perceived societal injustices. According to their self-analysis, serial killers are not responsible for their behaviour.

If the seeds of a serial killer's warped psyche are sown early in their life, so too the warning signals of what may follow are often shown when they are young. A fascination with pyromania frequently precedes a serial killer's first murder. The Son of Sam, who delighted in torturing his mother's pet bird, kept records of the 1411 fires he deliberately lit. Watching property go up in flames is often a sexual stimulant, fuelling the need to burn and kill a human being. More than 60 per cent of serial killers wet their beds long past childhood, keeping this secret to themselves until police raid their bedrooms. Most move on from pyromania and bed-wetting to the torture of defenceless animals, using them as a yardstick for pain, knowing they can't speak or fight back but enjoying their tormented screams. Animals are the dummy runs, until they find the courage to move on to human beings. Now they are getting even with society. American necrophile Ed Kemper, who killed 10 people including his grandparents and mother, buried the family cat while it was still alive, dug it up again and chopped off its head. Dahmer also cut off his dogs' heads and displayed them on sticks in his backyard.

Whatever the cause – bitterness at the world, bitterness at themselves – the compulsion to hurt and kill another individual becomes overwhelming. Somewhere in the serial killer's circuitry, the normal revulsion at seeing another person in pain is switched off.

Who are these monsters? The FBI characterises a serial killer as a person who commits three or more murders at different times, with a 'cooling-off' period in between. While many are statistically young, white males from a low- to middle-class background, that description doesn't always apply. Some, such as Ted Bundy, are of above average IQ. The victims are not always strangers, and while most killings are not for profit, there are cases that prove this is not always the case.

While there is expert disagreement on the phenomenon of serial killing, what is not in dispute is that to understand the psychology behind their depraved actions, ongoing study needs to be undertaken. 'The journey into the mind of the violent offender remains an ongoing quest of discovery', wrote criminologists John Douglas and Mark Olshaker. 'Serial killers are, by definition, "successful" killers who learn from their experience. We've just got to make sure we keep learning faster than they do.'

There are generally six phases between a serial killer preparing to commit murder and the 'cooling-off' period before he does it again. In the Aura phase, the killer can lose his grip on reality, before he moves into the next phase of Trolling, when he searches for the next victim. In the Wooing period, the killer seduces the victim into trusting him, which leads directly to the Capture phase, where the victim is entrapped. The Murder period represents the emotional high for the killer, the peak of his achievement, when he experiences great pleasure in inflicting pain before committing the ultimate act of exercising the power of life over death. American John Wayne Gacy enjoyed this phase so much that he sometimes resuscitated his victims at the point of death, asking them, 'How's it feel, knowing you're going to die?' as he sang them the 23rd Psalm and slowly inched the life out of them by strangulation. John Bunting recited the names of other people he had killed, to heighten his victims' fear.

In the crucial Depression phase which follows, the killer loses all feelings of joy and slides back into self-loathing and rage, trapped again with his demons until the only release is to start all over again.

The FBI classifies serial killers in two distinct groups: organised and disorganised. The disorganised killer – psychotic and out of touch with reality – will depersonalise his victim, leave evidence behind at the scene and not use a vehicle to escape. The organised killer is far more violent; with no conscience, although he recognises the difference between right and wrong, he continues to torture and kill despite the consequences for himself or his victims. This type is far more likely to use restraints – gags, handcuffs, threats of continuing violence – to maintain the upper hand and to control his victim, and is also more likely to use a vehicle.

But they don't necessarily fit snug definitions. A confused mix of a need for power, of lust, of fantasy or of mental imbalance may drive them, but even within that, there are sub-groups.

Investigators have profiled four distinct groups: the missionary oriented, who are driven to eradicate individuals they perceive as evil, such as prostitutes, or those of a different colour to themselves; the visionaries, who are directed by 'voices' of God or Satan to wipe out certain people; the hedonists, who kill entirely for pleasure; and the fantasy-oriented killers, who equate dominance with sexual gratification. Within these groups are sub-types. Lust and thrill killers make a mental connection between sexual gratification and the act of violence. Sex is not the main motivation for thrill killers; what drives them is the exquisite joy they gain from the actual act of taking someone's life. The comfort killer is rare – one whose motive is financially based, who kills for gain.

Ressler notes that medical examiners frequently marvel at the precision with which the killer has performed a dismemberment, and accordingly recommend that investigators look for a perpetrator who may be a medical doctor or a butcher. But in so doing they have missed an important psychological point. When a killer removes himself from the horror of his crime and depersonalises his victims, he is able to dismember without the emotional baggage that a normal person would carry with him to the process of, say, cutting off a person's arm. When we cut off a chicken's leg in the process of preparing our dinner, we don't think of the human ramifications of the act. Serial killers who have reached the point of dehumanising their victims can dismember them in that same disinterested way.

The weapon of choice for most serial killers is the knife; strangulation and suffocation follow. Guns are deemed too impersonal, the bullet capable of killing from a distance. Watching someone die up close is the ultimate aphrodisiac and Bunting added his own peculiar fantasies to fuel his need for power. 'Master. My Lord. Sir.' Controlled enough to avoid police. Controlled enough to continue killing despite the risks. Controlled enough to choose who lives and who dies.

Most serial killers prefer to work alone; of those who choose to have an accomplice, one is normally dominant, the leader. Rarest of all is the serial killer 'pack' which again has a dominant leader whose ideas and actions are followed by others in the group.

Serial killers often trawl among their own: the lonely, the deserted, the forgotten, the poor. Feeling like just another ant on the sidewalk, they strike out at those closest to them, the ones whose experiences reflect their own: street kids, prostitutes, runaways, junkies. Prior to and after death, their victims are dehumanised, regarded as worthless objects whose bodies can be disposed of in any way the killers desire. Serial killers have a history of problematic relationships, possibly caused by being victimised physically, emotionally or sexually, or by being neglected or abandoned by one or both parents. They are either unnaturally intimate, or coldly detached in their relationships with parents, brothers and sisters.

Their behaviour is compulsive, and obsessed with certain events or types of people; they take pleasure in watching or discussing sadistic violence. Intimacy and trust eludes them and they are often misogynistic. Above the law, they have contempt for people in authority but may wish to be part of a group – either one that is already organised, or one they form themselves.

But serial killers are always loners, with a deep hatred for people.

Many criminologists believe that the 20th century has spawned both killers and victims, the nameless, faceless people who are numbers on a government roll, who live in huge, impersonal cities and now fall through the cracks as never before. Ted Bundy called it the 'anonymity factor'; David Berkowitz, the 'Son of Sam' who was isolated and alone in New York, understood it all too well. 'Hello from the cracks in the sidewalks of New York City', he wrote, 'and from the ants that dwell in these cracks . . .'

The first time Major Crime meets with Elizabeth CIB in relation to Bunting and Wagner is mid-December 1998. The first time Haydon's name comes on their radar.

By February 1999, South Australian investigators have been given the go-ahead for telephone intercepts and extra surveillance has been prioritised. But they need more. Bunting, Wagner and Haydon – a trio Gail Sinclair will later describe as 'the three amigos' – are now suspects in the suspicious disappearance of four people: Clinton Trezise, Suzanne Allen, Barry Lane and Elizabeth Haydon. Serial killings. Investigators access call charge records, including subscriber details and addresses, for Bunting and Wagner's mobile phones. All up, they will execute more than 5800 hours of house and phone taps. They are hampered by a legality: they cannot listen to the tapes in real time. But even this legal stumbling block cannot disguise the stark truth: that in the eight-week period from late February through to May 1999, covert surveillance operations tracked the killers' movements on only 25 occasions. Not nearly enough.

John Bunting's cooling-off period has long passed. He needs to play.

30

Vlassakis hangs up his mobile phone and shifts, agitated in his seat as his stepbrother, David Johnson, powers along the deserted Port Wakefield road that runs north toward Snowtown on this Mothers Day, 1999. There is little traffic on the bitumen strip in this early evening, as they pass rows of houses silhouetted against a darkening sky in Adelaide's northern suburbs. Suburbs with working-class people and English-sounding names – Elizabeth, Salisbury, Smithfield Plains – that peter out and become Highway 1. Soon the highway becomes desolate, lonely, where stunted trees bent over like old men are ravaged by the winds that hurl with wild abandon from the flat lands that border it to the left.

David Johnson had jumped into his vehicle gleeful as a child going to his first show. Jamie has told him there is a cheap computer at Snowtown, and he is now on his way to buy it. It has taken weeks to get him here. Bunting has become agitated with the hold-up and Wagner has started whining. They want to play.

David revs the Turbo Exa into fifth gear and glances out at the deepening dusk. It's becoming more deserted by the minute now, as the Clare Valley wine region becomes a speck in the rear-vision mirror and the wheat-belt country looms ahead, arid and undulating as a moonscape. It's as quiet as space, too. So quiet, you can almost hear the wheat growing.

At 24, David is four years older than Jamie, and they usually get on well. But they have their moments. Having graduated to heroin, with a raging habit, when Jamie is stoned and on the nod he's easy to be around. But when he is hanging out to score, he is a pain in the arse, dark and edgy, hassling people to lend him money with the desperation only junkies understand. But David appreciates him helping find a cheap computer. It's nice of him to do this, to drive with him all the way up here. 'Thanks, mate', he says, when Jamie first mentions it to him. He says it again as they climb into the car but his stepbrother barely acknowledges the compliment. He just gives a twisted smile.

The cops have had Vlassakis and his mates, Bunting and Wagner, under close surveillance for weeks, tracking their movements via phone intercepts. The recordings are intercepted by police monitors who pass on any information they deem relevant to investigators on the case. The sharing of information can take 24 hours. When they can, they also put surveillance crew – known as 'dogs' – on the suspects.

Two days before, the phone monitors have heard Bunting ask Vlassakis if he has had any luck luring Johnson to Snowtown. 'No, not really', he replies. 'He's spending the night over at this sheila's place. But I'll get him out if you like.'

'No, let it go tonight', Bunting grunts. 'It's getting a bit late.'

Meticulous, patient, rigid. Bunting can wait. But he is becoming toey. He can't wait much longer.

Two nights later – Mother's Day, 9 May 1999 – police intercept other calls. At 6.40pm, Vlassakis answers the shrill ring of a mobile phone.

'Where are you?' It is Robert Wagner, puffed up and important.

'I'm just at my Mum's house now, taking the car home', Vlassakis replies. 'Then we're leaving.'

'Right. So you've got pus head with you?'

'Yeah, he's just behind me.'

'Ring when you are leaving Adelaide', Wagner orders. Sixteen minutes later, another call.

'This is the voice of happiness.' John Bunting's voice wavers with excitement. Jamie Vlassakis's hand hovers nervously over his mobile phone, snatching to answer it the moment Bunting rings. Vlassakis forces his response to sound upbeat, relaxed; instead, his gaiety suggests he is suppressing panic. He hopes Bunting doesn't notice. 'Ha ha', Vlassakis replies. 'We're on our way up there.'

A heartbeat, before Bunting responds.

'Cool. Just walk straight in.'

John Bunting is waiting quietly at Snowtown for them to arrive. Calm, inert, save for the occasional blink of his eyes and the beginning of the stirring in his groin, the thrill of anticipation. Robert Wagner stands behind him, closing and unclosing his fists, smirking with dumb bravado. Jamie has been given his instructions, and everything is going perfectly to plan: the side door to the disused bank is open; all they have to do is walk straight in.

Vlassakis accidentally kicks the metal gate that is the side entrance to the bank as he and David walk through. He curses under his breath. *Fuck.* The last thing he wants to do is attract attention or incur Bunting's wrath. The racket reverberates on the quiet autumn air and he nervously glances up, sees a curtain flutter and the face of the old lady who lives in the former bank manager's house next to the bank, peering out her window. He gives her a cheery wave, and she acknowledges his presence with a cursory nod of her head before she closes the curtain. Vlassakis releases a shaky breath and walks into the bank with David.

For four hours, there is nothing from the mobile phone but dead air, silence, until Bunting's voice again crackles over the intercept. It is 10.40pm.

'How is it?' he asks Vlassakis.

'Um, not authorised. Cancelled.'

'Oh, in other words there's no money.'

Later, much later, Vlassakis will recall how David thanked him for taking him to Snowtown, recalls the look on his stepbrother's face, smiling as he enters the bank, greeting Bunting and Wagner who usher him into the manager's office to look at the computer. David grinning and then being grabbed from behind and handcuffs placed on his wrists. Not smiling now, his mouth twitching as he tries to speak, 'What the hell is going on here?'; hoping this is a game. His dawning horror as Bunting tells him he can go home soon, but first he has to hand over his wallet and PIN and has to speak into the micro-phone attached to the computer. Names: 'Lisa, Nigel, Linda'; numbers: '1, 5, 60, 90'; words: 'not, off, who, yeah'; phrases: 'Why are you phoning me? Fuck off. How many times do you need to be fucking told?' Words that Bunting will manipulate on a 'Sound Forge' program, playing Johnson's voice, editing, changing.

Sophisticated. Clever. He's getting better all the time.

Ordered to sit on a black plastic sheet on the floor, reading from a script Bunting has prepared or repeating words after him, his eyes stinging and his words ricocheting around the bank as he is beaten and ordered to call Bunting 'Master'. David's blood-splattered words – 'Lord', 'Sir', 'God' – sounding tormented over the top of the ritualistic music playing loudly to drown out his screams, the music from the band Live's *Throwing Copper* CD, swelling to its chorus. A song about rape and scarring.

It takes an hour before David's jeans and t-shirt are cut from him and he is sitting naked except for his jocks. They are stuffing his own socks in his mouth, Bunting smelling them first even though he has no sense of smell, grimacing, 'How long have you been wearing these?' and putting tape over David's mouth so he can't speak. Forcing his legs open, booting him hard in the genitals, and David looking at his stepbrother now, pleading for his help. Vlassakis has to ignore him, knows what he has to do. Bunting has told him to go to the bank, to check that the prick has given them the right PIN. He has to do what he is told.

Fear. It is showing in the sweat that glistens on David's top lip, and his insides are rattling. Vlassakis leaves his stepbrother on the bank floor, walks out into the cool May night with Wagner, hears the mournful sound of a distant train on the breeze. Drives to the ATM at Port Wakefield, phones Bunting, and returns to the bank, David still on the floor but with welts on his face, his own belt around his neck tied in a tourniquet of death, eyes staring up. God only knows what else has happened in their absence. But Vlassakis can imagine, if it is anything like the other times, the other murders that he has witnessed, participated in; the small ceremonies, part of the pageantry.

Now there is silence, a terrible, black silence. Wagner is peeved, he has missed out on the fun and Bunting, a hideous look on his face, is clutching his sides in pain, devoid of emotion, like he is talking about the weather. 'Bastard kicked me in the ribs, I had to strangle him.' Ordering Vlassakis and Robert to pick up David's lifeless body and carry it into the vault. Barking orders: 'Put on your playsuit', and Vlassakis donning disposable overalls and gloves. Wagner grinning, 'This is a slice and dice', hacking off parts of David's limbs, trying to remove a leg. Vlassakis has been asked to help, but he can't watch. 'As he was cutting . . . I could see quite clearly that David was going to fit without having to cut and I told Robert . . .' Wagner keeps cutting. Keeping aside a sliver of flesh from his thigh and putting it into a glove, ramming David's head into one barrel and other bits into another.

There are other bodies in those barrels, and Bunting is pleased with the progress, grins. They are festering very nicely, he gloats. Wagner pulling his hands from behind his back when he comes out of the vault, showing Bunting his surprise, his ritualistic offering, the flesh in the glove. And Bunting smug, self-satisfied, enormously pleased with the handiwork and the precision of the murder, how he doesn't have to cart Johnson all the way to Snowtown in the barrel, like he did all the others. A stroke of genius, to actually kill this piece of waste in situ.

They have an unexpected visitor. Denis Cordwell has arrived home in Snowtown to a note on his door asking him to call Wagner's number. Bunting answers Wagner's mobile and – curious about what they are doing – Cordwell uses his own key, given to him earlier by Bunting, to enter the bank. Bunting's computer is in front of him, the screensaver on. Corpses, digging their way out of graves, grinning. Vlassakis and Wagner walk out wearing gloves and overalls. There is an atmosphere in the bank that Cordwell can't explain. Tension mingles with excitement. Vlassakis comes towards him, arms outstretched, giggling, 'Give me a hug' and Robert, he will recollect, has a very strange look on his face. 'Thinking back . . . I think he may have thought I'd seen something that I shouldn't have.'

31

Resealing the plastic over the door of the vault, locking the bank and using their mate Cordwell's shower at his rented sandstone house at Snowtown. Washing off the blood, Vlassakis trying to wash away the look on his stepbrother's face. And there is a smell in the kitchen, sickly sweet, the flesh of David Johnson, the colour of bleached tripe, frying in the pan. Wagner is grinning, proffering some flesh on a fork, saying, 'Try some', and Vlassakis is shaking his head, 'No, no way', feeling nauseated at the thought, wanting to throw up, heaving uncontrollably as he later tells police the story. Leaving the kitchen and driving David's Turbo Exa away from the house.

Repeating fabricated stories, parrot fashion as Bunting has told him to do, stories of why David, engaged to marry a girl in Adelaide, has suddenly disappeared. 'He's pissed off with another woman, he won't be back', and lodging a Centrelink form claiming social security benefits in his name. Offering Gail Sinclair – Bunting's part-time girlfriend – David's car for $1500. Sort of a Mother's Day gift, that she has to pay for herself. Going to David's house and rifling through his possessions – clothes, bits and pieces – and telling David's father, Jamie's stepfather, Marcus Johnson, 'David has asked us to collect his belongings'.

And later, much later, an ashen-faced Vlassakis will break away from the group, turn dog and give an 800-page statement to the police, change his plea to guilty, ruminate on what he has done. 'I was thinking, how can I stop John from doing this? How do I stop the murder? What would happen if I did stop the murder? If I told John the car had blown up. If I told David what is going to actually happen. I personally don't trust the police and I thought that if I did tell the police John would be arrested, he'd be given bail and he'd get me. Or we'd both be arrested and put in together in the same cell . . . I just had to make a decision . . . It was the wrong one to make but I believed that the more John was convinced that I was keen to be part of the plan, the safer I was.' Flashback to memories of he and David as teenagers, and saying to his stepbrother's broken family, 'I know the damage I have done to your lives, I wonder what went wrong and why I cannot change the terrible things I have done'.

David's long-term girlfriend, Linda, is dismayed to hear that he has got a young girl pregnant when she and her mother visit his flat four days after his disappearance. Wagner and Vlassakis are clearing out his furniture and greet them both uncere- moniously at the door. In tears, Linda warns that if she doesn't hear from David shortly, she will call the police. The message, intercepted by police, is relayed to Bunting by Vlassakis. 'If David doesn't ring her tonight or today sometime . . .'

'Yeah . . .'

'They are going to ring the police tomorrow.'

'Cool, that's okay.'

'They want to hear his voice to make sure he's alright.'

'Oh, no dramas.'

They road-test the messages they have forced David to say. 'Linda, how fucken hard is it? I'm not interested, fuck off.'

But Bunting has a better idea, an elaborate fraud to get Linda to believe that David is still alive. Vlassakis buys a pre- paid mobile phone and registers the SIM card, already issued in the pack, in the name of David Cheeseman – David Johnson's former name. This card has a built-in mobile number with it. Bunting then instructs Vlassakis to use the name Cheeseman and gives him a caravan park address with Johnson's birth certificate to complete identification. Finally, Vlassakis gives the number to Linda. It's David's number, he says.

They are in business.

When Linda calls, asking for David, a strung-out female answers the phone.

'Who is this?'

'A friend. Lyn.'

Gail Sinclair calls out to him. *David. David.* 'Sorry,' she mumbles, 'he must be on the toilet. I've got to go now. Bye.' She hangs up.

Sinclair has fallen for Bunting's glib lines again, buckling under his constant pressure to impersonate David's new 'girl-friend'. She is glad it's over, now.

Bunting is in a hurry, travelling north along Highway 1 toward Snowtown in David Johnson's Nissan Exa. He swears under his breath as the police flag him to pull over, but keeps his cool. 'No, it isn't my car', he says to the traffic officer who asks to see his ID. 'It belongs to a mate. I've borrowed it because my own car has broken down.'

Bunting takes the speeding ticket, gives a cursory nod to the cop and drives off. Fuck, that was close. Thank Christ the stupid copper hasn't done extra checks. David has been dead three days. His father, Marcus Johnson, hasn't twigged anything is wrong and hasn't reported him missing.

Bunting shoves the speeding ticket in the ceiling at Bunderra Court with his other trophies and laughs. The stupid fuckers will never get him.

It takes a huge amount of mental energy to operate at this level of deception, but that is part of the game. Beat the author-ities, beat the system. Cops are stupid. Doctors are dumb. Centrelink is a cumbersome government outfit run by fools. John Bunting will beat them all. He is the puppeteer, the ring-leader. He is invincible. The Lord Master.

Eight days later – 20 May 1999 – Bunting telephones Adelaide Auto Wreckers about a spare part for a car. David Johnson's Turbo Exa. The call is intercepted, recorded. The police will listen to it later.

Police are still searching for the four-wheel-drive that has disappeared from Mark Haydon's property. They will end up finding more than a car.

On 16 May 1999, Detective Patterson, travelling north on the Port Wakefield Road with Detective Brian Swan, gets a phone call from their telephone intercept area, advising that they have intercepted a call between Wagner and Bunting. 'They had swung our surveillance team onto the targets', Patterson recalls '. . . and we had the targets in their vehicles behind us, and the surveillance team behind them.' To avoid detection, the investigators pull off the road. A relaxed Bunting and Wagner cruise past in their vehicle. They are heading to Snowtown.

The police operation is now in full swing, but they have taken no action on the earlier phone intercepts that heralded the imminent murder of David Johnson. Why didn't they act sooner? Why did they allow Vlassakis to transport Johnson to Snowtown – and to his death – without making a move to stop them? They are questions South Australian police hierarchy will later be asked to explain, questions that will never be adequately answered. It is a simple case of economic rationalism, police claim. Lack of resources prevented around-the-clock surveillance. There was not enough money to put extra officers on the case and it is not legal to listen to the intercepts in real time. And even if they had, there are no guarantees they would have been able to decode the messages. There simply was not enough time to devote to this one case. Not enough officers.

Not enough. Not nearly enough to save David Johnson's life.

'As I understand it', Vlassakis's lawyer, Rosemary Davey, will later tell the court, 'I'm certain that the police would not have known what was going on because they would have taken action, of that I'm certain . . . but what I'm not sure about . . . is whether the police had listened to all of the telephone intercept material by the time of my client's interview – the first in May/June – certainly he was unaware of the phone intercepts and when he had that interview they weren't discussed.'

Late that afternoon, Patterson and Swan pull into Snowtown. They drive adjacent to the railway line and there, at 25 Railway

Terrace, is the four-wheel-drive they have been searching for since January.

They decide to leave it there for the time being. It will be another four days before officers are sent to investigate.

The task falls to Detectives Steve McCoy and Greg Stone. With them is Physical Evidence Section officer Bronwyn Marsh. They arrive in the sleepy hamlet of Snowtown on 20 May 1999 at 11.30am for a briefing at the local police station and nod good morning to local crime scene officer Senior Constable Gordon Drage.

It is a low-key start to what will, within the hour, become the biggest serial killing investigation in Australian criminal history, one which will dominate most of their lives for the next seven years.

32

McCoy flashes his ID when Cordwell answers the door. 'We believe that a four-wheel-drive may have been, or is, involved with the disappearance of Elizabeth Haydon. We need to speak to you in relation to the four-wheel-drive in your driveway.'

Cordwell, tall with a rangy beard and shabby clothes, does not appear fazed. They move outside and sit in McCoy's car, and he begins to take a statement. The vehicle, Cordwell says, had been brought up to his premises at Hoyleton sometime in November 1998 by John Bunting and Robert Wagner. It was brought to that address because it stank, and people had complained about the smell. The vehicle has had black barrels on it, but they have been moved. He indicates with a vague gesture and hands McCoy a key. 'The barrels are in there. In the vault.'

McCoy immediately stops the statement. Black barrels. In the vault.

McCoy's gaze follows to where Cordwell is pointing, to the bank across the railway line. He gets out of his car and speaks to his colleagues. 'I think', he murmurs, 'we've found the bodies.'

Police have a perfunctory look inside the bank. They touch nothing, recording in notebooks what they see. They urgently need assistance, but that will have to come from Adelaide. Bronwyn Marsh, a police officer in SAPOL for 12 years, starts gagging immediately, overwhelmed with the disgusting stench of what she will later describe as that 'ghastly bank'. She stumbles out. She is going to vomit.

There's an odour of death in here that is overpowering and unmistakable. The automatic reaction of the police officers is to recoil, back away. The senior cops have smelt it before, the

Bunting loved thrashing around the salt pans at Lower Light where he buried his first victim. (Photos courtesy Elizabeth Harvey)

Bunting hid a .38 revolver under his motorbike seat. He used the gun for target practice and to kill animals for fun.

Behind the face of youthful innocence, Elizabeth Harvey's home life was violent and tormented. She is seated second from left, front row.
(Photos courtesy Elizabeth Harvey)

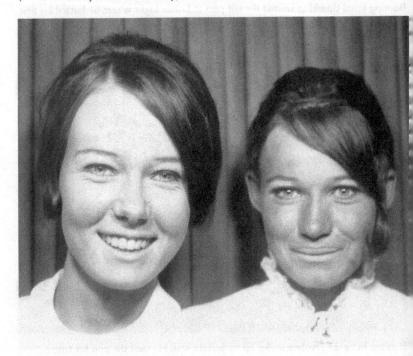

A young Elizabeth Harvey (right) with her sister, Diane.

Troy Youde, 4. He had a playful side – and a very dark one.
(Photos courtesy Elizabeth Harvey)

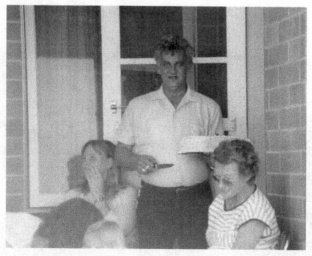

Spiros Vlassakis with birthday cake. There was little to celebrate
in the household. He raped his sons and his wife, Elizabeth
Harvey.

The sunless housing trust home at 203 Waterloo Corner Road, Salisbury North, where Bunting killed and buried his first victims.
(Photo: Newspix/News Limited)

Troy Youde, 16. Like his half-brother, Jamie Vlassakis, Troy had scant hope of forging a decent life given his family background. (Courtesy Elizabeth Harvey)

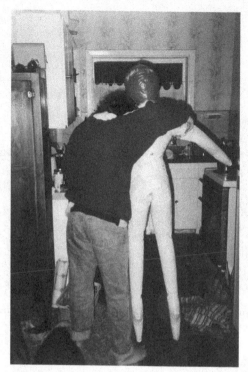

Cold comfort. John Bunting preferred the frigid
charms of a blow-up doll to real intimacy.
(Photos courtesy Elizabeth Harvey)

Life with Bunting took its toll. Elizabeth Harvey, 40, looks stressed and anxious.

Benign façade. Snowtown residents had no idea what was stored in the former bank. (Photo: Newspix/News Limited)

Police Superintendent Denis Edmonds examines the Snowtown bank vault where the bodies in barrels were stored. (Photo: Newspix/News Limited)

Backyard burials. Police excavate the gravesite of two victims at 203 Waterloo Corner Road. (Photo: Newspix/News Limited)

Detective Sergeant Brian Swan was overseer of the grim excavation site. He is carrying a bag with human bones. (Photo: Newspix/News Limited)

203 Waterloo Corner Road is demolished to prevent it becoming a macabre tourist attraction. (Photo: Newspix/News Limited)

Déjà vu. Superintendent Paul Schramm briefs the media on *another* serial killing case in South Australia. (Photo: Newspix/News Limited)

Family photograph of Clinton Trezise, 19. His was the first body found, but the last identified. (Photo: Newspix/News Limited)

Ray Allan Peter DAVIES
DOB 01 Jun 1969

Ray Davies, 26. Davies's body was found interred in the gravesite at 203 Waterloo Corner Road. (Photo: Newspix/News Limited)

Suzanne Allen, 47. Bunting repaid her loyalty by dismembering her and disposing of her body parts in garbage bags on top of Ray Davies. (Photo: Newspix/News Limited)

Barry Lane, aka Vanessa, 42. A paedophile and Wagner's former lover, Lane did not stand a chance of surviving Bunting's hit list. His body was found in the Snowtown vault. (Photo: Newspix/News Limited)

Gavin Porter, 31. Jamie Vlassakis's mate and a hard drug user, Bunting regarded him as 'waste'. He was a perfect target. (Photo: Newspix/News Limited)

Fred Brooks, 18. The young man endured unspeakable horrors before his murder. Death, when it finally came, was a merciful release. (Photo: Newspix/News Limited)

David Johnson, 24. Lured to his death at Snowtown, David was the only victim murdered in the bank.
(Photo: Newspix/News Limited)

Elizabeth Haydon, 37. Betrayed in life and death, the terrified woman pleaded desperately to be spared, but none of her torturers listened.
(Photo: Newspix/News Limited)

This photo of Troy Youde, 21, was taken shortly before his birthday. He would not live to celebrate another.
(Courtesy Elizabeth Harvey)

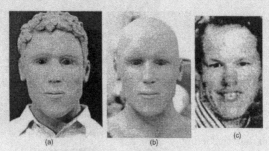

Fig. 2. The facial approximation constructed by the first author (CNS) with hair (a) and without hair (b), and the target individual to whom the skeletal remains belonged (c). The image of the target individual is adapted from the "Sunday Mail" newspaper, 6 June 1999.

The facial reconstruction by Dr Carl Stephan proved to be uncannily close to Clinton Trezise, the first victim. (Courtesy Maciej Henneberg and Dr Carl Stephan)

Fig. 1. Facial approximations constructed from the skull of the remains found at Lower Light. (a) Different versions of the same facial approximation constructed by interstate forensic scientists using computer methods, as advertised in "The Advertiser" newspaper on 19 April 1998. (b) Facial approximations produced by different individuals using two-dimensional drawing methods, some of which were advertised on television during 1996 (Channel 7, "Crime Stoppers").

Despite the advertised images, Clinton Trezise remained unidentified.

No remorse. Snowtown killers Robert Wagner (far right) and John Bunting (centre with beard) walk with a security guard into the committal hearing. The 'passive manservant' who helped hide the bodies, Mark Haydon (far left), follows behind. (Photo: Newspix/News Limited)

The sale of fridge magnets capitalised on the shocking murders. (Photo: Newspix/News Limited)

Artist's sketch of day one of the Snowtown committal hearing, 27 November 2000.
(Photo: Newspix/News Limited)

Formidable team. Prosecutor Wendy Abraham (left), QC, with her junior,
Sandi McDonald, at the opening of the Snowtown trial, 14 October 2002.
(Photo: Newspix/News Limited)

Justice Brian Martin (left), the trial judge, walks outside the 'death house' –
3 Burdekin Ave, Murray Bridge – during jury views.
(Photo: Newspix/News Limited)

The scene of the crime. Robert Wagner opted to return to Snowtown
during jury views, September 2003.
(Photo: Newspix/News Limited)

Quiet reflection. Marcus Johnson, father of David Johnson, has a beer after the guilty verdicts. (Photo: Newspix/News Limited)

Garion and Rae Sinclair at their former home. They knew the victims and killers. (Photo: Newspix/News Limited)

reeking, fetid stench of a body in decay, a smell that stays with them and permeates their nostrils, clothes, car for weeks, sometimes years, afterwards. Nothing else comes close to this, not rotting household rubbish or dead animals; nothing invades the senses like a corpse, the sickly-sweet, cloying smell of human intestines and guts.

Every person, regardless of their job, has an instinctive, emotional response to the sight of a dead body, particularly the first one they encounter. It's an automatic reaction, like a kick in the guts from steel-capped boots. It doesn't matter whether they're male or female. Rookie cops removing a mangled corpse from the wreckage of a car, or medical students in the mortuary, often react the same way; reeling with shock, passing out or vomiting. Some never get used to it, and quickly learn to wrap a hankie smeared with Vicks over their nose and mouth to try and dull the stench. Vicks is a good police tool, it helps for the moment, but it doesn't help when they wake in the middle of the night and re-live what they have seen.

'Floaters', experienced coppers know, are the worst; bodies that have been submerged in water and finally rise to the surface, bacteria mingling with the natural gases that ooze from their body. But none of it is pleasant; every person, regardless of how they meet their death, smells of decomposing fat. It is part of a cop's job to deal with it, but that doesn't make it any easier.

One of the detectives who has been working on this Missing Persons investigation that has culminated at Snowtown braces himself against the smell and swings a torch around the darkened, airless room. The concrete walls are 600 millimetres thick and without the light on, the vault is pitch-black. Six barrels, randomly lined up against the back wall of the vault, immediately become apparent. It doesn't take much to work out what is in them; the foul odour is a sure give-away. Thirty seconds in here is enough. Knives, gloves, handcuffs are also dotted around the vault. This is a death chamber. The officers exchange a quick look but say nothing before they beat a retreat from the stuffy tomb, into the main body of the bank and out onto the street where they take greedy gulps of fresh air.

They will stay with them, these images, long into their old age, and like war veterans who survived the mud and lice and filth of the trenches, some will talk about it, and some won't: what they saw that night as they flashed their torches into hell. The stinking morass of arms and legs, the nauseating stench, the sickening, appalling reality that these have once been human beings, now dismembered like animals. It will stay with them, but right now they need to secure the site, keep a professional distance and call the head of Major Crime, Detective Chief Superintendent Paul Schramm. The news is blunt. 'Boss, we've got bodies.'

Schramm has been half expecting this call. He reclines in his seat for the briefest moment, gathering his thoughts before he picks up the phone on his desk to call forensic. It appears, finally, that their work has borne fruit. The year-long Missing Persons investigation has moved up a gear.

By late afternoon the Cordwell's house has been thoroughly searched for evidence. Police are drawn to a slip of paper inside one of Cordwell's cars. 'Lord, Grant me the serenity to accept the things I cannot change, the courage to change the things I can and the wisdom to hide the bodies of those I had to kill because they pissed me off.' It is a coincidence, but no one laughs.

Led to the car with blankets over their heads by police, both Denis and his partner, Anne, are taken in for questioning and later released. When they return to Snowtown, they stay only long enough to hastily pack up their house and shoot through.

It will take a few hours for Schramm, Patterson, Swan and the forensic team to get up here, so the detectives wait in their cars. It is unusually warm on this May afternoon – 27 degrees Celsius, markedly above the average – and they wind the windows down a fraction and try to look unobtrusive. They don't want to alert the locals that anything unusual is afoot. It is, they know, the calm before the storm.

33

With military precision, Schramm mobilises his troops, starting with the phone call to the forensic unit. 'They've found bodies at Snowtown', he tells Superintendent Andy Telfer. 'Can you organise your team?' He keeps his voice impartial, controlled, using the professional approach etched with warmth for which he is renowned. He guesses there are four bodies in there, but there could be more. It is vital that forensic is there from the beginning to ensure that no evidence is tainted. Soon, unmarked police cars are on their way, travelling out of Adelaide CBD towards the Clare Valley region and on to the rural hamlet. The mobile phone never leaves Schramm's hand as he hangs up from one call and immediately goes on to the next. Gut instinct warns him this case is going to be huge. He has a hunch that the identities of whoever is in those barrels will match the names on the Missing Persons list his colleagues have been investigating for over a year, and he knows for certain that the families of those people are about to take a roller-coaster ride to hell.

It is late afternoon when the cavalcade of vehicles rolls into the town. Businesses are starting to close for the day, and the officers jockey for positions in the main reception area at the local police station, waiting to be briefed. They don't need to be told that what they are about to face will be horrifying; a sense of expectancy hovers over proceedings. One of their immediate problems is staying one step ahead of the media, who they know will swarm. They've also got to decide how to deal with the locals if they start nosing around: the sudden arrival of about 20 police officers in a small town like this will hardly go unnoticed.

'What do we tell people if they ask?' a detective inquires. They need a game plan, and with the speed that this is moving, they need it fast. 'Tell them we're just making routine inquiries', Schramm responds. 'A drug bust.'

As surreptitiously as possible, the officers stroll down the street at the end of their meeting, reconvening in the bank's backyard that offers the protection of a high fence. There is none of the usual banter between them. 'Shit', a young detective murmurs under his breath as he stamps out a cigarette underfoot. 'What the hell have we got here?'

By nine o'clock, the forensic team starts the grisly task of collating evidence. They move around the vault, dressed in protective overalls, their hands covered with specially designed gloves. Schramm had made the decision to get the barrels out of the vault and back to Adelaide, where the police can work without fear of locals or media sussing out what is going on, but he now gives the directive that the barrels will be opened. Wearing a breathing mask, an officer from Schramm's old posting at Kadina, Senior Constable Gordon Drage, moves in, closely followed by Senior Constable Cramond who films his every movement. The red eye of the video camera blinks and casts an eerie glow as it slowly pans around, recording the contents of the vault.

Even through the breathing mask the smell is nauseating, but it will become a lot worse when they unscrew the lids. Made of plastic, the lids come off easily, releasing the pungent odour of acid decaying flesh. Drage instinctively steps back as the smell engulfs him. 'Ch-rist', he splutters. 'That's rank.' It is as though someone has thrown a blanket sodden with sewage over his head and he gags, forcing himself to move forward again to peer inside. 'Oh my God', he whispers, staring into the morass of skeletal remains: legs, arms and skulls floating in their embalming fluid. There is no way of telling how many people are in here, but indications are there are more than five. He glances at the other barrels, nods to the officer behind him to keep moving and methodically keeps working. The sooner this is over, the better.

No one will ever forget this smell. 'The stench was unbearable,' Steve McCoy will later recall. 'It permeated your hair, your clothing, everything you had on, the stench got into. It was horrific.' His descriptions are graphic. 'It was the stench of what I would say was rotting flesh, rotting bodies, human bodies. It was putrid.'

Through the night, Schramm has watched events unfold with an eagle eye. He has already been on his feet for almost 48 hours; the night before, he had been called out to a stabbing murder at the beachside suburb of Glenelg, the same area where the three young Beaumont children went missing on Australia Day, 1966. But adrenalin has kept his tiredness at bay; that, and the gnawing realisation that this is far worse than he could have imagined. By the time he gets back to Adelaide, he knows this case will surpass any he has ever worked on.

An area is cleared on the floor of the bank foyer, where each exhibit is individually described, photographed, recorded and packaged. Some of the exhibits are left overnight, secured by police. Disposable gloves found inside the vault are inside out and soiled, with dark discolouring on the fingers and palm areas. Items found in the doorway of the vault include keys, a notebook in which the victims' PINs are kept, a wallet, a hammer and packing tape. Also found are sneakers, water bottles, socks and windcheaters. The killers have left nothing to chance, and are well stocked for the eventuality that they may need to spend longer in the vault than they had anticipated. The items of clothing are wrapped in a quilt, and some are covered in hydrochloric acid. Six plastic bags are also found inside one another, containing tissues and cigarette butts.

Nobody disturbs the officers as they complete their grisly work. The Snowtown residents are fast asleep.

The team works until 2am, gathering forensic evidence. Almost full of fluid, the barrels are impossible to be moved by only one person and can't be tipped over, in case of leakage.

A trolley is used to slowly move them along. A detective organises a trailer large enough to hold all six barrels, which are securely strapped in place. There is no chance of them coming loose during the drive back. The exhibits too are removed to

Angas Street, Adelaide, then headquarters, where they are laid out on long sheets of brown paper.

Exhausted and filthy, at 4.30am the officers off-load the evidence and re-assemble in the office for coffee and a quick clean up.

As they were driving back from Snowtown, a network of staff – forensic investigators, CIB officers and back-up support in Adelaide – were being woken from sleep by an order to report to the office for a 5am briefing. Annual leave is postponed for investigators whose experience is needed and some are summoned back from holidays. Some of the older blokes have worked the bigger murder cases in South Australia and have a foreboding sense of déjà vu. This feels like travelling backwards in a time warp.

A TV screen is set up to show the video footage taken inside the vault as more than 50 people cram into the Major Crime room, some still rubbing their eyes from being rudely wakened. Schramm – reed thin, balding and bespectacled with a greying moustache – takes a long, deep breath before he starts speaking. It is one of his idiosyncrasies that allows him time to prepare his thoughts before he begins to background brief the officers on the Missing Persons inquiry that has led to the discovery at Snowtown. The room is silent as they watch the video footage of the barrels being opened in turn.

The shock is evident in the room when the fluorescent lights are turned back on. For a few seconds nobody says a word, and it is up to Schramm to break the silence. 'Any questions?' he asks. There are plenty, but not a lot of time. It is imperative that they move fast.

Schramm assigns different squads to set the next series of events in place before he heads back to his office. The phone is ringing on his desk and he ignores it at first, buying time to think. But it starts again, incessantly demanding attention. He picks up the earpiece. 'Paul Schramm', he says, with just a hint of impatience. He groans when the voice on the other end identifies himself as a reporter for the local newspaper. He had desperately hoped the police operation could stay covert until they finished their initial investigations, but he now knows they can't operate in secret. This reporter is a nosy bastard, specialising in police rounds, and he won't give up in a hurry. 'I believe that something is going on in Snowtown. Can you give me some details?' he asks.

'It was then', Schramm recalls, 'that the avalanche broke.'

PART TWO
Retribution

Where the carcass is, there shall the eagles be gathered together.

Matthew 24:28

PART TWO

34

It could be any outback town, anywhere. There is nothing to distinguish it; neither spectacular views nor natural land-marks. Flat farmland stretches as far as the eye can see, broken only by a low range of hills.

Snowtown has fallen on hard times, is struggling to stay afloat. The train used to stop in the middle of town but it hasn't done so for years now, part of a government drive to cut costs. They still blame the late, flamboyant state premier Don Dunstan for that, for his part in selling off the railways to the Commonwealth. Now, the locals listen to the haunting whistle of the trains as they roar past, day and night, each carrying around 300,000 tonnes, mostly grain. For light sleepers, the night trains are an irritant. In summer, the hum of air conditioners helps to block out the noise, but summer is also the season when the power regularly goes off without warning. The younger people can get a bit toey when the trains streak past, watching as they disappear and wanting to jump the rattlers. But older people don't want to leave. Others can have their big cities and large towns. This is home.

The glory days for Snowtown were when the banks were open, the train stopped and it boasted its own water supply. Now, the dole forms that are sent to Adelaide each week are testament to the stagnation that has slowly eroded the town, the unemployment and creeping sense of despair. Half the population is unemployed, and there is a high percentage of single mothers who wheel their babies down the street in prams and share idle gossip in the wide, deserted streets. They stand outside the closed-down bank, an unimposing, red brick affair with a bull-nose veranda, or the two-storey Federation-style hotel, which has seen better days and could do with a facelift. The interior of the pub is run down and dark and reeks of beer and cigarette smoke, but there are concessions to modernity. Ubiquitous poker machines litter the back room, and are frequented by locals with time on their hands and coins to spare.

The water board was shut down years ago and the town's two banks have long been closed: ANZ in 1998 and the State Bank, where they found the bodies, in 1995.

Barry Drew used to own the second-hand shop next to the bank and made a joke about that after the police raided the vault. 'They closed the bank down, but they're not averse to making after-hours deposits', he chortled. It was typical of the sort of comment he came out with, using his black humour to cope in the same way that other people used organised church services or refused to discuss it in the hope it would go away. When police took away the evidence, some of the locals cringed when they heard Drew comment that 'they counted the toes and then divided'. He didn't care for political correctness. 'Snowtown was just the burial ground for these people', he insisted. 'In that respect, it drew the short straw.'

The local newspaper, the *Northern Argus*, is primarily concerned with rural issues – cattle auctions, shows, resignations of council members, births and deaths. But on 1 August 1995, it reported on the State Bank's closure. 'Bank closure angers residents.' It was a masterly understatement.

The locals didn't take the closure lightly. Incensed that the banks were catering to their shareholders, not customers, they organised a protest. The farmers don't like to get involved in politicking, but they made an exception this time, parking their expensive farm machinery outside the bank with signs plastered over them asking, 'Where do we make our payments now?' They built a gallows, 6 metres long and 3.6 metres high with 13 nooses hanging from it, each representative of 12 board members and the shareholders. A coffin was placed near the gallows with a plastic skull peeping out of the top, a nail hammered into it and a black wreath laid on the footpath for passers-by to step over. The bank got the message, loud and clear, but it didn't make any difference. Within a week, the 'For Sale' sign went up.

As a salve to community anger, the bank opened Giropost and an electronic service at the local post office, but it took a while for the residents to adjust. They don't like change. Still, the electronic service has proved a godsend. They'd be buggered without it.

A few more hitching rails and Snowtown could be the perfect location for a Western film – Clint Eastwood as Wyatt Earp striding down the street at high noon. Ugly grey wheat silos that hug the side of the railway track, dominate the landscape and the track itself has become a symbol for a town divided; the demarcation line that runs through its heart.

But the locals are fiercely loyal to this place they call home, having lived here for generations or moved from other areas in search of the peace and quiet they can only find in the bush.

Snowtown has the nostalgic feel of another time, another place, far removed from the traffic jams and high crime rate that characterise cities. The 'Welcome to Snowtown' sign is as pockmarked as the face of an old whore, but it is a necessary guide. The town's name has been removed from the UBD street directory, a bureaucratic decision that left the locals outraged. Things are hard enough, God knows, without the added indignity of being left off the map.

In summer, when temperatures soar to a blistering 46 degrees, tumbleweed rolls down the broad streets, pushed along by the hot winds carrying red dust that permeates everything. Sticky black flies – 'so big you could stick a saddle on 'em', as the locals like to say – cling to face and clothes. There is no respite from the heat, save for air-conditioned offices and homes. The locals are constantly at war with the electricity board, to do something to stop the power going off, but it's a losing battle. Those city bastards with suits and attitudes just don't seem to care.

In winter, the days are mild in this semi-desert climate, but the nights are freezing, three-jumpers weather. The police who raided the vault were grateful they found the bodies in May, when the autumn weather was cooler, and not at the height of summer. The trauma and stench were bad enough without having to cope with unbearable heat as well. Some cops were so distressed by what they saw, they require ongoing counselling for post-traumatic stress disorder. They just couldn't handle it.

This is farmers' territory. Some families go back generations to when Snowtown was first settled, and they are proud of it. The district is renowned for its grain, barley and canola, and there is some stock breeding and sheep farming. Things are tough right around rural Australia, but these farmers are tough, too; glad that they've got soil that pays dividends and sheep that have survived the crippling droughts. The wool from these sheep is high quality and the smaller surrounding townships rely on Snowtown as their main service centre. With all of them pulling together, they'll survive. There is no question of these farmers, unlike many of their rural counterparts, needing to walk off. The problem they have is getting their kids to take over when they retire.

The young are leaving in droves. From the time they reach adolescence, they start looking over the horizon, not content to stay on the land. They have to go to the big smoke if they want to further their education, or leave home to go to agricultural college, and only about 20 per cent of them come back. The heavy burden of farming – dealing with the vagaries of nature, getting up before dawn, keeping the machinery oiled – is of little interest to most of them. It's too hard. 'My great-grandfather had this place', their fathers tell them. 'We've gotta keep it going, son.' But the young ones aren't interested in the history lessons, stories of the pioneering early settlers who ventured north seeking space and pastures for their flock, settling around Snowtown in the 1840s.

So when the time comes they pack their bags and make off to Adelaide, and their parents can only hope the call of the land brings them back one day. If their kids don't return, the ageing parents have to either appoint a manager or sell out to nearby farmers. They admit there's not a whole lot for young people to do here: the average age in Snowtown is around 60 and there are no cinemas, no nightclubs. If the teenagers aren't interested in bowls or the local sports teams, they can become pretty despondent. And that can lead to trouble.

The most remarkable aspect of Snowtown is its name. In its 150-year history, it's never snowed one flake. In 1878, the then governor of South Australia, Sir William Jervois, named the town after his secretary, Thomas Snow. Some residents thought it would be a grand idea to change the name after the spotlight was put on the town, but that wasn't a very practical solution. It wouldn't change what had happened here.

Five hundred people live here, many of them old-timers with weather-beaten faces that hint they have a host of stories to tell. They say g'day in the slow, laconic way of country people, in tones as flat as the surrounding land. There are a few shops – a newsagent, takeaway, supermarket – where the shopkeepers know the locals and the checkout counter doubles as a news exchange. 'Poor old Agnes is really crook, not long for this world, they reckon'; 'Michael's put in for a job in Perth, don't like 'is chances; so much competition in the city.' And sometimes better gossip, the sort that prompts them to put their heads down when they share it and look around furtively to see who else is listening: 'Won't be a second, be with you in a tick' – whispering now – 'She's on with 'im, has been for months but he's a playboy; won't stick with her, no chance' – then waving them away with their newspaper and milk and the bonus of gossip to take home.

At the local pub, where they might amble in for a beer and to catch up on the weather, they are friendly but guarded; not hostile to strangers, but not loquacious either. Apart from the usual pleasantries – where are you from, what are you doin' here? – they have little to say. But their patience ran thin in the months following the discoveries of the bodies. They hate the carnivorous press. When a reporter shoved a microphone into the face of one of the elderly locals, he got more than he bargained for. Glowering at him, the old bloke shoved the microphone back into his chest, squared him in the eye and yelled at him to

'Piss orf!' City slickers with their suits and attitudes. Big mouths giving their town a bad name. Strangers. Blow-ins. 'Piss orf.'

In Snowtown, the definition of a local is someone who has a relative buried in the cemetery. But they are used to strange sights. Push-bike riders who straggle into town with no water left in their jerry cans, bloody fools who risk their lives in this part of the country, or the 'mad dogs and Englishmen' who slumber through the heat of the day under the table diagonally opposite the pub, before taking off again at dusk. They don't see many tourists, and certainly not the types who go to the Clare Valley for wine tastings and dip their continental bread in nutty olive oil. There is nothing here to entice that kind to visit.

The out-of-towners, particularly television crews for commercial stations used to big chequebooks, taxis, mobile phones and a nice glass of red at the end of the day, were in for a rude shock. 'They'd arrive by helicopter and ask that a taxi pick them up to drive them into town', Barry Drew said. 'The town is only 50 metres from where the chopper lands and the nearest taxi is 30 kilometres away. So we had this situation where the cab was driving all that way to pick them up and taking them an incredibly short distance. They'd try to fire up their mobiles, but you have to go to the edge of town to get the best reception, which they found inconvenient. I'd see them outside the shop, punching newsroom numbers into their phones and bellowing "Hello, hello?" but they couldn't get a signal. I'd tell them to stand on top of the picnic table opposite the shop to get a better reception, and those who were gutsy enough to do that in front of their rival colleagues did it. At the end of the day, when they knocked off, they'd head to the one pub here, but it doesn't sell wine. We're only 30-odd minutes drive from the Clare Valley, one of the richest wine producing areas in Australia, but we don't sell wine. That used to really amaze them.'

Off the main drag sprawls a labyrinth of streets where houses boasting backyards filled with broken-down cars, cement water tanks and TV antennas squat next to each other. In this jaded rural landscape, only one house stands incongruously apart from the rest, its front yard littered with Australiana – a spectacle, a kaleidoscope of colour – that catches the eye: painted cement swans, butterflies, a snake, an Adelaide Crows mascot and a kookaburra. The locals scratch their heads and say they don't know why there is a zebra there as well; they've never thought about it not being an Australian symbol; but whatever, it's a harmless eccentricity, that's all. Which is more than they can say for those garish fridge magnets that Barry Drew sold from his second-hand shop across the railway line.

It takes the locals a long time to embrace strangers, and they don't take well to change. The town's former policeman, Ray Andt, had worked there for more than six years, but that wasn't nearly long enough for some elderly residents, who still regarded him as the 'new copper'. But they liked Ray, thought he was a good bloke – fair-minded, community spirited and settled – and they eventually lowered their guard around him. The police station is only a few doors from the bank, and Ray wasn't involved in the operation to retrieve the corpses. That was left to those higher up, the boys from Adelaide. But at the beginning of 2001, Ray packed up his family and moved to another station at Gladstone, leaving the locals to grumble that they now had to break in the new copper.

Change. They don't like it.

Like many small communities, Snowtown feeds on the rumour mill that moves from mouth to mouth. At the height of the media scrutiny, one resident asked a photographer how he could have the audacity to still be there, considering he'd been barred from the pub and ordered by the copper to leave town. Both rumours were untrue. He had neither been barred nor asked to leave.

The suppressions throughout the committal hearing also helped oil the rumour mill, ensuring that South Australians knew very few details of the case. 'We didn't hear anything during that time, absolutely nothing', Drew said. 'They released so few details that my mother in London knew more about what was going on than I did.' In many ways, the suppressions only served to heighten speculation about what had really happened, and led to lurid imaginings. People locked their doors to escape the press, and the hardware store ran out of padlocks immediately after the discoveries, locals petrified because the last murder had taken place in the vault.

And locals started to piece together memories. Three months before the discovery, some Snowtown residents had noticed that the vertical blinds shading the bank's external window were closed and never re-opened. Now they knew why. Over cups of tea, at the supermarket checkout counter, in farm kitchens, at the pub, they pondered out loud: what happened behind those closed vertical blinds? More than that, why didn't anyone notice anything? Strangers, coming and going in their town: how did they go unrecognised? No one asked why the bank was being rented, what it was used for. No one saw anything, the barrels being rolled into the vault. No one heard anything, strange noises. And no one smelt anything. Here, in this rural farming community, the locals are used to the putrefying stench of dead cattle and kangaroos, and they consoled themselves with that. But still, it is a chilling thought: that here, in this quiet, rural backwater where even the trains don't stop any more, this quiet and safe hamlet far from the city slickers with suits and attitude and the high crime rates, killers moved about, undetected. And right under their noses to boot.

The sense of shock in the community was overwhelming, and most residents heard about the bodies the same way that many people in country towns get their news – over the back fence.

And so as the days wore on and became weeks and months, and the brittle blue summer sky changed to a metallic grey; media left town and moved on to the next story; old Agnes died and Michael missed out on his job in the city; and the town's playboy took off just as they predicted he would, life returned to normal. They grappled to find some meaning in it all, an umbrella they could shield beneath, and they found it in the comforting, sure knowledge that it could have happened anywhere. Snowtown was just a sleepy little backwater, chosen at random. The victims weren't locals and neither were the killers.

They are not from here. They are not one of us.

They took heart in that.

35

At their respective homes Bunting, Wagner and Haydon are fast asleep in the pre-dawn hours of 21 May 1999. Well before 8am, detectives in squad cars are quietly, unobtrusively, pulling up outside their houses, holding warrants for their arrests which will happen simultaneously. The detectives knock on the doors.

At 6.47am, Jamie Vlassakis, groggy and half asleep, answers the knock at Bunting's door. Major Crime investigators Bob Stapleton and Kym Presgrave show their warrants. They quickly dispense with the courtesies, taping the conversation. 'Good morning. Police. We would like to speak with John Bunting, please.'

They move past Vlassakis and head towards Bunting who, awakened by the commotion, is standing in the hallway. Introducing themselves, they reel off the names of five victims. 'We believe you might be able to help us with our inquiries. I'm now arresting you on the suspicion of murder at this stage of an unidentified person, body found in a drum at a disused banking premise at Snowtown yesterday, the 20th May 1999. I am now required to advise you of your rights and to advise you that anything you say will be recorded and may be given in evidence.'

They read Bunting his rights. He can make a phone call: have a solicitor, friend or relative present during interrogation at Adelaide police station. Bunting ignores them.

'Do you wish to make a telephone call?' Stapleton persists. 'Can you answer yes or no, please?'

His response, a half whisper, is barely audible. 'No. I don't wish to make a call.'

Stapleton asks him to speak up. 'You are entitled to refrain from answering any questions while in custody. Do you understand that?'

'Yeah.'

He is entitled to apply for bail. Bunting answers, petulantly. 'Yep. Yeah.' They advise him they need to do a body search. Is there anything else on his person? 'Nup.'

Elizabeth, fast asleep, is rustled awake, told to get dressed and to go with police down to the station. A female officer tells her to strip but turns her head away respectfully when she sees she has only one breast.

Elizabeth walks past John as he is being handcuffed in the kitchen and he smiles reassuringly at her as they read out the murder charge. Handcuffed, he has a split second to speak to Jamie. 'Get rid of the stuff from the cars', he whispers. He is calm on the drive to the watch house, but this calm is not to last. Within the hour, Bunting shows police the obstreperous streak they will come to know only too well.

He wants a lawyer. He won't move closer to the microphone in the interview room. He doesn't wish to do an interview. 'I told you I'm not doing this', he snarls. 'I would like my phone call now. I wish to ring Legal Aid.'

They have no doubt he will be a tough nut to crack. A cool customer, he had previously rung Detective Greg Stone to complain that the coppers were harassing him. He maintains his cool throughout the interviews.

Formally charged with one count of murder at 8.19am, he is asked to give blood and hair samples to the police medical examiner, Dr Ernest Flock, who treats him with affable respect. He has been asked to do two things, he tells Bunting; take a sample of blood and some hair samples, for comparison purposes during the investigation. 'Fine. We will just pull your chair a bit closer to here and then we will get you to rest your arm, get a couple of things ready and then we're in business.'

Bunting turns to Stapleton. 'Do I have to give a blood sample?'

'Yes, you are required to and we are able to use as much force as necessary to obtain that sample.'

A slow flicker of his eyelids. 'It's not necessary. I'm just asking.'

'And I'm just advising you.'

Bunting glares at Stapleton. 'Why are you here?'

'I have to be present.'

'You're not the doctor.'

'I'm required to be present during the examination.'

Haydon isn't as verbose as Bunting when he is arrested by Detective Greg Stone and Steve McCoy. Accepting the handcuffs with little more than a sour expression, he sits bleakly in the back of the car, his expressions obscured by facial hair as he is led into the station, where he is formally charged and his rights repeated.

Wagner is silent too, surly and silent save for the grunt that indicates he's not happy. Early in the arrest, Detective Craig Patterson asks him if he would like to exercise any of his rights.

'Yup,' Wagner says.

'What would you like to exercise?'

'I'm not saying anything.'

He opens up when he gets to the watch house, wanting to know if anyone else has been brought in. His question is ignored. He will find out soon enough. All in good time.

After Wagner's arrest, the DPP knocks on Nicole Zuritta's door and asks her if she will look after Maxine Cole's kids while she goes down to the station. Nicole stands in her doorway, bewildered. 'Excuse me?' she says. 'He's been charged with what?' Maxine is hysterical. 'They wouldn't let me kiss Robert goodbye', she screams.

Of course she will baby-sit, Nicole says, her words wrapped in a sigh. She and Maxine are first cousins. They share a special bond.

By mid-afternoon and each handcuffed at the front, Bunting, Wagner and Haydon step out through the watch house doorway into a blaze of waiting flash bulbs from media photographers. They have staked out their places hours before, balancing on ladders like circus trapeze artists, desperate to get the best vantage points. Adelaide Magistrate's Court is packed with onlookers but the four-minute hearing, in which all are charged with the murder of a person unknown between 1 August 1993 and 20 May 1999, is unremarkable. Lined up together in the dock, the three do not change expression when they are remanded in custody to reappear at a later date, apart from bestowing benign smiles, bordering on smug, to their court guards as they leave the dock.

Jamie Vlassakis's stomach is liquid. He needs to talk to someone. He needs help. He needs some smack. His friend Wally Fitzgerald answers his call. Vlassakis is babbling that his mother and Bunting have been arrested for fraud and murder, but Fitzgerald can't be bothered listening to his bullshit. He hangs up.

Vlassakis rings again within the hour, says he is coming over in a taxi. This time, Fitzgerald believes him as he pours out his story between heaving sobs. There are things he knows, he tells his mate. Lots of things. Like where bodies are buried in a backyard.

The next day, Fitzgerald passes the information to Crime Stoppers.

Police speak to Vlassakis the same day Bunting, Haydon and Wagner are arrested. He is not a suspect at first, but within 24 hours he speaks to his solicitor, who contacts the police. His client, he says, has information regarding the bodies found at Snowtown. Taken in to the station, he is questioned for six days – not all consecutive – by Steve McCoy and Greg Stone on the basis that immunity from prosecution be considered in return for any information he gives. It will be 10 months before he is told his request for immunity has been rejected.

Elizabeth Harvey, too, has information but she is reluctant to share it at first. Even as she is interviewed by police straight after Bunting's arrest, and admits that she hasn't seen her son, Troy, for eight months, she stays silent. Even as she recoils in shock when she is warned that her stepson, David's, wallet has been found in the bank vault, she still tries to protect John. Nothing is sinking in: it is too unreal. It was, she would later say, just too big to get her brain around. The John that she knows is the same John they are saying possibly murdered her son and stepson? It is just too unreal.

She is not under arrest, and for two hours denies all knowledge of anything. She doesn't believe John would be involved in murder, she says; doesn't believe that he has accessed the social security benefits of dead people; doesn't believe that she was involved in impersonating Suzanne Allen. She doesn't believe, doesn't know. She is stressed out. It is all too amazing.

The police don't share her amazement. They are tired of her denials, particularly after they find a letter addressed to Suzanne Allen in her handbag. 'Can you', Detective Williams asks in a cool tone, 'explain to me what you are doing with that document?'

No, she can't.

She hasn't, he asks, been impersonating Allen to obtain her social security money?

No, she hasn't.

Harvey changes her mind on the drive home, and is promptly returned to the police station. This time she talks. Bunting, she says in a voice slurred by Valium, had found Suzanne Allen slumped over the bath, dead, when he and Wagner had gone in to rob her house. He had told her to 'shut up' when she asked what they had done with Allen's body, but he told her enough. They had buried her, he said, so they wouldn't be done for robbery. They had sold her property and Harvey, for the next 12 months, had impersonated the dead woman and received her social security pension.

Harvey is charged with fraud and driven home.

She'll keep.

Taskforce Chart is a name belched out by a computer just days after the vault is raided. Police feed in some preliminary details, and the first suggestion it throws back is Taskforce Barrel. This isn't even an option: the media have already got wind of what is going on in Snowtown and are salivating over this story. The less they give them now, the better. Best to play it down, keep it under wraps until it blows off. In Paul Schramm's experience, that won't take long. A veteran at the game, he knows this one is a definite pressure cooker, with all the ingredients to get an editor's nose for a good story twitching like a hound on the scent of a fox.

Acting Police Commissioner Neil McKenzie has given the go-ahead to Taskforce Chart and has chosen Schramm to head it up. He is a good choice: Schramm has been in the force for 34 years, starting out in 1965 as a fresh-faced young copper. Raised on a farm north of Port Lincoln in South Australia, he joined up when his family moved to Adelaide and his career included a three-year stint as head of the CIB at Kadina, an area whose jurisdiction stretches to Snowtown. He knows all there is to know about the South Australian police force and – central to this case – the nuances of small country towns, how the rumour mill feeds on innuendo, and the blurred line between fact and fantasy that can spin out of control like a game of Chinese whispers. He has proved himself to be calm and competent under fire and has a finely tuned ear and an eye for detail; his experience enabling him to balance the ability to give orders with the knack of keeping his officers on side. Of equal importance, he is a deft media player, knowing how to feed information to the press without giving vital clues away. In this age of technology, it is paramount that the police stay one step ahead of the game, but that proves harder than any of them can imagine.

At a press conference on 24 May 1999, to announce the formation of Taskforce Chart, attended by the world's media, Acting Police Commissioner Neil McKenzie deems it necessary to pick his way carefully around the issue of the serial murders. 'Never before, in the history of South Australia', he intones, 'has the challenge been so great to investigate a series of crimes as a single event'. It is a telling statement: whoever is responsible for the murders has obviously not been working alone. McKenzie knows only too well what he is talking about. He joined the force in 1959 as a 17-year-old and, after graduating, opted for a 12-year stint in the CIB. In 1978, as a divisional inspector at Nuriootpa, he was chosen to lead the search for other murder victims in the so-called 'Truro' murders. Truro was shocking – the senseless theft of young lives. And other memories from his long career cling, reminding him to watch closely, empathise more.

And now this. Snowtown. He needs a colleague as steady as Schramm to handle this.

Taskforce Chart is a team of 33 officers and Schramm has his work cut out for him, not least of which is to allay the public's fears that a maniacal serial killer is on the loose and picking targets at random. 'We believe there is a distinct association between the alleged killers and victims and from that point of view there has not been that random risk to the public', he said. 'There's a difference between people being randomly grabbed off the street and people forming an association and becoming victims.' Schramm is also quick to point out that not all the victims have been social welfare recipients and those who were had received a range of different benefits. 'It may not have been the Missing Persons collecting the money', he added.

Centrelink paid money to some people after they disappeared. Of the thousands of people who go missing every year, many don't want to be found, hiding from family and friends for their own reasons while still continuing to receive benefits. Even when Centrelink is notified that a person is officially missing, the benefit can still be paid, although most Centrelink offices are vigilant about checking the death notices each day. Paul Schramm refuses to be drawn into this debate. 'There are different levels of checking depending on the different type of payments', he says. 'Disability payments may not be checked as thoroughly as dole payments, for example.' Disability pensions – at the time of the murders – average $361.40 per fortnight, and parenting payments are similar, rising according to the number of children.

In a 'best case' scenario, the killers could have netted $100,000 a year. Divided by four. $25,000 each.

Rich pickings.

★ ★ ★

During his career in the force, Schramm has seen it all: delivering the news that a family member has been killed in a car crash or has committed suicide, and hoping against hope that the people left behind have a network of support to get them through the grief; distraught parents, half paralysed with fear, begging him to find their missing child; naked bodies lying open to the weather, stripped of any shred of decency; the corpses of the old and the lonely, lying in their beds for weeks without anyone knowing they are dead; people who remain unidentified because no one has reported them missing; the bruised bodies of victims subjected to unspeakable horrors before they died. It never gets any easier, never gets any better, but he has long ago learned how to switch off, how to operate on automatic pilot while still maintaining the sensitivity his job requires. It takes skill not to register the disgust he feels, for example, when he interviews the paedophiles who shrug and recount with icy calm how they raped and murdered a child, the men who finally crossed the line and killed their wives after years of systematic violence, or psychopaths with no conscience.

When he goes home at night, Schramm divests himself of the day's events, sharing time with his family, doing the normal things a husband and father does. Normality is important: it is the only way he can cope, he and all the other cops who come face to face with the darkness of the human soul on a daily basis. Sometimes, though, it's damn near impossible to wipe out the memories, and he knows that this investigation is going to be incredibly tough on everyone who is involved with it. Very early, he makes a mental note to ensure that all his team know there is a counsellor on hand.

Other people are going to need counselling, too. The police now have the unenviable task of contacting the relatives of those who they believe may be in the barrels, warning them to prepare for the worst. It is a hideous catch-22: when someone disappears in a vacuum, they leave a trail of doubt behind.

Without knowing the fate of a missing person, families cling to hope and live in dread. Every time the phone rings, their stomachs lurch; every time there is a knock at the door they pray that there is good news. They watch for signs that the missing person has accessed their bank account, anything to signal they are alive, and rush to get back home in case they miss a call. Their imaginations play tricks. They find themselves endlessly searching faces in the street, running after people who look similar, stumbling away, apologetic and humiliated when it is the wrong person, again. Dreams become night-mares, despair is their constant companion and they go over and over the past, for a hint or a clue about what might have happened. As birthdays and Christmases come and go, as the days roll into months and then years hope fades, replaced with an emptiness, a fear that this is it and this is all there will ever be; a bitter acceptance that they may never know what happened. Did they say something to drive the person away; have they committed suicide, been in an accident, been murdered? At least knowing offers closure. But death is so final and they haven't said goodbye.

For the police, it is a long walk to the front door to impart the news: waiting while someone answers their knock, the hope on their face replaced within seconds by shock and grief; the tears, the hysteria and crumpling to the floor, their world shattered, splintering like shards of glass. If forensic identifica-tion is needed they enter a twilight world: more waiting, more hope and more prayers. They want to know, but death is so final.

And so it is when they start the gruesome task of warning families that they have found bodies they believe to be connected to a Missing Persons case and that they should be prepared for the worst.

Clinton Trezise's sister takes the news that they may have found her brother with the same mixture of emotions that police know to expect. Weeping, she speaks on behalf of her family. 'I pray it's not him. I don't want it to be him, but if it is, then we can bury him and get on with our lives. When the forensic reports come back, we'll know one way or another.' Barry

Lane's mother, Sylvia has a similar reaction. 'In one respect it's a relief because, if it is Barry, then we'll know what's happened. We haven't known whether he's dead or alive. I'm hoping that if he's been done in, that we have found him. I do want to know, to put him to rest – and us to rest as well.'

The agonising catch-22. Wanting to know. But death is so final.

36

Shell-shocked at John's arrest, Elizabeth watches as half her household goods start walking out the door. Furniture, white goods, all loaded onto the police truck and then other things: computers, CDs, even computer games. 'I mean', she says indignantly, 'they took a camera with no roll of film in it. Now you tell me how that is going to help with their investigation.' She always told John, 'Don't bring any stolen stuff home here', and she got the shock of her life, she reckons, when police started checking serial numbers to see if gear was hot. And they are crawling through the manhole now, coming back down with armfuls of paperwork and other people's things. 'A lot of it was paperwork. I mean, what do you do with a dead person's things – you can get rid of their big items, their TVs, and you can get rid of radios and CDs and things like that, but what do you do with things like sheets and towels and knick knacks?' What do you do with the trophies?

Crawling over the house, searching every room. Emptying the freezer, taking the contents for forensic testing and Elizabeth thinking, 'Oh God, where does it end?'

'How do you think you'd feel if the police come down, they send your little kid out of the room and say, "You're not allowed to come into the kitchen", and they start pulling your meat out of your freezer and taking it all away for forensic testing', Elizabeth's sister, Diane, later says. 'They thought they were into cannibalism, and you start to wonder how many times John cooked and what in hell he was using for ingredients. It's bloody scary.'

The fallout is scary for Marcus Johnson, too. Gutted at the news that his son, David, and stepson, Troy, have been murdered, he is also deeply distressed to learn that his other stepson, Jamie, has had a hand in their deaths. It is a shock from which he will never fully recover.

Elizabeth Harvey and Jamie arrive by taxi to meet Marcus at his workplace. When they return to his house, he finds out for the first time that David might have been killed. Marcus has been aware for two years that Jamie is a drug addict. He regularly hassles his stepfather for money and is highly nervous and disturbed when he needs to score. The atmosphere in the house that night is laden with grief and anger and there is no easy way to break the news to Marcus. 'We believe that David is up there', Elizabeth tells him, indicating towards the sky. 'Yes, he is up there', Jamie replies, his head down. 'I'm sorry, Marcus.' It is a statement that hangs in the air, a simple apology for the deaths of his son and stepson. 'I'm sorry, Marcus.' And all Marcus can do is pace the floor, around and around in a circle. 'How could you, Jamie? How could you?' That's all he can remember saying.

Memories of his son spin in Marcus's head. He articulates it in his rambling, convoluted way. 'He was lazy, he hated putting his hands in the dishwater that's for sure, I cleaned up the house. But he kept his room immaculate, he did not drink or gamble excessively and he was not into drugs. He loved chasing skirt but he was just not into anything that would put him out into left field with his behaviour. His behaviour was so structurally sound that it's incomprehensible that this should have been done to him.'

Jamie and Elizabeth go outside; when they come indoors again, Jamie offers another apology. 'Elizabeth told me that Troy was in the barrels too', Marcus recalls. 'Jamie then asked for some money and he gave the impression that he would try to commit suicide. He was full of shame and remorse but I was quite prepared to give him the money to do it, the way I felt at that minute.'

Marcus tries to explain why he didn't notify the police of his son's disappearance. 'Well naturally, being 24, I looked upon him as a young man able to look after himself and I didn't get too apprehensive after the first three or four days that he'd not come home. I then started to get a bit wary but I waited until that weekend and then my eyebrows were going up and I thought, "Now it's been a week now", and I thought, "Now he hasn't come home". I thought, "If he's around at his girlfriend's he could at least contact me", but I thought, "Well, if anything has happened to him well then like anything in life it will come. If it's bad news it will surface, if it's not, then I'll hear about it". So that was my philosophy at that time, but I thought, "If this goes on much longer I will go to the police".'

Jamie spares him the effort of wondering where David is, showing Marcus bankcards that belonged to David and other victims. It is all starting to sink in. How they spoke in code, and why. Marcus explains: 'It was like being on another planet the way they talked. They'd say things like, "We've got to do something about the engines tonight, this one's going to need a super-charge". Things like this, a code about who they've done in, when they're gonna do the next one, all this. They liked to talk in front of people, and the code was all about that. It was, "We know a secret and you don't", and you always felt on the outer. You weren't good enough to know what was going on.'

Elizabeth can't get her head around it at all. John now arrested and her son, Troy, dead. She feels absolute disbelief. 'I started to cry and asked Jamie if he was lying. And he put his arms around me and he said, "Sorry, Mum, it's true". I just didn't want to see Jamie after that.' Elizabeth wrestles with the idea of calling Major Crime. 'We went to the pub and I said, "I've got to ring the police." Marcus said, "Now, you're sure?" and I said, "Yes, they've got to know." So I rang Major Crime and said, "Jamie told me that Troy was one of the victims." And they asked me how Jamie knew. I said, "I don't know; I can only assume that he was there." They said, "Right, we'll be around to speak to Jamie sometime during the weekend." Well, that didn't seem enough. So we went and saw a solicitor on Sunday . . . But the police would never have known Jamie's involvement unless I'd actually phoned and told them.'

She can't bring herself to accept the murders. Police take months to officially notify all the families, and she checks with a female officer, clinging onto her arm. 'You've seen the bodies. Are you sure Troy's up there?'

'Did he have any markings, any scars?'

That rough tattoo, the iron maiden. The one that looked like a jail tat. Elizabeth describes it and the policewoman nods. 'I'm sorry, but yes, he was found at Snowtown.'

Only then can she start to grieve, to believe. All those stories that John and Jamie had told her – that Troy was okay, that he was with a family, grape-picking – all lies.

Elizabeth is often bemused by the behaviour of the police. 'Sunday morning, not long after the arrests, I get a phone call from Brian Swan and ask what I can do for him. "Well," he says, "it seems like your sister's disappeared." She was visiting me and I said, "No she hasn't, she's in my bed asleep. Do you want to speak to her?"'

Diane's daughter, who did not have Elizabeth's phone number, had alerted the police to her mother's 'disappearance'.

'Well, the report went to the local gendarme and from there it went straight to Major Crime. They put two and two together and came up with six. "There's another body missing! It's Bunting's girlfriend's sister!"' She shakes her head and coughs. 'Like they didn't have enough real murders to worry about.'

Twelve days later, Jamie moves to answer the knock at the door of the Craigmore house. He glances quickly at his mother who is standing with him at the door before he nods to police. 'Yes, I am Jamie Vlassakis.' Sitting in the squad car as it pulls away, he inclines his head backwards, craning to catch a last glimpse of his mother, who is leaning into the doorframe. She is thin and lined in the face; the thin, haggard look of a woman dying of cancer. Before the car reaches the end of the street, she closes the door.

Jamie's lawyer brokers a deal: he will pass on information from Elizabeth Harvey regarding the location of two more bodies, in return for assurance that the statements can't be used in evidence against her.

Detective McCoy outlines the terms of the interview: 'We will not be issuing you with a caution and, as a result, the statement you make will not be issued against you in any proceeding. Once this statement has been made, it will be forwarded to the Director of Public Prosecutions. It is only then that a decision will be made by the Director of Public Prosecutions as to whether or not full immunity will be granted to you.'

Jamie sobs through the six-day interview that starts in the late afternoon of Monday 24 May 1999, as he recounts in harrowing detail everyone's role in the murders. Distressed, breaking down and vomiting as he recalls the details to detectives McCoy and Stone. He overdoses on bad heroin at the police station, later admitting, 'In the interviews I was quite stressed out and pretty much stoned all the time.' Ringing his mother, a call that is intercepted. His counsel will later describe his conversation as not the speech of a callous killer, but of a young man whose life is out of control.

Another call details his fear of jail: 'If I go to jail, I will do myself in; I don't care. It's hard enough sleeping at night now without sleeping in a four-by-four cell . . . After tomorrow I might be in jail; I might have to put John in for everything; then I might have to say he did a couple of others, you know, unfound bodies that were found and stuff.'

Charged with David Johnson's murder in the late afternoon of 2 June 1999, Vlassakis is taken into custody, starting a second round of interviews with Brian Swan and Craig Patterson that begin in winter and conclude in spring. Almost 2000 pages of disturbing, chilling detail that will take 18 days and be referred to, compendiously, as the 'second interview'.

Fear. It hangs over all his words, all his past actions. Knowing that Bunting, who sometimes called him 'waste' because he uses drugs, killed people he regarded as waste. Fear that his family would be murdered and that all of them would end up in barrels like the others. Fear of the police. Fear that he would be sent to jail and be locked up with paedophiles. And the overwhelming fear that John Bunting – the sadistic psychopath – would be bailed and come and get him.

It is his mother's greatest fear, too, that John will get to Jamie, turn his head around, try to seduce him into changing his mind to not give evidence against the other three. It would fit with Bunting's game plan, his philosophy. 'Keep your friends close. Keep your enemies closer.'

Charged at the end of April 2000 with a further four murders, Vlassakis is locked up in G-division at Yatala Prison in close confinement. His safety is paramount: the 19-year-old's eye-witness account will form the backbone of the prosecution's case.

37

Vlassakis's mental state – at best, fragile – deteriorates rapidly in the week following his arrest, and he twice attempts suicide at Adelaide's Glenside Psychiatric Hospital where he is being held. He is transferred to the secure psychiatric facility of James Nash House, under the auspices of the South Australia Department of Corrections. Some of his mates visit him in the hospital and notice he seems far away, not quite there. It is a bit spooky, Jamie's state of mind and the atmosphere at the hospital. They watch him intently, wanting to know what is going on inside his head, where he mentally goes to when his gaze fixes on a spot on the floor and stays there, unflinching, like a subterranean being. They wonder what he is thinking about when his voice trails off, mid-sentence, and he closes his eyes, or jumps up and starts pacing around the room before slumping back in the chair and looking at them again, unseeing. Sometimes he talks in coherent grabs and other times he looks close to tears, his chin trembling, his hands curled into fists covering his dark eyes, lost in an aloneness that is disconcerting to witness.

There is something childlike about Vlassakis, surreal almost. There are glimpses of the emotionally stunted boy who was serially abused; the boy who would always be a follower, never a leader; the boy who needed a hero and found one in John Bunting. And so his visitors mumble small talk and stare at the other patients before taking their leave earlier than they had expected. They walk along the corridor back out into the fresh air, stammering, unnerved. 'Shit, that joint is full of zombies'. Back out into the everyday world, leaving this strange environment: the shuffling feet, the pale, phlegmatic faces, some just like vegetables, just existing, like subterranean beings.

The allegation that Jamie Vlassakis committed murder at Snowtown is initially kept from the public. Prosecutors successfully gain a suppression order on most of the details surrounding his involvement and Adelaide's media organisations, including the *Advertiser*, immediately launch an application for the suppression to be lifted. They are partly successful.

On 3 June 1999, Magistrate David Swain, with the Director of Public Prosecutions, Paul Rofe QC, and a defence lawyer present, holds a bedside hearing at the psychiatric hospital. Vlassakis is formally charged at this hearing with one count of murder. Swain also imposes an interim suppression order but allows for legal argument to be heard the following day. At that hearing, Swain agrees to lift suppression of Vlassakis's name, location of the offence and date it occurred.

Although still living with her parents, Veronika Bunting has kept in touch with her husband; four years after they separated they still have a joint bank account. The address on the account is Mark Haydon's house, though Veronika will claim she wasn't aware of that.

Veronika is on a disability pension and considers it a friendly gesture that John allows her to take money from the joint account. But she always has to clear it with him first, and it is always the same amount. He only ever leaves $20 in the account for her. Sometimes she visits him at the houses he has shared with Elizabeth Harvey. There are no hard feelings.

Last time she saw her ex-husband, around Easter 1999, they went shopping together to buy his mother a birthday present. And she will always remember how she heard the news, eating lunch a month later, when she saw on the television that John, Robert and Mark had been arrested. The things the reporter reckoned they had done made her almost choke on her sardine sandwich. Terrible things. Shocking.

Veronika has been ever faithful and loyal, but this is too much to bear. She put up with his black moods, his obsessive talking about the abattoir, his digging the giant hole, the strays who wandered into their home, even Elizabeth Harvey. She never asked any questions. She loved him, even after they separated. But now he is charged with murder. This is too much to bear.

The media attention is overwhelming. Journalists practically camp outside her parents' house, sticking a camera in her face because she is his ex-wife. They are a flippin' nuisance.

Her father stands behind the door when she answers it, instructing Veronika on what to say.

'Tell them to fuck off.'

'Fuck off!' she yells.

'And don't come back.'

'Don't come back!'

The door slams. And still they come back. They just won't get the message. A flippin' nuisance.

Veronika's housing trust flat where she now lives – a grey, concrete edifice – is as dingy inside as it is out. A single bed in the corner, like a nun's cell. That suits her. She has had nothing to do with men since she separated from John, and their divorce was finalised in August 1999, three months after police opened the vault. Veronika is determined to stay single. She occasionally thinks she might contact her ex-husband, in the rare moments when she doubts what he has done. She has heard that he has no visitors in prison, not even his parents. She frets about him sometimes, reckons he must be lonely.

She is expecting my visit, but when she opens the door, her greeting is brusque. 'Well? What do you want?' It takes her a while to relax. Veronika has no reason to trust the press.

Being John Bunting's ex-wife has taken its toll on her health. She takes anti-depressants for post-traumatic stress disorder, and is borderline agoraphobic. Art helps her relax. Once, all she would draw and paint was intricately detailed birds and animals in beautiful colours; now, she also paints crocodiles and sharks, predatory creatures with cold eyes and teeth that can tear a person apart.

Peaceful sleep evades her. The police have told her she is lucky to still be alive and she is haunted by nightmares of living in a house that had bodies buried in the backyard. And she still cries when she thinks about Troy Youde. She liked him. Veronika is, apart from her parents, alone. Even her school friend, Caroline – the only real friend she has ever had – has died from an epileptic seizure.

On her doctor's advice, Veronika is writing her story as a way to try and expunge the past. It is simple, child-like, and she struggles with spelling and expression. She has titled her memoir, 'I Married a Monster – the Snowtown Murder Story'.

She keeps guinea pigs and a pet mouse, talks to them as if they are human. She doesn't know, she says, what turned the man she married into the fiend she now hears about. It seems to her he was just never the same after his mother cut his hair.

'They reckon things happened to him in his past, like he was raped as a boy and all that', she says. 'But trouble is, you never knew when John was telling the truth. I was married to him, and he never told me nothin' like that. It's flippin' news to me, sunshine.'

Veronika will later carry a teddy bear with her to court, clutching it close as she gives evidence, her answers measured and painfully slow. The jury, warned that she does not have the normal mental capacity of a person her age, watches as she strokes the bear through the lengthy cross-examination.

Why, the defence asks, if Barry Lane told her Bunting had killed a man in their lounge room at 203, had she not noticed anything different when they returned home that night? Why had she initially failed to tell police anything she knew about a body buried at Lower Light? Why did she tell detectives that other than some of the books he read, TV programs he watched or the hole he dug in the backyard, her husband just seemed normal?

Veronika's eyes, mirrors to a brain short-circuited against nuances and subtleties, dart sideways as she speaks and her answers are delivered in her trademark loud voice: blunt, sing-song. As though she has stomped on them as they fall from her mouth; though the sub-text of all her conversation is: 'There, I've answered you. Can I go now?'

Justice Martin instructs them on how to assess her when she leaves the witness stand. 'Some witnesses, such as the one you've just seen, have what can be generally described as an intellectual impairment. That doesn't mean they can't be truthful or reliable. You might have observed that, in some respects, Ms Tripp had almost childlike reactions; sometimes a little bit of petulance, you might think, crept into her responses, almost like a child who was confronted with the situation, although that's a matter for you obviously. She told you herself that she has, all her life, had a poor memory.'

Robert Skewes is bathing in the winter sunshine of his backyard on Sunday, 23 June 1999, when police knock on his front door. Introducing themselves, they tell him they are inquiring about the hole in the backyard next door. Used to officious cops, he takes up his customary stance, scratching his belly and stroking his beard. 'It's over there', he says, pointing to the hole. 'I helped them dig it.' Later that afternoon, the State Emergency Services and police arrive to dig it up.

Armed with their latest investigative weapon, ground-penetrating radar that has already been used to detect bodies in Britain's House of Horrors, they set to work demolishing the concrete slab outside the back door. Now down to bare earth, they wheel the bright-yellow radar over the spot, and wait. The read-out from the machine comes within minutes: a 2-metre square area of earth had been disturbed and re-filled. They are on target.

Skewes has scored, too. His house has a clear view to Bunting's backyard and he offers a TV crew the opportunity to use it, giving them an uninterrupted vista and the edge over their rivals. In return, they give him a t-shirt as a memento of the occasion. He is the man of the moment, reporters asking questions – 'How long have you lived here? Tell me what you know about the people who used to live next door?' – as they peer past him into his darkened lounge room. And he answers them, awkwardly at first, then slowly gaining confidence. Skewes lets two names slip: Ray Davies and Suzanne Allen. The names don't ring a bell. Are they murder victims, too? How much does Skewes really know? Living so close, and he doesn't know anything?

Working under tarpaulins to keep out the rain and the mawkish gaze of onlookers who have gathered outside to watch, forensic experts meticulously dig to a depth of 2 metres, as if searching for buried treasure. The delicate operation is supervised by Detective-Sergeant Brian Swan, who had ordered the dig to start at 11.30am. Five hours later, smashing through cement and rock, they finally find what they are looking for: a dismembered corpse, bundled into plastic bags. The police report details the find in unemotional language. '. . . There was a strong odour of decomposition released on the opening of the bag. All of these bags were marked and taken to the Forensic Science Centre . . .' Forensic testing confirms their suspicions that the body has been in the ground for up to four years. There is nothing left, bar skeletal remains. Suzanne Allen.

Schramm has to face more inevitable questions from an excited press who now have another salacious angle on the Snowtown story. He gives them little. 'You can appreciate now, as the saga unwinds, we have a lot of information coming in from a lot of different sources. That, coupled with the investigation and information we have already been aware of, has led us to these particular premises.'

Detectives again speak to Elizabeth Harvey, questioning her information. 'They have only found one body. You said there were two.' 'Tell them to dig deeper', she says. 'They only went down 8 feet, yet I told Jamie's lawyer to tell them, go to 15.' She squirms with her guilt. 'If I hadn't opened up me big fat mouth, those bodies would never have been found.'

Within hours, police unearth the second body, buried beneath the first, 1.9 metres deeper. Detective Patterson has the unenviable task of sifting through the dirt to ensure no bones are missed. This body, tossed unceremoniously into the hole, was not given any burial rites. The skeleton is unclothed, except for a green parka hood around the skull, covered in maggot casings. It too is removed and taken to the Forensic Science Centre. Ray Davies, thrown in and splattered with dirt, just as Bunting had said he was. Waste; died clutching his balls.

Horrified neighbours immediately dub 203 Waterloo Corner Road the 'death house' and Skewes, who had once leant against the side of his neighbour's house, rubbing his massive belly and scratching his whiskers and asking Bunting, 'Do youse wanna hand?', makes hurried plans to move out.

Later, he will say this is the part that haunts him: that he helped dig a hole that would be filled with human beings, two human beings who were just thrown into the earth like garbage. He is obsessed by the fact that he has been living next door to corpses, people he had known, who once lived and breathed and who have lain in there through summers and winters, invisible from the world, covered in dirt and spider webs and cement while their mouths became cavities for the worms to play in and their flesh rotted away. Skewes had lived rough on the streets but nothing compares with this, nothing he has seen or heard compares with the depravity of this. And so he tells the story over and over again, like a mantra, as if by repeating it he can exorcise the demons. 'The police told me they'd found body parts in the hole. I couldn't believe it. The first time was bad enough, and then they come back a few days later with a front-end loader and did another dig and found another body. I had no idea. I just got the shock of me life.'

Skewes leaves the street before they raze 203 Waterloo Corner Road, the bland, housing trust home that competes for sunshine along with the other bland housing trust homes in the street. Leaves before they fill the backyard graves with cement and level the house as if it never existed, to prevent it becoming a macabre tourist attraction, people tramping up to the front door like grim tour guides: 'This is where two bodies were buried and no one knew'.

There will be speculation as to why, when Bunting had so many chances to move the bodies from their suburban graveyard, he chose to keep them there. But it was his obsession. His own private hiding place, where he could keep his junk. The place where no one rummaged. Part of his bizarre desire to collect things; his trophies, his grand mosaic. And part of his personal philosophy: keep your friends close; keep your enemies closer.

Elizabeth asks Jamie why John risked keeping the other corpses in the barrels, but he can't answer her. And she suddenly understands, now, why he wanted to buy that boat. Realises if she hadn't kicked up about it, he would have bought the boat then. Would have filled the barrels up with the concrete he stored in the bank, taken them out to sea and dropped them. They would have fallen heavy as a ball and chain; instead, they sat out at Hoyleton before being moved to the bank, when he started to stockpile cement.

If she hadn't kicked up, those stinking barrels would have been long gone, sitting on the bottom of St Vincents Gulf with sharks cruising around them. Sitting on the bottom of the seabed, and no one would ever have known. Later in court a conversation between Bunting and Wagner, recorded on intercept a month before the arrests, is played.

'I thought you'd like it, a nice fishing trip', Bunting says.

'It's not that far from the water where we are.'

'Lot of deep water . . . We could get ourselves some big fishes . . . We might catch a big shark.'

Elizabeth watches the television footage of police carting away the bodies from 203 Waterloo Corner Road. Two bodies, 14 garbage bags: the shock hits her, hard. 'I nearly died. I still don't know whether Suzanne died of natural causes or whether John just said that to me because I would have freaked if he told me he'd murdered a woman.'

Skewes's trust in his former neighbour has now turned to scepticism and fear that he might have been next. 'I was on the hit list, I'm sure of that', he repeats. It is said with a hint of bewilderment and a dollop of pride. This case has attracted world-wide attention and he is part of it, the biggest thing that has ever happened to him in his dreary, tough life. The attention puffs him up – having lived next door to a crime scene and knowing the people involved. He is darn sure, he says, that he was next to go. Robert Skewes hasn't enjoyed a lucky life, but he reckons he scored the ace card this time. 'I've had a lucky escape. A lucky escape.'

38

As the story breaks, national and international journalists board flights to South Australia. They know little at first, except that something is going on down there, and that it involves deaths by foul play. But beyond that, when they are asked what the story is, they say they have few details: they are heading to a small country town outside Adelaide. A 'blink and you'd miss it' sort of place called Snowtown. It won't take long for the whole world to know what happened here.

Radio and television break the story ahead of the *Adelaide Advertiser*, which misses the deadline and runs it the next day under the banner, 'The Snowtown Killings: 6 Barrels, 8 Bodies, Bank Vault's Evil Secret'. The following day's *Sunday Mail* asks 'How Many More?' and details what was found inside the vault. Superintendent Edmonds outlines the police theory: '. . . there was a chain of events involving people which brought us to Snowtown', he says. 'We cannot rule out that other arrests may be possible. This investigation could take us months . . .' By now, papers are comparing the bodies in the barrels with the depraved activities of British couple Fred and Rosemary West, the House of Horrors. By Monday 24 May 1999, the *Advertiser* is reporting new developments. 'Two more bodies uncovered as toll rises to 10. Grim find under number 203.' An editorial in the *Advertiser* is indicative of the interest the case is attracting. The headline in one of the Sunday interstate newspapers sums it up: 'Bodies bring infamy to sleepy Snowtown'. 'Very much more of the same can be expected', the editorial continues, 'and nothing can be done about the subject, intrinsically lurid as it is. What can be done is to commiserate with the residents of this pastoral community for having drawn this very short straw. It could have happened in any of the hundreds of other Australian post codes . . . they, too, are for the time being victims, the classic innocent bystanders.'

In comparison to overseas outlets, the Australian media is circumspect in their reporting of the case. 'Death on the Dole', announces the *Sydney Morning Herald*. But internationally, imagination runs riot. 'The Case of the Casked Cadavers in the Crypt', screams one American tabloid. 'Pandora's Vault', trumpets another. In an American newspaper, Adelaide is called a 'Shrine in Australia's Gruesome Crime Capital'. In the breathless story that follows, readers are assured that the 'acid vat killings were not the first to haunt the area'. Already, truth is a casualty.

SAS 7 *Today Tonight* producer and reporter Graham Archer stands somewhat remote from the South Australian press pack of newspaper reporters, radio and television journalists, a lone figure snapping at government, police and judicial heels. It is a position with which he is comfortable: distance, he reasons, lessens the chance of clear vision being fudged.

Archer recalls the reaction when the news first broke. 'Initially it was shock and disbelief. For some, there was a sense of déjà vu, a feeling of "not again". From the media and possibly the public's point of view, one of the instinctive reactions in this state is whether such events could provide links to other similar unsolved crimes where people have disappeared or been weirdly murdered. The immediate thought, which is never far below the surface, is of course for the Beaumont children and for Joanne Radcliffe and Kirsty Gordon. A shiver runs through you when you ponder if the perpetrators could still be at work and could this finally bring those terrible tragedies to a close? It's almost as if two generations of South Australians are frozen in time, waiting for answers.

'The other nightmare cases are the Family killings. It is a natural response to hold your breath and wonder for a moment if we are finally about to get the answer to an aching mystery which has haunted this state for decades.'

Reality kicked in fast. 'The need to cover the events quickly took over,' Archer continues, 'and there was a media frenzy to learn more. Who were the victims; who could do such a thing; was it as truly evil and bizarre as the first reports suggested; and most challenging, could there be other victims? Just how big is this thing? The rush to discover more was tempered somewhat by the fact that the police had made arrests prior to the news being released, but this posed another series of challenges; to discover who these people were, what were their backgrounds and their possible motives. The chase was then on for relatives, friends, neighbours, anyone who might have had any contact with the accused or their victims. It was a 24-hour-a-day scramble, everyone looking over their shoulders to check what their rivals had unearthed and what might still be left to discover.

'Amongst the people we found were those who had unwittingly moved into John Bunting's home in the northern suburb of Salisbury. This was the couple's first home and, shortly after moving in, they were greeted by police wanting to dig up the yard in search of bodies. We also spoke to Skewes, who told us he had just discovered he was on the extensive hit list, to be done away with. By this time the police were excavating the backyard for bodies, while cameras hung over the fences trying to get images of what they were doing. It was this close scrutiny from the media and the contact with the relatives and witnesses that caused Superintendent Paul Schramm to make the comment that "we will have to start to call the press as witnesses". Needless to say, despite the $20 million frolic that the Department of Public Prosecutions indulged themselves in during the prosecution of the case, no journalists were called. We conducted a long interview with Gail Sinclair, too, but for legal reasons were forced to hold it for several years.'

The discovery of the bodies spells the end of siesta for the Snowtown residents who, from that time on, will feel under siege. Hundreds of national and overseas media descend on the town like locusts, falling out of the sky in flashy helicopters, staking their places with microphones and satellite dishes in the main street and positioning themselves in the one pub opposite the bank. Over the coming months they are followed relentlessly by more police, forensic experts, lawyers, criminologists and ghouls who get down on their knees and sniff the air vents outside the bank.

Barry Drew immigrated to Australia in 1968 and eventually moved to Snowtown for its cheap housing and the hope of early retirement. He opened the second-hand shop and set it up as something of a draw-card for the few tourists who wander into the town, mostly in caravans and four-wheel-drives.

Drew watches the passing media parade from his vantage point next to the bank. It is impossible to miss them: if they aren't asking to use his generator to fire their recording equipment, they are doing pieces to camera outside his shop, staring down the lenses with the intensity of generals organising the deployment of troops. They come from all over and they all want the same thing: a look inside the vault. It doesn't bother him, helping them out. At least it livens the place up. 'Snowtown goes to sleep at 10 o'clock at night and the most exciting thing that happens is the changeover of the nursing staff, or when the trains derail', he laments. Drew repeats the same things over and over, but at least, as they say in the game, he is good talent. And he is willing to talk, unlike a lot of the locals who avoid the press at all costs. He becomes something of a celebrity, and that gets up a lot of people's noses. Here he goes again, talking to the media.

Drew lights his umpteenth cigarette. 'Look, I don't think that what happened is right. But it did happen, and it happened here. Before the bodies were found, we were lucky to have 10,000 tourists bother to drive off the highway and come through. Afterwards, I stopped counting at 80,000 people in 1999.'

Many locals don't think much of Drew. They regard him as a blow-in, with no ancestors buried in the local cemetery. 'You've got to be able to prove your family goes back 200 years in this area', he scoffs, 'which is funny really, considering the town only started 150 years ago.' He has no time for the 'churchy do-gooders' who organise feel-good festivals and services after the cops discover the bodies. He thinks they're a waste of time. 'What bloody good is a festival? It won't change what happened.'

Local kindergarten teacher and member of the Snowtown Action Group, Cindy Growden, is vocal in flying the flag for the town after the discoveries. She organises a church service for the victims, demands the bank be razed to the ground and leads the charge against the selling of crass souvenirs. To lift residents' spirits, Cindy garners community support for a Snowtown Festival – a curious affair where hay is wrapped in white plastic to resemble snow.

Sleeting rain falls on the roof of the Snowtown church on 7 June 1999 as residents hold their service for the victims and accused. The service is open to all denominations, yet less than 60 people attend. Eight candles, representing each victim found in the vault, are lit as the small congregation prays for the souls of the dead and for those on remand for the murders. At Snowtown's tiny school, the children are gathered together and told that an evil had been visited upon the town. Counselling is made available to them and to any other residents who are finding it hard to cope. There is a common thread running through the messages: this is not the fault of the townspeople; they have done nothing wrong. They are not from here. They are not one of us.

They take heart in that.

Soon after the discoveries, bad-taste jokes start circulating at dinner parties and in pubs in the same way that dingo jokes proliferated after Azaria Chamberlain disappeared. Why is it difficult to get a bank loan in Snowtown? Because it costs an arm and a leg. Why is service so slow at the Snowtown bank? Because they've only got skeleton staff. On the Internet, a wag ventures: 'Police believe that the Snowtown bank vault killings may only be the tip of a murderous iceberg. Police today admitted that they were investigating the possibility that other Australian banks may have dead bodies in their vaults. Police first became suspicious when bank tellers started to go missing a few years ago . . .'

Drew has a litany of horror stories about the 'ghouls' who made the pilgrimage to Snowtown when the story broke. 'The media was here hunting for stories and then the wackos arrived, hunting for souvenirs. Here were these well-dressed people down on their hands and knees in the middle of the pedestrian path sniffing the air vents outside the bank. They would pose outside it, getting their friends and partners to take pictures of them to send home to Mum and Dad. And they would lift their kids up to the windows and get them to peer in, giving them a running commentary on what had happened inside.' He rubs the grey sideburns that hug the edge of his face and rummages in his packet for another smoke. 'I thought the souvenir hunters were even more repugnant than the air sniffers. They used to knock off pot plants from around the bank, take bits of soil, anything they could get their hands on to take back as proof that they'd been to Snowtown.'

Shirlee Randylle buys the infamous bank for an undisclosed sum months after the corpses are discovered. The eccentric 65-year-old recluse lives next door in the adjoining property, and is surprised that a garage sale she holds at the site attracts few genuine customers. 'Most people came out of the vault a bit disappointed, saying they thought it would be different, more eerie', she says. An Internet auction garners some interest, including sale of the double solid steel doors to the vault. 'I'm not in this for profit. But I do have to live and the more funds I can generate to help make this a restful and peaceful place, the better. I want to put a skylight in the room where the barrels were, perhaps turn it into a garden courtyard – a place where the families of the victims can come and feel at peace.'

Drew's shop groans with furniture, bric-a-brac and seventies kitsch: china dogs named Alf, brown-robed monks that double as money boxes and plastic faces saying 'Smile'. But he admits they didn't exactly walk out the door before the bodies were discovered; Snowtown was hardly a tourist's dream holiday destination. The consummate businessman, he sees a golden opportunity to cash in on the discoveries by selling souvenirs. It is a decision that will divide the town as surely as the railway track that winds through its centre. The souvenirs are high tack: pictures of skeletons hanging out of barrels, captioned, 'I've been to Snowtown and Survived'; barrels with the inscription, 'Snowtown, SA – You'll have a barrel of fun'; and the Snowtown Snow Shaker – plastic body parts floating around a hillside scene, the perfect gift for someone who has everything. And it is high risk. The shocking, gruesome deaths of eight people whose bodies have been dismembered and rammed into barrels will have a ripple effect on the victims' families and on a community already sensitive to the publicity.

If Drew is surprised at the vitriolic backlash he receives from some quarters over his decision to stock the souvenirs, it doesn't stop him. 'I received abusive phone calls and letters from victims' families and anti-homicide groups, but it didn't faze me. It was simply a case of supply and demand. Tourists were constantly asking for mementos. This could not be pushed under the carpet.'

The Victims of Crime Support Group in Adelaide is as appalled as some Snowtown residents. The souvenirs, they say, are insensitive and outrageous, and seek only to make a profit out of pain and suffering.

Despite the *Adelaide Advertiser*'s front-page headline, 'Selling of Slaughter', Drew continues to stand in his shop offering a cheery 'good morning' to the tourists who come through, giving a run-down of what has happened in the bank next door. Spruiking about how these fellows from out of town dumped the barrels in there. 'No one knew what was going on, no one guessed and let's keep this in perspective, they weren't locals who were murdered, they weren't locals who killed them and frankly there isn't a whole lot of sympathy around here for either the victims or the killers. And the fridge magnets are $2.50 sir, a bit of a laugh although of course – don't get me wrong – there isn't anything very funny in what has happened but it has happened now and people are up in arms about these souvenirs, they could become a collector's item, madam.' The trains roar past and he keeps talking over the din and wrapping the magnets and saying, 'Thank you, sir, have a nice day'. The next tourists come in and he lights another cigarette and says a cheery good morning and no, he doesn't think it is a good thing to have happened but it has and let's keep this in perspective.

Some locals tut-tut as they walk past his shop, shaking their heads in disapproval.

They wouldn't be caught dead going in there to buy one of those magnets. They get their visitors from out of town to buy one for them instead.

39

Desperate to establish just what they are dealing with, South Australian police turn to their international counterparts at the FBI and Scotland Yard to help them piece together the psyches of the Snowtown killers.

Forensic psychiatrist Dr Park Dietz, who works with the FBI and the New York State Police Forensic Sciences Unit, is gracious in imparting his knowledge. He has looked closely at the Jeffrey Dahmer case, the techniques Dahmer used in disposing of his victims' bodies; and he now turns his attention to the men who worked together in a predatory web to kill their own. His professional opinion – that the killers' motives were financial and not sexual – will go against the thinking of the DPP and is based on the knowledge that there were more than three people involved. 'It's very unusual. When we see somebody putting bodies in vats of acid, you naturally think "weirdo individual" and how unlikely it is for two weirdos to get together and unthinkable for three to get together.' The bigger the number of killers, the bigger the risk of one leaving the group and breaking down. There had to be something to keep them there, a lure. 'You don't tend to think of them as serial killers but organised crime figures. They are doing it for profit, it's business and that of course is the suspected motive here.' Dietz is astonished that so many people could keep the secret for so long. 'The same characteristics that cause people to commit crimes cause them to lack judgment in other things as well. They tend to shoot off their mouth and get caught.' The means by which the bodies were disposed of is also highly unusual. 'That's something that Dahmer did – he had a very elaborate system in which he would remove the flesh from bones and put the flesh in a vat of acid and then he would ladle the acid with the dissolved soft tissue into the toilet. The bones he would either preserve, baking them and painting them or else dispose of them in large trash bags and have them hauled off.'

For serial killers, the first murder is the one that opens Pandora's box and it is this kill that sets them apart from normal people. Guilt and feelings of self-disgust can eat at them, but the gnawing has started, the excitement, the sense of power it gives, and they can't help themselves: they have to do it again.

Bunting started in 1992, with the murder of Clinton Trezise. Less than four years later, Ray Davies; and now the cooling off period becomes shorter and shorter. Suzanne Allen about 10 months later, near the end of 1996. Michael Gardiner 10 months after her. Barry Lane one month later. Thomas Trevilyan one month after him. And then 1998, when they really hit their straps. Gavin Porter five months after Trevilyan. Youde four months after him. Brooks one month. O'Dwyer one month. Haydon one month. And Johnson, the last victim, six months later.

Dietz is unequivocal: they would have kept killing if the cops hadn't got in their way. No doubt about that.

The idea for a new colony of free men untainted by a convict past was conceived in a dank jail cell at London's Newgate prison in the early 1830s by Edward Gibbon Wakefield. Wakefield, though blessed with a substantial inheritance from his late wife, abducted 15-year-old heiress Ellen Turner from her school in 1826 and fled with her to Calais after their marriage. Enraged, her furious family forced Ellen's return to England where the marriage was annulled and Wakefield, convicted of a statutory misdemeanour in 1827, was sentenced to three years jail. There, with precious else to do with his time, he began to record ideas that later spawned the colonisation of South Australia with free settlers and parcels of land. Convicts were decidedly unwelcome: the new colony worked on Basil Fawlty's principle of 'No riffraff here'.

No convicts, no Irish ancestry; instead, a society whose

architecture and attitudes are still overwhelmingly British. Established in 1837, Adelaide was planned with military precision using the engineering skills of Colonel William Light, whose vision encompassed spacious gardens and parklands, wide streets and city squares. The city would lie between the mountain and the sea, and through it would snake the River Torrens.

Adelaide does not move to the same beat as Sydney, with its brassy, carefree lifestyle, nor does it resonate with the classy elegance of Melbourne. Conservative, quiet and cultured, Adelaide has built a reputation as a city which hosts an internationally renowned Festival of Arts and which is outwardly tolerant of its large gay community.

But the city's benign facade did not fool author Salman Rushdie when he visited in the 1980s. In what would become a trademark, over-used quote, he observed: 'Adelaide is a perfect setting for a Stephen King novel or horror film . . . Sleepy, conservative towns are where those things happen'. By the time Rushdie had visited the city, its reputation for ugly crime and bizarre abductions was already well known. The city that had tried so hard to keep up its conservative appearance had failed. Underneath the make-up, there are hideous scars.

Their small, smiling faces stare out from the yellowing pages of newspapers. The Beaumont children – Jane, 9, Anna, 7, and Grant, 4 – who disappeared without trace from a beach at suburban Glenelg on Australia Day, 1966. Despite a massive police search and heartbreaking appeals to the public from their parents, they were never seen again. Had they been dumped in St Vincents Gulf? Abducted by a cult? Taken by Adelaide's so called 'Family'? They would come to symbolise the end of Australia's innocence in the buoyancy of the postwar years, their disappearance a mystery that would rivet the nation in the same way the disappearance of Azaria Chamberlain did 14 years later. Short of a deathbed confession, police now believe there is little hope of ever solving the case.

While the rest of the world fixated on the extraordinary events that were to characterise the 1970s and 1980s – the end of the Vietnam War, the peace movement, the Chernobyl nuclear disaster, AIDS – South Australians were forced, time and again, to confront horror on their own doorstep.

In September 1971, the quiet sanctuary of Hope Forest, near Adelaide, was rocked by the shooting murders of 10 people – eight children and two women – who were all related to the gunman, Clifford Bartholomew. Bartholomew was sentenced to death but served only eight years in prison. The following year, gay Adelaide University law lecturer Dr George Duncan drowned after being thrown into the Torrens River. Eventually, two detectives from Adelaide's vice squad were charged with and acquitted of his manslaughter.

In 1973, four-year-old Kirsty Gordon and her friend Joanne Radcliffe, 11, disappeared on the way to the rest rooms at a football match at Adelaide Oval. Thousands of people attended the game, but no one noticed the children, who were never seen again. The spectre of the Beaumont children's abduction again raised its head; was the same person responsible for the Gordon and Radcliffe disappearances?

In 1978, a man stumbled upon the skeletal remains of a young woman in dense scrubland at Truro, 80 kilometres north of Adelaide, close to the internationally renowned wine-growing region of the Barossa Valley. Mobilising their resources, police soon discovered corpses in a garbage dump in a northern suburb and at Murray Bridge. In all, the remains of seven women aged between 15 and 26, who had gone missing between Christmas 1976 and February 1977, were uncovered in what was christened the Mass Murders of Truro. Hysteria gripped the city as body after body was found.

Eventually Jamie Miller, who had worked hand-in-glove with his criminal partner and lover, Christopher Worrell, led police to the bodies. Worrell, a handsome, charming bisexual, had been killed in a car accident just two days after the last victim was found and it was left to Miller to carry the can. In March 1980, he was convicted for his part in six of the seven murders and sentenced to life imprisonment without parole.

In June 1979, a week after he suddenly, inexplicably disappeared, the mutilated body of 17-year-old Alan Barnes was found on the banks of a reservoir north of Adelaide. Barnes had suffered an excruciating death and an autopsy showed that the cause was blood loss from massive anal injuries while he was still alive. It was to be the start of a horrific murder spree that would continue between 1979 and 1983. Most of the five victims endured unspeakable savagery before they died.

Accountant Bevan Von Einem, a pale-faced, sexual sadist, who favoured cardigans and lived with his mother, was committed for trial by Magistrate David Gurry, who would later preside over the Snowtown committal hearings. In 1984, Von Einem was convicted for the rape and murder of 15-year-old Rob Kelvin and sentenced to life imprisonment at Yatala Prison. Worldwide, the five shocking murders for which Von Einem was implicated were dubbed the Family murders, an alleged homosexual paedophile conspiracy involving high-profile establishment figures in Adelaide's elite: lawyers, judges, doctors, politicians. Rumours persist that Von Einem did not work alone, that he took the rap to cover for others. Later, an associate of Von Einem's will also come forward to claim he had admitted killing the Beaumont children, as well as Gordon and Radcliffe, claims that have not been proved. As the details of the perverse Family abductions, drugging, imprisonment, sexual assault, torture and murder came to light, South Australia would be forever tarnished in the public psyche as a state of depravity. And Adelaide, once the 'City of Churches' would become known as the 'City of Corpses'.

Von Einem's committal will come back to haunt Magistrate Gurry. In 1990, attempts were made to try Von Einem for the savage murders of two other Adelaide men in 1979 and 1982. The supreme court ruled that vital evidence was inadmissible from the original trial and the new challenges collapsed. Gurry had imposed suppressions at Von Einem's committal, but lifted them a week later on appeal, allowing room for his defence to argue, six years later, that he could not receive a fair trial. The memory will claw at Gurry when he makes the suppression orders in the Snowtown case. He is determined that history will not repeat itself.

Melbourne writer Mark Ellis arrived in Adelaide as an eight-year-old British migrant with his family in 1971, and has since lived and worked extensively overseas. But, he writes, no city has terrified him more than the dark, empty suburban streets of Adelaide at night, so vivid are his macabre childhood memories of snatched children, buried bodies and dis-embowelled boys. Ellis returns to Adelaide when he can, but, he ponders, 'On the dark and empty streets, surrounded by silence and brush fences, I often wonder: would anyone come running from behind the twitching net curtain if they heard you scream?'

In September 2001, tough-talking, Magistrate Peter Liddy, who had served longer on the bench in Adelaide than any of his colleagues, was sentenced to 25 years jail for the sexual abuse of junior lifesavers aged from seven to 13. Some of the incidents occurred in the court cells and included six counts of inter-course with a person under 12 and three of indecent assault. All but one offence occurred in the mid 1980s while Liddy was a magistrate. Reporters, green to their gills, could not hide their shock. 'The abuse is sickening, but the hypocrisy is worse', one commented. 'Some days, you just wonder where it ends in this city.' The inevitable questions rear their ugly heads: Did Liddy operate alone? Did other influential people in the city know of his depraved activities? Is he part of the Family network of wealthy, secretive deviants? Within hours of Liddy being sentenced, the jokes started doing the rounds. Q. How do you address a paedophile who wears a wig? A. Your Honour.

★ ★ ★

South Australian legal eagles, used to prosecuting and defending the macabre cases that reach court in Adelaide, grimly joke that a police Crime Scene ribbon should be strung right around the city. Writer Paul Kidd goes further. 'In the annals of Australia's most horrific crimes', he writes, 'laid-back Adelaide's sinister past (and present) makes other cities look like Camelot.'

Not all criminologists agree. Some argue that South Australia has been unfairly branded as having a higher rate of deviant murders than other states and that the homicide rate, based on figures in the past decade, is below the national average. Professor Paul Wilson, who has written 25 books on crime and criminology, agrees that statistically there is little difference in the amount of crime committed in South Australia per head of capita than any other state. What is different, he says, is the deviant nature of the crimes committed.

'South Australia has a social atmosphere that is distinctly its own. In this, it is very like Christchurch in New Zealand, which is also a Wakefield-designed city, flat and ordered, and which also has a higher percentage of deviant, bizarre crime. There is a sense of correctness, politeness, conformity in both places, a social hierarchy in that the pioneering families who go back generations hold the prestige and those who don't aren't in the same league. The social atmosphere of a city or state contributes to the crime rate. Where people hold onto their feelings, are repressed and uptight, you might expect that some will develop deviant behaviours that will explode in violence. There is a sense of isolation in South Australia, and that can also help to give rise to anti-social or psychopathic behaviour. South Australians will undoubtedly deny this, but the unlocking of the Snowtown secrets, the psyche of the offenders, will also reveal a great deal about the psyche of the state.'

It will take years for the details of those secrets to be unveiled.

40

The Victim Support Service originated in Adelaide in October 1979 when the distressed parents of the Truro and Family murder victims met with a retired police commissioner to discuss their grief and the lack of support services for victims of crime. From that meeting the support service was born, offering counselling, companionship, support and information.

The people who attend Victim Support Service sessions are the walking wounded, an eclectic group from all backgrounds, struggling to come to terms with their loss through shared communication. They come to the group to seek comfort, to share stories, to offer solace and advice to each other, to say – unlike everyone else with their trite throwaway lines – 'I understand what you're going through', and mean it.

There is ongoing confusion and controversy over many aspects of the reporting and discussion of the Snowtown murders. For years, there has been debate in police, judicial, media and support circles as to what name these crimes should be given, what they should be called. And how best to support the families and friends of the victims. Staff at the Victim Support Service try not to refer to the 'bodies in the barrels' crimes by labelling them as 'Snowtown'. They reason that other places were involved and they want to avoid an unfortunate repeat of what Truro residents had to suffer.

In March 2001, this letter from David Kerr appears in the group newsletter, *Victim's Voice*. '. . . For 19 months, [South Australian] newspapers generally used the term "Missing Persons Killings" to describe this case. As the Committal hearing approached and the newsworthiness of the tragedy increased, a deliberate marketing shift was made such that from the start of July 2000, the event was repackaged to become the "Bodies in the Barrels" case . . . For decades to come, the perception of these murders will be defined by the way the media report this event now . . . Victim Support Service urges a return to ethical, victim-sensitive reporting that is considerate of the needs of family and friends.'

For the media, it ends up being a two-sided coin. Heads they win, tails they lose. No murder, except for that of David Johnson, actually took place at Snowtown, but it is there that the story broke, there that the bodies were found, and hence the name 'Snowtown' has come to be linked in the public's mind with the serial killings. Given South Australia's sinister history, labelling the crimes as simply 'the serial killings' creates confusion. Which serial killings? Truro? The Family? Or 'Snowtown'? Do editors, needing short headlines to engage the readers' attention and to clarify what the copy is about, deliberately upset the sensibilities of their readers? When the Missing Persons are identified as murder victims, is it still appropriate to call the case the 'Missing Persons murders'? And when further charges are added, are they then to call the case 'the Lower Light/ Snowtown/Salibury North/Kersbrook Missing Persons murders'?

Heads they win, tails they lose.

Paul Schramm wants to understand what they are going through. He wants to see how the victims' families are coping with sudden loss and senseless violence, to take a measure of their pain back to the office, a mental snapshot of the individuals, a reminder that these people are victims, too. The room is crowded tonight at this regular meeting, and he does a quick head count: about 40 people; 40 more than there should be, the air oppressive with their grief. He knows quite a few of these people by name now, having dealt with them when they first contacted the police, and he notices some have aged way before their time, sorrow indelibly etched on their faces. At times like this, Schramm wonders just what makes human beings tick, but hard experience has taught him that even if the people locked up for the crimes could witness the damage they have wrought, a lot of them still wouldn't care.

Each year in South Australia, up to 5000 people are reported missing. Of these, 99.8 percent are located. Following the discoveries at Snowtown, the number of Missing Persons reported and collated through the National Missing Persons Unit in Canberra rises dramatically, with concerned people ringing in to add their relatives' names to the list. Telephonists who answer the calls are often bemused or saddened. One woman calls to report her son missing, and when asked how long it has been since she last saw him, she replies, 'Five years'. The boy would have been 11 when he disappeared; no, she says, she hadn't thought about reporting him earlier. Another rings to check whether her husband has been identified as one of the Snowtown victims; she is disappointed, she says, that she hasn't yet seen his name released.

For the police, the fact that four of the victims have not been reported missing by either their family or friends makes identification more difficult, an issue Schramm refers to as an 'inhibiting factor'. But police have statistics which help them: 80 per cent of homicide victims are known to their killers, which narrows the field.

As Schramm juggles the responsibilities of feeding the media on a need-to-know basis about the identities of the victims without prejudicing the on-going investigation, fate conspires to work against him in an Adelaide courtroom. In late May 1999, sentencing submissions for a case totally unrelated to the serial killings are heard in the Magistrate's Court. Michelle Kovarskis – the sister of David Johnson's girlfriend, Linda – is convicted by a judge of social security fraud and her lawyer, Amanda Carter, advises the judge of the pressure under which the Kovarskis family is living. Without naming victim David Johnson, Carter says: 'Apparently the situation was that he was

lured to Snowtown to purchase a computer and has been
missing ever since'. Police have been reluctant to name
Johnson, but they now have no choice.

41

Schramm's working knowledge of the media has given him an insight into how they operate; what he calls the 'three Cs': co-operation, competitiveness, controversy. Co-operation is the first step, and is short-lived. Reporters who are on the ground when the story breaks have all the material they need, but within 48 hours, competitiveness kicks in. Media outlets from all over the country and overseas send in their teams, and the need to find a new angle and fresh material becomes paramount. That, in turn, leads to the final stage: controversy. With no fresh leads to follow for their stories that have now been picked over like vultures, reporters start searching for something – anything – that will spark renewed interest.

Within the first seven days after the Snowtown discoveries, the major crime unit takes more than 500 calls from national and overseas media outlets, all pushing for a new lead, all wanting an up-to-the-minute breakdown of events.

Schramm feels that press conferences are the best way to feed information to reporters; they ensure that what is said cannot be misinterpreted and that information is evenly distributed. He nods to the journalists he knows and sits down in front of the microphone. After delivering his statement he faces a barrage of questions, which, as usual, come thick and fast. Have they identified the victims yet? Are the victims the same people who were the subject of the year-long Missing Persons investigation? Are police expecting to find more bodies?

And then, predicably, the questions turn. Why did the investigation take so long to lead to the bodies? Is it true that the last victim was killed while the accused were under surveillance? Were enough police resources thrown into it early in the piece? For Schramm, this is the worst phase: busy enough with the on-going investigation, the last thing he needs is for his officers to have their attention diverted to putting out other fires.

Some of the reporters use sheer rat cunning, lying to Task-force Chart investigators that they have been told by Schramm that his team can speak to them. This happens often, and Schramm's officers always get the same reply from him: 'Bullshit! Absolute bullshit!' Nobody – nobody – talks to the media but Schramm or those he has anointed.

And Schramm has an ace up his sleeve when dealing with the press. At the outset, he contacts the head of the English investigation into the macabre 'House of Horrors' murders. Schramm takes the advice of the superintendent, heeding his words each time he steps in front of the media scrum. Tread carefully. Avoid sensationalism. Give them only what they need to know. Today's word out of place becomes tomorrow's screaming headline.

The House of Horrors case, in which 10 people were brutally murdered and their bodies hidden under a house, concluded in 1996 when the jury found Rose and Fred West guilty. It dominated headlines around the world and the super-intendent understood only too well the pressures on police to satisfy the media without prejudicing a future trial. There are chilling similarities between the Snowtown murders and the House of Horrors case. Both involve treachery and betrayal, torture, de-fleshing and death, and the addictive, sadistic power of murder. As with the Snowtown investigation, some of West's victims were not reported missing and the choice of victims was also close to home.

The public cannot get enough of the gruesome details, and the reporters do their best to feed them.

Within weeks, the sheer size of the investigation warrants a movement of the team from police headquarters at Angas Street to their barracks at Thebarton on the northern outskirts of the city. The building needs renovating to house the large number of detectives, crime analysts and back-up teams now involved in the case and to accommodate the high-tech computer systems and the increasing pile of evidence that is supervised under tight security. Computers are proving helpful. It is a far cry from the old days when the evidence of suspects and witnesses was taken down long-hand, inviting allegations of police verballing and the loss of crucial material that was required for presentation at trial. But still, hard copies of everything need to be stored. The days of using pen and paper are a long way from obsolete.

The amount of detail the computer is required to handle is staggering, and at the peak of the operation more than 60 police and support staff work on it, almost 40 officers at any given time. In this, it is not dissimilar to the Milat backpacker murder investigation, when within three months, the holding of information increased from 10,000 pieces to more than 1.5 million. An unprecedented six prosecutors are assigned by the Director of Public Prosecutions (DPP) and by March 2000, the South Australian government is forced to provide another $1.3 million towards funding for Taskforce Chart.

A sophisticated bar code system, using software imported from Germany, is used to keep track of all the evidence. Every item, regardless of how insignificant it may seem, is issued with its own code that is later matched with the computer data. From that, investigators can establish all essential details: who found what and where, who has checked it and where it is now being held.

A computer program is specifically designed for the Chart investigation. By the time the case is finished, the system will need to prove capable of handling 3500 exhibits and more than 730 witness statements. Chart also has another police tool, a relatively new technique borrowed from colleagues in Queensland who have successfully trialled it. The crime scene is recorded on video and transposed onto computer. A 360-degree view is recorded, allowing the observer to visually 'walk through' the area. With the click of a mouse, all entrance and exit points are shown and any other peculiarities at the scene. The data needed by the Chart team is now, literally, accessible at their fingertips.

Schramm's second-in-charge is 56-year-old Detective Senior-Sergeant Mick Standen, a 40-year veteran of the force who joined as a lad of 16. Modest, with a self-deprecating sense of humour, Standen is highly respected among his officers, not least for the way he gets out of bed in the dark every morning to allow himself time to drop off food to charities before he signs on for a day's work.

Computers may make life easier for investigators, but they cannot work without human input. For every major crime, officers are required to fill out a 300-question Violent Crime Linkage Assessment System form that details all the information regarding the scene, suspects and victims. It is a tedious and time-consuming job, but one which can produce results. When the information from a crime is fed into computers, matched with data held at the Australian Bureau of Criminal Intelligence in Canberra, and sorted through by analysts trained specifically for the task, links are often found between that crime and similar cases in other states. At the height of Chart, six analysts worked full-time collating the mountains of evidence, using their expertise to pinpoint areas that needed further investigation. One analyst was Chief Inspector Bronwyn Killmier, Australia's answer to the FBI profiler Clarice Starling in the movie, *Silence of the Lambs*. Killmier is the only Australian profiler trained by the FBI, and she has the added experience of having spent three years at the helm of the South Australian Missing Persons Unit. All up, it is a strong team, but they will need it. The tighter they keep it now, the better the chances for a successful prosecution at trial.

In the last, rare interview given before the police are silenced from speaking to the media, police psychologist Sergeant Ray Dowd describes to the *Bulletin* the pressures police are under during a long investigation. 'We're in an organisation that values strength and control and deals with everybody else's crises', he says. 'You see a whole range of very frightening and bizarre things happen and those things can start to filter through into your own personal life.'

Dowd, now in his 50s, still looks like a young John Farnham. His role is an essential part of policing; if officers feel they are not coping, he is in the front line of defence. He joined the force in 1975, armed with youthful ideals and a psychology degree, starting out in the graveyard shift, monitoring and tagging the bodies that came into the then decrepit old morgue, since closed down. Dowd and the team called themselves the 'Bod Squad'. He saw things he wished he hadn't, but it afforded him an insight into what other coppers go through.

By the early 1990s, Dowd had transferred to internal counselling, where his role was to be on hand to help both serving and retired officers and their families. The signs of someone not coping can be subtle – blowing their stack at the slightest provocation, dwelling on events of the day long after they get home at night, having nightmares from which they wake in a cold sweat.

Check the composition of the team, Schramm instructs Dowd and chief psychologist and civilian Milton Kelly. Make sure they are all up to it – detectives, analysts, even the secretaries who prepare the background reports. It's vital that they can cope. Satisfied with the team, during the critical phase of the early investigation Schramm organises a police barbecue, ostensibly a low-key affair where the officers share a steak and chat. Dowd moves amongst the crowd, making quiet observations.

'Everyone is going to be changed by the experience of these serial murders,' he later recounts to me. 'The trick is to prepare them to have strong defences but not so strong that it jeopardises their health or their personal life. Part of the police psyche is to be in control and resolute because, in a lot of situations they go to, people are out of control. It is a physically and emotionally confronting job in which they are exposed to disconcerting, confusing and often bleak situations. Snowtown was certainly one of those cases. No one could come away unchanged.'

Milton and Dowd's job is to get to them before they lose it, before it is too late.

42

In normal circumstances, a relative undertakes identification of a corpse; when this is not possible, identification has to be proved by scientific means. The pathologist's work is to ascertain cause of death, whether by natural causes, accident, suicide or murder. DNA samples, which provide the human blueprint for profiling, are matched against samples from living relatives and tissue checked for unnatural substances such as alcohol or poison. Where a body has been dismembered, comparative samples are taken to match marks on the bone with any weapons – knives, saws, axe – that may have been used. The Coroner will not release a body for burial until he is satisfied that identification is complete and police have enough evidence if the case is to go to trial. Pathologists also have the gruelling task of finding which part belongs to which body: in some cases, it is necessary for them to hold a separate autopsy for each limb or skull. When their work is complete, the corpse is then passed to the team member next in line.

Post-mortems involve examinations by different professionals in their field, and each case is meticulously studied by a small group; first the pathologist, then an assistant, a police photographer and exhibits officer. When necessary, the deceased are x-rayed to find projectiles – foreign material in the body – which is photographed before the clothing is removed. An external examination is followed by an internal: the testing of liver, stomach contents and effusions in the chest cavities. Where no blood is present, bone marrow, a molar or hair can be provided to biologists for DNA testing.

The pathologist's work in no way mirrors the glib, unruffled persona of those who solve crimes miraculously before the advertisement break on commercial television programs. The work is laborious; often slow, often harrowing, always demanding.

It is 24 hours after the discovery. Forensic pathologist Dr John Gilbert, a veteran of almost 3500 autopsies in his lengthy career, has seen his fair share of deaths by homicide. The rule of thumb is for between 20 to 30 murders a year. Gilbert carries out four of the post-mortems, and he details his involvement from the beginning. At 9am on Friday, 21 May 1999, he is shown to a trailer placed in the secure vehicle area at the Forensic Science Centre where he observes six large plastic barrels on the back of the trailer. The police have labelled these A to F inclusive, and they have opened the tops of the barrels and inspected the contents. It is immediately obvious that there are decomposing human body parts and watery fluid in each of them. The liquid is murky, but some contents are disturbingly clear. A hand, disconnected from the arm. A foot, floating alone. The pathologists have seen it all before, the grisly results of psychopathic murders, but it shocks them nonetheless. They work in silence. The pathologist has been alerted that acid may have been involved in the treatment of these bodies and because of that, he asks one of the forensic chemists to sample the fluid from each of the barrels and ascertain how acidic they are.

Five of the barrels have a neutral pH; in other words, they are not acid. But one, barrel F, has a pH of 5, indicating that it is weakly acidic.

Assisted by forensic pathologist Roger Byard, a team of mortuary technicians and the unit manager, at 1.20pm Gilbert starts the gruesome task of decanting the fluid from each of the barrels, tipping each onto its side and sifting it as it is being decanted to catch any material floating around inside. Finally, they record the contents of each barrel. Including all barrels, the mass is a combined 903.5 kilograms.

The process of decanting the fluid and inspecting the sieved contents of the barrels is an agonisingly slow three hours and twenty minutes. Gilbert checks his watch. 4.40pm. Time to call State Coroner Wayne Chivell to report the findings. Six barrels. Eight people. It has been a long afternoon. As he will comment in court, 'All of the bodies were quite remarkably putrefied, [and] they were quite unpleasant to work with.'

Prolonged periods of immersion in the barrels, combined with lack of oxygen, has drawn putrefaction – the active destruction of cells and body tissues caused by bacteria, fungi and other organisms – to an end. With two of the four cases Gilbert examines, there are no specific features identified at autopsy which indicate a cause of death. The problems highlighted by severe putrefaction of the bodies render identification of injuries very difficult. For the same reason, date of death for all the victims, apart from Johnson, cannot be established. In effect, the bodies have been held in suspended putrefaction.

Under a headline in a chart marked 'Mutilation', Gilbert notes the disarticulation of David Johnson and Troy Youde. The nature of the injuries to the various joints where attempts were made, successfully or not, to remove a limb indicates no particular detailed knowledge of anatomy. They were, Gilbert thinks, relatively crude attempts. He also lists, under a column 'Toxicology', the three drugs he has found in the barrels' liquid. Diazepam, better known as Valium: a tranquilliser. Methadone, used in the treatment of heroin withdrawal. Benztropine, a drug that is normally used to control the side effects of other drugs used in the treatment of psychotic illnesses such as schizophrenia.

Elizabeth Haydon's body is coated with semi-solid, brown grease-like material, particularly offensive in smell. In Gilbert's opinion, it has come from her body.

A syringe is found in the barrel that held the body of Gavin Porter: easy to explain, as he was a heroin addict. But Gilbert cannot explain everything that is found in the barrels, particularly the crystalline particles in some faecal matter. To the naked eye it looks like glass, but it is, in fact, particles of magnesium and phosphorus. 'We still don't know what on earth they are and where they come from', Gilbert frowns, as if the question baffles him as much as whether aliens exist, or there is life after death. 'They shouldn't be there. I've never seen anything like it in faecal material before.'

Troy Youde died from strangulation by ligature, which resulted in fractures of his thyroid cartilage and probable fractures of the hyoid bone. Parts of his body have been retrieved from two separate barrels: his torso and head from barrel F, and parts of his lower limbs from barrel A. There is also evidence of de-fleshing of the femur of each leg, though pathology has found no particular features which indicate that it occurred while he was alive. It is the evidence of the 'de-fleshing' which ups the ante, changing the case from one in which the victims were probably murdered for material gain, to one in which it has become hideously apparent that the killers delighted in taking lives. There would have been a great deal of work and cutting involved in getting all that flesh off the bones, probably involving the use of a sharp knife.

Asked by the police to provide a report on what, specifically, was the cause of death of each individual, Gilbert notes in relation to Troy Youde: 'I was aware that one of Dr Ross James's bodies showed evidence of electrical injuries and obviously that meant all the other bodies had to have that aspect considered'.

Cause of death is attributed in only five out of the cases. Gilbert explains why. 'If the bodies had very large oral gags in the mouth, and those gags were of a sufficient size to obstruct the airway, then, given the condition of the body, that reasonably could be attributed as the cause of death. Equally, if there was a rope tightly around the neck . . . not unreasonably that was attributed as the cause of death. That much is not difficult. What is difficult is that in some cases there were some such items present on the body and an examination, externally and internally of some of the bodies did not allow a confident assessment of the causes of death. The important thing, though, is that in those cases by no means does the absence of a cause of death preclude the prior use of something around the neck, or an oral gag to have in fact caused the death.'

The victims' families can perhaps take some small comfort from the fact that it appears the amputations occurred after death. The pathologists will testify that there is no reason to believe they were inflicted during life as there were no so-called 'vital reactions'. But there is clear evidence that some of the victims were tortured while they were still alive. Gardiner's cause of death is from strangulation by rope; like two other victims, he also has blackened skin on his legs, arm and scrotum. Its appearance indicates that damage was inflicted during life.

The gruesome evidence continues. Barry Lane has a gag in his mouth, 176 centimetres long – by itself potentially lethal – and was also strangled by rope. Fred Brooks also has an oral gag.

O'Dwyer has lacerations on his scalp, but the post-mortem fails to positively show whether he was alive or dead when he received them. Davies's body has been in the grave for at least two years, and there is only skeletal evidence remaining.

Some of the victims' bodies have what appear to be electrical burns on their chests, some have been tied with thumb cuffs and handcuffs. One has his legs folded back with wire to shorten them so they would fit into the barrel. Another has a foot and ankle removed.

Reporters spell it out: eight bodies found in the barrels, but only 15 feet. Where is the other foot? Has it been it lost, or kept as a grisly trophy?

Later, in court, Gilbert will specifically break down the contents in each barrel; the blunt, harsh reality of each victim's undignified end. He will start with Barrel A and end with F.

Barrel A. Total weight of 113.5 kilograms. A male body, intact wearing a jumper. Tattoos on the victim's chest. Four slices of skin and some muscle. Two clumps of hair, matted, and two femurs with attached muscle and tendon tissue, clearly 'largely de-fleshed'. A left lower leg with foot attached. Right lower leg with foot missing. Rubber gloves, electrical wire, plastic.

He will pause briefly before detailing the contents of each barrel, maintaining a stoic expression that does not allow any emotion to show.

It doesn't take much imagination, either, to understand just what had gone on during lengthy torture sessions, particularly when Edmund Silenieks, the Evidence Recovery Technician gives his evidence regarding the examination of exhibits such as clothing and bedding for biological staining. Some of the male underpants at the U-Store-It, he says, show faecal and blood stains.

A reporter winces as she takes down notes. 'Too much information already,' she mutters, her face draining colour.

Geral Feltus from Major Crime spells out to the court what he found in the ceiling at Bunderra Court, an Aladdin's Cave of information. 'I could see a lot of documentation in various names, which I thought at the time . . . I would get documented or videotaped prior to any disturbance . . . I was in possession of information prior to going to that location in relation to what we should direct our attention to, and amongst all those items were specific things that related to other names which I thought certainly required further investigation.'

Sandi McDonald knows exactly what he is referring to. 'Other potential victims?'

'Possibly, yes.'

In her capacity as a forensic dentist, Jane Taylor is frequently asked by the police to help in the identification of bodies. It is labour-intensive, close work, undertaken in the post-mortem area deep in the bowels of the Adelaide Forensic Science Unit. The work suits only those with a calling to it, but even Taylor sometimes finds it confronting and upsetting, facing the harsh realities of death, either accidental or deliberate.

This investigation, she knows, will be one of the worst she has ever dealt with, exacerbated by the fact that there are so many bodies this time. Taylor sees her job as a community service, sees herself as a cog in the wheel of crime analysis. She rarely lets her professional mask drop, but there are glimpses of it slipping when she starts on the Snowtown identifications.

There is a hum of activity and unusual noise in the post-mortem room this morning as Taylor begins her day's work. She is, as usual, well prepared, but there is something about this case that is edgy, different. The room smells different, too: there is the usual trace of antiseptic and formaldehyde, used as disinfectant, but there is also an overwhelming stench of death, a smell that seems to seep into the walls. Later, when the pathologists move premises, there are whispers that it is because they can't get the smell out.

The area is crowded with people, and ladders have been pulled up to the end of each table to afford the forensic photographers a height advantage when they are taking their pictures.

The mortuary assistant wheels a body from the refrigeration unit as Taylor calls out the number. Even if the identity of the dead person is known, no names are used here. There are reasons for that, not least of which is the necessity not to personalise the victim. Each tooth of each victim is recorded on a chart and double-checked by another odontologist; later, they are photographed and radiographed.

Despite advances in forensic science, teeth are still the best means of identification when every other body part has disintegrated. Not everyone has a fingerprint record, but most people have been to the dentist and their charts are on file. Tough and hard, teeth can often offer information that has survived even the furnace heat of a fire.

A pathologist's job is not about drama: it is about completing a puzzle, built up piece by piece. The make-up of a mouth – moistness and thickness of muscles – protects teeth. Nature has provided scientists with a great tool, but there still has to be a match for odontology to produce results. If they don't have that, then they look to things such as a DNA match with living relatives.

While most of the pathology for the Snowtown investigations is done in the laboratories in Adelaide, there is double-checking when they deem it necessary. Pathologist Katrina Both takes a number of samples to the United States for DNA analysis: teeth and extracts from relatives of Troy Youde and David Johnson, and pathology in relation to Suzanne Allen.

★ ★ ★

Chief forensic pathologist Dr Ross James, employed at Adelaide's Forensic Science Centre since the late seventies, has undertaken five of the victims' post-mortems, which are carried out on 24 and 25 May 1999. James's pathology background in South Australia includes the gruesome, heartbreaking evidence he gave about Von Einem's victims in the Family murders. He is also the pathologist who made the initial examination of Clinton Trezise's skeletal remains before passing it to Jane Taylor. Now he is to give evidence on these serial killings: how the pathologists identified the deceased; the chart that classifies name, date of birth, the date the victim went missing, and the location in which the body was found. Each case is then allocated a number, which will, eventually, help to piece together the jigsaw puzzle, to link toxicology or other forensic reports with the victim. That each barrel has been given a letter from A to F so that when the contents are transferred to body bags, they have a corresponding number and letter, helps. Some of the barrels contain more than one body, or parts of more than one body. The cessation of putrefaction, he says, renders it difficult to know precisely how long the bodies have been in the barrels. Not unlike, he continues, putting meat in the freezer for months at a time.

When the pathology reports are complete, they are peer checked. No pathologist can put out a report without another of the team checking for discrepancies.

Forensic evidence given at committal or trial can be, and often is, extremely lengthy and excruciatingly dull. Scientific jargon can lull the most intrigued onlooker to sleep, and many a reporter has returned to the newsroom with little more than a pad full of doodles after hearing a day's evidence. But forensic material is vital in linking together the pieces: when people are innocent, it can prove to be a defence lawyer's dream; when they are guilty, it can be their nightmare.

43

The newspapers run only one photograph of Elizabeth Haydon: her narrow eyes stare out from a bloated face above a triple chin, and an awkward grin exposes a missing front tooth. Her lank, dark hair, pulled back from her forehead, hangs loosely about her shoulders and she is bereft of make-up. It is a photo of a woman damaged by life, defeated by circumstance, who looks older – much older – than 36, the age she was when the photo was taken a year before her death.

Her family has to wait two months before they can give her a funeral service, during which time her oldest brother, Garion, haggles incessantly with the police to release her remains. They aren't happy about letting them go: knowing this case will be the most complex and lengthy in Australian history, they need to keep every shred of evidence they can. The committal hearing is still 17 months from opening, but Garion stands firm: without a service, his sister's soul can never rest.

Elizabeth's mother, Pat Sinclair, attends the funeral, the toll of the murder showing on her worn face. There is an obscenity in burying your own daughter, especially under these circumstances, and she is taking it hard. She has been hunkered down at Taree, where she was staying when she heard the news of Elizabeth's murder, only returning to Adelaide just before the funeral. There isn't much to go back for: this is hardly a family that will nurture each other through shock and grief.

Elizabeth's sister, Christine, is here, pale and quiet, holding the hands of two of Elizabeth's children, now both teenagers. Christine is so upset, Pat thinks she might have to be hospitalised. One son isn't coping at all, angry at his mother's death and because he doesn't know who his father is. Elizabeth wouldn't tell him: he wasn't much chop, was all she had said, and now she's dead, he's got Buckley's of finding out.

And Garion is here with Elizabeth's two youngest boys. Since Elizabeth died, his wife, Rae, and he have had custody. It's hardly surprising: ever since he was a kid, Garion claims, he is the one who has regularly stepped into the breach, to take charge when Pat took off. Christened Guy, he has tried to reinvent himself with a name change. Now he only answers to Garion, Celtic for 'Chieftain'.

His wife understands his background only too well. Her childhood hadn't exactly been a bed of roses, either. Without fail, every Thursday night her father's pay cheques were spent on grog. From then, until Sunday night when he passed out, he would drink himself into a brutal rage, screaming and swearing at the family, looking for someone to belt. Upturning furniture, smashing glasses, stalking them in their own home. A childhood blighted by poverty and fear and violence.

Four of Elizabeth's siblings – Wayne, Tony, Gail Sinclair and Diane – don't attend her service.

Wayne has been in and out of jail interstate for horrendous crimes, described by the judge as being representative of 'conduct at the epicentre of depravity', and the family no longer has anything to do with him.

Tony reckons he is always in strife with the family, one way or another, and doesn't want to stick his head in the noose again. He hasn't spoken to Gail for 12 years, and says he is the 'outsider', the black sheep. He says goodbye to Elizabeth in his own way, spending some time alone and thinking about the sister who looked for love in all the wrong places.

Gail Sinclair hasn't exchanged a word with her mother, Pat, since Elizabeth went missing. Pat screws up her face when Gail's name is mentioned. 'I hate her', she says. 'I know she's my daughter, but I hate her. She's a bitch. I don't want to never see her again.' A key witness in the case, protected by the state, Gail has had a gutful of the whole thing, and prefers to lie low. But even if she had wanted to go to her sister's funeral, she doesn't have a choice. Pat has told her in no uncertain terms she isn't welcome there. Gail retaliates by barring Pat from attending her grandson, Fred Brooks's, funeral.

Diane scarpers from her new-found family when the publicity about the case hits the news, and she doesn't intend to go back.

But the cops are present, moving among the small crowd and distributing business cards as if they are hustling at a bar. They try to be as surreptitious as possible, but it's difficult. 'I'm from Elizabeth CIB. If you have any information I'd appreciate you calling me on this number.' Garion is apoplectic. 'You blokes stand out like dog's balls. This is an invasion of privacy, a disgrace. Can't you leave the family in peace, just this once?' He has had a lot of run-ins with the law over the years, even though he's staying on the straight and narrow now, but old habits die hard. He doesn't have a whole lot of time for them, so he vents his disgust. 'Piss off, for Christ's sake!' he tells them. 'Get going! You're not welcome here.'

But the cops stay. This is a funeral but it's also, for them, a murder investigation. Grief and conscience can make strange bedfellows, and detective work can reap results in the least likely places. *Where the carcass is, there shall the eagles be gathered together.*

The hideous details of Elizabeth's murder stun the mourners, and they don't discuss it at the funeral. But the questions won't go away.

The Sinclairs can't afford to pay for Elizabeth's funeral. Pat is on a pension and none of her children holds down a job, but the state government kicks in $3000 for expenses. That helps. Pat can't find the words to express what the funeral is like, so she says the same thing every time the subject comes up. The service, she repeats, is 'beautiful. Just beautiful'.

Elizabeth's two youngest boys have chosen their mother's white coffin and also the flowers – red and white carnations. Pat would have preferred roses, but she bows to the boys' decision. God knows they are upset enough.

The funeral service is held at the Church of Jesus Christ of Latter-day Saints in Elizabeth Downs on a mild mid-winter's morning in July 1999. Elizabeth hadn't exactly proved to be an outstanding church member; the Mormons hold to a strong moral code of sexual and other behaviours, but they accept her anyway. Her day will come at the Resurrection, where all men and women will be shown to be children of Christ, and when the mistakes of this life will be forgotten and sinners forgiven. For Mormons, the body is the tabernacle, the temple. Some family members shift a little from foot to foot when the bishop speaks about this.

The bishop is reverent in his prayers for Elizabeth. Her spirit, he says, is now reunited with her body and the ills and pains she suffered on earth will be overcome in the next world. There, she will be reunited with her family. Had he known the whole truth, he would also have said a prayer for Elizabeth's unborn child.

She was eight weeks pregnant when she was murdered.

And so it is a handful of mourners who say their farewells, offering Elizabeth Haydon, nee Verna Audrey Sinclair, a little dignity – perhaps the only dignity she has ever known – before her coffin exits through the curtains of the crematorium. As the Church of Jesus Christ of Latter-day Saints had blessed her and heard her wedding vows three years before, it now sends her on to her God.

May heaven prove kinder than earth.

Some of Elizabeth's ashes are scattered around a rose bush that Pat plants in the tiny garden of the housing trust unit where Pat used to live in Elizabeth Downs, inside a light yellow and green tyre painted with flowers. Pat also has some secreted in the gold locket she wears around her neck, so that Elizabeth can always be close to her heart. Garion has some at his home near Ballarat; and the teenage boys raised by Christine and her husband, also have some.

44

Pat Sinclair has an exhausted, martyred air. 'This whole business has knocked the hell out of me', she sighs. 'Elizabeth and I were very close.' She has no reason to trust the press: a slip of the tongue here, a slip of the pen there and she is forever damned in print. Pat claims to be a practising Mormon; she joined the Church of Latter-day Saints in 1994, 10 years after Elizabeth; but religion doesn't offer her immunity from pain. She is a victim, too, trapped with her memories and nursing wounds like a soldier. It is little wonder she is guarded: since the police found the bodies, her family life has been exposed to the world and increasingly, she has wanted to run. If she refuses to talk, she is hiding something; if she does speak, she can only hope her story isn't misrepresented. 'I'm damned if I do, and damned if I don't', she reckons. She speaks in a whiny drawl, as if at any moment she will start to cry.

I query the conflicting media reports: did Elizabeth have seven children, or eight? She jumps in to reel off her grand-children's names, finishing the sentence in triumph. 'Seven children. Only seven! The media have got so much wrong.' But they hadn't. 'Well, I suppose if you add the baby Elizabeth was carrying – well, I suppose that makes eight', she concedes. Mark Haydon's baby, the child he had harped at her to conceive.

Pat is at pains to point out that she isn't close to her son, Garion. She doesn't know, she says, why another of her boys is in jail in Queensland, doesn't know, doesn't want to know, but she loves him anyway. It's a mother's protective instinct, she murmurs. It seems odd, that a son can be charged and jailed for a crime so loathsome that reading the details makes your flesh crawl, but she claims not to know the details. Pat shrugs. 'I can't be blamed for me children's actions once they reach a certain age. It's not my fault.'

Elizabeth, Pat says, was loyal – extremely loyal – but she grapples to find other adjectives to describe her daughter. Happy-go-lucky. Outgoing. Outspoken.

'How outspoken?'

'Very. She needed to be the centre of attention, and she was foul-mouthed. Oh, yes she was.' Pat wants her to be at peace, but doubts her soul will ever rest. 'How can she rest?' she asks. 'Murdered like that. How can she?'

Her voice seems to shrink away, coming back strong and defiant when Haydon's name is mentioned. 'She married him, more to my sorrow. I didn't like him from the start, and I told Elizabeth. We had the biggest row we'd ever had over that mongrel. He was a mean man all round, though I never seen any violence.'

She is savage, too, that Garion delivered the eulogy at Elizabeth's funeral. 'He said he loved his sister, but he did not, he did not. Some of my kids have given interviews to the press, but they've twisted everything about my life, my marriage. We had our problems, for sure, like any marriage, but consider this: I had seven children in 10 years, and five miscarriages. It wasn't easy.'

A month later, Pat agrees to meet with me at her home and gives me directions on how to get there. Keep driving, an hour north of Adelaide. Turn left at the roundabout. Pass two streets on the right. First turn left. That's it.

The small unit is chaotically untidy; stove top stained with food, kitchen table cluttered with overflowing ashtrays, the lounge room floor littered with orange peel to match the striped brown and orange couch and ripped chairs disgorging foam. Videos of John Wayne – Pat's hero – are stacked on the shelves. A plump matriarch with white hair and brown eyes ringed with tortoise-shell glasses, she almost disappears in the chair: a diminutive 147 centimetres, there is little of her. There is a cacophony of noise, the TV blaring with afternoon soapies and advertisements offering credit cards, bonuses and discounts on luxury items this family could never afford.

Four of Pat's grandchildren are here, squabbling and staring at me, this stranger with a notebook; and her son Tony with his partner, Tammy McKenzie. Pat has asked Tony to come, to help set the record straight, and he feels the need to explain Tammy's 'condition'. 'She's a bit intellectually disabled', he says in front of her. 'Aren't you, Tammy?' She smiles and goes to see to one of her kids. Pat and Tony contradict each other on virtually every subject, their voices getting louder and louder to compete with the background noise, and they rarely reach a point of agreement. 'Noo, noo', says Pat, shaking her head. 'Ye-es, ye-es', says Tony, nodding his. A picture of Elizabeth adorns the wall, and pictures of some of her children. 'I've got 30 grandchildren and 20 great-grandchildren', Pat says proudly. 'Not enough room on the walls to put them all up.' In a faded black tracksuit and denuded of make-up, she is reticent to reveal too much, but she warms up as the afternoon seeps into early evening. She has a lot to talk about. She has lost a daughter and a grandson. She understands grief.

Pat's grandson, Fred Brooks, went missing a few months before Elizabeth. 'Freddie was Gail's son, and she rang me and said he'd gone to the shop to get cigarettes and hadn't come home', Pat says. 'But she told me Mark Haydon and John Bunting were looking for him. The next day she phones back, says it's okay. They've found Freddy, he's shacked up with a married woman and her two kids. So I thought, he's all right, then. He's just sowing his wild oats.'

The last time Pat saw Elizabeth – late November – they were planning a get-together with Diane to celebrate her return to the family fold. On that weekend, Sunday, Gail told Pat that Elizabeth had taken off, that she was drunk and had walked out. 'I knew she was dead, straight away. It was a gut feeling that I would never see her again. Mark Haydon came over the next day, sat on my lounge and said, "She's gone", and then he was gone, too. Just took off out of the house.' When detectives spoke with Pat, they wanted to know where Elizabeth may have gone to. She wanted to scream at them, 'You fools, she doesn't have a passport, she doesn't have any money, she hasn't gone nowhere of her own accord', but she didn't. 'Yous wouldn't believe me if I told yous', she told them.

Pat was in New South Wales six months later when she heard the news about her daughter. 'One of the detectives rang me from Snowtown, said he wanted me to know before the media got a hold of the story, said, "Sorry to tell you this, but we've found Elizabeth", and I dropped the phone and cried. Oh, how I cried.' The next night, while she was cooking a meal, she heard a news report about the barrels being found in the vault. 'I went in to watch it, and they flashed up a picture of my grandson, Freddy. I went into total shock. I loved that boy. I started grieving for him, as well as for my daughter.'

Some weeks after my initial visit, Pat is to have her photo taken, the first time she has been in front of a camera since her wedding day. She has applied make-up and the black tracksuit has been discarded in favour of a blue and white striped dress. She fusses like a girl, running her hands over her frock, asks, 'Do I look all right, do I look OK?' 'This is the only dress I own', she says, smiling sheepishly. She looks fresh, different, as if the years have been rolled back and she is again a child, following her mother around the family's guest house, learning to set a table and glowing with pride at her achievement.

A neighbour, in his mid-40s but looking more like mid-60s, comes through her door and slouches down in the seat. He could be anyone; there are no introductions and he doesn't utter a word for 10 minutes. When he finally speaks, he addresses Pat. 'Got any coffee?' he asks. 'Me pension doesn't go in till Thursdy night, and I'm right out.' Pat offers him some in a jar, and smiles at his retreating back. 'We look after each other around here. Oh, my word we do!'

Pat is well aware that Elizabeth made mistakes in her life and that she wasn't the greatest mother. 'She dumped the kids, in her own way, but she loved them, oh yes she did. She didn't deserve to die like that: she had too much to live for. She was only 37, still had her life ahead of her. They snuffed it out of her. Oh, they did some terrible things to her that night. Shockin'. I close my eyes, and I see the horror.' Pat now takes tablets to help her sleep and to try to keep the nightmares at bay. But she takes comfort in small mercies. 'The coppers assured me Elizabeth weren't dismembered', she says. 'And she had her own barrel.'

The children are becoming fractious, squabbling among themselves and edging closer to me, their eyes fixated on this stranger with a notebook who has walked into their grandmother's lounge room and talked all afternoon about nasty things. Now I am juggling four on my lap, all under the age of six, not given anything to do to distract their attention from the gory details. They are fractious and tired, so tired that one child cuddles into the folds of my coat and falls asleep, tucked against my shoulder.

The journalist in me knows to remain objective, but the woman and mother in me has taken over and I want to protect these children, wrap them up safe and warm from the horrors of the outside world, the horrors that are being discussed so openly in front of them. And they give me warm hugs when I leave and I suddenly want to take them with me, all of them. But instead I walk back up the path to the car as they call goodbye and I turn out of their street and cry all the way back to Adelaide. Cry for these children who have little chance of escaping the endless cycle of poverty and hopelessness, cry for Pat's murdered daughter and grandson, and cry for Pat Sinclair too who, for all her admitted failings, is still a mother, and for whom Elizabeth – the child she christened Verna – will always be remembered as her last born, her 'flying baby'.

45

Elizabeth Harvey is given the all-clear after chemotherapy but a month later she loses mobility with horrific pain in her back and is bedridden for six weeks. Initially, she is told it is arthritis, but when they finally run tests they find that the breast cancer has spread to her bones. Added to the trauma of Troy's and David's deaths and Jamie's arrest, and having the cops from Major Crime on the phone every day, she now knows she will die from this cancer within two years. She will not see her 48th birthday.

And in the last throes of her cancer and her life, Elizabeth wrestles with it all: guilt at her own silence and bewilderment laced with bitterness at the police role. 'The police started surveillance after Barry Lane disappeared. Our phones were tapped, yet all those murders were committed under the police's nose. They had enough evidence to charge them, according to Jamie's lawyer, after Barry disappeared. Not for murder, but at least for fraud. They had video tapes of them going into the bank, getting the money. But they didn't act.'

She tipped off the police, told them where bodies were buried: Ray Davies and Suzanne Allen, in the backyard at 203 Waterloo Corner Road. Now she is scared rigid. The police want to talk to her, to hear her side of the story; and her lawyer is warning her she could be charged with murder because she was present in the house.

It haunts her right up until her death, why she said nothing, did nothing. 'I did nothing about it at all and David and Troy are dead. I kept shut about it and that's why I kept going into Murray Bridge hospital with nervous breakdowns. And I told John I would never, I made John promise me that he'd never do it again and that's when he said he was doing breaking and entering. I thought it was better than going around murdering people. So there he was murdering people all the time. I never dreamt that he was doing that.'

There will be time – years – while the court cases roll on, for people to piece together the jigsaw. Elizabeth Harvey will remember how Bunting made her continue to receive a pension after they lived together, even though it was illegal and he was also on the dole. He said he couldn't afford to lose the income and it makes her laugh, bitterly, when she finds out he collected thousands of dollars from dead people's welfare while she was always on the bones of her bum. She never saw a cent of the money. The strangest irony of all, she thinks, is that only a week after she finally convinced him to come clean to the government about their living arrangements, the bastard was arrested.

Marcus interrupts, defends his ex-wife. 'Elizabeth never saw a cent of the money, right, she was always dead broke. Bunting and the rest never had a penny between them. What was done with the money God only knows. I know they were running what I think you might call it an industry in a sense, that they had to move bodies around the state but . . . there was no co-ordinated structure to make it worthwhile as far as finances go because there's no benefit there; it's only craziness.'

Bunting, Marcus recalls, was the master of distraction, 'He made sure that there was always trouble. It was never a well-structured life, right, and so when somebody died, it accelerated. So right at the time that he was involved with somebody's death, he made sure that the madness was well and truly there. The house would get broken into or the windows would be smashed in the yard. He made sure that every time somebody disappeared a catastrophe was going on in the house. So you could half blame the person who disappeared, and it got Elizabeth's mind away from thinking "why isn't so-and-so coming to see me any more?"'

★ ★ ★

Now Elizabeth is fitting it all together. Remembering her second youngest telling her that John, Jamie and Troy had taken him down the back paddock, made him wear a dress and rubbed him in the dirt. He was 20 years old, borderline intellectually handicapped, crying for them to leave him alone. Bunting's plan was to make him a vegetable by forcing him to breathe glue fumes for a few hours.

He tried to tell John he had it wrong; that his younger brother had lied when he said he had molested him. But John wouldn't listen and it would be years before the truth came out: that it was Troy who had touched up the youngest boy. John would have killed his brother. He was on his list to go. In his mind, he had sexually molested the boy and he wouldn't ever hear any different. But he escaped from him, twice. It made John hate him more.

The first time he got away was pure luck. Elizabeth had to go down to Adelaide but didn't fancy going alone, woke the boy and asked him to go with her. 'I was going to take Troy as well, and I peeked in his room but he was dead to the world, he'd been up smoking dope all night, so I didn't wake him. So I just took my boy with me and John got a little bit upset, asked, "Why do you want to take him?" and I told him I couldn't face the drive by myself. They were going to do my boy and Troy and make it look as though they'd just taken off together, because Troy always told me he'd take him grape picking. So my boy was supposed to go that day as well.'

He could only kill Troy that day.

The second time her son leaves the house without telling Elizabeth, John looks for him in a temper. 'I didn't know why he wanted to take him for a drive so badly,' Elizabeth says.

She knows now.

Elizabeth didn't hold anything back from John. 'There's always a secret bit that you hold back from anyone in any relationship, I don't care how much you say you love one another, there's always that self-preservation that you hold back, and I didn't. I gave it because I didn't think John would ever hurt me or abuse me in any way like other men. At that time I had no family. There was no contact with my brother or Diane; my mother had died; and John replaced all that. He put all the pieces back when I had my nervous breakdowns.'

And she had thought she understood why John often disappeared to Adelaide for days on end. He told her he had got his truck licence and that he was working part-time hauling for a trucking company. But there was no truck company. He was just hauling barrels with bodies in them all over the place.

Truth and lies, the stories rolling along and picking up speed. John coming home with yarns about how he was moving grand pianos around the state. The exotic lifestyle he led in his imagination, the stories he told other people: he'd just bought a BMW; just paid off his house; just gone on an overseas holiday with his girlfriend. On and on for months. And then one day he came home with a puppy and he was crying, cut up. A drunk had roared through an intersection, he said and knocked his mate and girlfriend off their motorbike. They were both in a coma, not expected to live, and he was looking after their dog.

Elizabeth recalls that the whole household tiptoed around John for weeks, while he waited for news of his friends. And when they both died, he was speechless with grief. The household jarred to a halt, while Elizabeth consoled him.

But his friends didn't exist.

She got the shock of her life, too, when she picked up the newspaper and saw an article from Gail Sinclair saying that she'd been engaged to John for 12 months. Elizabeth never had a clue. Didn't know Sinclair existed.

His other life. The life Elizabeth Harvey knew nothing about.

John had become increasingly aggressive, shitty about the cops hanging around and targeting Gail Sinclair. He called them 'little boys' for the way they protected each other, and fantasised out loud about what he would like to do to the 'wastes', particularly Greg Stone and Steve McCoy, who always seemed to be on his case. Desperate she was losing him, by May 1999 Gail snatches any moments she can with Bunting. She writes him a letter and he tells her she has nothing to fear. She is the only woman in his life, he says, the only one stupid enough to have him. And she has him, he assures her. She has him.

There are echoes of her sister Elizabeth Haydon's story in Gail's own past, a childhood riddled with sexual abuse and horrific domestic violence. And as with her sister, the cycle continued into her adulthood, through seven children and numerous partners.

But now Gail knows her son Freddy and sister Elizabeth are dead. Darkness closes in, just like it did in 1997, the last time she had a breakdown.

She rocks back and forth to try to escape the noise in her head. Sits on the floor of her housing trust unit, rocking, and cradling a porcelain doll. Clutching the doll close to her chest. She won't let it out of her arms, even when she gets to hospital and staff at the psychiatric ward say to her, 'It's okay, you're okay, and tell us, what's your dolly's name?'

'Gail Bunting', she says.

Gail is just existing now, her children all taken by welfare after her voluntary admission to the psychiatric hospital days before Bunting's arrest. Vomiting when the police confirm her sister and son are dead, and bitter that her family accuses her of knowing more than she has let on. She is sick of the whole damn world.

Elizabeth Harvey only begins to question John Bunting after his arrest. She says the police confirm he had a daughter, but beyond that, she can't be sure where reality and fantasy blur. Her lover is an enigma. 'I don't know how much is true from what's fiction. All I know – he was a damn good actor because he sucked me in for many, many years over all his friends committing suicide and him being devastated by it.'

There was always so much chaos. Like the time Jamie and John went down to the supermarket in Elizabeth's car, came back and the windscreen, front headlights and door were caved in. John told her a junkie had smashed the car up with a crowbar because her son owed money for drugs on credit. Elizabeth walloped him around the face and he looked stunned, innocent. It cost her a fortune to put her car back together and then she found out that John had done it himself: taken to the car with a crowbar, while Jamie helped.

Chaos and lies. Mayhem.

Her youngest son was due to be groomed next, Elizabeth realises. John bought him a disposable camera and they went down to the shopping centre to take pictures of physically handicapped people in wheelchairs.

John started talking to him about paedophiles – dirties, wastes – and Elizabeth couldn't stop him, though she tried. In hindsight, she could see what was happening. He was going to recruit him as the next generation. His next protégé.

Elizabeth Harvey remembers and soul-searches about so many aspects of her life with John. 'Keep it in the family', was his catch-cry, she recalls. 'He always used to say, "We might not be blood, but we're all family and we will look after ourselves as a family unit, we don't break apart". To hell with everyone else. To hell with the police, to hell with bureaucracy, we were all going to look after one another. I think that's why it came as such a big shock, because he slept with me, he said he loved me, and I was with him for five years. Didn't that count toward anything? If we were family, why did he kill Troy? That's what I don't understand.'

She visits her son Jamie Vlassakis at Yatala Prison and watches, listens as he struggles to disconnect mentally from his hero, to work out the emotional dynamics. He has been suborned by John for so long he finds it difficult to separate the psychopathic serial killer from the father figure.

And Elizabeth struggles with it, too. She is dying, and it all seems so surreal. 'I want to see this John that I never knew, who has killed my son. I want to know who this John is that I lived with for five years and I didn't know existed. He was very domineering. The whole house revolved around John. You never rocked the boat with him. I ended up in hospital three times and it was really basically through John but I didn't see it at the time. Everything had to be his way. Sometimes I thought he looked at me to be his mum that he never had, but not in an incestuous way, if you know what I mean.'

His mum that he never had. She wonders: was that at the heart of John's problems? Why he was so profoundly disturbed? The reason he was so detached from normal human emotions? The boy, now a man, seeking maternal attention. *Look at me. I'll show you. Look what I can do.* John's father, Elizabeth knows, is weaker than his mother, dominated by her. Lives in her shadow. It was his mother's attention he wanted. Craved.

Elizabeth phones John's parents to tell them he has been arrested, and gets their answering machine. She is stunned that they never return her call. 'They've never seen John in jail . . . they've never even gone up to see if he's innocent', she says. She is puzzled how parents can act like that, simply ignore their own flesh and blood. You still love them, she says, no matter what they do. No matter what.

'If Jamie had never come back to Murray Bridge, he wouldn't be in jail now', Elizabeth Harvey muses. 'John's very manipulative, he can make the plausible sound implausible, and the implausible sound plausible. Jamie thought, like me, that John could walk on water.' She loves her son with a mother's fierce instinct and tries not to dwell on what he has done, instead providing what she can for him – a Walkman and television – to give him some comfort in jail.

46

Joanne and The vehicle had travelled around John Vou-

Around the courts, Wendy Abraham QC is referred to as the 'Princess of Darkness' – a reference to the tough cases she takes on and her 'take-no-prisoners' approach to justice. With short dark hair cut into a crisp, spartan style accentuated by pillar-box red lipstick and large glasses, pencil-slim, 40-something Abraham commands respect and a little fear. She lives and breathes the law, striding through the Supreme Court building, offering cursory nods to her colleagues as she passes.

Abraham first cut her teeth on a murder trial in 1988, building on her expertise with cases involving multiple offenders and convoluted legal arguments. As the Prosecutor in the Snowtown case, she and her legal team start work long before the committal opens, wading through mountains of police and witness evidence. Stephen McEwan will be gone by the start of the trial, departing the office of the DPP to become a defence lawyer. But her trusted junior prosecutor Sandi McDonald – the antithesis of Abraham in personality – is by her side throughout the committal and trials, ensuring the nuts and bolts of the case are well oiled, stepping in to fill McEwan's shoes and cross-examine wherever required.

It will fall to Abraham to present the opening address for the Crown, the transcript of which is more than 26 pages long. This will be the longest committal hearing in South Australia's history, a huge, systemic juggernaut involving the accused, witnesses, police and lawyers. It will, on occasions, severely test the patience of the legal teams for both the prosecution and defence, turn the stomachs of the court reporters and stenographers detailing the evidence and frustrate the legal representatives of media outlets with its unprecedented number of suppressions. It has been 19 months since the accused have been arrested. Starting on 11 December 2000, the committal hearings run for a marathon 49 sitting days over seven months; during that time, 68 witnesses are called, 1458 witness statements and 18 exhibits tendered, 172 suppression orders made, revoked or varied and 3242 pages of transcript recorded.

Television footage of the killers leaving the prison van on their way into court for their early appearances show the grim pleasure they took in being the centre of attention. This is their moment in the sun, their crowning glory, and the memory will become part of the videotape that will be played over and over again in their minds as they sit out their sentences. Despite being handcuffed, Vlassakis executes a perverse little dance, whooping 'woohoo!' and grinning widely at the cameras. His final gestures before he moves out of sight are to poke out his tongue and put his hands up in a salutatory gesture, much like a boxer after winning a bout in the ring.

The lawyers file in like horses to the barrier. The front row is dominated by the prosecution team: Wendy Abraham QC, Stephen McEwan and Sandi McDonald. Sitting in the same row, representing John Bunting, are Mark Griffin and Elizabeth Sheppard. Behind them are John Lyons and Sam Abbott for Haydon, flanked by Stephen Apps, Mark Twiggs and Bill Morris, for Wagner. Nick Vadasz and Rosemary Davey, for Vlassakis, have drawn the back row. For Magistrate David Gurry, one face is hauntingly familiar. Mark Griffin had defended Bevan Von Einem.

It is a packed court when the accused are led in. First into the dock is John Bunting, walking with his peculiar gait, like a draught horse trying to canter. Wagner and Haydon follow, and all look directly at the magistrate and say nothing. Twelve months before, when they appeared in court under heavy guard to hear argument over the reporting of their case, their hair had been cropped to prison regulation length and all but Wagner wore jail-issued clothing. Around his neck, he had boasted a gold crucifix, which is noticeably absent. Today, they look slightly older and slightly less smug. A year in remand is taking its toll. It's a nasty place to live. Bunting has developed a noticeable paunch, but his eyes, behind his large glasses, are cold and unrepentant. Wagner steals a quick, sly look around the courtroom, huge and oafish next to his co-accused, but trimmer than he has been in the past, and his hair is close-cropped. Haydon shuffles in, as though an old man walking to the gallows. His complexion sallow; his look vacant. Their clothing is nondescript, hair and beards trimmed. If they weren't standing in the dock, no one would afford any of them more than a fleeting glance. Except the police.

Bunting, Wagner and Haydon – each charged with the murder of 10 people between January 1996 and May 1999 – maintain a belligerent silence as the charges are read to the court. Vlassakis, jointly charged with the murder of five people between April 1998 and May 1999, is the only defendant to speak, telling the court he reserves his defence.

Magistrate David Gurry tells the men their silence will be interpreted by the court as a denial of guilt. Mark Griffin, sombre and thin, immediately rises and asks that the court be closed for the prosecution's opening address, as some breaches of suppression orders have already occurred and no action has been taken. He continues, claiming that some of the material to be aired at the committal would be objected to at trial, and therefore should not be published within South Australia. 'Some of that material won't see the light of day', he said. 'We are concerned there is the potential for publication of material that is highly prejudicial and harmful and for which there is no safeguard against.' Griffin gets his way: the Crown's opening is suppressed, as is the scientific evidence given by the pathologists. It is the start of what will be unprecedented numbers of suppression orders.

The court is closed as Abraham, in the calm, measured voice that is her trademark, holds the floor for an hour, outlining the state's case, delicately unravelling strand after strand of the spider's web. Her slender fingers flirt with the palm of her hand as she speaks, but her body remains still. Abraham is a master of control. She needs to be. Brilliant on her feet, she will juggle the start of the committal with her role as prosecutor in a murder trial held in a nearby courtroom. She begins with the disappearance of Elizabeth Haydon, and the subsequent disappearance of the Land Cruiser that was towed from the Haydon property after police started making inquiries. 'The evidence to be led in this case, very broadly, falls within a number of categories', she continues. 'These include – although this is not an exhaustive list – the following: evidence of association between the various accused; evidence of association between the accused and the deceased; evidence of what was found in the bank and the bank vault – this is relevant to not only determining what had happened, but provides links with the bank and the accused, and the deceased and the accused.

'There is evidence of surveillance. This includes observations by the police relevant to the question of association between the accused. There is scientific evidence. This takes a number of forms, including the evidence of the post-mortem examinations. There are also a number of civilian witnesses that naturally relate to a number of topics. These include, for example, evidence of association, motive, explanations provided to them by various of the accused as to the disappearance of the deceased . . .

'The accused were well known to each other. And it is alleged the deceased were known to various of the accused . . .'

It is a marathon address, and Abraham pauses. 'They are my opening comments', she says, inclining her head before sitting down.

The suppression orders hold no weight beyond the South Australia border. Invoked to prevent prejudice to the proper administration of justice or undue hardship to a victim, witness, potential witness or child, they frustrate the media and the *Adelaide Advertiser* fires the first shot in what will become an ongoing war. The South Australian public, it rages, will possibly never know the full details of the prosecution's case against the four men accused of the Snowtown killings; the blanket ban on information is 'unprecedented' and 'extremely uncommon'. Magistrate David Gurry, it writes, has not only permanently suppressed from publication all details of the prosecution's hour-long opening to the committal hearing and the pathologists' evidence, he has also 'even suppressed his reasons for the suppressions . . . which has been reported extensively interstate and overseas where local court orders have no jurisdiction . . .'

The following day, Richard Ackland, editor of the *Gazette of Law and Journalism*, writes a piece for the *Sydney Morning Herald* on the suppressions. In his article headlined, 'Echoes of Bryant as Snowtown Prepares for Trial', Ackland argues that the concept of finding a jury totally free from prejudice is far removed from reality. And he pulls no punches. Describing Gurry as a 'nervy magistrate from the boondocks', he continues, claiming that Gurry is prepared to suppress all the 'seamy details that could infect potential jurors in his jurisdiction . . .' Ackland scoffs that a state of being where everyone is 'clinically free from prejudice' is well nigh impossible and describes the idea of 'the proper administration of justice' a 'doleful legal principle'. 'In this advanced technological age', he writes, 'news and information are no longer simply a local commodity.' He has made his point. But nothing changes.

The following day, the *Advertiser* – the newspaper most affected by the suppressions – runs an editorial that leaves readers in no doubt as to where the newspaper stands on the issue. Calling it a 'test of our freedoms', it roars that 'the principle that an accused should face the accusers in open court before an independent judge or judges . . . should be undeniable'. The media extend that courtroom to the wider public who are unable to attend. Allowing that there are circumstances when proceedings shouldn't necessarily be open to the media, such as issues of national security, the right to privacy, family and juvenile courts, it argues that this case is not one of them. '. . . Grave crimes are alleged. Because of them, rumours of the most lurid nature are rife. There is public disquiet. The best means of allaying it is to report the facts as presented to an open court, its proceedings fully and responsibly reported . . .'

Anyone with access to the Internet can read the material, it thunders. Readers' rights are being determined by lawyers and the judiciary in secret for reasons which cannot be divulged.

Journalist Penny Debelle returned to Adelaide in 1998 to work for the Melbourne *Age* and the *Sydney Morning Herald*. She describes the suppressions as an 'angst ridden debate' about what could, and could not, go into the copy. 'The lawyers ended up with the view that the suppressions could only extend to the jurisdiction of South Australia – beyond that, a full account of proceedings could be published. It was a real concern that publication of material could result in a mistrial. The forensic evidence was gruesome, but the courtroom setting is so de-personalised that it tends to buffer you from the evidence to a degree. Also, everything we were hearing was on such a huge scale that it was beyond belief, almost beyond experience.'

Debelle first hears about the story after police have discovered the bodies. 'My initial reaction was that I didn't believe it. There was some talk that it might be a ring of paedophiles, and I was at my desk making calls to Major Crime who were correcting misinformation. I had to file within the hour for two papers and so the pressure was on to get the story right. The weighty nature of the whole event was hard enough, but for the local reporters it was enormously frustrating. They would spend hours compiling a piece and then most of it would be removed because of the suppressions in place in South Australia, so local TV reporters, for example, were going to air with virtually meaningless stories, through no fault of their own.'

Debelle files two stories every day: one to suit the local market and the other for interstate readers. It is the only way the papers can get around the suppressions but still, it is a minefield. She is denounced in court one day by South Australian Attorney-General Trevor Griffin, who names her and implies that she has breached suppression orders because a copy of the *Sydney Morning Herald* has been sold in a south-east

South Australian town, on the border. He claims that, effectively, it has been published in South Australia because people can easily buy it, and he wants her media accreditation to gain entry into the court hearing revoked. Debelle copes with the public embarrassment by keeping her head down and reporting on the events as if they were happening to someone else. 'It was uncomfortable', she laughs. 'Humiliating. But the magistrate made it clear that any complaints of that nature had to go through the Department of Public Prosecutions and that there was no argument as far as he could see with regard to contempt of court.'

The debate widens, filling the airwaves. Everyone, it appears, has an opinion.

Try as hard as they might to stay in line with the suppressions, sometimes the media makes mistakes. In February 2001 an ABC news broadcast inadvertently shows images of the four accused that have been suppressed. Their lawyer, Mr Short, has some explaining to do. '. . . As I understand it there's been a breakdown in the procedure arising out of human error, and I suspect that Sir Donald Bradman's death has played a part in that. With people being busy with other matters, they were not paying the attention that they ought but, as I say, that's a matter that will be looked into . . .' The ABC is fined.

Debelle recalls seeing the defendants for the first time in court. 'Vlassakis had his beard shaved off, and it was as if the things he was hearing about in the court – what he had allegedly done – were a revelation to him. He just looked like a scared little boy. Haydon, Wagner and Bunting were calm, but Vlassakis wasn't.' She finds herself in a situation that reporters frequently face: torn between the need to remain objective while being drawn to the story on a human level. 'Vlassakis had got mixed up with the others circumstantially because his mother had lived with John Bunting. It was a bit sad, really.'

With the suppressions in full swing throughout the committal, the police are also jittery about witnesses talking to reporters.

Schramm is well aware that in some cases the media has got to witnesses before the police have had a chance to interview them, some stitching up contracts for exclusive story rights. So the problem has now become, what to do with the media? 'We will have to start to call the press as witnesses', Schramm says. 'Who was the first person to speak to this person? Can we have your notes because we want to make sure the story they told you is the same one they are telling us. That is the potential dilemma we have got.' Police solve this 'dilemma' by hitting the phones and also by talking to witnesses face to face. 'Don't speak to the press', they warn. 'Hang up. Say nothing.'

Concerned that some stories might prejudice a fair trial, the Director of Public Prosecutions, Paul Rofe QC, issues an unprecedented warning to all press outlets. 'Trial by media', he says, 'will not be tolerated under any circumstances.'

As Debelle notes, the very last thing the police want is to see their case fall over because the media gets there first.

Some witnesses take the order seriously. Following Paul Rofe's announcement, Sylvia Lane, mother of Barry Lane, retreats behind the door of her home in Parafield Gardens, from where she had previously given interviews. On the door, she pins a note saying that her remarks have been twisted and that if any other media approach her, she will call the police.

But for every person like Ms Lane who closes their doors to the press, there are plenty more people willing to talk. Despite the order, there is no shortage of stories. People come out of the woodwork, claiming to be neighbours, friends and long-lost relatives. The three-ring media circus is in full flight, and everyone, it seems, wants to be a part of the act.

47

From the beginning of the committal, there is a clear demarcation line between Jamie Vlassakis and his co-accused: a security guard provides distance between him and the others and he arrives separately at court. It will become a familiar ritual: Bunting and Wagner slowly turning their heads to stare down their former co-conspirator, Vlassakis staring fixedly ahead at the magistrate, struggling to contain his terror.

At the end of the first week of the hearing, with legal arguments and suppressions seriously slowing proceedings, Vlassakis rises in the dock. Bemused, Gurry tries to stop him from speaking out by suggesting his counsel have a word, but it is too late. 'What I am about to say does not reflect upon my co-accused', Vlassakis says. 'I'd like to say I'm terminating my counsel.' Gurry closes the court: when it resumes two hours later, Vlassakis is no longer in the dock. He has been excused until January, Gurry explains, on medical grounds.

By the middle of January 2001, Vlassakis's head counsel, Nick Vadasz, has quit the case. Rosemary Davey moots that lawyer Eugene McGee should replace Vadasz, but adds that Vlassakis will need to confirm whether or not he wishes the proposed team to act for him.

The hearing is again adjourned until 12 February, and a transcript of the proceedings provided to the media. For the reporters covering the committal, the adjournments, added to the suppressions, are frustrating. And it will get a lot worse before the committal hearing finishes in July 2001.

Gail Sinclair is pissed off. It's bad enough that she has to take the stand as a witness at the committal, where they air her aliases for all the world to hear. Jodie Elliott, the name she is presently using; Gail Spek, Anne Knudson, Gail Sinclair, the list goes on. Perched wanly on the stand, she scratches the top of her head and looks around the court.

She has been seeing psychiatrists for years to treat depression, and had a mental breakdown in 1997. With all this added stress, she figures she could easily have another one. She changed her name from Gail Sinclair to Gail Elliott before she went back into hospital in 1999, and other name changes, she says, were to avoid an ex-husband who was giving her a hard time. But they can come in handy for other reasons, too, particularly when she wants to avoid paying debts. Once, someone came to her door inquiring about payment for electrical goods, asking if Gail Sinclair was there. 'Nup, she doesn't live here', she said, opening the door just a fraction. 'I dunno who she is. I'm Gail Elliott.'

During the committal, Gail Sinclair has to answer whether or not she screwed John Bunting. You'd think they'd leave her alone. After all, her sister Elizabeth and son Freddy are dead. She's still in mourning. She stares at her inquisitor with glacial eyes, hoping he will retract the question, but he doesn't. She has to answer. 'I think [I did] on one or two occasions. It was that rare, it's very hard to remember.'

'Could you forget such a thing?'

'Well . . .'

He won't give up; he's going to keep digging and digging until he draws blood. She waits, eyeballing him. His tone, when he speaks again, is slightly raised, sarcastic. '[Could you forget] whether you had sexual intercourse on one or two occasions, or not at all, with a particular man?'

'Well, I've forgotten about it with a lot of other men as well', she says, her lips pursed and her head slightly cocked to one side. 'So, yes.'

It's only the beginning, and already Sinclair feels like she is being hammered. There is now no mistaking the sarcasm in this lawyer's voice when he asks what possessions she has kept of her sister's. 'I kept Elizabeth's jewellery', she responds flatly. 'It sort of made me feel closer to my sister.' She is reluctant to say any more, but he is asking her about the furniture – lounge, kitchen table, fridge – that she has also kept. 'What, did you keep that because it made you feel closer to your sister?'

She squirms. 'No, mainly because I was required to have some furniture at the time.'

The public gallery is tittering, but Sinclair is beyond caring. Let them gasp and gawp at her, let the lawyers put their heads down with their polite coughs and sly grins. Let them. She is in mourning. She doesn't give a shit. She just wants to get out of here.

They are asking her about her sister, Elizabeth Haydon, about the tape recording that was made before Elizabeth died, whether or not Gail believes Elizabeth was forced to make the recording. She shakes her head. She doesn't know if Elizabeth was forced to and no, she wasn't present when any such record-ing was made. But she has heard the tape, heard Elizabeth yelling – yelling, ranting, raving – and then foul abuse, crying; the 'distressness', as Gail puts it, of someone crying. She says she only listened to it once. And the people in the court only want to hear the description once, stomachs churning as they imagine Elizabeth yelling, ranting, raving, the foul abuse that follows and then her begging, crying; no one listening to her begging and crying as she does what she is forced to and splutters the words into the tape recorder before she is murdered.

Gail Sinclair is telling them what she knows, has stood there during the committal and enough's enough. She is in mourning. She doesn't give a shit. She just wants to get out of here.

But at least she has been offered immunity from prosecu-tion. 'I might indicate Mrs Elliott – I'll call her by that name – has an immunity from prosecution for Social Security offences offered to her by the DPP', the lawyer tells the court. 'That was supplied to her via her solicitor . . . and she's also been given a letter of comfort by the state in respect of any offence short of murder.'

Sinclair admits trying to obtain Centrelink payments on behalf of Suzanne Allen, who was buried in the backyard of Bunting's former address at 203 Waterloo Corner Road. Bunting knocked on her door, she says, and asked her to go for a drive. But it wasn't what she had hoped for, not exactly a romantic run to the country.

She tells the committal her version of events. Mark Haydon is also in the car, and she is relegated to the back seat on the hour-long drive to Berri. Bunting asks her to make a phone call to Social Security, because Suzanne Allen has received a letter from the department which states she has been reported as missing. He wants her to ring up and let them know that she isn't missing, that she is all right. Gail is a bit confused about all this. 'Why can't Allen ring up herself?' she asks. 'That's not possible,' Bunting tells her. 'She doesn't want to communicate with people, she doesn't want to answer too many questions and she doesn't want her family to know where she is.' And so Gail agrees, because she understands from previous conversations with John Bunting what Allen has been through with her family. She can relate to this: she has been through similar stuff herself. She feels she has a bit of a bond with Suzanne Allen in that respect. And that is why she is standing in a phone box in Berri calling Social Security on behalf of this stranger she 'has a bit of a bond with' while Bunting and Haydon wait in the car. But the Social Security officer tells her she has to be sighted, to physically go into the office, and she isn't prepared to do that. No bloody way.

Maybe she wouldn't have done anything at all to help Bunting, if she had known he had called her the 'village idiot' behind her back. He sniggered she was a nut case, but he figures her time will come. He has plans for her. He is going to give her a 'hot-shot', an overdose of heroin, while she sleeps. But for the moment, Gail has her uses. Bunting offers to personally speak to Suzanne Allen. He'll talk to her and fix it up. He'll fix it.

Sinclair and Bunting also tried to rent a house in Allen's name, but the property fell through. And now the lawyer is on her back about her representing herself as Suzanne Allen to get discount cards and books, and asking about her discussions with John Bunting with regard to stolen goods. Gail Sinclair denies she knows any specific details, and her patience has now run out. The only reference to stolen goods that she has ever heard was that occasionally Bunting and Wagner's reason for not spending a great deal of time with her was because they had to go and do their shopping. No, *obviously* they weren't going shopping for food, she sneers, rolling her eyes upwards, as if the roof will open and beam her out of here. Obviously, it was a colloquial expression that she took to understand meant breaking and entering into people's houses and stealing their property. She is familiar with that expression, she has heard it a lot over the years. How has she heard it? Because, she says, she has some dubious brothers. That's how.

And now she is affronted, being asked if she has also dealt in stolen goods. 'Of course not', she indignantly replies. Of course she hasn't. But she 'kept nit' while Bunting and his two mates moved what she thought was stolen goods from the ceiling. More questions.

'Did John Bunting ever suggest he could ever do anything about your identity?'

'He did state to me that if Social Security got a bit heavy with me that I could acquire an identity that also had a Social Security going in it, and I said, "Sorry, any time I change my name with them I will let them know and my debts will follow me, with Social Security".'

She strokes the teddy bear she is holding as she finally steps down. Thank Christ that's over.

It is months into the committal, 2001. The witnesses at the hearing are picking up pace and sometimes provide unexpected entertainment. Barmaid Suzanna Dickenson, cross-examined by Bunting's counsel, Elizabeth Sheppard, is asked about her notation in the diary that police had asked her to keep, relating to the movements of her next door neighbours, the Haydons. Why, Sheppard asks, did she record the sighting of a red Volvo in the neighbourhood? Dickenson spits out her answer in a strident voice. 'It's as plain as the nose on your face. We live in Smithfield Plains. We don't drive Volvos or BMWs around there.'

But light entertainment is rare. Most witnesses provide gruesome insights. Greg Cannon met Bunting in 1984 and stayed mates with him throughout the 1990s.

Cannon's former de facto, Raelene Brown, met Bunting on a few occasions and as part of her evidence recalls a conversation she had with him in her kitchen in late 1993. 'He was just talking about different things you could do to people, like the way you could blow up houses and torture people; how you could hurt people', she says. 'We were sitting around talking. We were having a few problems with Mark Day, the bloke Bunting moved to Adelaide with, and Bunting said, "You can fix these problems by getting rid of people".' Some of his methods, Brown remembers, were 'torturing people, skinning people, putting salt on their wounds, razor blades in their feet, putting stuff through their air conditioning to make the house blow up'. Asked why she didn't tell Cannon that she was disgusted, why she didn't tell him not to bring Bunting around, she looks surprised. 'I would have deserved a punch in the head if I had done that, sir.'

Several witnesses comment that the killers spoke in code, using their own lingo to communicate with each other. Their 'code' evolved around cars: a broken down car that needed fixing signalled it was time for action. They were always fixing cars.

Like many of the other women who orbit in their circle, Tony Sinclair's de facto wife, Tammy McKenzie, learned a long time ago not to ask questions. She testifies that she heard Mark Haydon brag to Tony about how he 'got rid of someone' and that the person was one body 'they'll never find', but it didn't occur to her to inquire what he meant, or ask who he was referring to.

For Tammy, being somewhat intellectually impaired has its

advantages. People don't expect a whole lot of her. Her face, pleasant and bland against hair the colour of wet sand, doesn't change expression when she speaks. It is a blank canvas on which nothing is drawn. Tammy, sweet-natured and quiet, is used to the undercurrent of bad blood that swirls around her; she lives with a Sinclair and can't escape it.

Elizabeth Harvey does not make the committal hearing. Earlier, in an application to suppress her name and address, a lawyer tells the court: '. . . The names Elizabeth Harvey, David Johnson, Marcus Johnson, Christine Youde, Christine Vlassakis, and so on, don't hang in a vacuum. There's obviously, in this case, a web of interconnection, and some of those interconnections continue . . . Her health continues to be extremely poor, in fact, if anything, it may have taken a significant turn for the worse. On one possible prognosis she may have less than 12 months to live, but we're awaiting further tests to determine that.'

They come in droves, one after the other taking the witness stand, voluntarily or otherwise. By the time the witnesses have finished giving evidence about their association with Bunting, Wagner, Haydon and Vlassakis, the tawdry, sad lifestyles of the killers, witnesses and victims are well and truly hung out for public scrutiny. Many are unemployed and most are barely educated.

One witness at the committal hearing, Adam Solowitz, who met Wagner at the Country Fire Service in 1996, states that Wagner had a propensity for 'bashing poofters'. Apps cross-examines.

'To put it bluntly, you hated his guts and he hated yours.'

'I wouldn't go that far.'

'Not that far, but close . . .'

'We disliked each other, I would say.'

'You say that he admitted to bashing people you called poofters.'

'No, they are not my words.'

'Whose words are they?'

'The police officer who took the statement.'

The irony of Wagner 'bashing poofters' is not lost on the public gallery.

Tina Dowling, who once shared a house with Wagner's de facto, Maxine Cole, appears at times to be impatient with the questions that are put to her. Her blunt views raise eyebrows in the court. 'There were all sorts of stories going around', she says, 'from they were cannibals and they were doing social security fraud, to the coppers could have saved some of the victims.'

It is obvious that the evidence is going to be grisly, but just how foul no one could have predicted. On occasions, it is as though the very air in the courtroom is fetid, polluted by details so vile that onlookers gag, so obscene that some stagger out, unable to hear any more. Evil up close, the darkness of the human soul laid bare. And as it continues, people come to understand why Vlassakis vomited when he spoke to police, sick to his stomach as he recounted the hideous details. Depravity up close. A human parade of the banality of evil.

Maxine Cole's obese frame dominates the witness stand. Her evidence is damning. Declining to take the exemption offered to her in return for information, she explains that she met victim Gavin Porter at a friend's funeral and that eventually his car, which was by then being driven by Vlassakis and Wagner, was registered in her name. She testifies that she also knew Thomas Trevilyan, Barry Lane's last de facto.

She tells the court that Bunting, Wagner and Vlassakis – Bunting, particularly – liked to brag about what they had done on 'shopping' trips. If the property belonged to someone they disliked, they delighted in tearing the house apart. It was their signature, the calling card they left behind. Bunting, according to Cole, disliked quite a few people, particularly Michael Gardiner, David Johnson and Troy Youde.

But it is her testimony about a 'hit list' that chills the court. Jamie Vlassakis, she recalls, told her about it after Robert and John were arrested and before Jamie himself was charged. David Johnson had been on the list. Marcus Johnson also. She isn't sure about a man called Philip Gee, she says, but his partner, Roslyn, told her he was on the list. And there are other names: her cousin, Robert Wheeler; and another man by the name of Daffyd Cochrane. Her cousin, Nicole Zuritta, told her Jamie had mentioned those people. She isn't sure about someone called Fred Webb. The lawyer is asking her to just deal with the names that Jamie told her, rather than ones she has heard from someone else.

'What names did Jamie tell you were on the hit list?'

'Mark and Marcus', she says, 'and my cousin, Robbie. And Jamie said that Mark was the next one on the list to go.'

Mark Haydon. The rats had been planning to scavenge their own nest.

If Mark Haydon knew that he was on the 'hit list' he gave no indication of it. Aware that the police were starting to sniff around, he made a panicked phone call to Wagner. Maxine Cole had answered the call, and shortly after Bunting and Wagner went to Mark's address to move something from the shed. But Bunting didn't scare so easily. On another occasion, outside Haydon's house, a witness overheard Bunting talking about the cops having a look around the premises. 'The fat fucking cunts didn't find what they were looking for', he sniggered.

The evidence grinds on for a gruelling 49 days. On the pavement outside the court, smokers stand in a grey shroud as more details emerge about how the victims met their deaths. The faces of their families are turning as grey as the smoke that is exhaled from their mouths.

48

Elizabeth Harvey is too ill to sit in her chair anymore, but she constantly frets about Jamie: what he did, why he did it, why she did not do more to stop it. She tries to let it go but it haunts her, especially when the pain comes on bad in the middle of the night and she can't get any rest. Why didn't Jamie just take off after he saw Gavin's murder? Why didn't he make an excuse and leave? 'He should have made a better choice', she says, 'instead of allowing John to suck him in. Because we all have choices and even though he was in drug heaven, I still think that choice was open to him.'

Dying, and trying to work it all out. The deception and betrayal. 'I did see the money come in but it was in dribs and drabs and obviously it was when they killed a person and cleaned their house out, they would take their goods to cash converters if they didn't want them.' Robert would ring up and say, 'Tell John the money's in the bank', but she never got any of it. 'Robert used to call me his second Mum, and . . .' The monologue is interrupted by a phlegmy cough, and a sigh, before she resumes. 'He lived with us for quite a considerable time and he ate my meals, he looked at me to solve his problems for him with Maxine Coles and all the time he'd strangled my son and there was not one time that he looked at me funny.' She doesn't understand how they could sit at her table, or how John could sleep in her bed, knowing what they'd done.

She can't understand any of it. 'I learned not to rock the boat, but underneath all our arguments I still felt he was a rock that I could lean on, that he was there to protect me. That's why I can't understand how he could turn within the family and have murdered Troy and David and Gail's son. He was supposed to be engaged to her for 12 months, well he obviously charmed the pants off her. How could he do that to her son and still look her in the face? How could he do that and still sleep with me and make me feel safe and secure? You know, I didn't pick up that anything was wrong.

'So when Jamie said to me "There's a John that you don't know", he was referring to the John that I hate. But I've somehow got to put the two Johns together and, until I meet this John, I don't think I will be able to. It's very hard to get my head around. Because I never believed he would hurt me. Never.'

The details run over and over in her head, a recurring nightmare. Deception and betrayal. Worrying about her kids. There are holes all through the unit where the boys have thumped the walls and doors in grief and rage. Elizabeth reckons her youngest and Troy were so similar in thought, they were like bookends. Troy held his brother when he was just two hours old, and she figures they bonded from that moment. Now Troy is dead, John is in jail, and she is dying. Her youngest son will be alone.

She wishes he understood she has cancer and that the time they have now is the only time they will ever have. She tries to explain to him that she won't live until she's 200 years old but he cries when she says it. These are her biggest worries: that she will die before the boys are old enough to take care of themselves.

And in the end, all she has is regret and grief and bitterness. She tries to get it all said, sputtering it out in wheezy gasps. Journalist Alison McClymont takes down Elizabeth Harvey's story:

'Do you ever regret John Bunting coming into your life?'

'Mmm. Even now. I mean, it's worse now than what it was in the beginning. Now – murder, murder, murder. So, yes. The answer is yes. Yes.'

'But you really loved him, right?'

'I thought I did.'

'But now in retrospect you don't think you did?'

'Oh, in retrospect, I felt tremendous compassion and love.'

'Do you think Tammy really existed – you know – his daughter?'

'Yeah, apparently, according to the police she did. I thought she did.'

Marcus Johnson constantly adds his two-bob's worth, sitting next to Elizabeth as she talks, frequently interrupting. He is determined to make it clear that no one outside Bunting's immediate circle could have known what was going on, crashing through the sentences in his bumbling style. 'They talked in code', he repeats. 'There was always this . . . when you had the two of – any two together, that is, out of the four of them, including Jamie, right, when you – you had two out of that four together in any . . . or more, they gave you the impression that you were almost inferior, you would feel inferior in the sense that you would get the message that they had a secret code and they would now and again speak in code. They did, they absolutely spoke in a code.'

The day she returns to Adelaide at the height of summer, 2001, for the last series of interviews with Elizabeth Harvey, McClymont records her impressions on tape. 'I get to Marcus's house, it's 39 degrees, he doesn't have a fan in his house, it's like being in a sauna. He tells me that Elizabeth is unconscious and I can't interview her, that he will have to do the interview himself. He starts immediately talking about money and how he's going to get the money . . . I immediately ask to go to the hospital, we go over and all the time he's talking about money . . . We go into the hospital room and Elizabeth is sitting propped up in a chair, one that reclines, with a catheter bag, and her head on one side, tubes coming out her nose, in a hospital gown and sheet covering her torso and legs. In the room is her sister, Diane, who has been staying with her day and night. And Elizabeth wants a drink and she can't get it down, she is making the most horrendous noises. It was really distressing. Dreadful.'

It is the last time Alison sees Elizabeth.

Twelve hours later, she is dead.

In the end, there just isn't enough time. The death of Elizabeth Harvey, a prominent witness, on 6 February 2001 is a savage blow to the prosecution. Right to the end, she cannot figure a reason for John Bunting's overwhelming compulsion to kill. It is, she says, just like he waved a wand, anointing who would live, and who would die. All she can reason is that he killed because he could.

Because he could.

John Bunting does not apply to go to Elizabeth's funeral. Agitated, restless and grieving for his mother, Jamie Vlassakis tells McClymont that Bunting lost control when he found out about Elizabeth's death. 'He trashed his cell, but said he wouldn't be applying to go to the funeral because he knows they won't let him go', he told her. 'And I would have said, "Look, Mum didn't want you around anyway, after all this, you know what I mean?"'

Like his mother, Jamie struggles with the demons of guilt and regret about his association with Bunting. 'Basically, I'm not too sure how I feel, I mean I used to hero worship him . . . I grew up with him from an early age and then I got led down the wrong path. I didn't walk away, I didn't trust the police, I felt in a no-win situation. I got in deeper and deeper. Too deep. Shit happens. I feel sorry for the fact that it should never have happened, you know what I mean?'

Thrilled that prison authorities have allowed him to attend his mother's funeral, Jamie gets his Auntie Diane to organise him an outfit to wear. 'Auntie Diane will be getting me a shirt and tie and slacks and shoes', he tells McClymont on the telephone from James Nash House. 'My old clothes don't fit me any more. I've put on so much weight. I used to be 65 kilos before I come to jail, now I'm 85.8 or something!'

'The food must be good.'

'Aw, not really', he laughs. 'I've been exercising. But my

daily routines aren't the same now. You know what I mean?'

'Don't they get you doing much exercise?'

'No, when I'm at Yatala, none at all. It's 21 hours a day in the cells.'

He has no sleep the night before his mother's funeral, fretting that he won't get the chance to say goodbye properly, that he will be handcuffed and the private family service will be turned into a circus.

Handcuffed to his trouser belt and flanked by prison guards, Vlassakis is forced to stand apart from his family at the funeral. Fascinated with the handcuffs, a toddler crawls over to him and starts playing with them, thinking they are bracelets.

Even after the funeral, Jamie can find no peace of mind. 'Now we've had the funeral, said our goodbyes – you know what I mean, now we've still got people hassling us all the time, the media, other prisoners. Now they'll write all the bad shit in the paper about it, instead of saying who she was, it'll be, "Mother of Snowtown killer Jamie Vlassakis, girlfriend of John Bunting". But you know, for me, my Mum was my Mum.'

He tries to keep a low profile in jail, and prefers the peace of James Nash House. 'People in here get to know me for who I am, not for what I've done. You know what I mean? Like, a lot of people in Yatala, they turn around and try and hero worship you. It's a big ego thing. I mean, you go into jail and, you know, you're arrested on five counts of murder and you know what I mean, no one else is. But I've made friends with a couple of lifers in there and they understand the situation, they know what happened. They've accepted who I am and really, I'm not after friends.'

He will need them for what lies ahead.

49

The Supreme Court in Adelaide, surrounded by squares and parks on the corner of Gouger and King William Streets, does not have holding cells. Criminal cases are heard across the road in the Sir Samuel Way building, and the accused, flanked by security, are brought up to the dock from the holding cells below.

Sir Samuel Way has 17 holding cells, starkly modern and each containing nothing more than a bunk, a toilet and a sink. These cells are a world away from the drunk tanks in police holding cells where people spend a few hours sobering up before they face court. It is virtually silent down here, save for the sounds of nervous hands being wiped on trousers, the shuffle of feet, up and down, up and down the cell, and occasionally the muttered, muffled prayer of a man fearful of losing his freedom. The lawyers, in last-minute consultations with their clients, hear every sound: a hawking man clearing his throat, the flushing of toilets and the hollow bravado of people in their late teens who have finally made the dubious graduation to the Supreme Court.

Upstairs in the courtroom, people are taking their places: the public, lawyers, media and police, rising and bowing to the judge as he enters court. Downstairs, the prisoners wait for the jangling of keys to open their locks, signalling it is time to follow their jailers through the corridor, up the steps and into the dock. This is always the worst part, when they are suddenly on show; downstairs, they can hide from the world but here, it seems to be lined up in front of them. Some look out to the body of the court, returning fire with fire, hatred from the victims' families or the victims themselves. Some keep their gaze directly on their defence lawyers, as if by staring them down they will cause them to magically pull a rabbit out of a hat and convince the jury – that nebulous group of individuals – that they are innocent, wrongly accused and should be set free. And some don't look anywhere, save down at their hands, their affirmative reply about their identity muffled in the witness stand and by the unfamiliar shirt collars that chafe their necks.

If they walk free, they will exit through the front door of the grandiose building, formerly one of the oldest department stores in Adelaide, from 1912 until its closure in 1980. A wide marble staircase dominates the inner entrance and sunlight filters through multi-coloured leadlight set in the ceiling's massive dome. It is a rarefied world, quiet and controlled.

If they are found guilty, they are escorted from the dock, bundled into a prison van and given a free ride to prison.

Dr John Raeside, Vlassakis's treating psychiatrist from the time of his arrest, is cognisant of John Bunting's hold over his patient. He had, he notes, expressed a wish to have some contact with Mr Bunting within the prison environment. This was not so much to discuss whether he should or shouldn't enter a plea; he simply wanted to see Bunting and get a feel for what would happen if he pleaded guilty.

These were tense times for Vlassakis, and the prison rumour mill was rife that Bunting and Wagner were going to do something to him. 'When I saw John in Yatala, I said straight out to him, "Listen, are you going to kill me or what?",' he later confesses to Alison McClymont. 'And he turned around and said, "I can't believe you'd fuckin' ask me that question because you know I'd do anything to get out of here". So basically, he just wants me back under the thumb where he had me before, so that if something happens to him in jail I'd be there to help save his arse.'

Justice Brian Martin is waiting in chambers for the court to open. Appointed to the bench three months before police opened the vault at Snowtown in May 1999, he spent two years before that as the Commonwealth Director of Public Prosecutions. In Western Australia during the turbulent days of WA Inc his name was inexorably linked with the highly publicised prosecution of corporate larrikin Alan Bond in his role as senior counsel with the royal commission into the affair. He was also the lead prosecutor on the Von Einem case.

Court 7 of the Sir Samuel Way building is quiet on this Thursday, 21 June 2001, for the surprise arraignment of Jamie Spyridon Vlassakis. Dark-haired, fresh-faced and boyishly handsome, Vlassakis doesn't display the same leering demeanour today that he has shown in the past. Gone is the confident swagger, the little jig he performed for the cameras as he was led into court for the start of the committal months before; gone, the poking out of his tongue and obscene grin, the smile that often played on his face in the courtroom. Now, as he stands in the dock clean-shaven and dressed in open-neck white shirt and blue denim jeans, he is a nervous and sombre young man who swallows hard and often, his Adam's apple bobbing up and down in rhythm with his hands that shake in their cuffed restraints.

For the six months of the committal hearing, Vlassakis refused to enter a plea, his silence construed by the court as a plea of 'not guilty'. But today is different. Today, 25 months after police opened the vault at Snowtown, he falters, his chin quivering as he rises in unison with his counsel, Rosemary Davey, who is still acting for him. The charges are read out.

Today, in a dramatic courtroom confession, he makes a trade-off, hoping for leniency in the handing down of a non-parole period. The arraignment has been brought forward to allow him to enter his pleas.

'Guilty', he murmurs to the joint charge of murdering his half-brother, 21-year-old Troy Youde, between late August and early September 1998. He does not look up, his eyes riveted to the courtroom floor as the clerk of court prepares to read out the second charge.

'Guilty', he says, to the joint charge of murdering Frederick Brooks in September 1998. He is weeping now, tears splashing down his cheeks, but his emotion attracts little sympathy. 'Sick bastard', someone mutters in the public gallery.

'Guilty', for his part in the murder of Gary O'Dwyer, between October and November 1998. Quietly crying now, his response barely audible as his lip quivers. In the body of the court, an onlooker breaks down in a paroxysm of sobs, oblivious to the strangers around him.

'Guilty.' David Johnson, his stepbrother who had trusted him; who was thrilled Jamie had gone with him to Snowtown to buy a cheap computer.

'Ha ha. We're on our way up there.'

'The side door is open. Walk straight in.'

Johnson, the last victim, murdered in the vault at Snowtown in early May 1999. Betrayed, tortured and dismembered, parts of his flesh fried in the pan before being eaten.

Vlassakis slumps back in his seat and buries his head in his hands.

He was 18 years old at the time of the first three murders, 19 by the fourth. He is now 22 years old.

Justice Martin, whose genial face belies his sharp intelligence and fine legal mind, asks Vlassakis to stand. 'Mr Vlassakis, the law prescribes only one penalty for the crime of murder and that is life imprisonment. Accordingly, on each of the four counts to which you have pleaded guilty, I sentence you to imprisonment for life.'

Vlassakis does not flinch.

Explaining that Vlassakis has been charged, at his request, with four murders on ex officio information − charges initiated by the Crown rather than those that result from police information − his counsel, Rosemary Davey, continues her submissions. 'Our client has, by his pleas, and will, by the submissions which will be made on his behalf, acknowledge his involvement in what must be described as, and he agrees are, horrendous crimes. Yet there is a lot that can and will be said for this young man and there is a large amount of material as to the factual circumstances of the offences which must be put before the court, and we need the time to gather that to put before Your Honour. There is a great deal of material about my client's personal history and circumstances, including, it is hoped, material as to his psychiatric state. In this case, we will be asking the court to fix a non-parole period [and] we understand the DPP does not oppose that course. We understand that the charge of murder in relation to Gavin Porter will be withdrawn in the Adelaide Magistrate's Court. Our client is not guilty of that offence.'

The implications of Davey's address are clear. A guilty plea, side-stepping the necessity for a lengthy and expensive trial that will save the state millions of dollars in legal costs, could attract significant remissions.

Justice Martin does not reveal to the court the reasons for his decision to indefinitely continue suppression on the image of Vlassakis, placing the order in a sealed envelope. In adjourning for sentencing submissions until 20 July 2001, he warns the media that Vlassakis's plea has no relation to the charges facing his co-accused.

Vlassakis, a blanket over his head, is chaperoned from the court under heavy police guard and whisked away in the back of a car to an undisclosed destination, where he will begin serving his life sentences. Reporters, milling with the small crowd gathered outside the court, query whether the surprise confession means that Vlassakis will be called to give evidence against his co-accused. Director of Public Prosecutions, Paul Rofe QC, refuses to answer their questions.

For the time being it is over and done with, and Vlassakis at least has the compensation of knowing that the fifth and final murder count he faced – his mate, Gavin Porter, killed in early April 1998 – will be dropped.

On 4 July 2001, Magistrate David Gurry hands down his decision, which takes less than a minute to deliver.

'Having over a number of months had the opportunity to consider the declarations and to consider the oral evidence of various witnesses who were called, I have formed the view the evidence is sufficient to place each of the defendants on trial for each of the offences as charged. The defendants will be committed for trial in the Supreme Court, where they will appear on arraignment on August 13 at 10am.'

Gurry rises to signify the committal hearing is over. Bunting, Wagner and Haydon remain as impassive as they have been throughout and leave the dock in an orderly manner. Bunting turns his head as he exits through the dock's doorway, his eyes scanning the faces of the Taskforce Chart police, who have come to have their day in court. Only after he is gone do they register any relief at the outcome.

The state dips into its coffers to organise special legal aid payments to ensure the men all receive a fair defence. Wagner's lawyer also has to purchase equipment that will facilitate the evidence being read into an audio file, as his client cannot read or write.

That this case will be kicked upstairs to the Supreme Court comes as no surprise to the reporters who have covered the committal for months on end. Now they have the trial to face, one that promises to be an epic: long and complex. The logistics alone are boggling: a $6 million budget to cover lawyers' costs, a courtroom tailor-made for the cast that will attend, and an empanelling of 15 jurors, instead of the usual 12. Attorney-General Trevor Griffin makes this decision in order to minimise the risk of the trial being aborted in case of death or illness of a juror.

Chris Paraka QC is under no illusions about the peculiar stresses that will be placed on the jury in this particular case. 'The trauma will be significantly more than in many murder cases; that follows just from the number of deaths and the circumstances of the disposal of the bodies, the necessary evidence about the forensic work that that will entail. That's of course not to take away from the enormous trauma and difficulty that jurors would face in assessing the evidence of any murder trial. Jurors are pulled off the street without previous exposure to matters such as this, they then have to listen to very detailed evidence about the forensic examinations involved and view photographs that would be completely outside their day to day experience.'

To their distress, some jurors will discover how right he is.

50

Delayed until October 2001, Vlassakis finally appears in court for submissions on the fixing of a non-parole period. It is a dramatic moment. For the first time, it is made public that he will be called as a Crown witness against his co-accused and his image will remain suppressed to the public. 'I do not know where he is [being held] and I do not know the name under which he is being kept', Justice Martin tells the court. 'He is to be a Crown witness in what is a trial which . . . has been quite an extraordinary matter. It's generally accepted that when witnesses who are in custody as offenders are to be Crown witnesses, there's some cause for concern about their security.'

Like his guilty plea, his decision to turn Crown witness is not taken lightly. Vlassakis has wrestled with the dilemma: whether to join Bunting and Wagner for his own safety, as an insurance policy against the possibility of being killed in jail, or to make a deal with the DPP, go on the witness protection program and hopefully win himself a non-parole period. It is a weighty decision, made in the pressure-cooker environment of jail. But the journalist's hunches were correct.

Jamie Vlassakis will roll over. Turn dog.

Sentencing submission hearings, before Justice Kevin Duggan, begin eight months after Vlassakis pleads guilty. His counsel, Rosemary Davey, has asked for an adjournment on the submissions pending further psychiatric reports, but makes it clear that her client had expressly asked to be sentenced before he testifies. 'My client, more than anyone, is really anxious to know his fate', she states.

Davey is passionate. 'The events leading to the death of four people', she says, 'were evil, marked by unparalleled barbarism, cruelty and sadism . . . But the story of James Spyridon Vlassakis is not the story of an evil young man. It is the story of a person who participated in evil and why he did so . . .' Davey pauses before continuing a lengthy address, outlining Vlassakis's tragic life, the harrowing police interviews to which he has willingly submitted, his remorse, guilt and fear of John Bunting and his traumatic childhood.

'John Bunting', she continues, 'is a depraved, disturbed if not deranged, vicious and dangerous killer. The relationship was one of power and corruption of my client . . .'

Davey does not shy from the issue of cannibalism. 'My client was going to have a shower and he comes out to find Robert Wagner cooking the flesh of David Johnson in a frying pan in the kitchen. He was offered some, told effectively, "Try some", as was Denis Cordwell.' Vlassakis declined the offer, she continues, and volunteered this 'whole horrible revolting scenario' in his first record of interview.

There is no escaping the evidence now: how her client described the 'extensive use' of instruments for torture – 'like sparklers in the torture, the blows, the use of devices to crush toes, the burns, the electric torture, the injection of material'. The public is wincing, kneading tissues, crossing and uncrossing legs, putting their heads down as the revelations continue, descriptions of evil at work, the bizarre ritualism of the killings: the playing of music, the subjugation, 'Lord, Master'.

Davey calls on two psychiatrists – Professor Mullen and Dr Raeside – to offer opinion about Jamie Vlassakis. Their evaluation is bleak. Bunting, they believe, has moulded and shaped the impressionable, damaged young man like a piece of pottery. Vlassakis's development through childhood and adolescence occurred in a context of disorganisation, inconsistency, emotional deprivation and frank abuse, any or all of which might be expected to disrupt his subsequent personality and emotional stability. His drug use, unstable mood, recurrent suicidal impulses and incapacity to maintain any stable social or work roles could all have been contributed to by such disturbances of personality. His history has led to both depression and post-traumatic stress disorder. He was extremely vulnerable because of his on-going sexual abuse and lack of any consistent care from a role model. Mullen notes that: 'In my opinion, one of the many tragedies in this case is that a vulnerable, immature and dependent adolescent, desperately seeking adult love, care and concern, fell under the influence of John Bunting'.

But Mullen adds that while Vlassakis did not take pleasure in the infliction of pain and was not detached in a psychopathic sense, his fear of Bunting could only partially explain his 'silence, acquiescence and active participation' in the murders. He was often separated from the older man and able to escape his influence. In his opinion, Vlassakis's involvement 'did not stem primarily from fear, but from having come to share Mr Bunting's views about a number of matters and from coming to view him as a figure of such power that acquiescing in his wishes was the only option . . .'

Their conclusion is positive. With maturity, James Vlassakis could one day re-emerge into society, no longer damaged or anti-social.

Then Vlassakis speaks, offering his 'sincere and unconditional sorrow' to the victims' families and friends. Neatly dressed in white shirt, slacks and tie, he appears bowed. 'I hate myself for the fact I have done these degraded crimes. I have to live with the pain and suffering I have caused to the victims, families and friends and it sickens me to think that I could even be involved in taking away precious lives from their loved ones. When I lie in bed at night, I think I don't know myself any more . . . in the mornings I wake up and think "Why?" . . . and when I look in the mirror and look at my face, I think, "This is not me. How did I end up in this position?" I could kill myself tomorrow, but then I think this would be the easy way out, and then I realise that the choices I've made are the ones that will affect my life forever . . . Now is the time to face up to my mistakes and own up to my responsibilities . . . I am so sorry for what I have done and I could never forgive myself . . . I would like to say to the loved ones of the victims, I know that nothing I have said today nor anything else would ever make up for the pain I have caused you. I know the damage I have done to your lives and the suffering you will have to experience, and I know you can never forgive me, but I am sorry.

'As I look back and reflect into the past I wonder what went wrong and why I cannot change the terrible things I have done', he says. 'I know the damage I have done to your lives.'

There is a moment, a brief heartbeat, when there is no sound in the courtroom, like a minute's silence for war veterans; a stunned, sad silence where the spirits of the victims – Troy Youde, 21, David Johnson, 24, Gary O'Dwyer, 29 and Fred Brooks, 18 – seem to hover over proceedings, hover over Vlassakis's words. '. . . what went wrong . . . the terrible things I have done . . . I am sorry.'

And then it is gone, replaced by Wendy Abraham QC recounting the gruesome details all over again.

What Bunting, Wagner and Haydon think of their mate turning state's witness – turning 'dog', in the prison vernacular – is not made public.

But the feelings of David Johnson's natural mother, Carlyne Cheeseman, about the death of her son, are. In a harrowing victim impact statement, she spells out her pain. 'David's death ended his dreams of becoming a journalist or a cartoonist . . . I will never see him again. I will never hold his children. I have lost the grandchildren I thought would bring me joy in my ageing years . . . Family and friends all deserted us as if a son murdered is a contagious disease . . . The only thing I got was the body, which I had to collect from Adelaide and transport myself in the farm ute because the state did not supply any funds for transportation . . . I was told, because I lived in Victoria, all "Support Victims of Crime" help stopped at the border . . . It was a gathering at the graveside of [husband] Ron and I, his twin brother Michael, a girlfriend who loved him very much and her parents . . . We had to sell the property in Hamilton . . . The lack of information made available to the public caused people to fear us. Ignorance breeds gossip, slandering [sic] and suspicion . . . Our lives lack the peace, happiness, joy and freedom we once had . . . [I] cry each Mother's Day, the anniversary of his murder, and his birthday, which he shares with his twin, is no longer a day of celebration.

'To Jamie I would like to say, I forgive you, but I don't condone your actions. I feel sorry for you because you have robbed and defiled yourself. What has been done has been done, but can't be changed, not in heaven or earth. Just as Judas gave Jesus to his murderers for 30 pieces of silver, so you gave up my son for his possessions and money . . . David was no angel, but his life was not yours to take.'

There is little left for Rosemary Davey to say. '[My client] has shown great moral fortitude in owning up, and knows he is both morally and legally a murderer. The persons who should have protected my client failed to do so. Elizabeth Harvey left her son in the care of a man she knew to be a callous and wicked killer. John Bunting did nothing but initiate my client into a world of evil and malignancy. He will spend a long time in prison. He has never had a life, he has no proper joy, he has had no family, and is now without anyone else to care for him. He is truly alone. He is unlikely ever to marry, he is never to have children. He will be denied his freedom, and that, he acknowledges, is how it must be. But he is not evil . . . he is worthy of redemption . . . mercy should prevail.'

This sober, sorrowful Jamie Vlassakis is very different from early depictions of him whooping and grinning outside the courthouse. For Marcus Johnson, father of victim David Johnson, who has to make submissions both for and against his stepson, Vlassakis, those early images are obscene. In the months leading up to Jamie's sentencing, Marcus wrestles with the enormity of what he has to do. 'I can't find it in my heart to hate him, even though he killed my lovely David and my lovely Troy. I thought he had the capacity to love his family, but he obviously never did. He must never walk the streets again. I don't know him as a human being. I obviously never did.'

Justice Duggan's sentencing remarks recap Vlassakis's disruptive, unsettled life, reading like a sad resume. In conclusion, Justice Duggan tells Vlassakis: 'If it had not been for your plea of guilty, your extensive co-operation with the police and your undertaking to give evidence for the prosecution in the forthcoming trial, I would have imposed a non-parole period of 42 years . . . I fix a non-parole period of 26 years to date from 2 June 1999, the date when you were taken into custody . . . After that, it is up to the authorities as to whether and when you will be released.'

51

Seasoned journalists know that while murder trials are often harrowing, lengthy trials can also become very dull. Regardless of how big the story is, it's a struggle to keep up the momentum, to titillate the public and keep them informed, to create a story that commands attention, to stay awake day after day, week after week, and not let boredom creep into the copy.

Lawyers, tugging at their forelocks, mumbling into their colleagues' ears, addressing the judge, 'I respectfully . . .', 'Your Honour', 'May it please the court . . .' The forensic evidence, the exhibits, the protracted silences as the junior lawyers awkwardly search for relevant pages in their notes. The rustle of gowns, the scratching of wigs, the exasperated looks from the eminent silks, the judge stifling yawns, the 'All rise!' every time the judge enters and leaves the room, the swearing of oaths, 'Do you promise to tell the truth, the whole truth, and nothing but the truth, so help you God?' The heartbreaking sound of the victims' families crying as they listen to the evidence, the shuffling in the dock of the accused, the grim set of the coppers' faces, the adjournments, the legal arguments ad infinitum and, finally, the ticking down of the minutes and hours that can turn into days, waiting for the jury to return.

There is a long, long wait for the trial of Bunting and Wagner to start. Vlassakis's submissions – hundreds of pages – slow down the system, and then there is the legal argument about admissibility, closed to the media, and the empanelling of a jury. It will be March 2002 before it gets under way. It is not for nothing that the press wryly nickname the case: Slowtown.

It is three years since the bodies were discovered; three years since the first headlines when Australians thought: 'Oh God, not again!' as they had thought when the backpackers were found in the Belanglo State Forest and when toddler Jaidyn Leskie's little body was found in the dam. And in that time, Sydney has hosted the Olympics, the world shifted a gear on September 11, Elizabeth Harvey has died, Jamie Vlassakis has changed his plea, there has been the committal and the long, legal argument at the start of the trial.

And now this. On 21 May 2002 – exactly three years to the day after his arrest – two further murder charges are laid against Bunting, for the murders of Clinton Trezise and Thomas Trevilyan.

It is eight years since the remains of Trezise were found in that lonely paddock at Lower Light: Trezise, the first victim to be found, the last to be identified. In his small lounge room at Waterloo Corner Road, dominated by a television set, Bunting could not have failed to see the nightly news broadcast of the farmers who stumbled on skeletal remains. And as the years passed, and the body remained unidentified, he must have privately gloated that the cops would never connect him with that murder.

Wagner is also charged with the murder of Trevilyan and with assisting offenders in relation to Trezise. Haydon, too, is charged with the murder of Trezise, but without enough evidence to implicate him in all 12 killings, he will eventually stand trial only for the murders of his wife Elizabeth and Troy Youde.

Without preamble, Justice Martin orders that to ensure Haydon receives fair trials, his proceedings will not run jointly with those of Bunting and Wagner. 'I doubt that the separation of trials will add greatly to the public expense as individual trials will be shorter and more efficient', Justice Martin says. The Bunting/Wagner trials are to start first.

Robert Wagner is on his feet on this 27th day of September 2002. He has changed his plea to guilty on three counts of murder. Barry Lane. Fred Brooks. David Johnson. A smile flickers around his bulbous lips. There will be no more admissions.

'Ladies and gentlemen.' Wendy Abraham momentarily pauses at the start of her opening address. There is not the slightest movement in the court. It has taken four years to get to this and the jury of 15 is intent on absorbing her deliberate, clear sentences. They do not take their eyes from her. A face that could be chiselled from porcelain. Skin the colour of whipped cream. Her voice is slightly clipped, unemotional as she turns page after page, unravelling the sordid details of a story unimaginable in its savagery. The Crown is not required to prove a motive. But Abraham and her team know there are common themes underlying *why* particular victims were chosen. They are themes that will be woven throughout the trial. Some victims know too much and, therefore, pose a greater risk of exposing the group's activities. Some were murdered because Bunting believed they were homosexuals or paedophiles. Others were killed for financial gain. And some just presented opportunity.

'On the 20th May 1999, when the police opened the vault of the disused State Bank at Snowtown, they were met with the pungent smell of rotting or decomposing meat...' Abraham quickly moves to warn the jury about what lies ahead. 'The Crown alleges that what the accused, John Bunting and Robert Wagner, did in committing these crimes can only be described as horrific. What you will hear at times will be very unpleasant and distasteful. The description of some of the events will be chilling...' After the first hour, the faces of the jury appear to have been dunked in bleach.

Steady, unimpassioned, on and on. By late afternoon, the judge calls stumps. Tomorrow, he tells the jury. We will continue tomorrow. But first he needs to warn them to take care when leaving the building. He draws an unsteady intake of breath. 'I am afraid I have just received some extremely distressing news. A senior public servant has been gunned down outside her [city] office... The Star Force is in the streets and on the lookout for the killer. I urge you to take care.'

Margaret Tobin, the former director of South Australia's Mental Health Services, has been assassinated in broad daylight and her killer, a deregistered psychiatrist, will be jailed in late 2004 for the murder. With the world's press present for the opening address, it seems an ominous beginning.

It is.

A female jury member, unable to stomach the gruesome evidence, has bailed out, on day one. On the back of her decision, so early in the trial, Justice Martin discharges the jury and empanels a new one. The second jury of seven men and eight women is older, more conservative. Bunting stares hard at each of their faces, Wagner looks uninterested. And from the beginning, Justice Martin – at pains not to have to start again – nurses and mollycoddles them. Now Abraham has to start all over again. She rises, steady. 'Ladies and gentlemen . . .'

Now she is reading out the victims' names and other details.

Wagner is salivating, Bunting cold as stone.

Clinton Trezise, 22, August 1992. Ray Davies, 26, December 1995. Suzanne Allen, 47, November 1996. Michael Gardiner, 19, September 1997. Barry Lane, 42, October 1997. Thomas Trevilyan, 18, November 1997. Gavin Porter, 31, April 1998. Troy Youde, 21, August 1998. Fred Brooks, 18, September 1998. Gary O'Dwyer, 29, October 1998. Elizabeth Haydon, 37, November 1998. David Johnson, 24, May 1999.

Abraham's junior, Sandi McDonald, sits quietly next to her. It has been her task to interview witnesses, to lay the groundwork for questions. Fair where Abraham is dark, warmer by nature but with the same dedication to the law, she will take over cross-examination whenever necessary.

It is a monumental address, an epic two-day journey on a highway littered with signposts and clues that were not detected for years. One lawyer switches off to the sections of the address he has already heard, idly trawling the Internet on his laptop, looking at the latest model Porsche. A British documentary maker, in court for the opening address, raises his eyebrows. This trial, he whispers, will prove to be a gravy train for lawyers.

Bunting is casually dressed in open-necked shirt and jeans; his co-accused, Wagner, incongruously dapper in a blue suit and tie. There is little their lawyers can do to counteract Abraham's lethal address, apart from trying to negate some of the damning evidence. And they try hard.

After every recess, Bunting and Wagner emerge from the cells beneath the court, as though the earth has opened up and delivered them; silently re-appearing in the dock, their faces expressionless and still.

Wagner's blond hair is receding. Thickset and dumb, he uses the middle fingers that had tightened the rope on his victims' necks to push his glasses back up on the bridge of his nose. He occasionally glances around the court with his customary dull blankness or hideous smirk, but mostly he is absorbed in the theatre of witnesses and lawyers or his computer terminal. His lead counsel, Stephen Apps, is an antipodean Rumpole, a loud, rambunctious larrikin completely lacking in pomposity. The court and its precincts are his stage. On one occasion, I pass him in a narrow corridor, his horsehair wig tucked under his arm; he raises an imaginary bowler hat, grins broadly as he bows deeply from the waist and says in an exaggerated voice, 'After *you*, my dear'.

There are no such theatrics with Bunting's lawyer, Mark Griffin, who has the air of a travelling preacher with the Devil on his tail. Curt, serious and frugal with his smiles, Griffin – dark hair and slim shoulders curved into well-cut suit – never lets his mask slip. Defending John Bunting is the most thankless job in the land, and the points he scores are rare. But he stays focused, his mind on his client. There is no time for theatrics.

Mark Griffin tries to trip Veronika Tripp up. 'John never said to you that he did it, or that he killed anyone, or that he buried a body at Lower Light.'

'What I wrote in my statements are what I remember and that's all I can remember,' she replies, scowling. 'I wouldn't – I don't make false statements to police. It's against the law.'

He returns to the subject later. 'I put to you that you never said to John anything about a story from Barry about killing someone and burying a body at Lower Light. You didn't ever talk to John about that.'

'I did, I remember I did. I wouldn't be able to remember something if it didn't happen. Of course it happened.'

He deals with Tripp they way one would a slow child. 'Do you understand the question? Then I'll break it down into two parts.'

She pouts at him, strokes her teddy bear.

Bunting declines to return to Snowtown for the jury viewings; give the press and the jury anything to cogitate on, about his demeanor or emotions. But Wagner goes, marching down the middle of the road handcuffed at the front like an overgrown schoolboy in too-short trousers and wearing his usual dense expression.

All up, the jury views would take five days, trawling through the accuseds' houses and other locations, watched over by curious locals come to ogle this legal sideshow. But if the media had hoped for some recognition from Wagner, on the searing hot day, that he is moved by his return to Snowtown, they are disappointed. Nothing but the vague suggestion of a smile that plays around his mouth.

Brian Swan intervenes with the owner of the bank to stop her pulling it down. 'She was going to demolish it,' he tells the court, 'and when we found out about that, bearing in mind that if there is going to be a jury view, it would be nice to leave the premises, so I approached her and she was in agreeance with that. She said, "I'll do that if you can arrange for the [vault] door to be back on its hinges." So I contacted the local police officer at Snowtown and . . . the door was put back on.'

And if anyone was in any doubt about just what was hidden inside that vault, pathologist Dr Gilbert reiterates what he and the pathology team had found in those barrels. 'We needed someone with anatomical knowledge to ensure we could work out which bits went with which bodies,' he says.

During the trial, thousands of exhibits are put up to the jury, displaying the filth that wrapped itself around every daily event in their lives, scribbled on pieces of paper, stuck on the wall of spiders. 'I'm in Barry's AIDS hole.' 'Ray is a homo.'

Court 3 has entered Hades. They are watching video footage taken inside the vault, the police camera slowly panning the opening of each barrel. Severed, bloodied hands and feet. Gloves. Clothing. Hair. Gut-churning.

It is three years since police opened the vault, and the barrels have been professionally steam cleaned. But they still reek. They are so putrid, still, that they cannot be exhibited in the courtroom. The jury is shown, instead, barrels of similar design and size, and photographs of the empty drums.

And as at the committal, witness after witness takes the stand. Clutching teddy bears, breaking down in tears, averting their eyes from the dock, trembling or belligerent. Regardless of the jury's sympathies, it doesn't always go well.

Detective Stone is asked by the prosecution to elaborate on what he means by the 'smell of death'. Was it like rotting flesh, was it like decomposition? Or what?

There was, Stone says, what he considers the peculiar odour of a body.

'A peculiar odour of a decomposing body?'

'Correct.'

'Because of this odour, did you give the shed a thorough search?'

'There were no bodies in the pit. It was obvious.'

'I take it that the smell, when you say you detected a smell, that would have had a big effect on you in relation to the investigation of Elizabeth Haydon.'

'Correct.'

'It would have been the situation that upon smelling this odour, in your view, we are talking about not just a possible murder investigation but a *probable* murder investigation. Would that be right?'

Bunting and Wagner are staring at Stone. His face betrays nothing.

'Not necessarily.'

'Let's put it this way: you were certainly more convinced in your thinking that Elizabeth Haydon was murdered.'

'The smell heightened my suspicion, yes.'

John Bunting is calm, implacable in his surroundings until he hears something to which he objects. Then his ears prick up and his mouth opens in voiceless anger as he gesticulates to his defence team from the dock, or turns slowly to stare down a witness, resembling a clown's head on a stick in side-show alley. And in that moment, that split second – his eyes bright, his face grotesque and contorted and his mouth wide open – he looks as though he is unravelling into madness. Then, just as suddenly, his face shuts down again, draining to an emotionless vacuum.

They move, silently, out of the dock and down the stairs, back into the basement cells. Bunting is so short, so unremarkable. I watch him disappear, and think of a line from Truman Capote's masterpiece, *In Cold Blood*: 'Gosh, I didn't know he was such a shrimp'.

'Yeah, he's little. But so is a tarantula.'

It is February 2003, time for the prosecution's star turn to take his place in the witness stand. The trial has been active for four months. Vlassakis – 179 centimetres tall, perfectly groomed in shirt and tie and perfectly nervous. Bunting, now recovered from a three-day illness that necessitated an adjournment in proceedings, turns to stare him down. But Vlassakis stares straight ahead, a tactic he will maintain throughout his 32 days on the stand.

Abraham cuts to the chase. 'Were you involved in the murder of Troy Youde?' She waits, with solemn poise, while he answers in a voice sliced thin by a whisper. 'Yes.'

And were other people present?

Yes. John Bunting. Robert Wagner. Mark Haydon.

So it begins.

Bunting's food of choice is cold meats and cheese, which he eats on most days when the trial adjourns for lunch. Eating in the cell downstairs, except on the days when his ulcer plays up, and he sticks to a glass of milk. His ulcer plays up a lot when Vlassakis is on the stand. Sometimes, he doesn't show in court at all; once, it is a dose of diarrhoea that stops his attendance. 'There's the proof', a security guard grins. 'Vlassakis's evidence must be really giving Bunting the shits.'

For a time, before he gives evidence, Vlassakis is housed in a cell next to former copper Wayne Maddeford, who is serving 13 years for armed robbery and for taking a court stenographer hostage at knifepoint.Vlassakis denies he bragged to Maddeford about enjoying watching people begging for their lives before they were murdered. He talked to him about the killings, he says, but never bragged. But his name is on the cell door and the other prisoners snicker, yell out as they pass, going up and down from wing to wing, laughing, 'Barrel boy is in that cell over there'.

But it is no laughing matter when he is moved after he completes his evidence to one of the toughest prisons in the South Australian system, the location suppressed for his safety, and where he is held well removed from the mainstream population. 'They have to be very careful who they put in the cell next to him', Elizabeth recalls. 'It can't be a sex offender 'cause Jamie gives them hell.'

52

Justice Martin keeps his sang froid throughout the extra-ordinarily long trial, but there are moments – albeit very few – when he shows an overt, cool disdain for the press. He once asks counsel to supply him details on specific media coverage, and the unsolicited answer, instead, is offered by the *Australian*'s Adelaide reporter, Andrew McGarry. 'From our recollection of the coverage,' McGarry begins, but Justice Martin cuts him short.

'I don't think I need to worry about that, Mr McGarry.'

But it is not always the press who cops it. When Apps asks a witness if it was his belief that Mr Trevilyan had been living with Mr Lane prior to his death, Justice Martin interrupts.

'Prior to whose death?'

'Prior to Mr Trevilyan's death, quite clearly,' Apps replies.

'Was it?' Martin responds. 'Maybe I'm being pedantic. I just thought there was a latent ambiguity there.'

Apps suppresses a sigh. 'Let me rephrase it.'

Two hundred and twenty Crown witnesses. Twenty million dollars. One hundred and twenty-three days. And yet, nearing the end, it takes less than two hours for the defence witnesses to give their evidence. Three witnesses for Bunting. A forlorn man who thinks that he killed Ray Davies when he punched him for planting an unwelcome kiss on his mouth. A friend of Vlassakis, who repeats to the court that Jamie said he was going to kill a teenager and assume his identity to avoid going to prison. And another 'friend', who claims Vlassakis boasted to him that he hated gays and planned to kill Michael Gardiner.

Wagner can only muster one person to speak in his defence: Troy Trengrove, who admits that he is the author of a strange poem about serial killers. Wagner copied the poem and sent it to notorious convicted killer Paul Page in September 2000. Prison authorities pass the information to police, who search Wagner's cell. Written in rhyming verse, the poem, complete with spelling mistakes and amateur phrasing, claims he has never been to a Snowtown bank.

> I'm a CFS man – my uniform's swank
> And I've never been to a Snowtown bank
> Yet bodies in barrels – hey I wonder who's there?
> Paedophiles I'm told so who really cares
> See so many people are murdered each year
> Yet just how many answers can you find around here?
> Plus everyone's listening to the media hype
> A psychotic killer – hey do I look like the type?
> Now in months to come it's my judgement day
> You can be sure I'll have my say
> And I will not ever be held in contempt
> For everyone knows my time was well spent
> See you know I only provided a service that's needed
> For just like your gardens our streets should be weeded
> So fuck off Judge Chester in your silly white wig
> I only make the streets safe for all of our kids
> Now can anyone say what's really what?
> For I could be innocent then again maybe not
> So fuck all the media and fuck the police
> For I know where you live in case I'm released
> Now my poem must end with thought of my life
> Where did this start – what caused all my strife?
> And if my life reads like a Steven King thriller
> You know I'm not a bad guy . . . for a serial killer.

Finally, Abraham is on her feet again. Polished, calm, measured, just as she was at the beginning. Through all the storms that have raged around her in the DPP office – taking over as acting director following Paul Rofe's sick leave, the incessant, prying press and the baying of an outraged public – she has kept her cool. Working to the letter of the law, never putting a foot wrong. So pedantic, so meticulous that when it all ends, she and her junior counsel, Sandi McDonald, can boast there was not one ground in law for appeal. They are a formidable team, the yang and the yin. Abraham: married to the law, ambitious, aloof – who allows few to see her soft side, with an awesome intellect and a relentless determination to get the job done. McDonald: approachable, softer – who shares Abraham's determination but balances a mean juggling act between the law and married life. Abraham's final questions to Vlassakis are to elicit reasons why he came forward to give evidence and pleaded guilty.

'The absolute first reason was for being safe in jail,' Vlassakis responds. 'One was for getting a non-parole period set. To get it off my chest, to be able to speak about it . . . to put my hand up and say "I done this", and also to give other people a chance . . . the victims' families and stuff . . . to let them know what happened to their loved ones.'

'No further questions', Abraham says, sitting down.

Finally, Abraham opens her closing address. 'Ladies and gentlemen. Over the last nine months you have heard a vast amount of evidence that the Crown says implicated the accused. You have heard evidence from civilian witnesses, people who knew Mr Bunting and Mr Wagner, evidence from people who had dealings with them, evidence from police officers, from searches of vehicles and cars and properties associated with the victims of the accused, evidence of surveillance, telephone intercepts, listening devices, DNA evidence, handwriting evidence, fingerprints, pathologists, evidence from Centrelink and the hundreds of exhibits tendered before you . . .'

Bunting's lawyer, Mark Griffin, in his closing address, evokes the spectre of the OJ Simpson trial and reminds the jury of their obligation to apply the presumption of innocence, regardless of how shocking the evidence. 'They did not proclaim [OJ Simpson] innocent at the end; they said he was not guilty because they weren't satisfied that the charges had been proven beyond a reasonable doubt.'

Bunting and Wagner lean close together, whispering. Wagner has adopted his customary sour demeanour: eyes dead and thick lips turned slightly in a crazed grin. He is like a man called up on stage at an evangelical meeting, hypnotised by the lights and the audience, but bursting with excitement that he is the chosen one.

Bunting is still, grim.

Justice Martin starts his summing-up, a monumental address that recaps all the major points for the jury. Day after day they reconvene, go through the evidence. If this continues, it will go longer than the epic trial.

Tuesday 2 September 2003. The public gallery is virtually empty now, save for the occasional law student or a ragged poet, copy of Kafka stuffed into his shabby coat pocket, his hair lank from rain. Before the court opens, Marcus Johnson is outside, standing perfectly still in the shadows of a thorough-fare that runs alongside the building. A silhouette in the shape of a tripod, hands clasped behind his back and legs apart. Perfectly still, no movement even in the rise and fall of his breathing. Standing in the shadows, watching.

At 10.22am, the jury – an eclectic mix of men and women – finally files out to consider its verdicts. The punters have started already: 100–1 it will be out for at least 24 hours. It is too big a case for the jury to come back sooner than that.

A minute later, though, they are back, asking advice on legal direction. At 10.25am, they disappear through the jury room door once more.

Day 2, and the journalists who share floor space outside the locked courtroom, playing Scrabble and Trivial Pursuit, place their bets. Most tip that the jury will return between Days 3 and 4. As usual, there is no sign of anyone supporting Bunting or Wagner. No parents, no family, no friends.

Day 3, Thursday 4 September. It is Bunting's birthday. Thirty-seven years old, pacing in his cell downstairs. The jury arrives at the court and a reporter, whose bet is that they will reach verdict by 10.30 that morning, glowers in their direction. 'They're looking far too well fed and rested for my liking', he complains.

Day 4, and there is a restless change in the mood. The jury has only twice returned to the courtroom to hear tapes or ask legal direction, and there is no way of knowing how many counts they have still to consider. Bunting, increasingly belligerent and restless when the jury is out of court, targets people in the public gallery who may catch his eye. Too squat to see to the back of the court without springing from one foot to the other to afford himself a better view, Bunting cuts a comical figure, quickly navigating faces in the courtroom.

The clock is ticking and if the jury doesn't come back today – Friday – it will be all weekend in court. Saturday is the football finals, Sunday Father's Day. Given it is a special weekend, and jury members undoubtedly will wish to have some time out, Justice Martin offers them a concession: the opportunity to retire by no later than 2pm from deliberations on both days. They accept. Most journalists have lost the bet, their names scrubbed out on the makeshift betting card as each deadline passes. In their breaks, the male jury members boot a soccer ball around Victoria Square. Wendy Abraham, sitting at her usual spot outside chambers where she can see the comings and goings of court sheriffs on the next landing, is outwardly a study of calm composure but is so wound up, she can't even concentrate on reading a book. Her eyes quietly survey her surroundings, but there is not a flicker of movement in her body.

Day 5. A warm Saturday, the court closed to all but those involved in this case and suits traded for comfortable leisure gear. The jury has a question, and the court reconvenes. Bunting, with typical manic intensity, prances on the balls of his feet and scratches his head, his hair noticeably thinning on top.

My mother, Monica, has accompanied me to Adelaide for this part of the trial, helping me wade through the mountains of transcripts while the jury has retired. But we are booked to fly out of Adelaide later today or must forfeit the fare and an officious telephone staff member at Qantas assures me that, under no circumstances is it possible to change our flight. Frustrated that we are so close to verdict but will now miss it, we arrive at the airport disgruntled and disappointed.

'You look so tired,' a Qantas staff member remarks as we check in.

I nod, dejectedly, explaining our disappointment that we will miss the verdict. 'I'll change your tickets if you want to fly out another day,' she smiles. I want to jump the counter and hug her. Accepting that we won't be able to change the flight again, we opt to fly home two nights later. We jump into a taxi to return into the city.

Day 6, Sunday. Everyone is jaded and weary, the hours dragging inexorably toward 2pm. It's Father's Day, and people are anxious to get home. The jury returns, asking to hear a tape recording again in open court. And suddenly, Gary O'Dwyer's pitiful, petrified voice fills the room. The crackle of the recording and Bunting's girly, lispy voice follows, demanding that Gary repeat what he says. A hideous silence, a nanosecond as Gary struggles to dampen down his panic, tries not to cry and the desperation, the heartbreaking hope in his voice that if he does it right, they might just let him go. His eerie, haunting voice floats through the room. 'I'm Gary O'Dwyer. I'm a paedophile. Now I'm feeling really happy I've had treatment.'

Wagner's face erupts into a huge grin and Bunting, with the stature of a garden gnome, stares dispassionately out to the court.

And when it is finished, there is a shocking silence, a nanosecond as the voice of Gary O'Dwyer – intellectually handicapped, naive, trusting – fades away but his spirit lingers, as if to ask, 'Why didn't anyone save me?' There is a cold kick deep in our guts, icier than sub-zero temperatures, the chilling realisation that if Satan exists, he has just visited court; that if Bunting and Wagner have achieved even one decent thing in their entire lives it was smothered and extinguished in those hours of savagery, in the terrible, unearthly cries of that wretched, slow man begging for mercy and the gloating cackle of his tormentors. The jury shuffles out, ashen; Wendy Abraham is grim, eyes dark as coals against the determined set of her face. Police assemble in the court foyer. '*Where the carcass is, there shall the eagles be gathered together.*' Bob Stapleton, strong-jawed, with clenched hands plunged into his trouser suit pockets, pauses momentarily to speak to me. His forehead is heavily creased with fatigue, his whole demeanour that of a copper desperate for closure on this stinking case.

'I had to play that tape to Gary's mother, Maureen, so she could identify her son's voice', he says. His tone is level, but he can't hide the undercurrent, his abhorrence and disgust. 'Tape doesn't go for long, does it? Less than two minutes. But it took me more than two hours to get to the end of it with her. She kept breaking down, sobbed the whole way through. In all my years in the force, I've never heard anything like that tape and I've never seen anything so sad as that boy's mother as she listened to it.' He paws at the ground for a second before rejoining his colleagues.

Day 7. No sign yet of any decision. There is a rumbling of discontent – how much bloody longer? – and the prosecution team is looking frayed. Wendy Abraham has given up any pretence at calm, and prowls the perimeters of the court's interior. The journalists are playing Scrabble but they are distracted, jittery. The cops are in a huddle. And I am anxiously checking my watch. If the jury doesn't come back within half an hour, we have to leave for the airport, again. It seems our gamble hasn't paid off. We are going to miss the verdict after all.

There is a rustle in the corridor; Wagner's lawyers heading out of the cells where they have been speaking with their client. They are now heading towards Court 3. 'Is something happening?' I ask, falling into step behind them. They shrug, throw their palms upwards and I follow in the wake of their rustling gowns.

The landing outside Court 3 is packed, busier than it has been all week. Inside, there is a nervous sense of expectation, although word has filtered through that the jury is simply asking another question. Bunting, looking pale and sickly, does his now-familiar dance, craning his neck to stare at people in the gallery.

The forewoman stands; tells Justice Martin they are unable to reach a verdict on Suzanne Allen, the obsessive lover who adored her Johnny Angel, and whose badly decomposed body was found in the backyard grave at 203 Waterloo Corner Road. Suzanne Allen, who had been gutted, dismembered, skinned, her body parts thrown into garbage bags.

Elizabeth Harvey has been dead more than two years when the jury returns this verdict. She believed John, she said, when he told her he had found Suzanne slumped over the bath, believed him even when the coppers reckoned they thought he had killed her. But she had no reason to doubt him. He had given her Suzanne's card, but he didn't have the PIN. If he had tortured her before she died, Elizabeth figured he definitely would have forced that out of her. She had had to go and change the number herself, to stop him pressuring her for it. Thought she had better, in case he turned on her. Elizabeth collected Suzanne's pension for 12 months, but she just couldn't keep doing it. 'Get Veronika to help you', she told John. Veronika did a lot of things for him, even though they were long separated. Do this, do that, Bunting would tell her, and she did. No questions asked. But he didn't give the card to Veronika. He gave it to Gail Sinclair instead.

There was another reason Elizabeth hadn't doubted John's word on what had happened to Suzanne Allen. 'I'd seen him murder Ray in front of me', she reasoned. 'Why would he lie to me about committing another murder?'

Justice Martin is nodding to the jury. 'Do you have verdicts on the other counts?' There is an intake of breaths, a tense tightening of jaw muscles, a pause. 'We do, Your Honour', the forewoman replies.

Not a movement or a sound as the judge's associate stands. 'Do you find the accused, John Justin Bunting, guilty or not guilty of the murder of Clinton Trezise?'

'We find the accused guilty.'

'Is that the verdict of all of you?'

'Yes.'

Neither Bunting nor Wagner flinches. Breaths expel and Marcus Johnson, the only victims' family member in court, massages his hands together between the knees of his worn trousers. He momentarily drops his head as his eyes flirt with tears and his eyelids close as a dam against them.

The counts continue, the obscene roll call of the dead. By the time they finish, the guilty verdicts are Bunting, 11, Wagner, seven, not including the three murders to which he has already pleaded guilty.

Justice Martin, bewigged and red-robed, turns to the dock. 'Please stand', he instructs Bunting and Wagner.

'No', Bunting spits. All heads snap around to look at him. He eyeballs the judge with arrogant petulance, eyes smouldering behind his glasses. Not insane, not remorseful. Just coldly, psychopathically detached. 'I would prefer you did', Martin repeats, swallowing an impatient sigh.

'I would prefer you to tell the story about Jamie Vlassakis and the deal that he made.'

It is his final slap from the dock. But Martin ignores it, sentencing Bunting and Wagner to 11 and 10 life sentences respectively. He flags the possibility of not fixing a non-parole period, which would make them the only prisoners in South Australia with that stamp on their files, before he addresses the jury.

'It's been a long road, hasn't it?' he states with a wry smile. '. . . This trial actually began without a jury on 4 March 2002. There's something like 4724 pages of legal argument and rulings from me. We began on 16 October with you. The evidence was completed on 10 July. That evidence is 10,641 pages. It involved 148 sitting days . . . There was something in the order of 227 witnesses and there's well over 1000 exhibits. The addresses of counsel commenced on 21 July, they concluded on 7 August. There's something like 744 pages. My summing up commenced on 7 August and it concluded on

2 September . . .' Exempting them from ever doing jury duty again unless they wished to do so, he praises their fortitude in dealing with the stress and trauma of the trial. 'Can I say to you', he adds, 'with respect to your verdicts, for what it's worth, I agree with you entirely . . .'

The jury files out for the last time, and Bunting and Wagner stand and leave the dock. The shadow of a smirk plays around Wagner's lips and his tall frame dominates the doorway as he disappears through it. Bunting is callously aloof, pacing to the exit on his little legs before he vaporises from sight.

They will be back in court to process appeal applications, but for the moment it has wrapped. Reporters rush out to beam the verdicts back to their newsrooms, cops shake hands and the prosecution team give wan but triumphant smiles. They will celebrate with champagne at the Hilton next door to the court, but the celebrations will be short-lived. They still have Mark Haydon's trial to run.

Bob Stapleton has the air of a general at the end of a marathon battle. He grins at me. 'Bunting wasn't as smart as he thought he was, was he?'

Outside the court, Marcus Johnson is the centre of media attention, cameras trained on him as though he is the bulls-eye on a dartboard. 'Today is the pinnacle', he says. 'I have listened to the evidence – shocking things they did to David. To know your son died like that is devastating. I do really feel for the family of Suzanne Allen. I know the jury had a lot to think about, and I thank them. It has been a long, long road.'

There is little time left before our flight, and we pile into a taxi to go straight to the airport. The Croatian-born driver speaks only broken English, but he has just heard the radio news. 'Iz goot they get life, but those pigs, they should be strunged up for what they has did', he intones. 'But, you know, so much we not be hearing about this story. Iz a strange place, this Adelaide, that keeps its secrets even from its own peoples.'

As the taxi turns the corner, I glimpse Marcus Johnson trudging along the street. The television cameras have already focused on another target. He is pitifully, painfully alone.

★ ★ ★

'Evil ends.' This the verdict of the local Adelaide newspaper when the convictions are handed down. But it is not the verdict of Adelaide University criminologist Dr Allan Perry, whose inflammatory views and outspoken comments on a 'feral subculture' in Adelaide's northern suburbs divide the city and prompt South Australian Attorney-General Michael Atkinson to suggest Perry move to New York. Blaming Adelaide's stifling culture and conservatism as being partly responsible for outbreaks of evil, Perry continues that the decadent, degenerate subculture from where people like Bunting and Wagner are drawn provides a social crucible for crime, where the constraints that normally prevent people from committing murder fail to come to the fore.

Floored by the comments, Salisbury Mayor Tony Zappia hit back. 'Every city has its challenges . . . but the statistics don't support the assertion that specific communities are necessarily breeding places for people who ultimately become criminals.'

In the end, it becomes a war of words, a slanging match that no one wins. 'Identifying the nature and existence of this kind of subculture is going to become increasingly important in understanding the trends and manifestations of crime and violence in the near future,' Perry warns. 'The symptoms of this will occur with increasing frequency until eventually we will have no choice but to recognise it, because it will be ubiquitous. It will be everywhere.'

53

The verdicts have been handed down. It's all over now, bar the sentencing. But for the families and friends of the victims, the nightmare continues. For some, there will never be full resolution. For many, if not all, the pain will never completely subside.

Twenty-nine people – more than in any other South Australian trial – gave victim impact statements. Barry Lane's sister, Susan, moved to Queensland but said the notoriety of the case followed her there. 'I have had invaders in my home who have bashed me and left me with a permanent disability because my brother was a paedophile', she said. 'I am, and will always be, a victim of the Snowtown murders.' Suzanne Allen's sister, Joan Potts, spoke for all the families. 'I mean, look at all the families there are. They can't have . . . they've got no mother no more, no sister, no grandmother, daughters, no nothing. It's just all gone . . .' One of the boys did not mention his brother, Jamie, but told of his anguish at losing his half-brother, Troy and stepbrother, David. A court official read his statement, which captured his fear of Bunting and Wagner, to the court. 'I feel I have to watch my back', he said. 'I'm scared of John and Robert. Although they're locked up and stuff, I don't know who they talk to in prison.'

Gail Sinclair, glassy-eyed and fearful, swayed in the stand as she read her statement. 'They are cold-blooded killers and they have to be locked up and the key thrown away because, if they get out, there will be more murders. They live to kill and no one is safe. All there is now is hatred and I will never forgive them for what they have done.'

A heartbroken Allan Porter spoke of his son, Gavin. 'They say that the pain and grief gets better with time, but I dispute that – it only gets to the stage where you're resigned to it.

I loved my son but was not able to protect him and that has devastated me . . . it's incomprehensible that my son's life has been taken for someone else's indulgence.'

Gary O'Dwyer's mother, Maureen, choked back tears as she faced the pair in the dock. Bunting ignored her and read a book while Wagner stared back and smirked. 'What damage you have done to me and my family', she said. Maureen was utterly overcome by grief, and her daughter had to take over reading her statement. '. . . May you both be locked up in jail with no fancy amenities, and shame upon your souls', she cried.

Bunting, contemptuous throughout the proceedings, remained silent. But Wagner seized his opportunity to speak. Handcuffed, he stood and read from a brief prepared statement that he had had help writing in prison. 'Paedophiles were doing terrible things to children and innocent children were being damaged', he said. 'The authorities did nothing about it, I was very angry. Someone had to do something about it. I decided to take action and I took that action.'

The speech failed to move Justice Martin. Condemning them as cowards beyond rehabilitation and lacking contrition, he ordered both to serve mandatory life sentences without parole on each count.

'I'm satisfied that both of you derived pleasure from the physical acts of killing and the violence and torture that preceded some of the killings', he said. 'I am also satisfied that you derived pleasure from dismembering and de-fleshing some of the bodies. It's not an exaggeration to say by 1999 you were in the business of killing for pleasure.'

Refusing to set a non-parole period, Martin continued that he could not make an order that they never be released. But, he warned, 'If I had the power . . . I would unhesitatingly make that order'. He added: 'Many words could be used to describe the horrific nature of your crimes. But I will not employ those extreme descriptions because in some perverse way, within the prison environment, you might seek to benefit from or glorify in those descriptions.' All up, his address took 49 minutes.

Outside the court, Marcus Johnson again addressed the media. 'Sadly we still have an anomaly in our system where that judge was not allowed to say categorically that those two cannot get released. Now, we have to look at it and address it because those two must never get out again and I'm sure they would re-offend. They have absolutely no feeling of compassion and they are not sorry for what they did.'

Bunting showed no emotion as he was taken back to Yatala. To the end, he remained an enigma.

'. . . Without examining him, I can't tell whether this man has a peculiar set of beliefs which have arisen out of his experience, out of his real life knowledge, or whether they arise from a morbid process like a parallel illness . . .' Professor Mullen said of him. 'It certainly raises the possibility that this man is profoundly disturbed in this area, and the question is why and how he's come to be totally preoccupied and use that . . . to justify the most horrific of acts. I'm not for a moment suggesting that you can explain these crimes by Mr Bunting's preoccupation with paedophiles and the dangers they present. Clearly, there are other elements that came into this dreadful mixture . . . To explain these actions, one needs to look for other forces than simply a set of odd and extraordinary beliefs . . . questions about what and how this man came to be preoccupied and so forceful that he was able to carry others along with him.'

Back to Yatala, the questions unanswered.

It is my third trip to Snowtown on this hot March day, 2004. I have overshot the general signs, end up far from the town. The drought has reached here, as well; the paddocks are caramel, dotted with bloated, dead sheep. There is not a person in sight. I am lost and this barren landscape suddenly spooks me. It is irrational, I know, but I shudder, imagining Bunting and Wagner having taken a similar lonely road to get the barrels to Snowtown. I need to get out of here, spin the car into a full U-turn and accelerate, hard.

54

The Mark Haydon trial is yet to come, but for now the task of completing the first section of the manuscript for this book is becoming pressing. While I have already undertaken a great deal of research and have sat in court throughout much of the committal and the trial, I am also seeking to understand what really lies behind these horrific crimes. There are people I still need to talk to.

Mark Griffin, I hope, may be able to answer some questions about his client. I phone him at the end of April 2004, explaining what information I am seeking. Does he know when the Suzanne Allen re-trial might start, and can he tell me whether there are any psychiatric reports on John Bunting that I can access? His voice is wafer-thin, disdainful. He has, he assures me, worked on some 'very big cases', but he is 'frankly amazed' that so many lawyers tell journalists things about their clients. He can only assume that the reason they do is to get their names in print, but that is not how he operates. His role is to protect his client's interests, even though he no longer acts for him. And, he adds, it is not his job to give me legal advice. 'I didn't ask for legal advice', I rejoin. His bellicose attitude has caught me off guard. 'I just wanted to know what is happening with any possible Allen re-trial.'

'Who said there is going to be a re-trial?'

It hasn't started well, and it is to get worse. 'And what', he demands 'makes you think there are psychiatric reports?'

'I was just wondering if there are. I'd like some background on Bunting, and I'd like to get the facts straight.'

'Well the only way to do that is not to write anything that isn't checked.'

'But I'm trying to check. With you. You were Bunting's lead counsel.'

It's not his problem, he tells me, that I have chosen to write a book that is based in Adelaide when I don't live in that city. Yes, he's blunt, he admits, and that's just the way he is.

It is time for a different tack. 'I didn't call to be combative. I was just trying to check a couple of issues . . .'

No chance. He has cut me off, again. 'Well, I've taken your call.'

'Yes, you have. Thank you for your time, Mr Griffin.'

In November 2003, Channel 9's *Sunday* program aired a story that pointedly asked the question: 'How many lives could have been saved if Clinton Trezise had been identified in the mid-nineties?' The South Australian police, it said, tried but failed to put a name to the skeleton at Lower Light. But despite a world-wide search, the answer was right under their noses. 'Had the South Australian police done their job properly,' the program alleged, 'Clinton Trezise could have been identified three years earlier, leading the police to John Bunting . . . What is gradually dawning on experts in this case is the appalling realisation of how many victims might have been saved but for the appalling incompetence of the police.'

It took 12 months to research. Producer Ron Sinclair, a 40-year veteran of television, including *60 Minutes* and *Australia's Most Wanted* programs, waded into the abyss with reporter Graeme Davies to pull it together. It was, Ron Sinclair tells me, an 'amazing journey into the world of silence that permeates the South Australian police and judiciary'. Trying to get through the closed-door mentality of the state, where all information is funnelled through a filter before being doled out in edited portions, was frustrating and time-consuming. 'Many people simply freaked when we approached them to talk', Sinclair says. 'They claimed they didn't have access to their old records, or that they weren't in a position to say anything. When you drive through the leafy precincts of the city's elite areas, most of the shingles announce the professionals have been educated at the University of Adelaide. The evolution of this city is right there: very tight, very close. Self-preservation is paramount. Then you move out, along the North Road, past the takeaway shops and car yards, into the sprawling sub-suburban mayhem that is spreading like ground cover and growing wider every year; the industrial fodder of the post-war years.'

It wasn't just the police and judiciary that closed their doors on Sinclair and Davies. Most victims, they discovered, had drifted through the Assembly of God church at one time or another in their lives. A church that is hostile to homo-sexuality and behind the conservative Family First party in South Australia. 'But I couldn't get near anyone in there to discuss anything', Sinclair recalls. 'It was another closed shop in a state that has perfected the art of keeping out prying eyes.'

Relentlessly pointing the camera into the tawdry lives and shabby neighbourhoods from where Bunting and co. were drawn, Sinclair was astounded at the ugliness. Junk piled up in front yards, graffiti on every painted surface and the blank, lost looks of many of the people he sees. 'It's a putrid environment out there, and they're trapped in it. I came away from the story wanting to take a bath.'

Professor Maciej Henneberg took a circuitous route to arrive at the University of Adelaide in 1996 as the head of its Depart-ment of Anatomical Sciences. Imprisoned in 1981 in his native Poland for pushing change to the academic system – at the time when the Solidarity movement was banned – the activist spent 100 days in prison, held without trial, before fleeing the country in 1984. He arrived in South Australia after teaching in America and South Africa, and was given the task of identi-fying the skeleton found at Lower Light soon after he started work at the University of Adelaide. Unlike Jane Taylor, who worked in an adjacent building, he was not given the photo-graph of Clinton Trezise that Clinton's mother had handed to police when she reported him missing in 1995. It was the only adult picture of him in existence.

Trevor Couch, the now retired detective who headed up the Lower Light investigation, did not welcome Graeme Davies's line of questioning. The police, he said, had refused him access to his files and he could not remember if he had shown Henneberg the photograph.

But in Henneberg's line of work, dead people *do* tell tales; about how they died, how long they have been dead, their gender, race and height. He gently removed the cleaned skeleton from the box and laid it on the table. Male. White. European. Between 21 and 25 years of age and 171 centimetres tall. He was uncannily close: Clinton Trezise was 22, and 177 centimetres tall.

The web page of the University of Adelaide's Forensic Odontology Unit boasts that it applies dental science 'to the administration of the law and the furtherance of justice'. Established in 1980 and funded by the Government of South Australia, it was 'the first dedicated service of its kind in Australia and one of only a few worldwide at the time: truly a pioneer in the field'. The unit, the blurb continues, 'has contributed to the resolution of many well known and famous cases, many of them involving the identification of victims of murder when the condition of the bodies rendered identification by other means impossible . . .'

True, but not in this case.

The submission Jane Taylor made about identification of the skeletal remains will haunt her. 'We have been given a number of possible identities from Missing Persons and in all cases so far, we've been able to exclude those identities as being the Lower Light victim', she said in an interview in 1996, replayed on *Australia's Most Wanted* program. Taylor's opinion was unequivocal. The skeleton did not match the photograph, she told police.

At the trial, however, Taylor made a startling admission.

'With hindsight, probably it might have been fairer to say "we weren't able to say", but at the time I think we said, "we didn't believe it was him".'

Henneberg believes that had he been given the photograph, he would almost certainly have made a match. He shrugs and looks perplexed behind his huge wire-rimmed glasses when I ask him if he can suggest why he was only given the skeleton, and not the photograph. 'Don't know', he says. 'But it is a very sad mistake by an individual, or individuals. Something went wrong, and not only a lot of work could have been saved, but the lives of a lot of people, as well.' He shakes his head. 'A very sad mistake . . . If any case of major crime is not resolved to the best abilities of police and public prosecutors, it should cause disquiet.'

It did. After the *Sunday* program opened the lid on this Pandora's box, serving Queensland police officer John Garner – an expert in facial identification – contacted Graeme Davies. Davies's story was complete, and he passed Garner's contact to me.

'My involvement was as follows', Garner wrote to me. 'In 1994 or 1995 (I don't have access to my old records), I was approached by the South Australian police for assistance to create a facial reconstruction of an unknown deceased person. In these matters, I work with Dr Alex Forrest, Lecturer in Oral Biology and Anatomy at the University of Queensland and Consultant Forensic Odontologist to Queensland Health at the John Tonge Centre for Forensic Sciences.

'The facial reconstruction was duly done using the skull provided and was presented to the SA detective. In October 1997 I visited Adelaide on an unrelated matter and spoke to the detectives involved in the case . . . and asked if the reconstruction that we had done had produced any results. I was told that they had elected not to use the image on advice from their local experts who had stated that the image was not at all reliable and was not consistent with the true anatomy of the skull.

'I showed previous examples of our reconstruction work

and stated that there was no reason to believe that their face reconstruction was any less accurate than the examples shown. Their response was that they had to live and work with these people and did not want to antagonise them.

'When the Snowtown murders became public knowledge, I saw a TV news article featuring the Lower Light case and our facial reconstruction. I phoned a very senior SA police officer contact, who told me that there had been a stuff-up by the local forensic experts and that there had been a very serious mistake made in the identification process of the Lower Light body. The body had now been identified as Trezise.

'I obtained some video footage of the TV story and assisted Dr Forrest to make a positive identification using the available video images (a process which took about five minutes flat, despite the low quality of the images). We were able to super-impose the teeth of a photograph of the skull over those in the video image and demonstrate a perfect correspondence. I discussed the case with Dr Forrest at that time and realised the implication that a successful ID of Trezise in 1995 may have saved those other 10 lives. This issue greatly concerned both of us to the extent that in 2001 Dr Forrest raised it in the forum of the National Coroner's Conference in Brisbane. The SA Coroner responded to Dr Forrest's presentation by way of a very strongly worded letter of complaint addressed to the Chief Pathologist at the John Tonge Centre, claiming that Dr Forrest had exhibited unprofessional behaviour by naming one of his colleagues as being responsible for the mistake when, in fact, he had not mentioned any names or location as to where this had happened. The Coroner also notified the Adelaide forensic odontologists by sending copies of his letter to them without first warning Forrest . . . This concluded our involvement.'

By 1998, despite advertisements of facial approximations, the skeleton remained unidentified. Henneberg's PhD student, Dr Carl Stephan – brilliant, young and eager – applied his skills to building a clay model of a face based on contours of the

Lower Light skull. The resemblance was remarkable. But, as Henneberg would write for the journal *Forensic Science International* in 2005, 'this face was never advertised in the media.'

Something just does not seem to be adding up with Trezise. Why wasn't he identified? I mentally go over what I know. Missing since 1992; his skeletal remains found in 1994; reported as a missing person in 1995. Why was it so hard to find out who he was? The police and lawyers would not speak to me until after the trials, if then, so I needed to ask questions further afield. In early 2004, this email materialises in my inbox. 'From the vantage point of a person looking in from outside South Australia, may I suggest it is possible that there is much more to this story than has so far been revealed? And if that is the case, will people need to batten down the hatches as the cyclone heads towards them, the royal commission being at the eye of the storm? People want answers, and there will be a public demand for them.

'When the dam starts to break, get into the habit of reading everything several times, logging and cross-referencing and start asking, "Why?" and "What does this imply?" In the meantime: Keep the faith, be patient, be persistent and most of all, keep up the rage.'

'When the dam starts to break . . .' What dam? What is this person trying to tell me?

Back to the drawing board. What was known of Trezise? He had been Barry Lane's lover. Lane was hardly the most savoury of characters, so how did that association reflect on Trezise? Elizabeth Harvey said Lane was 'tangled up with the Family'. What family was she referring to? Bevan Von Einem's crimes were dubbed the 'Family' murders because of the belief that he had evil accomplices, none of whom, if they exist, has ever been charged. Lane had said, 'He was tangled up with the Family and he used to procure little boys for these little boy auctions . . .'

Trezise was a drifter. Gay. Who would a gay drifter mix with in Adelaide? What of the persistent rumours of a network of sexual deviants operating at high levels in the community? If they do exist, did he ever cross paths with them? What was his role, if he did? Was he a rent boy, shared by people with money and a powerful agenda to keep their liaisons secret? If so, did he know too much and was his murder, by rank outsider John Bunting, a stroke of good fortune for them? Was there any chance at all that his murder was a 'hit', not simply an opportunistic killing? Or did he hang out only on the fringe in Adelaide's northern suburbs with the likes of people like Barry Lane, AKA Vanessa, and never mix with the wealthy and powerful?

He was young, naive. Raised in foster homes. Who did he come into contact with in those homes? Was it in someone's interests to keep him quiet? And if so, who?

'Be patient. Be persistent.' The answers are not going to fall into my lap. And in fact, they never do, despite ongoing suspicions by many people that there is much more behind the scenes than anyone publicly knows.

From my perspective, one thing is clearly evident: that the conspiracy of silence in South Adelaide runs deep and is fiercely guarded.

55

A ghostly gum tree now stands outside 203 Waterloo Corner Road, and the house has been razed. But the neighbourhood still has the same melancholy air, the stench of hopelessness. I have come back seeking further insights. We pull up outside 1 Bingham Road, at Wagner and Lane's old address. A woman is standing outside her own house nearby and we engage her in conversation. She has lived there for years, she says – unusual in an area where people change homes as often as they do partners. She points her finger at the houses in the street, offering a running commentary. Her husband, she boasts, is the only person around here who holds down a job. 'What about in the next street?' I ask. 'Nup. No one works.' And the next? 'Nup. No one.'

Her daughter, she tells us, lived in 203 Waterloo Corner Road for six weeks until the police told her to move out. Summoned by her mother to come and have a chat, this daughter arrives with her husband, whom she introduces as Godzilla, and their sick baby, his eyes streaming from the flu. Cigarette smoke oozes from their car when they open the doors. Their uncle, the young woman says, lived next to the Snowtown bank – an uncanny coincidence given that she moved into 203. She shudders as she describes living there. It was, she says, a 'bitterly cold, creepy house'. She always had the feeling that someone was in the backyard. An icy draft would blow under the doors and they would slam shut on a still night.

They were glad to hightail it to another suburb.

Marcus Johnson is jumpy. His skin is as shiny as a wax effigy, and jug ears dominate either side of his face. He has lugged his small frame up the two flights of stairs to the hotel apartment where we are staying. The trials have taken their toll; the shadows of his past haunt him. He settles in at the dining table, slowly relaxing with each successive beer. Joining the dots to make a trail, he winces at the body count. 'Whenever there's a name comes up, police have looked for that person to be alive and they've hunted all over Australia and they've gone overseas as well. There is still two or three names that keep being thrown at us; I don't know who they're talking about, but they can't find them. So the bodies they have may not be their final figure, but they'll never know.'

Since David's death, he feels like a disconnected observer of his own life. His nightmare frequently recurs: taking David to the show, standing on the ground as his son straps into his seat and watching helplessly as the ferris wheel with barrels on the seats goes round and round without stopping. David is yelling at him to get him off, to stop the ride, but he can't. No one is listening to him. He feels like a pariah as he walks the streets of Adelaide, shunned, and paranoid about what people think. He courts the media to tell his side of the story; it is cathartic, he says, an act of cleansing. But sharing memories takes time. And time is money.

Memories. They come to him at night, tickling him awake. How Bunting told Elizabeth Harvey he wanted to bug Barry Lane's house. He is animated and excited when he speaks, wanting to get it all out in one rush of a sentence. 'I said to Elizabeth, I said, "It's very high time you got away from this man". I said, "How do you know that right this minute we're not sitting at the table and we'd look under the table, there and see there's a bug there?" I said, "What type of man are you dealing with?" I said, "This is madness". But she wouldn't leave him. He had some control over her, some weird control.'

Some weird control. 'Was it sexual?' I ask. He wets his lips, reaches for his beer. 'Well, how do I say this? Bunting was, ah, let me say it this way: well endowed.'

'Oh? How do you know that?'

He chuckles. 'Well, not from personal experience, you understand. Elizabeth told me. She said he was ordinary in bed, nothing to write home about, but well hung. Ah . . . well endowed.'

'Tell me what else you know about him. He's a mystery, isn't he?'

Marcus leans forward. His eyes are gleaming, partly from the beer, partly from something harder to define. Perhaps a secret he has been harbouring and is finally about to relinquish.

'If Bunting was here, talking to you now, he would be charming', he says. 'Sitting at the table, making conversation, and thinking, thinking all the time. Smiling at you and memorising the layout of the rooms in this apartment. Who is sleeping where. He would know that your daughter is with you, in one bedroom, and that your mother is in the next. He would smile when he left and in the middle of the night, he would quietly come back, climb up over the balcony, break the lock without making a sound, sneak into the apartment and kill you all.'

56

It is late at night and I am sitting on the windowsill of my swank, inner-city hotel room on this May night in 2004; the same hotel where earlier in the day the concierge smiled, and carried my bags. A national magazine has sent me to Adelaide to cover a feature story on the Snowtown killings. I am safe here, 14 storeys high, overlooking the city with its ribbons of light that stretch interminably, roads that lead to the suburbs where life goes on in the same endless cycle. Elizabeth Harvey has died, left behind one son she buried, another son in jail and two teetering to understand any of it.

Nicole Zuritta left Adelaide before Mark Haydon's trial started, desperate to try to erase the past, to start again. Desperate for the cycle of abuse to end, and determined that it will. She went into therapy to exorcise her demons and made a home for Jamie Vlassakis's half-brother for a few years to give him half a chance. She is tired of the generational repetition: incest, paedophilia, children raised by foster carers instead of their natural parents.

She sees herself as a survivor of a childhood she should never have had to endure, and grimaces at band-aid solutions to the problems. 'The type of abuse that Maxine Cole and I suffered stays with you for life. I always had a longing for a normal existence and a few years ago I finally found a counsellor who listened to me with empathy, not condescension. The government thinks that by razing the shitty houses in shitty neighbourhoods, they can move the people and fix the problem. It's going to take a whole lot more than that. People need to stop turning a blind eye to what is going on. The whole system needs changing, and a Royal Commission to look into how it got to this in the first place. I'm not interested in the do-gooders. I'm interested in the rights of the children who can't protect themselves. Change has got to come.'

I can leave that world but tonight the pictures replay in my mind, over and over again. Images of children locked in their rooms; children who are not protected from paedophiles, who steal food from cupboards and get a hiding for it, who are thrown away to welfare. I recall part of the judge's summing up in a case heard in another state that involved family members of one of the victims. 'In all my years of having to read victim impact statements I can't recall one where there seems to be less hope – almost no hope . . . [this child was] deprived of . . . its birthright to be protected and nurtured . . . That places it in the worst cases of offences of this nature.' The children. Growing up and having children of their own.

Deputy Police Commissioner Neil McKenzie retired in mid-2002, after 43 years with the South Australian police. I think about his description of the people involved in these serial killings, as 'a group that preyed on itself'. But just how far did the human network extend? I think of the code of silence. Did not one other person, beyond Elizabeth Harvey, guess that something was very wrong?

Denis Cordwell, who moved the stinking barrels from Hoyleton? His partner, Anne, who complained of the smell emanating from the barrels? Robert Wagner's former fiancée, Maxine Cole, who knew about the 'hit list'? Nicole Zuritta, Cole's cousin, who had also heard of the list? Tina Dowling, Cole's one-time house mate, who knew stories of cannibalism and social security fraud? Raelene Brown, ex de facto of one of Bunting's mates, who overheard Bunting talking about skinning and torturing people but who said she 'would have deserved a punch in the face, sir' if she said anything? Lenore Penner, who had been told by her cousin, Thomas Trevilyan, that he had been involved in the deaths of two other people and that the victims' social security money was being used? Michelle Bihet, who had lived with Barry Lane? Robert Skewes, who lived next door to Bunting? Tammy McKenzie, Tony Sinclair's de facto, who overheard stories but said nothing? Gail Sinclair, who was offered a letter of comfort from the state for any offence short of murder and who was once engaged to John Bunting?

Who guessed that Bunting and his cohorts were involved in illegal activity? If any of them did, no one said a word. In all the years that the killings continued, no one went to the police, raised the alarm, shared any suspicions they may have had about any aspects of the crimes. This, despite the fact that the targets were their own friends and relatives. Why the silence? Outcast from the mainstream, living in their blue-collar enclaves from where violent offenders are predominantly drawn and where homicide is overwhelmingly committed by males between the ages of 18 and 30, were they subdued into believing that strange behaviour is normal, that cops are the cultural enemy, and that saying nothing is a safer option?

I think about this country's under class, created out of a fatal combination of cyclical unemployment, crushingly low self-esteem and feelings that they have been overlooked. And the products of this class, the victims – their down-at-heel, uneventful lives and their gruesome, dreadful deaths – who could find no solace from the maelstrom that surrounded them, no framework to shelter them. Not even here, in this reverent, conservative city of churches.

Elizabeth Haydon hadn't had much of a go in life, and she was afforded no dignity at all in death. I have looked at her photo hundreds of times, staring at it to find something I may have missed. But it is always the same: the image of an intellectually impaired woman with little self-esteem, resigned to her lot, peering out at the world with eyes small as buttons set in an ample face, a woman the world neither cared about nor nurtured. There is a poignancy in the photo that makes me return to it time and again, as if by looking at it deeply enough Elizabeth, only a few years younger than myself when she died, might be able to talk to me. Perhaps she will tell me what it was like to grow up emotionally cauterised in a family that jumped around like jack rabbits, to grow up with no expectations of security, love or tenderness either for herself or her children. Perhaps she will explain how it felt to be uneducated, uninspired, unemployed, to grow up in a world where lives are measured by welfare cheques, where money is so tight that there is never enough to go around. And the more I look at her face, the more I understand that Elizabeth Haydon's life, defined by lack of income, lack of opportunity and lack of love, is as foreign to me as another country. The face of how 'the other half' lives.

How did they keep their secrets? More than one perpetrator is extremely rare. And to keep the group tight and safely operational, a psychologist noted, it requires that the people in it have a remarkable level of trust in each other. By and large, the people who perpetrate serial killings are driven by perverse sexual motivations. For a group to be involved there has to be a sharing of that sadistic drive, or the group members must somehow be persuaded to assist someone else in gratifying their perverse needs. One of the many tragedies in the Snowtown case is just how that group came to be together in the first place.

I think about Wendy Abraham's opening address, now so long ago. Her seemingly nerveless approach to the biggest serial killing case in Australian history. 'It has been reported . . . that the motive for killing some or all of the victims was Social Security fraud, with killing on the end', she intoned. 'That is just not so. This was maniacal killing and there was, in some instances, a Social Security benefit. So it is the wrong way around . . .'

There is a poignant, telling description by one journalist that stands out from the rest, a description of both the victims and killers as a 'ravaged, luckless lot'. Luckless by birth. Ravaged by life. Luckless in death. But Professor Paul Wilson, Dean of Humanities at Queensland's Bond University, has no doubt that, handicapped as they were by social and economic hardships, it does not automatically follow that they should become evil.

'These were coolly, coldly, calculated murders, not one but 11, and they stopped because they were caught – not for any other reason. These people knew exactly what they were doing; they were totally in control of their reasoning process, even if that process was warped. These killers are not psychiatrically ill.' Wilson says the level of planning by the killers was on a scale he has never before witnessed in Australia. 'They set about what they were doing with organised, ruthless efficiency, which makes this unique from other crimes in this country. The killers bonded together to keep their secrets, and not one of them broke from the group until they were caught. They were utterly focused on what they wanted to do. And they enjoyed what they did so much that they returned again and again to do it. Their victims were a nobody, a nothing whose deaths boosted the killers' low self-esteem, made them feel important, powerful, in control. It was a sick obsession, a need to kill. And the final depravity was to devour their enemies in an act of complete domination.'

Ingestion of another human being is a way of taking on their power, their spirit, their identity. A means of keeping them close. Like trophies. Was that also the motivation behind the macabre acts of de-fleshing and dismemberment? Hobart psychiatrist Professor Saxby Pridmore agrees to have a general conversation with me about the case in January 2006. He says very little literature is available on the subject – precisely *because* these acts are so rare. 'Normal' people have their own rituals.

'When a spouse dies', Pridmore says, 'the partner often keeps that person's belongings as a way of identifying them. But for Bunting, the ritual was much more sinister. Had he and his cohorts not been caught, they would certainly have continued, becoming more and more bizarre as time went on.'

I outline the little that is known about Bunting's past and his predilection for violence. Without examining him, Professor Pridmore says, and without a detailed knowledge of his childhood, it is difficult to comment beyond generalisations. He refers me to the Psychopathy Checklist, developed by psychiatrist R.D. Hare and used by psychiatrists as a rating scale to measure traits of psychopathic personality disorders.

John Bunting is a textbook case. A pure, unadulterated psychopath. He can check off all the items.

'I'd like to know what makes him tick'. I venture. 'Bunting is really an enigma.'

'Yes, but we know some things, don't we? You've told me he boasted about bashing "faggots" at a young age, and he tells us this is in revenge for the alleged rape. That may, or may not be, the case. The other possible mechanism is what's called "projection" – what we all use to project our own characteristics onto somebody else, our own failings. If you gossip about someone, for example, and are nasty, you are punishing that characteristic in yourself – but punishing it *away* from yourself so that you don't get hurt. There is a strong parallel of someone disliking something that they themselves are, but don't know it at the time. So there is a possible explanation for him bashing up "fags" at an early age, whether or not he was raped. Rape is an act of revenge; but if he wasn't raped, he probably has homosexual tendencies that he then projects onto others. He kills those others, rather than killing himself.'

'But what about his penchant for extreme violence? What's that all about?'

'He finds pleasure in causing pain to things that can't defend themselves: spiders, cats, dogs, humans. Freud said that to be normal, you need to be able to love and work. He was talking about having a normal intimate life. In deviant individuals, sex drive and violence is very closely linked. Anything that causes pain can be a sexual gratification. The anticipatory pleasure of pain starts right at the planning and entrapment stage.'

'And the blow-up doll?

'He would have inserted the other, small doll in the blow-up doll's rectum. And people who are into blow-up dolls aren't able to have a rewarding sex life with others. It speaks to his disturbed sexual identity and his reduced ability to express himself sexually. This man is incapable of intimacy.'

'Finally, Bunting has no sense of smell. Is this significant?'

It is as though I have lobbed a hand grenade into the conversation. 'It certainly is! What do you know about this? Was he born with it?'

'I think so . . . but one can never be sure with him. Why?'

'Because the sense of smell is a function of the frontal lobes, the front part of the brain. The frontal lobes control emotion and conscience. Loss of smell – the medical term is "anosmia" – strongly suggests damage to this part of the brain. Frontal lobe damage leads to frontal lobe syndrome; that causes irritability, apathy, callousness, lack of conscience and the abuse of rights and rules of others. Most people with anosmia are psychopaths because the frontal lobe circuitry is wiped out', Pridemore says. 'Unlike animals, we don't need to smell to survive, but imagine not being able to smell smoke from a fire, or your dinner burning. The sense of smell can protect a person from danger.'

Research into the phenomenon resulted in the infamous psychiatric surgery of the 1940s and '50s known as the frontal lobotomy, dramatised vividly in the movie *One Flew Over the Cuckoo's Nest*. 'Damage to the frontal lobes', Pridmore continues, 'does not disrupt the basic function of sensory, memory or emotional systems, but it interferes with a person's ability to engage in organised social behaviour. And Bunting uses his irritability and anger to control situations around him. He engages in manipulative chaos. The fact that he has no sense of smell probably speaks volumes about his personality.'

57

There was chaos in the Salisbury district's welfare offices when details of the Snowtown crime came to light. All the victims – and killers – had been through those offices, either as past or present clients. There would be scrutiny.

There is scrutiny elsewhere, too.

Known for his passion for investigating systemic corruption at high levels within South Australia, *Today Tonight* producer Graham Archer created a storm with his series of programs *The Takeaway Children*, which aired over two years. A bleak exposé of child abuse in South Australia, the stories peel back layers of grime to reveal the practice of vulnerable, orphaned children who have been raised in state welfare homes and community units, being used as sexual playthings by foster carers and others in authority. The first one aired on 10 February 2003. 'That initial story', Archer recalls, 'centred on a former ward of the state, Ki Meekins, who had been fighting in court for compensation for eight years. Remarkably, he had managed to get his file from the Department of Community Welfare, as it was then known, and the government settled his case out of court, in order to try and minimise the damage over what he was saying.'

Today Tonight took a calculated risk and broke the confidentiality agreement to tell Meekins's story. The reaction was explosive, particularly from other former wards of the state who, after years of silence, finally came forward to tell their shocking stories. 'This', Archer says, 'was probably the first occasion where the topic of the systematic abuse of children in state care had been so compellingly and undeniably exposed. In the stories that followed, there were also connections made to the so-called "Family", speculated to be a loose affiliation of well-positioned people within the state who used these boys and girls as playthings. Their actions sometimes resulted in children's disappearance and deaths.'

Archer continued to push, and to ask unpalatable questions. The government's response was first to repeal the 1982 Statute of Limitations on criminal proceedings in child abuse cases, which had prevented many, many victims from reporting their abuse and taking action. 'They also took the "soft option" of commissioning the Layton Report, a 12-month analysis of the Department of Youth and Family Services (now known as FACS – Family and Community Services), and its handling of abuse cases. This approach has a role to play, but in my opinion it was a sanitised attempt to deal with the system and not the victims.'

By now a thorn in the side of the government, Archer challenged the controlled air of a press conference by questioning the Layton Report's author, now Justice Layton QC, about the failure to address the crimes committed against the abused and whether a Royal Commission was in order. Ms Layton rejected the notion, saying nothing more would be achieved. When Archer reminded Layton of the magnitude of the problem by pointing out that there are hundreds of victims, Archer says her response was to retort, 'So you say!'

'The figures that have subsequently emerged', Archer says, 'confirm that my concerns were well placed.'

With the pressure now festering like an abscess that needed to burst, the government announced a Commission of Inquiry into the treatment of wards of the state, headed by retired Supreme Court judge, Ted Mullighan. (Robyn Layton took Mullighan's place on the bench.)

Archer watched the commission unfold with a critical eye. He was particularly concerned with the conflicts of interest that he believes haunt this isolated state. 'Robert Wagner's lawyer, Bill Morris, was a close friend of and, until recently, had power of attorney over, the assets of paedophile magistrate Peter Liddy', Archer says. 'He [Bill Morris] was appointed chief investigator to the Mullighan Inquiry. Morris resigned his position following agitation by *Today Tonight* in revealing his inappropriate connections to Liddy, but the fallout didn't stop there. Before Morris resigned, the minister responsible for his appointment, Jay Weatherill, used parliament to describe the *Today Tonight* revelations as "a scurrilous, appalling and dishonest attack on a decent South Australian".'

In May 2005, the Commission of Inquiry into Children in state care issued its Interim Report. Mullighan's terms of reference were to inquire into allegations of sexual abuse against children who were in state care, or criminal conduct resulting in the death of a person whilst in state care. By May 2005, 501 persons had approached the commission and the flood of people coming forward necessitated an extension of time until at least June 2006. The interim findings of the commission, including findings relating to the deaths of a high number of children in state or church care, proved a savage indictment against the carers in these institutions and all those who turned a blind eye to what was happening to innocent children.

Mullighan wrote of the conspiracy of silence: 'The culture in many of the homes and institutions discouraged in powerful ways disclosure of the conduct. That culture was reinforced and fostered by the perpetrators. In many instances those who did disclose, or attempted to disclose, were disbelieved and, in some instances, punished.' Well before 1970, he continued, the Welfare Department's accepted wisdom, based on professional advice, was that such allegations were fantasy. This later changed, with emphasis being placed on acceptance of the allegations as true unless there was good reason not to believe the children.

Ki Meekins, serially abused for years during his time in state institutions, seized the opportunity to address the commission. He is determined to keep fighting. 'Government's past sins create huge future shadows', he says. 'It is not possible to build a good future on a devious, heinous past.'

Somewhere between the haunted faces of those courageous enough to publicly speak on *Today Tonight* and the more formal arena of the Commission of Inquiry and the stories contained in the pages of its Interim Report, is the human toll. It is a testament of shame. Thousands of vulnerable children, over more than 50 years, were victims of physical, emotional and extreme sexual abuse; children from church and government welfare institutions, foster homes and detention centres. And the effect of this abuse is devastating. Abandoned by their parents, handed over or taken by welfare, the children are tragically vulnerable to on-going abuse from the people who promised to protect them: their carers. Many, boys and girls of all ages, were taken out on weekend leave and returned on Sunday nights, bleeding, traumatised and terrified. Often drugged, they were handed around groups of men and the occasional woman for oral and anal sex and further gross indecencies. Many were forced to perform sex acts on each other. And some children – far too many – never returned.

Archer can't hide his disgust. 'There was no monitoring of this large network of corruption with people who had dirt on each other. It worked on the theory that if you keep my secret, I'll keep yours. They protected each other. This is a system in desperate need of colonic irrigation. There has never been any kind of broad systematic inquiry into any aspect of the police or the justice system in this state. The reasons are that few in government, the various departments and the professions, want it and no one has made any sustained case that there are grounds beyond rumour for the need for such an inquiry.'

By October 2005, Mullighan had taken statements from 900 former wards of state claiming abuse and 60 cases have been forwarded to the prosecution branch. And still the numbers grow.

'As harsh as this may sound', Archer says, 'perhaps what happened in the Snowtown killings can be seen in this context. Perhaps it was the crime we had to have, the crime you get when repeated governments turn a blind eye to child abuse and domestic violence, as they have in South Australia. The chances are, you eventually create a monster.'

Archer winces when he admits that within South Australia – conservative, staid South Australia – the superficial view is that those involved in the Snowtown serial killings were lowlife welfare parasites feeding on the system and on each other. 'The public generally holds a harsh view: that no one of any value died and no one of any value was to blame, so good riddance to them all.'

There is, he continues, a serious lesson to be learnt. 'While the crimes may have shocked us, they should not have really surprised us. We are only now coming to grips with why it happened. Almost everyone involved, the predators and those preyed upon, were themselves the victims of abuse. The self-loathing, cold rage and the need to exert power over someone or something else are often the by-products of such abuse.'

He is cognisant that the issues are extremely complex. 'The overwhelming majority of people who have been seriously abused don't go on to become serial killers. But abuse is an essential component for those who do. Add to that the under class, the permanently unemployed, congregated in public housing ghettos: eventually there is a fair chance the ingredients will come together. It only requires an evil mind like that of Robert Wagner or John Bunting to exploit the situation. The frightening reality is that Snowtown is not just an aberration. It has a cause which needs to be treated and it is a dark beacon warning of the damage that results from neglect and indifference to abuse.'

Aware that similar barbaric crimes happen elsewhere, Archer says a small city has more of a culture of denial. 'The conflicts of interest, fear of reprisals and traditions of compliance ensure that those who should speak out, don't. And those who want to speak out have no one who is willing to listen.'

Archer sees the Snowtown story as being, in the end, a kind

371 Killing for Pleasure

of anti-climax. 'It has brought us no closer to understanding or solving the major mysteries which shadow this state. It also renewed the uneasy feeling about what humans are capable of and the reality that horrendous crimes are a constant possibility rather than some aberration of a particular period of history.'

With the issue now so blatantly in the public domain, Premier Mike Rann, with one eye cocked toward votes and a need to quell public outrage, supports an increase in the paedophile taskforce. 'I don't care whether the paedophiles are from the church, the media or within the public service – there is no hiding place left. We are coming after them. They must fear the tap at the door from police . . .'

The disadvantaged are confronting, and beg the question: what do we do with them? Outside the Adelaide courts, where justice is dispensed and lawyers drink cafe lattes in their breaks, the homeless, the mad and the destitute mill around, begging for money and for cigarettes. They sleep overnight in the nearby parks, Victoria and Whitmore Square, waking up for the day with nowhere to go, and nothing to do. 'What do you do with them?' a QC asks as he doles out loose change for the third time that morning. 'They don't go away, and these are the people we see, that we know about. There are thousands more in the suburbs, and we only hear of them when they hit the courts. Like the Snowtown story. Went on for years before they were apprehended. But can we stop it happening again? And if so, how?'

The QC lights another smoke and stirs a generous teaspoonful of sugar into his coffee. 'There's an expression you may have heard? "Some people walk in the rain. Others just get wet."' He hunches his gown higher on his shoulders, and heads back to the air-conditioned court.

58

At the end of July 2004, a jury of seven men and eight women are empanelled for the trial of 45-year-old Mark Ray Haydon. How do you plead? 'Not guilty' to the murder of his wife, Elizabeth Haydon, and of John Bunting's stepson, Troy Youde. 'Not guilty' to assisting Bunting, Wagner and Vlassakis in the deaths of six other people.

Five years in Yatala prison's E Division have changed Mark Haydon. Now he looks older, time-ravaged, like an ageing, feral country singer. 'You must be ultra-cautious', Justice John Sulan warns the jury. 'Justice needs to be seen to be done as well as deliberations with third parties . . . Just let the case unfold, pay attention [and] if you have any questions, we can deal with them in due course . . .'

On the opening day of the trial, the prosecution – again led by Wendy Abraham – goes for the jugular. The scheme, Abraham tells the court, was to get Gail Sinclair out of the house so Haydon's wife, Elizabeth, could be killed.

It is the same cool Abraham who prosecuted the first trial: immaculate, steady, poised to strike. 'It's the Crown case that Elizabeth Haydon was dead by the time Gail Elliott [Sinclair] and Mark Haydon returned home', she says. 'At least one motive for Elizabeth Haydon's murder is that she knew about a previous murder. By the time Elizabeth Haydon was murdered, Mark Haydon had been involved in two murders and had seven bodies in his shed.'

Haydon, she continues, stored dead bodies in his home and car before co-renting a disused bank vault at Snowtown with convicted killer John Justin Bunting. 'Mark Haydon', Abraham says with cool disdain, 'didn't do the physical act of killing. He wasn't even there at the time of the murder. But it's the Crown case that Elizabeth Haydon was killed pursuant to a plan made in advance by Bunting, Wagner and Haydon.'

Abraham rests her fingers lightly on the lectern before continuing her relentless address. Haydon, she says, was also involved in the earlier murder of Troy Youde, whose mutilated body was found in one of six barrels. 'The Crown does not suggest that Mark Haydon was involved in the mutilation and de-fleshing of the bodies, or that he derived any particular pleasure or enjoyment from it', she adds. Haydon, she admits, couldn't stomach the mutilation of victims, but his crime was no less serious. 'He rendered assistance and he kept the group's activities secret.'

Haydon's counsel, Marie Shaw QC, is taking a gamble, putting her sullen client on the stand on 10 November 2004. She gets straight to the heart of the matter.

'Were you involved in the murder of your wife?'

'No.'

'Were you involved in the murder of Troy Youde?'

'No.'

'Prior to your arrest on 21 May 1999, did you have any inkling that there were human bodies in barrels at the bank in Snowtown?'

'No.'

The questions continue. Heard of Michael Gardiner? Gavin Porter? Gary O'Dwyer? Troy Youde? *No. No. No. No.*

Mark Haydon, Marie Shaw will tell the jury in her summing up, loved his wife . . . [He] did not join with Bunting, Wagner and Vlassakis in these atrocities. The prosecution, at the very least, has not proved beyond a reasonable doubt that he joined with them . . .'

Wendy Abraham QC is steady as she concludes her address to the jury. 'I suggest that we've proved the case in relation to the murder of Troy Youde, Elizabeth Haydon and, indeed, that he was assisting them escape apprehension in relation to the other six bodies. That is a matter for you.'

On Wednesday, 15 December 2004, the jury retires. Four days later it convicts Mark Haydon of five counts of assisting Bunting, Wagner and Vlassakis to escape apprehension or prosecution. Five counts for the murders of Michael Gardiner, Barry Lane, Gavin Porter, Fred Brooks and Gary O'Dwyer. But the jury cannot reach a verdict over the murders of his wife, Elizabeth, and Troy Youde. It cannot reach a verdict, either, on one count of assisting in the murder of David Johnson at Snowtown.

The reporters' faces are dour, expressions glazed, as they file out of the courtroom, their fingers executing a now-familiar dance over mobile phone numbers as they call updates through to their newsrooms. A murder re-trial is now more than likely; this story will again leach into another year. It has already been more than six years since it first broke: more than six years of committals, trials, delays, legal arguments. They seem to do nothing, now, but take their places at the press pews and regurgitate, ad nauseam, the hideous details of miserable lives and murderous intent. It is like watching a tennis match, the interminable verbal lobby between prosecution, witness; prosecution, witness. They know the idiosyncrasies of the lawyers, the judges, the court staff; share their exhaustion after a day with an exasperating witness.

The transcripts are held in a windowless, makeshift office in the gloomy bowels of the court to which they descend, daily, as if entering a bar in the Middle East. Checking what the witness said, the often combative exchanges between witness and counsel; checking suppression orders; looking for a new angle.

There are few left of the original reporters who scored coveted front row media seats in the first round of the trial, striding around the court with the self-important air of privileged insiders. The press seats are now reduced to the odd straggler and their copy is pared down to the bare minimum. Cameramen wait outside on the street to stalk new prey entering and leaving court. One, leaning on his equipment, appears never to move from his footpath position. 'You still loitering?' a lawyer asks him as he sallies past. 'Yeah', he grins. 'With intent.'

The court ceremonies; the small details, too inconsequential to make the news; the snippets of gossip, once offered

as scintillating dinner party fodder to curious observers suspicious that the real story lurked beneath the suppressions,
have long ago withered to a plaintive plea by journalists to turn
the conversation to something else. It is starting to seem as
though it will never end.

Then suddenly, it does. With no warning, in mid-September
2005, prosecutor Sandi McDonald tells the Supreme Court
that new information has been filed, charging Haydon with
two counts of assisting offenders, to replace the two murder
charges. Haydon clasps long, milky-white fingers over his
mouth and stares forlornly at the floor. He appears to have
shrunken even further into himself since his last court appearance; his body is shaped into a bent half-twist as he slouches in
the dock seat. His once unruly hair and beard are now tamed
to prison regulation length and his former maniacal expression
dumbed down to a blank emptiness. He stands to plead:
'Guilty' to assisting Bunting, Wagner and Vlassakis – knowing
they had murdered Troy Youde – escape apprehension and
prosecution. He admits the same offence in relation to the
murder of his wife by Bunting and Wagner. His lawyer, John
Lyons, rises. Haydon, he says quietly, will not be pursuing his
appeal against conviction on the five other counts of assisting
offenders.

Haydon shuffles from the dock. After six years of living in
the glare of the world's media, he is virtually invisible even
before he exits through the door.

It would always have been an uphill battle for a lawyer to skew
the court towards some empathy for a client who, for seven
years, assisted Bunting and Wagner to avoid arrest. But, his
lawyer tells the court in October 2005, during a two-day
sentencing hearing, Mark Haydon was no more than a 'very
passive manservant', an ineffectual man incapable of aggression
who had fallen under Bunting's spell. He paints a portrait of
Bunting: a manipulator and consummate liar who preyed on
the weak and the vulnerable. His client did not stand a chance.

But the victim impact statements, aired to the court in October, reflect the lack of forgiveness for this passive man-servant. A mother of one victim encapsulates the general hostility toward him. She hopes he suffers, she writes, 'because he does not deserve to leave this world easily'.

If there is no closure for the victims' families, Haydon has an agonising wait for his own. In December 2005, his lawyers tell the Supreme Court Haydon is suffering severe anxiety and depression over the protracted wait for his sentence to be passed, delayed until some time in 2006. Haydon 'fell apart' when he heard the news. He is, John Lyons says, at a 'real risk of having a total physical and mental breakdown.'

Haydon's sister-in-law, Gail Sinclair, spits out her rage and grief. 'I have never hated anyone, but I feel hate and vengeance towards Haydon. I will never forgive him.'

Elizabeth Haydon's mother, Pat Sinclair, stares hard at Haydon when she delivers a statement about Elizabeth's two children. 'Her sons have lost their mother and they were so young,' she says.

Not a skerrick of emotion crosses Haydon's face.

59

With the trials over, appeals ended and this case finally having reached its close, I am hopeful of securing an interview with players involved in the marathon story. Robert Wagner's lawyer, Bill Morris, is unfailingly polite every time I make contact with him, though he will not disclose personal details about his client. But he understands my wish to try to get closer to the heart of this story. Bunting is a mystery; Vlassakis less so, by virtue of the admissions about his life made in court; Haydon, 'a passive manservant', according to the description offered by his lawyer. That leaves only one man: Robert Wagner. He has pleaded guilty to three counts of murder and, by any standard, had an increasing and insatiable blood lust. But why? Had something happened to him in his childhood to spur him to such depravities?

'They didn't really touch motive in the trial', Morris says, enigmatically. 'If Robert would tell you his story, that would be beneficial. I would like to see the whole story come out, but it can only happen with his permission. The best you can do is write to him, ask if he will talk.'

Robert Wagner has been in Yatala Labour Prison since 1999. I do write, including in the letter a series of general questions. Why did he do what he did? What does he now think of John Bunting? Does he regret his past?

No response. Months later, I try again. Still no response.

In October 2005, I approach the head of Major Crime, Detective-Superintendent Peter Woite, for an interview with both himself and officers involved in this case. On instruction from Woite, Detective Brian Swan returns my call. I have met him once, briefly, in court and generally outline the type of questions I hope police will answer in the interview. Swan indicates he will call me back. A week later, following another phone call from me, he rings with the news that Woite has declined my request. No one in his area will be talking to journalists or authors, he says.

I ask him if he is personally disappointed that, having spent seven years of his life on the biggest criminal trial in Australian history, he is not able to share some insights into the case? Given that his boss has stopped him from speaking, I canvass the question as off-the-record. He proffers a grim laugh. 'Nothing is ever off the record with the media', he replies. 'Well, it is with me', I respond, startled at his sharpness. 'Can you at least tell me the reasons why the decision has been made to not talk to media? After all, it is a huge case, funded by the taxpayer. There are questions that the public would undoubtedly like answered. Do you think the public has the right to expect accountability and transparency from the police? Why won't they talk to the media?'

'We are under no obligation to.'

This is hardly an answer to the question I had asked. 'No, of course not. But I would just like to be able to explain the reasons why this decision has been made?'

'Being pushy won't get you anywhere.'

'I don't think I am being pushy. It's just that I've waited five years to hear the police insights into this story, and I'm disappointed I'm not to be even told why they won't speak.'

That is an understatement. I have so many questions. Who did they credit as being most responsible for finally breaking open the case? What was the toll on the officers involved, personally and professionally? Why did victims die when the police had the killers under surveillance? Why weren't more resources made available earlier? What is their version of the Clinton Trezise debacle? It appears that the media won't even be treated to a corporate SAPOL version of events.

'I've spent seven years of my life on this case', Swan continues in his curt voice. 'You've done five, and you're getting paid for it.'

I am tempted to remind him that he is too, but I refrain. Being rude won't get me anywhere.

'Try Paul Schramm', Swan says, before he hangs up. 'He may talk to you. But no one from this office can.'

Paul Schramm is exceedingly polite, but bound by protocol. I need, he advises me, to float the idea past a contact at South Australia Police.

In an email, I outline what I require, and I spell out the deadline: 26 October 2005. 'I spoke with Paul Schramm a couple of years ago requesting an interview at the appropriate time', my email continues. 'I called Paul again two days ago, and he advised me to contact you with the request, and to explain the urgency, which is unfortunately out of my control.

'I would like to meet with Paul face-to-face in Adelaide for an interview regarding the trials and tribulations of running such a high-profile case. This would include personal or professional difficulties with the subject matter, leading a team through such a lengthy investigation and the highs and lows of it. It would also involve an examination of some aspects of the police investigation, such as admissions that police were under-resourced at critical times. I would expect that I would tape the interview and that the police would, also. Any questions Paul is not able to answer, or deems he does not wish to answer, he of course does not have to.

'I am simply looking for an overview of this case from the police perspective and hope that this request meets a favourable outcome.'

It doesn't. Schramm cannot speak to the media until after Haydon is sentenced.

At least, I hope, the DPP will respond favourably. Wendy Abraham has now left South Australia and moved to the Commonwealth DPP in New South Wales. There is a glimmer of hope that, despite having a natural reluctance to deal with the media, she just might talk. I speak to her by phone and she says she will consider it. The response comes back, via her former junior prosecutor, Sandi McDonald. 'I have spoken to the other members of the team about their views about participating in an interview for your book. The consensus was that it is inappropriate for a prosecutor to participate in such a way. This view was based on our unique role in the system. As you know, Wendy was very strongly of the view that it is improper and has referred me to some comments made by various judges to that effect. In all of the circumstances I have come to the view that I should not participate in such an interview. At the end of the day, Wendy is the QC and I should be guided by her.'

Three strikes out. Back to Wagner.

At my request, Bill Morris asks Wagner, during a professional visit, whether he will ever venture to speak to me, either directly or through a third party. He indicates it is not out of the question.

I contact the prison to inquire what permissions I would require for a visit should Wagner ever agree. The person on the other end of the telephone is blunt. Maximum security prisoners can't just talk to anyone, he says.

'Why not?' I inquire. 'If they wish to speak to someone whilst they are serving their sentence, why can't they?'

Because, he replies in a withering voice heavily tweaked with irritation, Yatala Prison is not the Hilton.

The book is nearing deadline and in October 2005 I give it one final shot, getting a message through to Wagner to please contact me by telephone if he can. From past experience, I know the chances are remote.

Then a phone call. 'I am calling on behalf of Robert Wagner. You have been asking him to make contact. What do you want?' It is a woman's voice; educated, cautious. She explains her relationship to Robert, and I tell her why I am desperate for answers. 'I suspect', I say, 'that there is more to his background than has so far been disclosed. Something darker, more malevolent. Something beyond one incident of child-hood rape. Something that gets to the heart of motive.'

The woman tells me she will think about whether to talk

to me, and asks for a guarantee that her identity will remain undisclosed. I assure her that it will.

We talk more in the following days; loose, general conversations. But if we are to do this story properly, we will have to meet face to face. I share with her a fact known about serial killers: that their histories very often show that they sustained trauma to the head in childhood. And my own theory: that Robert was more than likely serially abused, emotionally, physically and sexually; so severely abused that his view of the world was warped beyond any hope of healing when he reached adulthood. 'What is done to children, they will do to society.' Is Robert Wagner a man who wreaked revenge on behalf of the angry child within?

She suddenly starts weeping, and I have the sense that, finally, I am getting close to the heart of it.

A decent, brave woman, she wants the truth to be told. She doesn't condone what Robert did, she says. But knowing his story beyond the confines of what was aired in court may throw some light into dark corners and help ensure history does not repeat. Unless that happens, she warns, and the underprivileged, disaffected victims of childhood abuse – whether they be from private homes, government or church institutions – are illuminated and dealt with, Snowtown and crimes like it will always rear their ugly heads.

But we never meet. Scared that her anonymity will not be preserved, she shrinks as third-party negotiations fail to assuage her fears. It is beyond our control and, bitterly disappointed at losing this one chance at getting so close to a story I have hankered after for five years, I can only thank her for her courage in coming forward and calling me. She retreats back to the shelter of her family. I never even learnt her last name.

Robert Wagner's defence counsel, Mark Twiggs, agrees to speak generally to me about the case. In all the years of writing this story, it is the first glimpse I have into how it affected the legal teams. A former police prosecutor, Twiggs, 48, was admitted to the bar in 1995. He is exhausted from the

Snowtown trial and from the rigours of defending Bradley Murdoch, found guilty of the murder of British tourist Peter Falconio at the end of 2005.

'Our legal team all found Snowtown extremely stressful', he says. 'Not just that it was watched closely by the media but the allegations and the enormity of it all. We were all bewildered by just what went on. And we still are.'

Twiggs doesn't know if he suffers from post-traumatic stress disorder, but he frequently replays the gruesome facts of the story in his mind. 'I had no idea about the effect it would have on me', he admits. 'You think about the children, the filthy environments in which these people live, and then think: they had the children, why don't they look after them better? It's that sort of thing that stays with you, and just the violence and abuse permeates this whole story.'

'What about the idea of there being other murders?'

He hesitates for a moment. 'I suppose it can't be discounted. But if they are in Adelaide, they would have to be unsolved and the victims strangers to that group. Otherwise someone would have mentioned it by now.'

Twiggs regards their client, Wagner, as the 'enforcer' and Bunting the 'instigator'. 'I believe that Wagner is half-victim, half-killer. The stories we heard about the terrible sexual things that Barry Lane did to him during the four years they travelled around Australia when Wagner was a teenager – if they are true, little wonder he is so angry.'

He reflects on the years their legal team spent immersed in the gory details. 'Cases like this change you. You look at the world differently afterwards. If I had the chance to take on a case like this again, would I do it?' He pauses, takes a breath. 'Probably not. No, I don't think I'd do it again. It is truly horrific.'

60

Mid 2005. I am back in Adelaide for the last time, at the same hotel, watching the light fade over the City of Churches. And I think about the killers, how they all found each other; kept each other's dark secrets. Eleven murders, 12 corpses. And I think about what an Adelaide social worker said to me, how he casually threw into the conversation: 'There are bodies buried all over this city. God knows if they will ever be found.'

The concierge carries my bags to the taxi again, smiles and wishes me a safe trip home. The aircraft banks and I look down over the suburbs and think of some lyrics from John Bunting's favourite CD, *Throwing Copper*, by Live. *Reflection. What's been done. Sadness. Of everyone.*

I think about Bunting's parents. I cannot find them. Is it possible to so completely slip under the radar? To vanish into thin air? Have they returned to England, from where his father originally came? Have they changed their identity to avoid recognition as being parents of Australia's worst serial killer? Have they deliberately turned their back on a son who over the years has been nasty, manipulative and cruel? Wiped him from their lives and memory, as though he does not exist? Are they, in fact, still alive?

And I think about John Bunting. Sinister, obsessive John Bunting. How he has always been close-mouthed, secretive. Never told anyone anything he doesn't want them to know. Maybe we will never find out if there were other murders. Never know the difference between his truth and his lies. Whether his teenage friends really did commit suicide, or if they existed at all. Whether he cut a man up on the road between Adelaide and Melbourne, laughing and singing as the car sped along the highway, throwing pieces of his corpse out the window. Whether his faggot-bashing with Benny ever ended with murder, as he boasted to Jamie Vlassakis it had. And if his motive was to rid the world of 'wastes' – homosexuals and paedophiles – how to explain the murder of Gavin Porter, Frederick Brooks, Gary O'Dwyer, Elizabeth Haydon, David Johnson and the dismemberment of Suzanne Allen? None were gay. None were paedophiles. We may never know the real motive, locked deep in Bunting's secretive, warped psyche.

Like backpacker killer Ivan Milat, Bunting will not construct a story around himself to excuse or explain his behaviour. He will let them guess. Let them all guess. They only know what they can prove. What they can prove, and Bunting's own philosophy: *Keep your friends close. Keep your enemies closer.*

Postscript

- After Bunting and Wagner were sentenced to imprisonment, they were immediately remanded to a new trial for the murder of Suzanne Allen. In October 2005, the Crown decided against a re-trial on that count.
- Both Bunting and Wagner were granted leave to appeal against their convictions.
- John Bunting was refused legal aid to appeal in April 2004, and chose to represent himself. He asked Justice John Perry to force prison authorities to hand over his trial notes. He grumbled, 'I asked for a copy of all my legal paperwork in writing. They sent me a three-year-old incomplete copy of the Correctional Services Act.' Justice Perry agreed to help but was adamant he would not countenance Bunting's grudges against the prison system. Advising Bunting how to base his argument for appeal, Justice Perry warned Bunting that 'it would be a very difficult job for somebody without legal training' but he agreed to bend the court rules to allow Bunting leave to argue the majority of his appeal orally. Bunting frequently displayed violent outbursts in court. The appeal failed.
- Robert Wagner's 84 grounds for appeal were funded by the state. The grounds included a miscarriage of justice and the trial's length and complexity. His appeal failed.
- While Bunting reportedly menaces other prisoners he dislikes, Wagner has settled into prison life. The routine suits him. They are all in separate sections of the prison. Bunting does not share a cell; prison authorities will not risk a vicious attack on another inmate, of which he constantly brags. He talks incessantly of escape, revenge, and revels in his crimes.
- Jamie Vlassakis's image is still suppressed to protect his

identity and he is now studying to complete secondary education in prison. Prison officers find him pleasant and amenable. A psychologist noted of him during his sentencing: 'It was more than a dependent relationship. He was totally suborned by Bunting, caught up in the abnormal world and it's only with the passage of many months that he has been able to separate himself from Mr Bunting. Falling completely under the control and influence of someone else, you come to accept their bizarre and twisted views . . . as the natural and real world in which you live. It takes weeks or months for them to even begin to realise that these views were foreign to them, these beliefs are not theirs, but things that they have been caught up in and had imposed on them by the more powerful, the more dominating and intrusive other . . .' In a bizarre way, in prison, Vlassakis has found freedom.

- Media groups lobbied hard against the unprecedented suppression orders in the Snowtown trial. In September 2005, suppression on details of cannibalism was finally lifted.

- Vlassakis's lawyer and former police officer, Eugene McGee, was involved in a fatal hit-and-run accident which killed a father-of-three north of Adelaide in December 2003. McGee, who waited several hours before handing himself into police after the crash, was charged with causing death by dangerous driving, failing to stop and failing to render assistance. His sentence of a $3100 fine and 12-month driving suspension, regarded as manifestly inadequate, was greeted with outrage in South Australia. Following a Royal Commission into the accident, the new South Australian Director of Public Prosecutions, Steve Pallaras, recommended to police that Eugene McGee and his brother, Craig, each be charged with conspiracy to pervert the course of justice. If convicted, each will face four years imprisonment.

- Eugene McGee had also represented disgraced magistrate Peter Liddy and lawyer Scott Aitken, who received a suspended sentence after two of his children were killed in a car crash in which he was the driver and another two were injured.

- Robert Wagner terminated the services of his counsel, Bill 'Wags' Morris, after he found Morris had power of attorney over the substantial assets of paedophile magistrate Peter Liddy.

- In April 2005, maverick South Australian MP Peter Lewis quit as parliamentary speaker, after failing to produce substantial proof about his claim that one of the state's sitting MPs was a paedophile. Lewis also claimed there was a network of organised activity between a group of high society paedophiles in Australia, involving politicians, the judiciary and public servants. He said two gay men, since murdered, had separately told his office of an MP who frequented a known homosexual haunt in Adelaide's parklands. Two volunteers who worked from Mr Lewis's office also released statutory declarations naming four prominent Adelaide people as paedophiles. Two of those named were police officers, the other a retired Liberal MP. In his controversial resignation speech, Lewis declared: 'Removing me will not remove the stain or the shame'.

- The statute of limitations prohibiting the prosecution of a person for sex crimes prior to 1982 has now been lifted, largely due to the agitation by Graham Archer's *Today Tonight* programs, *The Takeaway Children*.

- Victims' families aren't the only people haunted by the Snowtown murders. Senior-Constable Bronwyn Marsh, who joined the force in 1987, has suffered a long and tortured battle with post-traumatic stress disorder since she entered the bank the day they found the bodies in May 1999. In a public letter published in the *South Australian Police Journal* in December 2005, Marsh writes of her illness and says that on the advice of many wise people, she is now looking for a position in another government department. She thanks particular individuals, including Deputy Commissioner Neil McKenzie, who showed there was life after Snowtown; Detective Brian Swan, for not letting her get buried in that 'damn excavation site' and Andrew Bosley, for his strength in putting up with her, day after day in that 'ghastly bank'. Excused from the committal hearing because of her illness, Marsh was supported – sometimes literally – through the trials by other members of the Taskforce Chart team. Chart, she writes, will always be a defining period in her life, working with incredibly committed people who achieved the best results possible in 'horrid' circumstances. The poignancy of the letter hits home. Bronwyn Marsh is yet another casualty, having to leave a job she loves, traumatised by what she saw and smelt in that ghastly bank.

- Pat Sinclair left Adelaide in 2002, and is now living in New South Wales. She has no contact with any of her family except Tony, and she insists she doesn't want any. Bad luck continued to dog her when she moved interstate: a friend, she claims, stole her few personal belongings and she now lives in a retirement village, where, she says, they feed her well and she 'finally gets some peace'.

- Paul Schramm no longer works at Major Crime, but is still a high-ranking police officer in South Australia.

- Sylvia Lane moved interstate to start a new relationship.

- Nicole Zuritta moved her family to country Victoria in 2004 to start a new life.

- Barry Drew died of a heart attack in 2003.

- Robert Wagner rarely contacts Maxine Cole, but he sees their son. Her other children have been taken into welfare care; their son is being raised by a close family member of Wagner's.

- Detective Greg Stone has left the South Australian police.

- Detective Senior-Sergeant Gerald Feltus has retired.

- Justice Brian Martin took up a position as Chief Justice Northern Territory in early 2004. In late 2005, he sat on the bench for the Peter Falconio backpacker murder.

- Marcus Johnson moved to rural Victoria in 2003.

- Former Director of Public Prosecutions Paul Rofe took sick leave as the trial ran up to verdict, leaving Wendy Abraham in the position of acting DPP. He later resigned from office citing ill health, in the wake of prolonged adverse media publicity following the findings in a controversial case.
- Rofe's position as DPP was filled by Nick Pallaras, whose public stoushes with government make it clear he will not abide their involvement in the workings of his office.
- In 2003, Professor Maciej Henneberg finally received recognition from Poland, being awarded the country's top academic honour with the title Professor of Biological Sciences.
- Many people involved in the case, including jurors, journalists and police, receive on-going counselling.
- Civilian psychologist Milton Kelly has retired.
- Many people mentioned in this book spent some time in foster care or state institutions, including Clinton Trezise and Barry Lane. Some children of people named in this book are now, themselves, in state care.
- In November 2003, the Opposition detailed in parliament the exorbitant costs of the trial up to that date: more than $7.8 million on defence lawyers, each comprising a senior counsel, solicitor-advocate, and solicitor. Bunting's team: $2.69 million. Wagner: $2.65 million. Haydon, pre-trial: $1.7 million. Vlassakis: $791,000. The final costs, including Haydon's trial and appeals, were in excess of $20 million. In 2004, three Australian newspaper companies were fined a total of $70,000 for contempt of court for publishing a photo of Jamie Vlassakis in their South Australian editions on 11 July 2002 – a day after he was jailed for life for his involvement in the murders.
- Privately, officers bemoan the organisational crisis with SAPOL, and the haemorrhaging of morale. Lack of staff and responses, they say, is showing at all levels, including the unacceptable clean-up rate for crime.

- The Queensland Department of Housing has initiated an urban renewal program of Bunting's birthplace, Inala, similar to programs in Adelaide's northern suburbs. But little has changed: Inala's unemployment levels are still far higher than the Brisbane average.

- Following the discovery of the bodies at Snowtown, the City of Salisbury council went into damage control, with a media campaign case study that highlighted the image problems in the area. It found that they needed to 'shift focus' away from the negatives and to extol Salisbury's virtues, as a 'good place to live, work and do business'.

- The author of a combined government/university study, Dr Helen Cameron of the University of South Australia, found that in Adelaide's poorer areas, nothing has changed and that crime cycles are continuing. 'You don't have any life chances', she wrote, 'so crime [like Snowtown] becomes almost an entertainment.'

Appendix

The people

Victims

Clinton Douglas Trezise, 19
Murdered between 9 July and 31 August 1992
Skeletal remains found in paddock at Lower Light, 1994
Ray Allan Peter Davies, 26
Murdered between 25 December 1995 and 21 January 1996
Found in shallow grave at 203 Waterloo Corner Road, Salisbury North, 1999
Thomas Eugenio Trevilyan, 18
Murdered between 3 and 6 November 1997
Body found hanging from tree at Kersbrook, north of Adelaide
Michael Jamie Gardiner, 19
Murdered between 31 August and 17 September 1997★
Barry Wayne Lane, AKA **Vanessa**, 42
Murdered between 15 October and 15 November 1997★
Gavin Allen Porter, 31
Murdered between 3 and 8 April 1998★
Troy William Youde, 21
Murdered between 25 August and 8 September 1998★
Frederick Robert Brooks, 18
Murdered between 16 and 19 September 1998★
Gary O'Dwyer, 29
Murdered between 27 October and 14 November 1998★
Elizabeth (Verna Audrey) Haydon, 37
Murdered between 20 and 26 November 1998★
David Terence Johnson, 2
Murdered on or about 9 May 1999★
★*All found at Snowtown, May 1999*

Suzanne Phyllis Allen, 47

Died between 20 November 1996 and 10 December 1996

The jury hung on cause of death. Allen was dismembered after death and her body interred with that of Ray Davies at 203 Waterloo Corner Road.

Killers

John Justin Bunting

DOB: 4 September 1966

Age at arrest (21 May 1999): 32

Address at arrest: 49 Bunderra Court, Craigmore

Former addresses: 203 Waterloo Corner Road, Salisbury North; Burdekin Avenue, Murray Bridge

Originally charged with 10 counts of murder, amended to 12

Found guilty of 11 murders, September 2003

Robert Joe Wagner

DOB: 28 November 1971

Age at arrest (21 May 1999): 27

Address at arrest: 36 Mofflin Road, Elizabeth

Former address: 1 Bingham Road, Salisbury North

Originally charged with 10 counts of murder, amended to 11 (Trevilyan)

Changed plea to guilty of three murders, October 2002; pleaded not guilty to remainder

Found guilty of seven murders, September 2003, plus three guilty pleas

Jamie Spyridon Vlassakis

DOB: 24 December 1979

Age at arrest (2 June 1999): 19

Address at arrest: 49 Bundarra Court, Craigmore

Charged with five counts of murder, dropped to four; changed plea to guilty

Sentenced to 26 years, non-parole

Mark Ray Haydon (real name **Mark Lawrence**)

DOB: 1958

Age at arrest (21 May 1999): 41

Address at arrest: 4 Blackham Crescent, Smithfield Plains

Originally charged with 10 counts of murder, amended to three counts

Pleaded not guilty. Found guilty of five counts of assisting offenders. Changed plea to guilty on two further counts of assisting offenders. Sentence not set at time of publication.

Other characters

Veronika Bunting, nee **Tripp**
Former wife of John Bunting.

Elizabeth Harvey
Died 6 February 2001. AKA Christine Johnson, Christine Vlassakis and Christine Youde. Natural mother of killer Jamie Vlassakis and victim Troy Youde. Stepmother of victim David Johnson. Two other sons. First husband, Spyros Vlassakis; second husband, Marcus Johnson. John Bunting's lover at time of his arrest.

Gail Sinclair
Went by the name Jodie Elliott. AKA Gail Spek, Anne Knudson, Galina Hyland and numerous other aliases. John Bunting's former girlfriend; mother of victim Fred Brooks; sister of victim Elizabeth Haydon.

Marcus Johnson
Father of victim David Johnson. Stepfather of victim Troy Youde and killer Jamie Vlassakis. Former husband of Carlyne Cheeseman and the late Elizabeth Harvey.

Sylvia Lane
Mother of Barry Lane.

Pat Sinclair
Mother of victim Elizabeth Haydon and Gail Sinclair (AKA Gail Elliott etc). Grandmother of victim Fred Brooks. Other children: (Guy) Garion, Christine, Tony, Wayne, Diane.

Tony Sinclair
AKA Anthony Stewart. De facto of Tammy McKenzie; brother of victim Elizabeth Haydon and of Gail Sinclair.

Gary Grey
Former husband of Gail Sinclair; father of two of her children. Also fathered one of her sister, Elizabeth Haydon's, children.

Linda Kovarskis
Fiancée of victim David Johnson.

Carlyne Cheeseman
First wife of Marcus Johnson; natural mother of victim David Johnson.

Denis and Anne Cordwell
Friends of killers. Barrels stored at their properties at Hoyleton and Snowtown.

Maxine Cole
Former fiancée of Robert Wagner; mother of his son (name suppressed); friend of Tina Dowling; first cousin of Nicole Zuritta.

Carol Bowers
Mother of Robert Wagner.

Nicole Zuritta
Cousin of Maxine Cole. Victim Michael Gardiner boarded with her.

Michelle Bihet
Lived with victim Barry Lane before he lived with victim Thomas Trevilyan.

Lenore Penner
Cousin of victim Thomas Trevilyan.

Robert Skewes
John Bunting's former neighbour; lived at 205 Waterloo Corner Road.

Geoffrey Williams
Former neighbour of Barry Lane and Robert Wagner at Bingham Road.

Jeffrey Payne
Neighbour of Elizabeth Harvey and family; sexually abused all her boys.

Andrew and Rosemary Michael
Owned the Snowtown bank; rented it to Bunting and Haydon.

Taskforce Chart police (major players)

Former head of Taskforce Chart: Detective-Superintendent Paul Schramm
Second-in-charge: Detective Senior-Sergeant Nick Standen, Detective Bob Stapleton, Detective Senior-Sergeant Brian Swan, Detective Senior-Constable Steve McCoy, Detective Greg Stone,

Detective Senior-Sergeant Craig Patterson, Detective Kym Presgrave, Detective Mark Wilson, Detective Jane Dickinson, Detective Senior-Sergeant Gerald Feltus
Police forensic team: Senior Constable Andrew Bosley, Senior Constable O'Neill, Senior Constable Cramond, Senior Constable Andrews
Crime scene examiners: Senior Constable Bronwyn Marsh
Local investigators: Detective Senior Constable Rick Day, Senior Constable Gordon Drage, Senior Constable Ian Young
Police psychologists: Milton Kelly (civilian) and Sergeant Ray Dowd
Major Crime: Detective-Superintendent Peter Woite

Forensic team

Forensic odontologist: Jane Taylor
Forensic pathologists: Dr Ross James, Associate Professor Roger Byard, Dr John Gilbert
Also involved: Forensic anthropologist Professor Maciej Henneberg

Legal teams

Committal Hearing Magistrate: David Gurry

	John Bunting	Mark Haydon	Robert Wagner	Jamie Vlassakis	Director of Public Prosecutions
Lead Counsel	Mark Griffin	John Lyons	Steven Apps	Rosemary Davey	Wendy Abraham QC (Senior Counsel)
Junior Counsel	Elizabeth Sheppard	Sam Abbott	Bill Morris	Nick Vadasz	Stephen McEwan Sandi McDonald
Solicitor	Patricia McCrohan	Lempriere Abbott McLeod (firm)	Mark Twiggs	Fiona Lindquist	

Bunting and Wagner trials

His Honour: Justice Brian Martin
Lead Counsel Public Prosecutions: Wendy Abraham QC
Junior Counsel: Sandi McDonald
Solicitor: Caroline Mealor
John Bunting
Lead Counsel: Mark Griffin
Junior Counsel: Elizabeth Sheppard
Solicitor: Patricia McCrohan
Robert Wagner
Lead Counsel: Steven Apps
Junior Counsel: Bill Morris
Solicitor: Mark Twiggs

Mark Haydon trial

His Honour: Justice John Sulan
Director of Public Prosecutions: Wendy Abraham QC
Junior Counsel: Sandi McDonald
Defence Counsel: Marie Shaw QC
Mark Haydon
Senior Counsel: John Lyons
Junior Counsel: Sam Abbott
Solicitors: Lempriere Abbott McLeod

Director of Public Prosecutions (when bodies discovered): Paul Rofe QC

Chronology of events

16 August 1994
Skeletal remains found at Lower Light. Identified as Clinton Trezise in June 1999.

November 1997
Thomas Trevilyan found hanging at Kersbrook. Coroner initially ruled suicide; later found cause of death to be murder.

20 May 1999
Eight bodies found in barrels at bank vault at Snowtown.

21 May 1999
Bunting, Wagner and Haydon arrested, each charged with one count of murder of a person unknown between 1 August 1993 and 20 May 1999. Remanded in custody to reappear 2 July 1999.

23 and 26 May 1999
Two bodies located in makeshift grave in the backyard at John Bunting's former address, 203 Waterloo Corner Road, Salisbury North.

2 June 1999
Jamie Vlassakis arrested, charged with murder of David Johnson. Later charged with further three counts of murder.

3 July 1999
Bunting, Wagner and Haydon jointly charged with 10 counts of murder.

11 December 2000
Committal starts. Sitting days: 49.

6 February 2001
Elizabeth Harvey dies.

21 June 2001
Vlassakis pleads guilty.

4 July 2001
Committal ends.

13 August 2001
Bunting, Wagner and Haydon plead not-guilty to murder counts in Supreme Court hearing.

4 March 2002
Pre-trial argument starts.

21 May 2002
Bunting charged with two additional murders: Trezise and Trevilyan. Haydon charged with murder of Trezise and his murder charges dropped to three. Judge orders Haydon's trial to be separate. Wagner charged with murder of Trevilyan and with assisting offenders in relation to murder of Trezise.

10 July 2002
Vlassakis sentenced.

16 October 2002
Bunting and Wagner trial starts. Sitting days: 148.

10 July 2003
Evidence completed.

7 August – 2 September 2003
Judge summing up.

8 September 2003
Jury verdict.

29 October 2003
Sentencing.

2 August 2004
Haydon trial starts.

19 December 2004
Verdict: guilty five counts of assisting offenders; deadlocked on participation in murders of Troy Youde, Elizabeth Haydon and David Johnson.

16 September 2005
DPP agrees to drop murder charges against Haydon in return for his plea of guilty to assisting Bunting and Wagner dispose of the bodies of his wife and another man.

Sentence: yet to be delivered at time of publication.

Acknowledgments

This book took five years to complete, and on the journey I made friends, both professional and personal. My thanks to the many people who helped me along the way.

In late 2000 and early 2001, journalist Alison McClymont undertook a series of harrowing interviews with the dying Elizabeth Harvey, Bunting's last lover. Present at those interviews were Elizabeth's sister, Diane, and her ex-husband Marcus Johnson. Alison also visited Elizabeth's son, Jamie Vlassakis, when he was at James Nash House. None of the material has been published before and Alison, in conjunction with Random House, gave me the tapes and transcripts of the interviews to use as I saw fit. Parts are reproduced in dialogue and some are presented as Elizabeth's and Jamie's memories.

My thanks to Professor Paul Wilson, Criminologist at Queensland's Bond University, for sharing his brilliant insights into the criminal mind; to Richard Ackland, for permission to reproduce his writings; and to retired Tasmanian forensic pathologist John Presser for his patient unravelling of complex pathology issues. Enormous thanks to courageous SAS 7 journalist and producer Graham Archer; to *The Bulletin*'s Garry Linnell; and to Graham Davies and Ron Sinclair for all being so wonderfully generous with contacts. Also to Professor Maciej Henneberg and Dr Carl Stephan for sharing their knowledge and not laughing when I almost fainted during a guided tour of the University morgue. Thanks, too, to psychiatrist Professor Saxby Pridmore and Dr Thomas Paterson, Senior Registrar in Psychiatry, for sharing fascinating – and scary – insights into how psychopaths think and why they behave as they do.

In her role as Media Liaison at Adelaide Supreme Court, Jenny Turner's calm assistance was invaluable. I owe you one, Jen. Appreciation also to Sylvia Kriven who went out of her way to help; to Natalie Charlesworth for her help during the committal hearing; to various court staff; and to the kind man, whose name I never found out, who waved a magic wand in my direction.

Many thanks to Joseph Bondin for helping me every time the computer crashed and for his patience in fixing it.

To Angelo Loukakis, Julia Collingwood and Jon Attenborough: much appreciation for your support at the beginning of this book and graciousness at the end.

Thanks to the many friends and family of the victims I interviewed who allowed me a glimpse into their sorrow and their lives. Particular thanks to Nicole Zuritta, whose incredible courage in speaking out about child sexual abuse just might make a difference; and to the people I interviewed, who did not wish to be named, who helped me understand the background to this complex, tragic story. Thanks are also due to the brave, anonymous people who bucked the system and made me think twice about taking things at face value; and to Bill Morris for his efforts in trying to help me secure Robert Wagner's story. We got so close, Bill! To Ki Meekins and all the others who put a face to their names in exposing systematic sexual abuse in institutions; keep rattling those sabres! Also to John Garner, for your insights – enormous thanks.

To Veronika Tripp, Marcus Johnson, Cyril Lane, Tony Sinclar, Gary Grey and the woman, whom I promised I wouldn't name, who was courageous in coming forward on behalf of Robert Wagner. Thank you all for your time in telling your stories.

During a two-month working stint at Adelaide's SAS 7 in early 2005, many people helped glue together the Snowtown puzzle. To the following people for their support, help and kindness: Mitch and Leonie Williams, Carol Vowles, Daniel Vowler, Shane McNeill, Kevin Hunt and the terrific team at 7 – huge thanks. Also to my colleague and friend Murray Nichol for your encouragement – it's been really appreciated. And to Graeme Pearce, who allowed me to juggle writing with a teaching gig and didn't growl at me flying in and out of the classroom in a rush.

In June 2005 we lost most of our home and almost all our possessions in an accidental fire. The seat of the fire was my study where I kept transcripts, notes and photographs that I had taken or had been contributed for this book. To those people who entrusted me with their precious photographs, my apologies for not returning them. And to all those people who were so beautifully kind and generous with us and who came out of the woodwork to help, we can never thank you enough. In times like these, you know who your friends are. We are blessed with many.

As always, cheers to my fabulous friends around Australia who buoyed me with their support during this incredibly long project, particularly Traceelea and David Peberdy, Joanna Thyer, Glen Pears, Peter Irwin, Kate Hansford, Heather and Geoff Hocking and Jenny Robinson. There are many I haven't named, who one way or another helped me continue when I sometimes lost heart, but I thank you all. Also to my huge family, particularly my brother, Wayne Marshall, whose warning to me not to touch this story I often wished, over the years, I had heeded. Right from the start, I was warned that writing this book would change me. It did; but it also made me treasure what the victims never had: loving family and friends. Finally, again, thank you to my 'road crew' – my daughter, Louise, and my mother, Monica. Louise, who metamorphosed from a girl to a lovely young woman during the writing of this book and whose patience was tested beyond endurance through my years of obsession with it; and Monica, my sounding-board and sidekick through the court cases, whose understanding of why this story must be written helped me keep my sanity through exposure to terrible, dark details. Both women for their lovely humour and positive attitude; I can't thank you enough.

It was a long road, and without the help of these fantastic people, I definitely could not have done it. Thank you.

Bibliography

Books

Wilson, C & Seaman, D (1992) *The Serial Killers*, London: Virgin Publishing

Kidd, P (1999) *Never to be Released* (Vol 2), Sydney: Harper Collins Publishers

Blundell, N (1996) *Encyclopedia of Serial Killers*, London: PRC Kiln House

Holmes, RM & Holmes, ST (1996) *Profiling Violent Crimes: An Investigative Tool* (2nd ed), Thousand Oaks, CA: Sage

Ressler, R & Shachtman (1997) *I Have Lived in the Monster*, Simon & Schuster

Kerry Greenwood, Editor (2000) *On Murder, True Crime Writing in Australia*, Black Inc.

Newspapers

Sydney Morning Herald, The *Age*, *Adelaide Advertiser*, *Courier-Mail*, *The Australian / Weekend Australian*

Magazines

Who Weekly, *The Bulletin*, *Good Weekend* (The *Age*)

Electronic media

Channel 9: *60 Minutes*, *The Sunday Program*
ABC Radio: *7.30 Report*

Journals

Gazette of Law and Journalism
Police Association South Australia, Vol. 86, No. 6
Stephan, CN; Henneberg, M (2005) *Forensic Science International*, 'Recognition by forensic approximation: case specific examples and empirical tests'

Pridmore, Saxby; Chambers, Amber; McArthur, Milford, *Australian and New Zealand Journal of Psychiatry* (2005) 'Neuroimaging in psychopathy'

Hare, RD (1991) *The Psychopathy Checklist – revised (PCL-R)*

Music

Live, *Throwing Copper.* Lyrics Edward Kowalczyk

Research papers/Reports

Arthurson, Kathy, University of South Australia: *Housing Tenure, Social Mix and Creating Inclusive Communities*

Blandyi, Richard, University of South Australia, Flinders University: *South Australian Business Vision 2010 Keynote Address*

Mullighan, EP QC (2005) *Interim Report of the Children in State Care Commission of Inquiry*